*The Lovelorn Ghost and the Magical Monk*

# The Lovelorn Ghost and the Magical Monk

## PRACTICING BUDDHISM IN MODERN THAILAND

*Justin Thomas McDaniel*

COLUMBIA UNIVERSITY PRESS

NEW YORK

Published with generous support from the Institute of Thai Studies,
Chulalongkorn University, Thailand

Columbia University Press
*Publishers Since 1893*
New York   Chichester, West Sussex

Library of Congress Cataloging-in-Publication Data
McDaniel, Justin Thomas.
The Lovelorn Ghost and the Magical Monk : Practicing Buddhism in
Modern Thailand / Justin Thomas McDaniel.
pages   cm
Includes bibliographical references and index.
ISBN 978-0-231-15376-8 (cloth : alk. paper)—ISBN 978-0-231-15377-5 (pbk. : alk. paper)—
ISBN 978-0-231-52754-5 (e-book)
1. Buddhism—Social aspects—Thailand—History.   I. Title.
BQ566.M38 2011
306.6'94309593—dc22
2010045092

*Cover image courtesy of the author*
*Book and cover design by Chang Jae Lee*

References to Internet Web sites (URLs) were accurate at the time of writing.
Neither the author nor Columbia University Press is responsible for URLs
that may have expired or changed since the manuscript was prepared.

For Christine, Henry, and Jane

*It was a long trip back*
*White lilies waved by walls*
*The sweat from blue grapes*
*Shone like glass.*
*A wind blown straight from the harbor*
*Brushed the long grass.*
*I suppose we thought of the harbor*
*And of how it looked with its blue water*
*And its sailboats moving.*
*But even though the wind smelt of the waves*
*And of the swamp grass nearer*
*Our thoughts were of the road . . .*

—PAUL BOWLES, song from *Six Chansons* (1930–1932)

# CONTENTS

We found a few small willows, about three inches in height, and
clusters of a small white flower, name unknown.

—OLIVER L. FASSIG, reconnaissance diary for Greenland Islands (ca. 1905)

## ACKNOWLEDGMENTS

My two-year-old daughter, Jane, and I share the same problem. We lack the vocabulary for describing the strangeness of the world around us. Slowly she is
figuring out a way to solve that problem by concentrating on naming the things
she can hold—leaves, crayons, french fries, and the occasional bug. Once she
successfully learns or makes up a name for something, to her the thing has
greater shape and significance. The act of naming thrills her. Deliberately she is
assembling the world. I envy her. I am lazy. I have yet to solve this problem and
still feel like I stumble through my explorations like Oliver Fassig—describing
but not naming, constantly tripping over a collection of unknowns, failing to
assemble the world. Instead of diligently working to solve this problem on my
own like Jane, I have instead retreated, quite happily, into the offices, monasteries, and living rooms of my friends and colleagues. Many objects, persons,
phenomena, texts, and ideas described in this book have been given shape and
significance by them. They have helped me name, date, place, and slowly understand. In many ways their ideas, experience, and enthusiasm assembled this
book. To her credit, Jane has been on my lap the entire way.

My debts are large. I received advice and inspiration from Damrongsak
and Anong Suksuksiang, Maechi Vimuttiya, Balee Buddharaksa, José Cabezón,

Malai Prachathorn, Suwanna Satha-Anand, Phra Sugandha, Caverlee Cary, Tamara Loos, Nai Somneuk, Jacques Leider, Nathan McGovern, Michael Jerryson, Sunait Chutintaranont, Penny Edwards, Vesna Wallace, Robert Briscoe, Thanissaro Bhikkhu, Kate Crosby, Phra Maha Silapa Dhammasippo, Stanley Tambiah, Ray and Susan Hewitt, Maritza Diaz, Sompong Duangsawai, Anake Nawigamune, M. R. Suphavat Kasemsri, Phra Maha Narongsak Sophanasithi, Bas Jarend Terwiel, Ven. Mahinda Deegalle, Phra Mahathawon Chittathaoro, Richard Ruth, Pornthip Kanjananiyot, Jeffrey Samuels, Chris Baker, Pasuk Phongpaichit, Lisa Onaga, Pram Sounsamut, Laurie Sears, David Chandler, W. S. Karunatillake, Pinit Ratanakul, Catherine Allgor, Andrew Jacobs, June O'Connor, Charnvit Kasetsiri, Juliane Schober, Phra Achan Sitikalo, Maechi Bunchuai, and the late David Wyatt.

I received materials in the mail or answers to very difficult questions from Kaviya Manavid, Somneuk Hongprayoon, Rassamee Maneenin, Erick White, Charles Keyes, Nonzee Nimibutr, Arnika Fuhrman, Adam Knee, Supachai Charusombun, C. Pierce Salguero, Kannikar Satraproong, Steven Berkwitz, John Listopad, Kamala Tiyavanich, Phra Khru Sunthapatthanaphimon, François Lagirarde, Rangsit Chonchansitto, Donald Stadner, Claudio Cicuzza, Anucha Thirakanont, Vivian Nyitray, Louis Gabaude, Alan Klima, Pimpaka Towira, Nu Khamsiang, Tamara Ho, Lan Duong, Sohail Wassif, Erik Davis, Pattana Kitiarsa, John Guy, Leedom Lefferts, Nicola Tannenbaum, Nasser Solomon, Catherine Newell, Michael Feener, David Biggs, Henk Maier, Sally Ness, James Lin, Kelvin Mac, and the late Henry Ginsberg. They all took time away from their own work to help me with specific problems with my research. It is this type of collegial support that makes the field of Southeast Asian studies and my professional and personal life so rich.

My friendships with Prapod Assavavirulhakarn, Suchitra Chongstitvatana, Arthid Sheravanichkul, Thongchai Likhitpornsawan, Chalong Soontravanich, Michael Montesano, Lisa and Edward Miller, Patricia and Leone Palagi, Jennifer Dee, Edward Leibman, Michael Keogh, Yara and Firmin Debraebander, Phanuthep Sutthithepthamrong, Ruangsasitorn Sangwarosakul, and Matthew Wheeler have sustained me through the process of research and writing. They provided in their own ways books, meals, rides, tours, apartments, child care, and jokes. Most important, they all reminded me not to take myself so seriously.

Rough drafts, chapters, and particularly troublesome sections were kindly read by Anne Blackburn, Anne Hansen, John Holt, Hiram Woodward, Thomas Borchert, and Craig Reynolds. Their harsh criticisms and insightful comments greatly improved this book. They cannot be blamed for when I chose to take comfort in my own mistakes. Peter Skilling, Pattaratorn Chirapravati, and Steven Collins were particularly supportive at every stage of this process, reading closely, recommending sources, identifying problems, and generally educating me in Thai and Buddhist studies. It is especially encouraging when scholars of such experience and integrity take an active interest in one's work. I owe them a great deal. As always, Luang Pho Sombun is my preceptor and Donald Swearer is my *achan*.

I received generous research funding from Chulalongkorn University, the University of California, Riverside, the National Endowment of the Humanities, and the University of Pennsylvania. My new colleagues at UPenn made the publishing and editing process go smoothly with their advice and friendship. Just west of UPenn, on the corner of Forty-second and Baltimore, preside Marie and Gus, whom I thank for several very good sandwiches. I especially thank Cecily and Jonathan Walton for their wisdom, warmth, and kindness. They made a particularly difficult transition from one coast to another much easier.

This book was published with direct funding support and the great generosity of Ann Matter of the University of Pennsylvania and the Institute of Thai Studies of Chulalongkorn University. The Institute of Thai Studies, directed by Suchitra Chongstitvatana, is the copublisher of this book in Thailand. Without this support, the project would not have seen the light of day.

I value the comments of the external readers. The editors at Columbia University Press, particularly Wendy Lochner, Leslie Kriesel, and Christine Mortlock, were supportive at every stage of the publishing process. Finally, it was the time spent with my complicated and wonderful family—the Fitzmaurices, Seips, Reddingtons, O'Dwyers, Coppingers, Brignolas, and Galvins—that gladly took me away from my work and gave me the renewed energy to write with fresh eyes. My brother Garvan, my sister-in-law Monica, my in-laws Wendy and Thomas have been constant supports. My dear parents, Adelene and Thomas, have taught me never to stop asking questions and rethinking my opinions. They have given my life a sense of urgency and joy. Jane makes life very sweet. I will never find a closer friend, better pretzel eater, or funner subway mate than my son Henry. Christine and I have followed each other around the world for twenty years. However, I have happily missed seeing most of it, since I can't seem to turn my eyes away from her.

# NOTE ON TRANSCRIPTION

I have geared the transcription system to a general audience without advanced skills in Pali, Thai, or Sanskrit. Experts will disagree over the importance of phonetic accuracy versus international conformity. I have attempted to be simple and consistent. For Thai, I follow, with a few exceptions, the Royal Institute's *Romanization Guide for the Thai Script* (Bangkok, April 1968), which also elides most diacritical marks for easy reading. This closely follows international library standards. Pali transcription is now relatively consistent internationally. This book includes the many hybrid Sanskrit-Thai and Pali-Thai words in Thai. I generally follow their Thai spelling without Pali and Sanskrit diacritics. I avoid the International Phonetic Alphabet and the Thai "graphic" system, so phonetically and phonemically it is not completely accurate but is clear and "unornamented" for the general reader. I follow the standard *CPD* (Helmer Smith, *Critical Pali Dictionary, Epilogomena to Vol. I* [Copenhagen, 1948]) used by the Pali Text Society. Certain Pali terms and Lao and Thai names like Buddha, Nakhon Pathom, *dhamma*, sangha, Chiang Mai, Luang Pho, *nibbana*, Mahathat, Vientiane, Pali, Chulalongkorn, and so on have become well-known without diacritical marks and even included in dictionaries in English and French.

I follow standard English spellings for them throughout. The bibliography includes many Thai-language texts, and they are ordered alphabetically according to the first name of the author as has become standard in many Thai bibliographies. If the author is a monk or royal family member, their formal titles are shown in parentheses before the first name.

*The Lovelorn Ghost and the Magical Monk*

The gun as well as the gun-owner have the potential for various actions: a gun can act as a collector's item, hunting gear, a murder weapon or a substitute for a hammer . . . [Still] a rifle will indeed resist being used as a toothbrush. However, artifacts routinely turn out to be capable of doing much more than what is intended by those who create them. The complexity of the real world setting in which the artifacts become situated can, perhaps, never be fully considered. The result: unintended consequences.

—FELIX STADLER

# Introduction

In 1928 those Siamese lucky enough to own or live close to a radio heard, through intermittent static and crackly dialogue, a sinister tale of loss, vengeance, and murder. A female ghost terrified a small village in the still thickly forested suburbs of Bangkok. With her long fingernails she gutted any person who attempted to tell her husband that she was merely the specter of his wife. All the while her husband, Mak, a poor soldier and woodsman, lived unaware that his beautiful and caring wife was indeed a ghost whose throat was coated with the blood of his friends and neighbors. When he realized her true nature, he was torn between the love for his departed and the fear of her ghost. In the end, a Buddhist monk used Pali incantations to release the ghost, thus freeing Mak and his village of her misguided love.

This was the story "Mae Nak Phrakhanong" (Mother Nak of Phrakhanong District) broadcast from Bangkok. Radio was not new to Siam, but it certainly was not a widespread medium. This was the first time the story of Mae Nak had been performed over the airwaves. The story itself was an old and well-known one. It had been told and retold by Siamese of all classes for decades. There were many versions with different characters and name changes. Even without access to a radio, most Siamese children had heard this story. Indeed it had been a novelette, a play, a poem, and an opera. Soon it would become a popular comic book and graphic novel, as well as the most popular genre of ghost films (over twenty-two films so far) in Thailand leading up to the 1997 blockbuster hit *Nang Nak*, the 1999 live opera *Mae Nak*, the 2003 *The Ghost of Mae Nak*, the 2005 *Ghost of Mae Nak*, written and directed this time by a British national, Mark Duffield, the very popular 2008 digitally animated version, and the full stage musical that premiered in 2009.[1]

In June 2007, seventy-nine years after that radio play aired, I found myself at one of the repeated funerals for this lovelorn ghost. It was 7:45 on a moonless night at a small monastery along a dirty canal at the end of a small city street. The monastery, Wat Mahabut, was founded as a rural village temple in 1793, but during the past two hundred years, Bangkok has grown to over 12 million people, and the forested grounds of the monastery have become fixed firmly in a grid of allies, tenements, and sidewalks. The monastery still had several large canopy trees, loosely intersecting dirt paths, and swarms of mosquitoes. It seemed more distant than its address would suggest. The boat, two buses, elevated train, and long walk necessary to reach this part of the city also gave me the feeling that I had taken a long trip into the countryside.

I had never been to such a funeral before, especially for a ghost. I did not know what to expect. As a monk, thirteen years previously, I had performed several funerals, and living in Thailand one always attends several funerals a year, since they are more public and social than private family affairs. However, this was entirely different, or so I thought. The shrine to Mae Nak is a small open-air pavilion flanked by three large trees with two altars, one to Mak and one to Nak. Mae Nak's is elevated above her husband's and is surrounded by new dresses, boxes of cosmetics, amateur paintings of the ghost as a beautiful young woman, and candles, incense, and thousands of colorful scarves. The trees (*takian* trees, which are considered especially inauspicious when adjacent to cremation or burial sites) are bound with the scarves. In the folds are hundreds of handwritten letters entreating Mae Nak to protect soldiers, children, and the sick. On the altar is a rather garish golden statue of Mae Nak with a long, black-haired wig. The image holds two plastic baby dolls also layered in gold leaf and paint. Mae Nak only had one child supposedly. The second doll is simply a replacement for the first doll, which was getting worn from all the touching and caressing from the steady stream of devotees. In front of Mae Nak is another doll lying in a glass coffin. The managers of the shrine had not removed the worn doll. Indeed, rarely are things ever removed from shrines in Thailand; abundance is valued. Piles of stuff show how much a shrine is honored. In front of the statue a television was turned on to a cartoon program for the baby dolls. Under the television were hundreds of plastic trucks, airplanes, beads, guns, and other toys.

I had been to the shrine numerous times and had interviewed many people either attending the shrine or working at the astrologers' tables and snack carts surrounding it. It is generally a bustling place visited by people from all over Thailand along with the occasional television crew. It is in an unattractive neighborhood on the way to nothing. It is not a mysterious place, though. It is just a shrine to ghosts. However, when I went to the recurring funeral, it was my first time visiting at night, and there was palpable spookiness about it. There were about seventeen people besides myself, a relatively even mix of women and men, with several small children sitting on folding chairs in front of the shrine. We were all offered bottles of Pepsi or Orange Fanta. The mood was light with chatting, cell phones ringing, and a couple of guys having a smoke. To the right of the statue of Mae Nak there was a temporary dais with four monks preparing to chant, holding ceremonial fans, joking with one another, relaxed, having some lukewarm tea.

The monks chanted very standard funeral chants drawn from the *Abhidhamma chet kamphi*. They took occasional breaks and resumed chanting. It was nearly identical to every funeral I had attended in Thailand. I found myself chanting along from rote memory. There was nothing strange about it. Kneeling, we presented gifts to the monks, smiled, and sat back on our haunches. Then we proceeded to pour water out of small metal vessels (some people just used plastic water bottles) into small bowls while chanting again. Since I had forgotten to bring a bottle, I held the wrist of the man next to me as he poured, to share the merit. This was all completely normal for a funeral. Then I was reminded that there was no corpse, the object of the funeral was a, perhaps fictional, bloodthirsty ghost. Why did I see this as a problem?

We stood up, walked to one of the large *takian* trees that had long been blackened by candles and softened by all the hands touching it (one person stated that it had been struck by lightning as well).[2] We put our collective foreheads against it. As our heads touched the tree in unison we silently entreated Mae Nak for protection. There was some bumping and light laughter. Supposedly Mae Nak's body is buried under the tree (or as the story goes, the tree was planted on top of her head—to hold her down). We offered gifts to both her elevated statue and her suppressed skeleton. The monks followed us and did the same. Then we went back to the statue of Mae Nak and her baby and offered them gold leaf, incense, and a little bit of cash. Then we all went home. It was late, everyone had buses to catch, and children had to be put to bed. We would all see one another again, depending on our schedules, next month. This recurrent funeral is performed once a month, at the same time, at the same shrine.

I had gone to the funeral of a ghost. While this was a ceremony unique to Mae Nak, the aesthetics, chanting, gestures, moods were not. They were common

Thai Buddhist activities. The repertoire was known by everyone, even me. There was nothing particularly sinister, mysterious, or esoteric about the event. In fact, there was another funeral for a nonfictional newly dead corpse going on in another pavilion at the monastery (often Thai monasteries have several funerals simultaneously performed a night, and many have new, high-capacity gas incinerators for the subsequent cremations). On many other occasions I had offered Mae Nak gifts and bought lottery tickets at her shrine. I felt comfortable at the shrine. No one seemed surprised. No one I had ever talked to had found the fact that there was a shrine and recurring funerals for a ghost odd. Mae Nak has become a standard object of worship at a Buddhist monastery. She is part of the pantheon of famous monks, "Hindu" deities, and Buddhas. Certainly she has her own qualities. She is feared and respected as a devoted wife, fierce warrior, and a protective mother. But she is not a hidden part of Thai "esoteric" Buddhism. She is a celebrity and universally known by Thais young and old. Thai Buddhists are attached to her and she is attached to them. Practitioners are happy to keep her haunting, and she is apparently not in a rush to get to her next life.

Despite her extreme popularity, I had never paid much attention to Mae Nak or her associated rituals. Being a researcher of premodern Southeast Asian Buddhism, I spent the majority of my time translating palm-leaf manuscripts, looking at stone inscriptions and monastery murals, and interviewing forest monks. Like many historians of Buddhism, Pali and Sanskrit, and Southeast Asian literature, I had little time for the modern, the celluloid, and the entertaining. Real research was done in monastic archives and cloisters with scholar-monks. I had no interest in ghosts.

It was during a period of manuscript research in 2000–2001 that I found myself living in a neighborhood called Wang Lang (also referred to as Phran Nok or Sirirat by locals) in the middle of the Wang Lang bazaar in Bangkok on the Thonburi side of the Chao Phraya River. Although this is arguably the oldest neighborhood in metropolitan Bangkok, today it is not marked by ruins, stately homes, or cobblestones but by a network of tailors, photocopying shops, temporary eateries, pharmacies, and toy stands. Nurses from the nearby Sirirat Hospital bump into ethic Lao and Khmer tradespeople hunting for bargains during lunch hour. Mangy dogs hide in corners, toddlers play in the alleys. The food is fantastic. Patience is enforced by foot traffic. Tangles of illegally tapped electric wires hang over carts of candied *matun* fruit. Teenagers regularly damage their hearing in computer-game cafés. It is relatively inexpensive to rent an apartment in this neighborhood, and it is a short boat ride to many of the most important monasteries in the city. I moved there to be close to the libraries and classrooms of Mahachulalongkorn Monastic University (across the river). Little did I know at the time that the neighborhood, more than advisers in graduate school or trends in Buddhist studies, would come to dictate the course of my research and the contours of my questions.

Down the main Wang Lang alley from my apartment on the river was a midsized monastery whose name I recognized but in which I had not spent time. Now that I lived so close to it, I went most mornings to Wat Rakhang Ghositarama (The Monastery of the Bells in the Hermitage of the Renowned) to meditate, listen to chanting and sermons, buy snacks, release turtles, eels, and birds for merit, and feed the fish. My wife and I liked a restaurant next door to the monastery, and I would occasionally play soccer with some of the children in the courtyards and allies. Because its library didn't have any manuscripts in which I was interested, and the monks in residence were not experts in the topic of my dissertation, I failed to ask any probing questions or even investigate the history of the monastery for several weeks. It wasn't until I started asking my barber questions about the statues, photographs, amulets, and images of Somdet To (pronounced "doe") in the neighborhood that I became enthralled with the history of the monastery and the significance of its most famous abbot, the most powerful magician and ghost tamer in Thai history. Interviewing laity, nuns, and monks, reading books, translating mystical diagrams, watching films, listening to incantations, collecting amulets, participating in rituals in the Wang Lang neighborhood and other places associated with this famous monk has dominated my professional life ever since.

This is also how I came to the study of Mae Nak. I hadn't spent much of my time watching films or reading ghost stories (Thai or other). When it came to my work, I considered myself bookish and serious. Trained in Indic philology and history, I had little commerce with film studies, ethnography, and social theory in general. However, as my casual interest in Somdet To turned into a full-time obsession, I found myself hearing ghost stories and watching horror films. In the most well-known versions of the story of Mae Nak, Somdet To was the monk who "cured" her and stopped her from haunting her husband and killing the residents of Phrakhanong District.[3] In order to understand Somdet To, I needed to know about Mae Nak, and vice versa.

As I spoke with monks, nuns, laity, amulet dealers, lay Buddhist practitioners, scholars, and even children, I discovered that my fascination with Mae Nak and Somdet To was neither obscure nor peripheral. Thai Buddhists of all classes and ages, even scholar-monks, were much more interested in speaking with me about them than about manuscripts, archaeology, or doctrine. It seemed that my side interest in ghosts and ghost tamers was the central concern of many Buddhists in the capital and in the countryside. Indeed, I discovered dozens of books, hundreds of stories, thousands of statues, tens of thousands of amulets related to Somdet To and Mae Nak. There were also the images, stories, rituals, and amulets related to the monks, magicians, and ghosts associated with Somdet To and Mae Nak. Thai Buddhism was there in front of me, but I had been looking right past it. Now it is painfully clear that any major study of Thai Buddhism is simply ludicrous if these two are not prominently featured. Ignoring them is ignoring what millions of Thai Buddhists know and value.

I found that without knowing why Somdet To was so popular and how he came to be a major figure in the amulet, magical, religious text, and image industries of Thailand I was unable to answer basic questions from my colleagues and eventually my students about Thai Buddhism. Why are some monasteries much busier than others? Why are some monks much more famous than others? Why did certain liturgies, rituals, texts, images, amulets persist and others disappear? What do Thai Buddhists wear around their necks? What images and photographs adorn their home altars? How much do these objects cost? What do most Thai Buddhists do? In order to make sense of the practices and images in Wat Rakhang, and in hundreds of Thai monasteries, I needed to ask better questions and write a different kind of book.

Despite the extreme popularity of this monk and this ghost, many prominent scholars have overlooked their central place in the study of Thai Buddhism. Whereas tantric and Taoist studies in India, Tibet, and China have taken magical practices as legitimate subjects in the study of religion, these protective and transformative practices have often been reduced in the study of Southeast Asian Buddhism to products of social anxieties, economic conditions, cultural artifacts, or political tools.[4] Too often in Southeast Asian studies, magicians and practitioners are seen as new reactions to globalization and Westernization (synonymous in most studies) or as persistent pre-Buddhist leftovers that are being lost in the hustle and bustle of present-day Thai society.[5] More generally, especially in Western-language books on socially engaged Buddhism and in introductory textbooks, Thai Buddhist practitioners are often depicted as "impacted" by globalization or "rampant" modernization. They are victims of political maneuverings or economic exploitation.[6] So often, studies of magic and worship in Thai Buddhism have been studies of oppression and loss.[7] These studies, while highly contextualized and well researched, often assume that ecclesiastical centralization and the promotion of monastic and pedagogical orthodoxy and orthopraxy have actually worked or have had a significant effect outside elite circles.[8] As I have shown previously, the central Thai government's sponsorship of ecclesiastical examinations, suppression of local religious practice, and training of Thammayut missionaries have had limited effect in standardizing Buddhist practice and learning over the past century.[9] The new Buddhist education and administrative structure created by the elite has little commerce among the vast majority of monks and novices throughout Thailand today.

Regardless of whether we depict Thai Buddhists as beings victims of globalization, of state centralization, or rebels trying to defend their way of life against Westernization, I warn that this type of approach establishes a dichotomy of victim-victimizer. It sees modernity as narrowly defined. It suggests that Thai Buddhism was a static entity that existed in a pristine state before modernization (read: the West) assaulted it and views modern Thai Buddhists as tools of powerful nation builders. I instead see Thai Buddhists as dynamic arbiters and sponsors of ideology and innovation. Thai Buddhists have not been merely supine receivers of modernization who choose to profit from it or be overrun. They are not simply responding to global changes or the anxieties of modern life. There are many people in modern Thailand who neither chastise the deleterious effects of magic nor claim that their practice is original, genuine, or pure. Many are both supportive or resistant to the state's role in religion depending on the circumstance. They negotiate with rather than blindly embrace the modern age. These people, like the worshippers of Mae Nak, dynamically respond and adjust according to the times rather than becoming one of the victimizers or victims of modernity. Many Buddhist scholars and practitioners in modern Thailand are socially engaged while being dedicated to the ascetic life.[10] Many are both students of Pali and practitioners of magic; many study in the city and practice in the forest. Speaking of monks and nuns, many come from wealthy backgrounds but live in forest monasteries. Many continually revisit their practice not by searching for a pure Buddhism that exists somewhere in the golden past but by responding to the changing needs of the time. They are neither static practitioners nor conservative reactionaries. They are reading new books, visiting new monasteries, watching sermons on television, attending monastery festivals, changing their opinions, changing them back again. They are having fun, they are working through problems, and they have their eyes wide open.[11]

The constant interpretation and reinterpretation of Thai Buddhism locally is not easily divided into elite-popular, urban-rural, or monastic-lay dichotomies. Therefore, this book aims to take individual Buddhist agents seriously and listen to the cacophony of their voices. It also pays close attention to the relationship these agents have with their material culture. Although images, gestures, the sounds, the ritualized relationships, the incense are the common denominators for Thai Buddhists worldwide, they are seen often as secondary to the meaning of the actions, the belief system, the social and political agendas, the theologies, the worldviews, the underlying causes of the practices and objects in a ritual space. These universal aesthetic expressions are seen merely as peculiar aspects of local culture. There is an assumption that there must be something "really real" beneath the accoutrements. In I. A. Richards's words, there must be a "tenor" behind the "vehicle."[12] Figural interpretation supersedes straightforward observation. Description is secondary to explanation. Astrology, protective magic, fortune-telling, ghost belief, "Hindu" deities, multiple Buddhas, amulets are ubiquitous at even most conservative Thammayut monasteries, but many scholars still dig and dig looking for their idea of Theravada buried under the weight of Thai culture. There are many reasons for this, perhaps more so than any other because up until recently Thai Buddhism was often depicted in opposition to something else more authentic, older, and more powerful—Theravada, Sinhala, or Mon Buddhism, or early Buddhism. Since Thai Buddhist practice is seemingly so different from its Indian origins, the why of a practice, the origin of a practice, the meaning of a practice, the Theravadaness of a practice are sought too quickly. The questions asked of "informants" are often too directed, probing, and irrelevant to the actual aesthetics of the room and the actions performed in it. It is not that there are not any aspects of Indic, early, Sinhala, or Theravada (often seen as synonymous) in Thai Buddhism. However, since Thai Buddhist practices are set against them, Thailand is seen as unique, corrupt, local, syncretistic, or cultish in positive or negative ways. Looking for the Theravada, the Buddhist, and the authentic often prevents scholars from seeing what is going on. Mae Nak and Somdet To, despite being extremely popular, are seen as strange because they do not fit in with early Buddhist ideals and impressions. Ghosts, various deities, magicians, astrologers, healers, amulet dealers, fortune-tellers are normative in Thai "Theravada" Buddhism, but they are depicted as marginal or as simply an "unfortunate" leftover of the past or unforeseen side effect of modernity by even the most progressive of scholars. This privileging of supposedly timeless elite state and scholarly knowledge(s) renders the particularities and material context of everyday Thai Buddhist knowledge(s) illegible. It also, as discussed in chapter 2, arbitrarily divides Thai Buddhism into esoteric and exoteric forms.[13] To get away from these unhelpful, divisive categories, we need, in Paul Ricoeur's terms, a "second naïveté"—to look at Thai Buddhism with fresh eyes.[14]

In 1968 an issue of the *SEATO Record*, a nonscholarly journal for mostly Australian and American development, military, and diplomatic advisers working in Southeast Asia during the Vietnam War, contained a three-page reflection called "Bangkok: Metropolis of Deities." While it might be dismissed as Orientalist, superficial, imperialistic, and amateurish by Buddhist studies scholars and anthropologists, this article is actually one of the most refreshing and accurate descriptions of Bangkok Buddhism that I have read. Monasteries and monks are described aesthetically in clear prose. There is no mention of the word "Theravada" or "Hindu." There is no mention of local culture. The often arbitrary dichotomies urban versus rural and modern versus traditional, folk versus orthodox, are left out. The article is set among others about French and Thai electricians working together in the city, canal management, fisheries, President Johnson's relationship with the Thai dictator Thanom, and a medical laboratory's new research on Japanese encephalitis. The unnamed author, a staff writer no doubt, wrote what he saw, what Buddhism meant or should mean did not get in the way. There were neither condescending, sighing reflections about what has been lost in Thai Buddhist modernity nor cynical mockery of Thai purveyors of magic and luck. The monasteries are described in their urban context. In fact, impressionistic travel pieces and Thai newspaper stories give the reader much more accurate and honest accounts of Thai Buddhism than many scholars trained in the Theravada and in Pali literature, who are overly influenced by a preconceived idea of what Theravada Buddhism should be.[15]

This book is not a travel piece or a diplomatic brief, though. Instead it is what some anthropologists would call a pragmatic sociological study of cultural repertoires. It is an ethnomethodological study in the tradition of Bruno Latour and Harold Garfinkel that is interested in the ways people make meaning, display this ever-changing understanding to others, and continually and mutually remake society and its explanations.[16] Instead of looking at the epistemic characteristics of macrolevel Thai culture or religion, I am concerned with the "practical reasoning and reflexive accounts that people use on a daily basis and that make social life an ongoing practical accomplishment."[17] I try to temper any macrosociological speculative analysis with the explanations and actions of individual agents, while always emphasizing that agents are in situated relationships with the art, texts, memories, and objects. This permits a study that takes into account individuals' capacity and authority to contradict themselves, switch codes (i.e., change justifications and meanings), hold and be comfortable with two or more contradictory thoughts, make decisions based on the economy of rumors and personal and collectively generated emotions, deliberately and assertively ignore facts and history, or simply act without reflection or meaning.[18] I also take into account the situated knowledges that become apparent when we acknowledge the agency of material objects. I emphasize that objects and people coproduce knowledge. Therefore, instead of trying to find what is "Buddhist" about what a particular person holds, chants, and values, I look first to how they do something, how they say they do something, and the material and social contexts they do it in. This is a study of repertoires, not epistemologies and epistemes.

A repertoire includes the words, stock explanations, objects, and images that a social actor can "draw upon while engaged in meaning-making 'on the ground'" in the context of interacting with others.[19] People who write about, worship, admire, and petition Somdet To and Mae Nak (among others) utilize a shifting set of words and actions in a wider cultural repertoire. They are not controlled by the repertoire of icons and tropes. They do not simply blindly follow saints, ghosts, and deities. In my interviews and reading, I found that these practitioners and purveyors of religion often question history, wonder about the veracity of stories, question the value of protective magic, are skeptical about the value of sacred objects, embrace new technology, consciously trade in rumors, take on social causes, read newspapers, go to work, and lead relatively normal lives. Studying this type of vernacular way finding shows that Thai Buddhists (and scholars) are all at different and evolving levels of knowing and learning Buddhism.

As with many Irish and Mexican Catholics, and Chinese Taoists, among others, magic and ghosts are part of a Thai Buddhist's normal life. Many of the practices of religiosity associated with Somdet To and Mae Nak are so pervasive and popular that they can only be called mainstream expressions (neither aspects nor features) of central Thai Buddhism. The practices are not confined to the poor and disenfranchised. Most practitioners are neither serving the state nor unwittingly being financially exploited. It is not a simple question of power (either oppressive or resistant). Homi Bhabha's postcolonial theories of resistance and Foucault's theories of oppression have limited use here.[20] This book is therefore not a series of "case studies" or interesting oddities articulating social scientific theories of habitus, power, and resistance but a study of mainstream Thai Buddhism articulating the repertoire and reflections of Thai practitioners and scholars. Therefore, I look at what Pierre Nora calls realms of memory, sites like the shrines and monasteries connected to Somdet To and Mae Nak where communal, familial, and national memories are "elicited, reinforced, and produced."[21] But instead of looking at these sites as simply reinforcing elite political agendas or articulating ideologies of resistance, I show how they reflect "everyday practices of relatedness" as well as difference and discomfort.[22]

The idea of a repertoire, Ilana Silber states, "has the double advantage of connoting the ready enactment and concrete performance of practical and practicable options; and of allowing for a measure of individual meaning and agency in mobilizing and choosing a specific configuration of cultural resources, while also stressing the public, and publicly available nature of those resources."[23] Culture, as Ann Swidler argues, is a "tool kit" that does not define the "ends of action" but rather provides "the components or tools used to construct recurrent strategies of action."[24] These repertoires are never identical for each individual, and there is never one reason a person does something ritually or religiously. However, there are similar tools that each individual can draw upon when performing and explaining the reasons for their performance. Understanding how individuals utilize these repertoires tells us much about why certain monks, certain texts, certain deities, and certain historical moments are seen as more valuable than others in modern Thai society. While I refrain from defining national Thai repertoires, I identify wider trends in Thai Buddhism, moving slowly from a micro- to a macrocultural study.

We might assume that the followers of a nineteenth-century magician or believers in a vengeful ghost are members of an all-embracing, mind-numbing cult who would wake up from their practices if they were exposed to a good liberal arts education. However, this ignores the complexity and pervasiveness of the practices, material culture, and texts connected with Somdet To. His supporters are not simply exploited or seek to exploit others. They are not necessarily followers or devotees or the faithful. They are best likened to dedicated fans of a particular or a group of local deities, saints, teachers, or ghosts. Like fans, their loyalty can waver, they can switch to be fans of other saints (like sports fans switching favorite teams when they move to other cities or when it helps them socially to jump on the bandwagon of a new team or player). They can add new teachers or ghosts to be fans of without losing their admiration and dedication to their original saint or deity. Some fans can become maniacal and purchase every piece of paraphernalia, go to every shrine, study every historical text, read every sermon, purchase their own poster, image, or amulet to keep at home on a personal altar, participate in online fan forums (yes, they exist for famous monks), join fan clubs (yes again) for certain monks, and the like. Fans can be mildly interested or unwaveringly devout. This attitude can evolve over time. They often admit doubt and have a healthy skepticism. The institutional history of Buddhism in Southeast Asia that has been written has generally overlooked the way a monk's, nun's, or layperson's personal teacher and personal ordination lineage trumps all other associations with monasteries, sects, provinces or regions, social classes, and language dialects. It is more revealing to know with which lineage of personal teachers within or across national sects like the Thammayut and Mahanikai or other lineages a monk, nun, or layperson self-identifies. Certain fans self-identify with certain lineages of teachers; however, loyalty to one lineage and one only is not common. In this way, being in a lineage (whether defined by ordination, ritual, text, or position on certain ethical issues) is more like being a fan. This great diversity in approach is possible because independent Buddhist agents work with a certain and evolving religious repertoire.

A study of repertoires has a distinct advantage of crossing boundaries of class, sect, and gender if centered on a particular place both diachronically and synchronically. It is, at its heart, a study of modern Thai Buddhist culture. Michael Carrithers has argued that culture can be seen not as a prescriptive formula but as a resource (or what I am calling a repertoire). Culture then is seen as "not only much more mutable than we had thought, but in fact much more a matter of persuasion of rhetoric, than of a determining software-like program. On this view it would be improper to say that culture works on people but proper to say that people use cultural tools to work on themselves and others."[25] Furthermore, he asserts that culture can only be understood as something that changes because of the "ceaseless action and reaction of people upon each other and so to match more closely our actual experience of the world." It is this "sensitive web of interrelatedness" and our "ability to recount convincing stories for others as fundamental to our ability to deal with the complexities of social life and the emergencies of historicity."[26] We will see that the Somdet To and Mae Nak movements have become increasingly useful in modern Thailand as the society has confronted foreign invasion, economic depression, crime waves, Islamic insurgency, and military coups.

My approach to the study of culture (or cultural data) differs from Carrithers's in some ways. I do not necessarily see the *resources that make up culture* being informed primarily by beliefs and ethical norms but also by what I call technologies. Scholars often privilege the beliefs of a particular religion when trying to understand the source of cultural expressions. Thai Buddhists are described as believing in impermanence, or in the importance of compassion. This is effectively vague enough to actually mean nothing. Anyone can believe in the value of compassion or selflessness. These values are not limited to Buddhists. If we are going to talk in useful ways about Thai culture, if we are going to learn from the various Thai ways of being Buddhist, then it is more useful to look at what complex technologies people actually employ to solve problems—the practical (and sometimes seemingly impractical) technologies of astrology, healing, protection, prognostication, precepts, and the like. Many people I interviewed, lived with, and ate with in Thailand espouse the virtues of indifference, impermanence, and nonattachment. However, this does not mean that they struggle with collecting amulets, entreating ghosts, the Buddha, and deities for protection or recite texts in hope of a long life and a good rebirth. They are comfortable with both seemingly incompatible sets of beliefs and practices. I argue throughout that while religious beliefs are hard to define and the reasons participants offer for conducting actions are often vague, technologies (including moral precepts, which are in a way technologies of self- and group control) are less mutable (or at least their changes are more easily tracked).[27] Culture in this sense is a dialogue between people who draw on different repertoires informed by often shared technologies as well as harder to define beliefs.[28]

In Thailand it is often hard to define someone's beliefs. Statements of belief are a rarity in Thai culture. For example, biographers of Somdet To almost never state what his beliefs were or what his ethical standards were. However, they do spend a great deal of time, as did he, on specifically explaining or displaying the techniques he used to protect a person or exorcise a ghost. Thai Buddhists often define themselves by what they do rather than what they believe. Some concentrate on learning astrological charts, some memorize protective incantations, some meditate and listen to New Age music, some master a particular way of giving specific offerings to specific images or monks, some entreat specific deities. Practitioners do not often try to separate these technologies into worldly and nonworldly, economically motivated or spiritually motivated. Many practice or learn numerous, overlapping technologies. While beliefs are rarely articulated, technologies are commonly defined, compared, and implemented.

By looking closely at several monasteries associated with Somdet To, Mae Nak, and related figures (most located in Bangkok and the farming communities of central Thailand, with a few in northern and northeastern Thailand) we can identify the morphology of practices reacting to and driving history over time with a great degree of detail. Samuel Johnson famously quipped that "example is always more efficacious then precept."[29] I concur. Wittgenstein called this a "methodology of examples."[30] By seeing multiple examples of these practices we can avoid overarching, explanatory theories and offer a less theoretically filtered view of the why of Thai Buddhism and begin to understand those things that are simply taken for granted by the practitioners themselves. The experience of being in a monastery, of listening and watching, undermines any comprehensive a priori theory about the nature of Thai behavior and religiosity. I do not want, as T. J. Clark has stated, to "oblige theories to work extra hard—improbably hard—to contain" the variety of art, texts, histories, and performances at any one monastery or shrine.[31] Somdet To and Mae Nak worship, as well as dozens of other Thai religious practices, are characterized like Thailand itself—there is a diversity of classes, ethnicities, accents, and personal motivations all interacting in a, sometimes quite literally, tight space.

This does not mean that the repertoires used in mainstream Thai rituals, texts, images, and liturgies, of which Somdet To is a major actor, are simply a random connection of resources. This does not mean that there are no "values" held by the followers of Somdet To and Mae Nak. Local repertoires are characterized, but not defined, by their emphasis on security, heritage, graciousness, and abundance (*khwam plotphai* or *kan pongkan, moradok, udom sombun, khwam sawatdiphap* or *kreng chai*).[32] I do not see these as universal and static Thai values or traits, but they are relatively useful technologies of enactment or perhaps axiomatic modes of articulation that characterize the motivation of stagers, performers, fans, experts, and devotees of Thai Buddhist religions. They are heuristic categories that we should not assume participants in Thai Buddhist culture necessarily would use to describe their own values but ones with which most would certainly agree. They are not foreign concepts but demotic modifiers. They might not be the ideal Buddhist values in which they are supposed to believe, but they help give shape and significance to what many Thais cherish and honor. Therefore, as a subtheme in this book, I want to suggest that the more an individual monk or monastery can show that they promote security, heritage, graciousness, and abundance (and others, of course) and use the images, objects, sounds, and movements in a widely recognized and shared repertoire, the better they will be able to compete for relevance in a highly competitive religious marketplace of ideas and objects, the better they will be able to speak to and hold the attention of their respective audiences. Each practitioner not only expresses but also employs these axioms to protect themselves and move smoothly through society. While on the surface this might seem incongruous with nonattachment, indifference, compassion, and selflessness, they are seen by most as virtuous nonetheless and by many as perfectly Buddhist.

I consciously resist defining any sort of alternative local Thai Buddhist ethics in the book. I purposely avoid the recent debates on narrative, cultural, and local ethics.[33] I also refrain from trying to determine the "popular morality" of Thailand.[34] However, I find "narrative ethics" as taken by some scholars of Buddhism (who are influenced by the approaches of Hauerwas and Nussbaum) as one of the most useful ways of investigating Thai Buddhist beliefs. They emphasize the importance of emotions in understanding the full range of reasons underlying maintaining beliefs and engaging in rituals. These emotions are often best expressed in narratives. Here I particularly agree with Nussbaum that "emotions, unlike many of our beliefs, are not taught to us directly through propositional claims about the world, either abstract or concrete. They are taught, above all, through stories, These stories . . . once internalized, they shape the way life feels and looks."[35] She continues, drawing on Aristotle, that human perception develops in response to "complex particular cases and of a willingness to see them as particular and irreducible to general rules . . . the correct perception of a practical situation requires emotional as well as intellectual activity . . . narratives are also the texts best suited to evoke [moral activity]."[36] In this book, I relate many of the stories about Mae Nak, Somdet To, and others I have heard or read. These stories often supplement and many times are recalled much more effortlessly than Buddhist canonical *suttas* or commentarial narratives. I often found that when people told me stories they heard about Somdet To, they related them to others they had heard about other famous monks or even stories about their own experiences with miraculous healing or ghosts. Stories often bled into one another quite seamlessly. However, I also find Nussbaum's approach limiting, since it focuses largely on elite literary texts. I want to "read" the ethnographic and textual narratives of Thai practitioners in ritual and social settings in the modern period. The way people relate stories, chant incantations, gesture, embed rumors and fantastical stories into popular Buddhist magazines and Web sites, interact with foreign researchers, and compile their own personal collections of amulets, *yantras*, books, images, photographs, and the like also, I believe, are narratives that need to be read. My reading of these idiosyncratic narratives has led me to identify security, heritage, graciousness, and abundance as axiomatic of the way many Thai Buddhists express their values in practice. However, readers of the following chapters may see my evidence as invoking other values. Indeed, I hope that readers will take the evidence I provide as a platform on which to debate the nature of Thai Buddhist ethics or even the very idea that there is a "Thai way" of being Buddhist.

Despite having certain cultural axioms, there is no core of Thai Buddhism. This is hard on both the student and the scholar. The practices of modern Thai Buddhists do not look much like those of early Buddhism or even Sri Lankan or Burmese Buddhism (which all show great diversity as well). In an effort to make sense of these diverse practices, observers have been prompted to identify origins, to trace influences, and to craft theories of syncretism. We retreat to a series of vague explanatory terms like "magic," "cult," "Indianized," "localization," and "folk" when attempting to describe what seem like local anomalies in the grand history of the world religion known as Buddhism. Since Thai Buddhism is so different from its Indic origins, one is compelled to ask, How could this have happened? This book asks the observer of Thai Buddhism to refrain from those urges. Various theories of syncreticism, synergy, domestication, hybridity, and vernacularization have limited usefulness when attempting to describe a Thai monastery, shrine, liturgy, or ritual.[37] First, no monastery is isolated from the economic and cultural morphologies (economic, social, political, cultural changes, as well as the congruent and contingent personal and institutional adaptations to these changes) in the streets and paths surrounding it. These morphologies and individual repertoires are in constant dialogue in every Thai Buddhist practice. Locating this study in that dialogue, I hope to offer a balance between a large general survey of Thai Buddhism and a highly detailed study of one aspect of the tradition's rituals or history.

Second, describing Thai Buddhism as a syncretistic blend of Brahmanism, Chinese religions, Theravada Buddhism, animism, and so on rests on the assumption that there is one thing that can be described as pure Brahmanism or Theravada that has been polluted, diluted, or borrowed. Indian, Chinese, Burmese, Shan,

Mon, Lao, Khmer, Portuguese religious implements, ritual technologies, ethi-cal justifications, aesthetic forms came into various Thai communities through individual traders, physicians, magicians, poets, and missionaries in bits and pieces over a long period of time. Lineages of teachers went in and out of favor in royal courts and among villagers. The content of any manuscript library in the region reveals the diversity of texts, crossing religious and secular lines, in multiple scripts and languages that were read and redacted. There has never been one type of Brahmanism or Buddhism or animism in India or China or Thailand. In this way, I am much more interested in the relationships between people and between people and their material goods and environment than I am in their traits, official identities (religious affiliations, stated ethnicities, places of birth, and the like).

Third, describing a Thai ritual practice or textual explanation as syncretis-tic, localized, or domesticized can also assume a hierarchy based on geography, age, or medium (textuality or orality). I consciously avoid using terms like "accommodation" or "pre-Buddhist" "or preexisting cultural belief." When Buddhism was brought to Southeast Asia, it was not corrupted by local beliefs in ghosts, spirits, and ancestors. Indeed, there is ample textual and art historical evidence that ancestor and animistic spirit worship was part of early Buddhism in India, as well as in Burma and Sri Lanka.[38] Therefore, the first monks who came to the area of what we call Thailand today brought with them undoubt-edly their own preexisting beliefs in the world of spirits, texts that spoke of ghosts, and complex understandings of hells. However, tracing antecedents is useful if it is done on a level of close detail. Practical technologies of healing, ritual, meditation, and magic are shared by various faiths regardless of world-view, sectarian affiliation, or belief. Broadly judging Thai Buddhist practices, explanations, and expressions against their Indic origins is suspect and arbitrary. If we are going to use the term "local Buddhism(s)" in contrast to early Indian Buddhism or a translocal Buddhist ideal, then we must ask, What form of Bud-dhism isn't local? Early Buddhism was a local north Indian religion. It was influenced by its Indian cultural context; indeed, its origins were impossible without it. There has never been a purely translocal or nonlocal Buddhist sect or school of thought. Even translocal movements like the International Associa-tion of Buddhist Universities or the United Nations Day of Vesak Celebrations Committee have their own particular cultures formed by their organizers and the types of nuns and monks and scholars that choose to participate in them. They do not represent a translocal Buddhism, they represent the idiosyncratic visions and imaginings of their founders and organizers. They are particular to a time and often to a place. However, that place is now not bounded by national borders but by religious professionals with Internet access and a sufficient command of English. They form their own local community but not necessarily geographically limited community.

Fourth, just as there is not one type of influence, Indic, Chinese, or Khmer, there is not one "local." Each monastery in Thailand is a site of accretion. Images, murals, teachers, texts are constantly being added, repaired, and rearranged. Monks, nuns, and lay patrons residing at any one monastery, especially in Bangkok or Chiang Mai or Nakhon Sri Thammarat, come from many different regions (and sometimes countries). They stay for a while and then move to another monastery. New students come, old students leave. Somdet To is depicted and described in a variety of ways at different monasteries. There isn't one type of local Thai culture or Buddhism that can be contrasted or compared with one type of Brahmanism or Chinese Buddhism. The very categories of China, India, and Thailand are barely a century or two old. Therefore, my approach also questions the usefulness of terms like "syncretic," "popular," or "local" that are often used to describe those practices associated with Somdet To, Mae Nak, and other famous Thai Buddhist saints, ghosts, deities, and spirits. In this way, the study assumes neither that every person has equal access to certain cultural tools nor that every person is a slave of predetermined and constitutive cultural and social forces. I argue, therefore, that it would be wise to stop describing different shrines, images, amulets, rituals, texts, and liturgies as Brahmanic, Theravadin, Mahayanist, tantric, esoteric, royalist, animistic, or even syncretistic. Thai religious practices reflect a great deal of what William Connolly has described as "tolerance for ambiguity."[39] I show that objects and practices are valued because of their relation to certain events, people, and places, not because of their ability to articulate Buddhistness, Brahmanicness, Thainess, or localness. While Thai Buddhists are not blind to the differences between Brahmanism, Buddhism, animism, and other religious categories, they do not generally avoid nonexplicitly Buddhist practices or beliefs. We will see in chapters 3 and 4 especially that liturgical handbooks and monastic altars are sites of accretion, where texts and objects from disparate religious origins are welcome. Therefore, it is more useful to understand certain Thai Buddhists has having tendencies instead of traits. For example, *mo wiset* (wizards) tend to be laymen who do not strictly follow monastic codes and tend to engage in prognostication or even aggressive magic. However, they might have been monks in the past, they might attentively participate in Buddhist ceremonies and celebratory events, and they may chant standard Pali liturgical texts. An ordained nun or monk may follow the monastic code strictly and preach about nonself and the impermanence of all things but produce amulets, offer gifts to ghosts, magically heal the sick, or use Pali chants to protect homes from fire. They have certain tendencies, but their professional and personal practices defy the compilation of a list of traits to describe them. They are trained in certain types of rituals and texts and tend toward different aesthetic and ascetic choices. They don't have defined identities but particular skills and preferences.

The following chapters offer a historical and contemporary study of some of the more widespread practices of Thai Buddhists in Bangkok and surrounding provinces. I attempt to describe the multiple reasons why figures like Somdet To and Mae Nak, among others, stay relevant in a cosmopolitan, highly techno-logical, and mobile society like that of modern Thailand. I suggest that the an-swers to the question of why they are popular can tell us much about the Thai Buddhist axioms of security (*khwam plotphai, kan pongkan*), heritage (*moradok*), graciousness (*khwam sawatdiphap* or *kreng chai*), and abundance (*udom som-bun*). I do not confine the study to the robed. The way texts, rituals, and build-ings are received and generated by the laity is also discussed throughout. How-ever, there is little reference to the larger Theravada communities, texts, and traditions, or for that matter to any type of universal "Buddhist ethics" or "Bud-dhist worldviews." I hope to offer a solid background of what a visitor to Thai-land, whether she is a scholar of Buddhism or an engaged tourist, will actually see, smell, and hear in a monastery. A full description of all the astrological, magical, liturgical, life-cycle, pedagogical, and artistic aspects in every region of Thailand would be impossible in one book. Instead, I structure the book like a composer or painter. I present variations on a theme just as a composer de-signs different movements in an orchestral composition that are performed over an entire season, or a painter paints the same scene in different lights, at differ-ent times of day, in different seasons. I attempt to construct a *Gesamtkunstwerk* (here, a complete work incorporating all media) by drawing on film, murals, manuscripts, printed texts, interviews, participant observation, rituals, statues, liturgies, amulets, photographs, and so forth). Although I lack any skill in music or art, I hope that from this evidence what has been seen before as local pecu-liarities, esoterica, exotica, and oddities in comparison with some ideal norma-tive Theravada (that is actually not found anywhere outside of textbooks) can be seen as mainstream Thai religiosity. Using this organizational rubric, I hope that this text opens up possibilities for asking new questions instead of providing well-worn answers. I make a concerted effort to cross boundaries between the past and the present as well as between the lay and the ordained. The "theme" is Somdet To and Mae Nak and the variations work as degrees of separation, variation, and connection to them. By focusing on a nineteenth-century monk and a ghost, many aspects of modern Thai Buddhism in general will be seen in high relief.

The chapters do not need to be read in sequence. Each could be read as an independent essay offering different perspectives and dismantling assumptions about modern Thai Buddhism. While the reader might, at points, wish I would stop describing different monasteries in detail, telling the stories of different saints and kings, and relating different ghost stories, I ask her or him to be patient. These stories and descriptions do not get in the way of reflective analysis or theoretical experimentation but instead demonstrate a new method of approaching Thai Buddhism. I pay particular attention to the way stories are told, objects cherished, and rituals performed by different individuals and small communities throughout the country over time. Like George Marcus I see following the story or even following an object as an ethnographic method.[40] Furthermore, in this following, one can see the lines between community memory and history disappear. They are both, as Jacques Le Goff has asserted, social practices.[41] This book is an exercise in following, listening to, and seeing individual Buddhist agents. I see all knowledge as situated and therefore pay attention to the often neglected evidence that comes from individual preferences instead of official documents or testimonies, including private amulet collections, regional handbooks, idiosyncratic murals, films, rumors, personal ritual practices, and the like.[42] I provide a number of examples of rituals, images, amulets, monasteries, and liturgies. I relate many of the stories I heard, read, or experienced. In this way, I hope that Thai religious repertoires become cumulatively apparent rather than systematically presented. I believe that this is the way many Thai practitioners come to know their own ways of being religious. They are not taught how to be Buddhist in a class or in a single conversation with a monk or their mothers. Their repertoires are being constantly developed and deployed in the relationships they form with others, as well as with images, murals, teachings, rituals, and stories. As Charles Hallisey used to repeat to me, we need to try to learn *from* Buddhists, not merely *about* them. I hope that this style is useful to anthropologists, historians, philologists, art historians, political scientists, and magicians.

Chapter 1 is about people. It is about the poor monks and rich kings who drive (and sometimes are driven by) the economic and artistic phenomenon that is Thai Buddhism. I avoid describing the rules and regulations of the Vinaya or the daily life or "social roles" of monks. This approach has been repeated by numerous scholars. Instead of describing the lives of monks, I describe how people in Thailand create the lives of monks; the creation and cultivation of the legendary-biographical process. More specifically it is about Somdet To, King Mongkut, and modern saint worship in Thailand. Here I place the numerous hagiographies and biographies of this famous monk in conversation. We will see that unlike numerous other political and religious hagiographical traditions in Asia, the tellers of Somdet To's life story do not attempt to create one ideal vision of him frozen in time. His is not a carefully crafted hagiography serving economic and political purposes. Moreover, although Somdet To's life certainly can be seen as a commentary on the rise of Thai nationalism and Bangkok-centrism over the past two hundred years, his handlers are neither agents of the state nor part of a gang of religious-opiate pushers. Somdet To might articulate many of the trends in Thai nationalistic discourse, but he and his followers are not part of a xenophobic and jingoistic top-down "movement." The stories of Somdet To instead articulate the value of the everyman of Thai, especially Bangkok, Buddhism. He can be seen as the ideal Thai Buddhist monk, although this ideal is very different from that most commonly described in studies of Theravada Buddhism. If the reader cares nothing about Somdet To or a ghost for that matter, I hope to convince her otherwise. However, if despite my best efforts, I cannot, this chapter offers some new ways of approaching the study of biography, film, and intellectual history in religious studies and related fields.

Chapter 2 is about texts. It sees texts not as objects or messages but as cumulative and contested phenomena that are as much a part of modern graphic culture as of textual history. It is a textual anthropological (or what I like to call an anthrophilogogical) study of one of the most common and powerful protective texts in Thailand, the *Jinapañjara gāthā* (*Verses on the Victor's Armor*). Tracing its history tells us much about what makes a text sacred in Thailand. It also tells us much about what a text can be. The *Jinapañjara gāthā* is found on cloth, in amulets, on CDs and cell phones, in symbolic form, and in tattoos. It is used in meditation, for healing cancer, and for protecting armies. Often magical practices are set in opposition to Buddhist textual study. However, magic is a textual practice. This text helps us question the very existence of Theravada esoteric Buddhism and start to define what Thai Buddhist magic entails. The last section of the chapter offers a critical reflection on the study of the so-called Theravada tantra, or magical/esoteric Buddhism in Thailand. It should have some value for scholars of ritual studies, tantra, new philology, and the history of magic.

Chapter 3 is about actions. I look at Thai Buddhist rituals and liturgies broadly regardless of their connection to Somdet To and Mae Nak. I argue that despite increased standardization in orthography, grammar, monastic orthopraxy, institutional administration, translation methods, print technology, and modernistic self-reflection, there remains a great diversity in quotidian Thai Buddhist liturgies and rituals that defies the stereotypical notion of state-managed, orthodox, and homogeneous Theravada Buddhism in Thailand. Liturgies and rituals can be used for multiple purposes, such as funerals, protection, offerings, dedications, and meditation. The study of liturgy is perhaps the most overlooked aspect of Buddhist studies, but it is the most common way Buddhists are introduced to their religion. Here I hope to dismantle the discrepancies between anthropological and textual approaches to the study of ritual and performance in Southeast Asian Buddhism.

Chapter 4 is about objects. I look closely at a variety of images, amulets, shrines, and murals. Here I speak not only to scholars of religious studies, Buddhist studies, history, and anthropology but also to art historians. Theravada Buddhism as it has been studied by scholars of religion has been depicted as a monastic movement that is desperately trying to stave off commercialism and materialism. This is part of the general Protestant devaluing of materiality that is often foisted onto Buddhist traditions. However, monks and devout Thai Buddhists are not victims of the trappings of a material world but are often the greatest purveyors of stuff. Following Morgan Pitelka and Cynthea Bogel I believe strongly that "Buddhism itself must be re-evaluated not as a purely textual tradition or a teacher-centered movement, but as a set of religious practices anchored to an active, transportable body of material culture."[43] Each statue, each amulet, and each monastery is a product of multiple and shifting intentionalities. The material objects are connected deeply to their urban and rural settings. These settings change rapidly. I support the idea that "we can profitably consider the object's (image, amulet, monastery) encounters with different communities of viewers and users who bring new interpretative lenses to bear on its value."[44] I seek to describe the great diversity of ways objects "act" in Thai religious life. This chapter, then, is a study of Thai Buddhist visual and material cultures. To this end, I first look at monasteries in Bangkok that have some connection with Somdet To and Mae Nak: Wat Rakhang, Wat Indrawihan, Wat Mahabut, and Wat Srapathum. Numerous other monasteries far outside Bangkok are also discussed. Instead of describing monasteries, amulets, and images along sectarian or institutional lines, I offer an aesthetic study of how they are received and described by patrons and clients in shifting ways over time. Each monastery must constantly adapt, articulate new histories, offer more services, and remain fun and beautiful to stay relevant in the competitive "city of deities." Instead of seeing this as syncreticism, localization, or even commercialism, which always implies a hierarchy, I record the cacophony of influences at every monastery. This cacophony gives voice to the modifiers of security, heritage, graciousness (a comforting blend of beauty and hospitality), and abundance.

The 1928 radio broadcast of the ghost story of Mae Nak and the shrine to her buried body are hard to categorize: Is the story of Mae Nak a religious or secular story? Is it a product of modernity or an expression of local tradition? Is her shrine Buddhist or animistic? Are her story and the rituals with which it is associated esoteric or popular? I look at moments and places such as these through-out the book. In each chapter, I use these moments and places to confront as-sumptions in the study of Thai Buddhism. In the end, I hope to offer a new way of approaching the study of Thai Buddhism through repertoire versus institu-tion or doctrine. It is only through a combined use of historical, anthropologi-cal, philological, and art historical approaches that we can begin to clearly understand the constantly broken and repaired lineages of Thai Buddhism that make any study of sectarian or institutional entities superficial and suspect. If this book is successful, it should be exceedingly difficult to talk about Thai Buddhism as simply Theravadin, or use adjectives like traditional, folk, urban, rural, orthodoxic, and orthopraxic in speaking of it. I hope to offer a study that makes describing Thai Buddhism in any general way an exercise in hesitation.

# 1. Monks and Kings

The first time I heard about Somdet To was in a barbershop. I was staring up at the top of the wall while getting a shave and noticed a framed photograph of a monk surrounded by cloth *phra yan* (Sanskrit *yantra*, "mystical" protective drawing). Below was a small, wall-mounted altar replete with plastic flowers and an incense bowl, hanging prayer beads, and dust. I had seen photographs of this monk in many shops, bookstores, monasteries, and taxicabs, but I had never thought to ask who he was. In between swipes of the razor and with my eyes watering from the menthol cream, I inquired. I was told it was Luang Pho To, of course, as if the question was downright stupid. "Why do you have a photograph of him versus other famous monks, like Than Achan Mahabua, Phra Achan Man, Luang Pho Wat Pak Nam (Phra Thepamuni), or Luang Pho Khun?" I asked. "Mai ru" (I don't know), my barber laughed, "I guess because he heals wounds like you are about to get if you don't stop talking." He finished the shave, slapped some St. Luke's powder on my face, and I paid my bill.

I didn't learn much more that day. My barber told me some stories about Luang Pho To (also known as Somdet Phra Phutthachan Phrahmarangsi To, Luang Phu To, Somdet To, Phra Maha To, Khru To, Khrua To, and Than Achan To), stating that he was a son of King Rama II, that he magically healed soldiers' gunshot wounds, and that he made powerful amulets, among others. What he did not know was when Somdet To lived, where he was born, what his Buddhist teachings were, when he died, who his teachers were, who his students were, and other basic intellectual biographical information. Over the next few years I began to see photographs and statues of Somdet To seemingly everywhere in central Thailand. He certainly is the most "imaged" monk in Bangkok. He is getting more and more popular every year. In fact, two new images of Somdet To in Prachuab Khiri Khan Province and Nakhon Ratchasima Province are now the largest statues of any monk in Thailand; each is over sixty-five feet tall. They were both finished in 2007.

Not only did I begin seeing Somdet To everywhere but I also started hearing numerous different and often conflicting stories about him. Sometimes he was a son of King Rama II, sometimes of King Rama I, sometimes from a poor farming family, sometimes from Tak, sometimes from Kanchanaburi, sometimes from Kampaengphet, sometimes a Pali scholar, sometimes a meditation master, sometimes from Bangkok, sometimes a forest monk, sometimes the abbot of a monastery in Bangkok (Wat Rakhang or Wat Indrawihan or Wat Rangsri or Wat Pho), sometimes he taught King Rama V, sometimes King Rama IV, and so on. He was always said to make powerful amulets and protect against ghosts. Collecting and sifting through these stories and the many published biographies of Somdet To became first my hobby and then my obsession. The conflicting stories and massive impact of this elusive monk, hidden in plain view, forced me to reflect on the nature of hagiography, the historical value of rumors, the connections between famous monks and powerful kings, esoteric versus mainstream religious practices, market forces, aesthetics, and competing and seemingly contradictory notions of prestige and virtue in Thai Buddhism. The underlying question that occupied me throughout was, Why this monk?

This chapter is a lengthy effort to dispel some assumptions often made in the study of Thai Buddhism and Buddhism more broadly. Through a close investigation of the creation of Somdet To biographies, I will first demonstrate that religious and political hagiographies/biographies are not simply top-down efforts to create national heroes for the sake of social control, nationalism, and economic manipulation. Somdet To's biography does not reify him or create a static picture of a state-supportive cadre. Somdet To's life story reveals competing discourses of cultural capital in Thailand. Even though many of the stories might not be true and many people telling them realize and admit that they are trading in rumors and hearsay, I am interested in what they reveal about Thai notions of human ideals and cultural heroes. Often scholars, especially political scientists and historians, overemphasize the power of the royal family's propaganda and consistently lament the tendency of the Thai people to display unwavering loyalty to their kings. The Buddhist sangha is often depicted as a tool of the state or royal family. This foreign and domestic scholarly outcry has become particularly acute in recent years with the public commentaries and books on the lèse-majesté laws in Thailand, the royal family's role in the coups of 1973, 1977, 1992, and 2006, the recent sangha administrative act, the intense propaganda campaign by the Thai Privy Council for the eightieth birthday of King Rama IX, and recent heated debates over abuses of the lèse-majesté laws. However, this commentary often treats the Thai people as a herd of uninformed, blind worshippers and monks as either political opportunists or pawns. It is well-known that every day Thai people trade in rumors about the royal family, openly share risqué photographs, and question their role in development, politics, and social welfare. This also seems to have been the case in the time of Somdet To, when, as we will see, he publicly insulted two kings. Perhaps the self-congratulatory attitude scholars have that they are the only people who question the wisdom of kings needs to be reconsidered.

Second, while Lao Buddhism is often seen by scholars as undeveloped, unscholarly, oppressed, and disorganized, a study of Somdet To (and indeed many Thai monks) shows that there is a "Lao mystique" in Thai religious discourse. Sympathetic scholars working in Laos, northern or northeastern Thailand often write in defense of the poor ethnic Lao people who have suffered at the hands of the Thai state and the hegemonic and centralized Thai sangha. However, what is often overlooked is the prestige that comes with a Lao connection in Buddhist practice and learning. "Laos" as well as northern and northeastern Thailand are often stereotyped in modern central Thailand as places of powerful magicians and meditators. A great part of Somdet To's fame is attached to his connections to Lao refugee communities in Bangkok, his possible Lao or northern Thai mother, his training under a powerful Lao magician, and his use of Lao and northern Thai recipes and incantations. He was not ashamed of his possible Lao or rural family history. He promoted it actively. His connection to these poor "Lao folk" is as powerful as his connection to kings.

Third, Thailand is promoted and promotes itself as a noncolonized, peaceful "land of smiles." Buddhism is seen as a peaceful religion that promotes meditation, world peace, and social harmony. However, Somdet To is lauded for his support of defensive and offensive magic, his protection of soldiers, his ability to save the nation from the French, the Germans, and the Japanese. He did not consider himself, it seems, a Theravadin monk but a Thai monk. He protected his land. In fact, the only known copy of his handwriting is a text containing recipes, protective drawings, and incantations to help people in battle. His only sermon witnessed by a foreigner states that Somdet To directly told Thais to be wary of foreigners and look inward. This chapter and the next discuss his nationalism, martial attitude, and outright jingoism and xenophobia. Thai fans of Somdet To are not embarrassed by these qualities but actively laud his nationalism.

Finally, I show through stories, films, and texts that Somdet To and his biographers did not necessarily promote the values of nonattachment and indifference (among others) but the local values of security, heritage, graciousness, and abundance. This will provoke students and scholars of Buddhism to question the universality of Buddhist ethics. That is a lot to pack into this chapter, but Somdet To is central to the history of Buddhism in Thailand and his story needs to be told.

## AMBIGUITY AS BIOGRAPHY

### DREAMS OF ELEPHANTS EATING MANUSCRIPTS: BIRTHS, PARENTS, AND NOVITIATES

Somdet To has consistently been the most-recognized monk in central Thailand for over one hundred thirty years. There are certainly more images, more biographies/hagiographies, and more amulets in Bangkok and the central region of Thailand directly associated with him or about him than of any other Thai saint, including the famous Luang Pho Khun, Phra Thepamuni, Achan Man, Luang Phu Tuat, Khrupa Siwichai, Phra Yantra Amaro, Buddhadasa Bhikkhu, among others. He still appears on more popular Buddhist magazine covers than any other figure, has the largest number of colossal images connected with him (including the largest image of any monk in the world), and has been the subject of major scholarly biographies in Thai.

There are over fifteen biographies that have been published, each of which, in very different ways, emphasizes his unique qualities; they range from simple chronologies to unapologetic apotheoses. There is even a children's book that devotes nearly an entire chapter to descriptions of Somdet To, explaining him as one of the wisest teachers in the history of Thailand.[1] Most books agree on the basic time line, major events, and special qualities, but the details are often vastly different and contradictory. There has been no sustained effort at establishing the "critical biography." I will make no such attempt here for two reasons. First, for Thai scholars and devotees there is no sense that there needs to be just one "true" story of Somdet To. Even serious scholars neither criticize conflicting versions nor attempt to promote the correctness of their own accounts. Critical research comparing and corroborating evidence is undertaken; however, once one story is established as historically genuine, the myriad others are neither chastised nor abandoned. Having access to one genuine biography is rarely claimed and not particularly valued. Certain books claim to be accounts based on the oldest evidence, but Somdet To's receivers often draw evidence when telling stories from many biographies without ranking them. Second, having multiple and conflicting voices adds both to the prestige and intrigue of Somdet To's life. The mystery created by having several unknowns in his biography adds to the air of his sacredness.

Telling different versions of Somdet To's story is furthermore an entertaining pastime among amulet dealers, scholars, devotees, nuns, novices, and monks. I often found myself among a group of scholars or dealers or novices who would laugh, gesture wildly, and speak in a wide range of different dramatic voices while telling stories about Somdet To. People would invite me to their personal libraries, offices, homes, or monastic cells to show me their personal collections of To-related books, amulets, and images. I was amazed at the range of people, from elite scholars who had received their doctorates from places like Chulalongkorn University, Banaras Hindu University, the Australian National University, and the University of California, Los Angeles, who seemed to be as fascinated by Somdet To as amulet dealers and fans who had received little formal education. Thammayut monks highly trained in Pali grammar in Bangkok seemed to be as intrigued by Somdet To as village Mahanikai monks from rural areas. Wealthy Chinese businesswomen, members of the royal family, Thai entrepreneurs, tailors, and shopkeepers all seemed to possess a Somdet To amulet and be able to relate a good story about him. I was even told stories about Somdet To by a waiter at a Malaysian restaurant in Washington, D.C., who collected amulets on eBay with his friends in Kuala Lumpur, as well as by a Chinese architect who lived in London and bought amulets at markets in Hong Kong.

As my own collection of Somdet To books, amulets, holy water, umbrellas, pillowcases, statues, and photographs developed over the years, I participated in this pastime, like showing off rare Coltrane or Clash record collections or baseball cards to friends in bars. No one could ever claim to have a complete collection. No one made firm truth claims about their version of Somdet To's biography. The telling of the stories and showing off of the stuff was the point and the pastime. There are amateur Somdet To biographers everywhere. They cross sectarian, age, gender, and class boundaries. Somdet To scholars come from multiple fields, such as economics, political science, history, and anthropology.

Somdet To was a high-ranking Thai monk in nineteenth-century Bangkok. He was given the royal title Somdet Phra Buddhācāriya in 1867, near the end of his life. From biographies, it seems that he was most often called Khrua To by his fans. Besides these basic facts there are few biographies that agree on the details of his life. Several versions state that he was born to an elite noble family from the once powerful northern Siamese city of Kampaengphet, on Thursday, April 17, 1788.[2] However, in one version his parents are relatively simple farming folk. His mother, Ngut, had fled to Ayutthaya during the Burmese invasion of Kampaengphet. His father is rarely mentioned, but it is believed by many that he was the son of King Rama I.

There is a famous story about his birth in which it is said that King Rama I, before he was king, was a general fighting the Burmese along the border of Kampaengphet and Tak. Between battles one day, he was riding his horse and met a young woman along the road. He was very thirsty, so he asked the young woman for some water. She, not knowing who he was but knowing that he was a nobleman from central Siam, gave him the water in a bowl. However, before she handed it to him she sprinkled lotus flower stamens in the water. Lotus stamens have a bitter taste. He took the water, and so as not to drink the stamens, he had to sip the water very slowly so they would not float into his mouth. He slowly finished the water and then asked her why she had polluted it with the stamens. She replied, "You looked very thirsty, I was afraid if I didn't put the stamens in the water that you would gulp it down and choke and fall off your horse. The stamens forced you to drink the water slowly and safely." The future king was impressed by her cleverness and kindness and asked her parents for her hand as one of his concubines. They, not wanting to offend this unknown nobleman and member of the powerful central Siamese army, granted his wish. He traveled on his campaign with the young girl, but he could not take her back to Bangkok. Therefore, he said, if you ever have a child by me, take my belt and come to Bangkok. If you show this belt at the palace, your child will be well taken care of. She was indeed pregnant with his child and went to Bangkok after having the baby. She stayed near Wat Indrawihan in a community of mostly ethnic Lao refugees and workers. Young To, as he was called (a common nickname meaning "first" or "big" and often used for children who are ironically particularly small at birth), grew up there. When he was about eight years old his mother took him and the belt to Wat Mahathat, next to the palace. The abbot showed the belt to the now King Rama I. King Rama I claimed young To as his son and sponsored his ordination.[3] I return to the significance of this story, but it should be stated that this is simply one of many stories of his birth and parentage.[4] Some published biographies and oral stories state that he grew up in rural provinces like Angthong, Pichit, Ayutthaya, and Suphanburi.

The oldest published biography is from 1923 (although there were many references to him before this). The life of Somdet To is briefly recounted alongside other biographies of famous nobles and warriors in *Ruang tang phra rachakhana phuyai nai krung Ratanakosin* (*Famous Noble People in the City of Ratanakosin*), by Prince Damrong and published on the occasion of the funeral of the *sang-harat* (the head of the Thai monastic order), who was an orthopraxic Thamma-yut monk.[5] The text states that the young To was born in Ayutthaya but says nothing about his father and little about his mother. This text states that he was a royally sponsored novice (*nak luang*) at Wat Sangwetwisayaram in Bangkok studying under the scholar-monk Phra Bowonwiriya and was ordained as a monk at Wat Rakhang in 1807.[6] He continued his studies at Wat Sri Ratanasasa-daram in Bangkok, where the *sangharat*, Phra Suk, was his preceptor and finan-cial support for his studies came from King Rama II. There he was given the title Phra Maha To for his ability to orally translate several Pali texts.[7]

The biography most cited by later accounts was written by Maha Ammattri Phraya Thipkosa (given name Son Lohanan) in 1930.[8] This is an atypical study, because instead of starting with the story of To's birth or mother, it actually be-gins with the author's discussing his skepticism about the oral traditions of Somdet To and describing his methods of combining interviews of students of Somdet To with those of local archaeologists and historians like Phrom Sutthi-phong and Phra Mahasawang, who were familiar with Somdet To's image, am-ulet, and mural production. He questions their accounts, compares sources, and occasionally makes sound speculations about Somdet To's travels, the places he gave sermons, consecrated statues, and so forth based on donation inscriptions, murals, interviews, and oral hagiographic traditions. Thipkosa states that Som-det To was actually born at Wat Bangkhunphrom (now Wat Indrawihan) in Bangkok. However, the author notes the difficulty in determining the exact place and shows that murals depicting To's life and oral traditions all disagree on the details. For the sake of accuracy, he bases much of his biography on the murals, which I discuss in chapter 4, since they were originally sponsored by Somdet To himself. He does not seek to resolve the discrepancies but presents conflicting evidence, allowing the reader to decide. He states that he spent his novitiate at Wat Bangkhunphrom under the tutelage of the powerful magician-monk Phra Arannik Kaeo. Many later biographies agree with these basic asso-ciations, and rather than deny Thipkosa's litany of facts, they expand the account. They pile on more stories, more connections, more village names, and more teachers who supposedly taught To. Some of these additions contradict Thip-kosa, but there is rarely any attempt to criticize him. History writing in modern Thailand often works this way. It is often not the duty of young historians to criticize or correct their predecessors. Instead they simply add.[9]

The only biography that makes an explicit claim to be the definitive account (although it does not criticize other biographies) was published by the National Library of Thailand. Here it states that Somdet To was indeed born in the vil-lage of Kaichon in Tha Luang District in what is now Ayutthaya Province. His

mother was not named Ngut but Ket, and she was from Tha It District, Uttara-
dit Province (in Thailand's far north along the Lao border). There is no mention of his father. It states, not in explicit contradistinction to any other claim,
that when he was a young boy his family did not move immediately as refugees
to the Wat Bangkhunphrom (Wat Indrawihan) neighborhood, but instead he
spent his youth in the farming provinces north of Bangkok as a relatively simple
young novice. First his mother moved to Chaiyo Village in Angthong and then
eventually to Wat Bangkhunphrom in Bangkok. The biographer employs art
historical evidence to establish authenticity for this biography. Somdet To established large Buddha images as an adult at Wat Satheu, which is next to Wat
Kaichon, and at Wat Chaiyo in Angthong.[10]

In this biography there is a wonderfully evocative little story. It tells how one
evening the abbot of Wat Rakhang, the high-ranking Somdet Phra Buddhagho-
sachan Nat, dreamed of a giant white elephant eating manuscripts out of Wat
Rakhang's famous library. After the elephant had devoured every leaf of every
text, the abbot awoke and immediately made an announcement that if anyone
knew of a bright young boy who wanted to study with him, that person should
bring him to Wat Rakhang. Phra Arannik of Wat Indrawihan presented his own
student—To. After a period of study at Wat Rakhang, To was seen as a prodigy
who could indeed mnemonically devour books, and he was sent for further study
with the *sangharat* (Suk) himself at Wat Mahathat directly across the river.
Somdet To was becoming an up-and-coming star monk in the kingdom.

This dizzying array of names does not make for good copy. The prose is
bogged down by the complicated shifting litany of monasteries, teachers, and
villages. However, the various biographies are written this way. The importance
of Somdet To's birth and youth is not the sequence of events but the people and
places to which he has been connected. The value of Somdet To's biography
does not come from his teachings but simply from his presence. Like the biography of the historical Buddha, there is an enormous amount of ink spilled in
telling the stories of his mother and youth. This attention seems unnecessary
since it tells us nothing substantial about why he was a great teacher or sacred
protector. Similarly, Somdet To's mother is not lauded for her methods of
raising children. In published biographies she never speaks, she is simply mentioned in association with place-names. Being from a particular town is enough.
Occupying space is sufficient. The variety of villages in which he was apparently simultaneously born and the various monasteries at which he was either
ordained or studied as a child are not, besides Wat Rakhang, particularly important for any reason other than that they are associated with the young To. This
association has paid great dividends. As we will see in chapter 4, there are entire
monasteries that base their reason for existence and center all their advertising

around loosely established oral traditions that young To or his mother lived or visited there. His supposed or actual presence at these monasteries, in some cases before he could even walk or talk, has generated a significant amount of income, led to the construction of sermon halls, the donation of statues of To, as well as to the sponsorship of festivals, museums, and memorials. One is reminded of plaques in small towns in the United States or Ireland that claim fame for the otherwise unimportant place because a famous writer or saint passed through or rented an apartment there once. The multitudinous claims of association to William Faulkner made by various towns in Mississippi are similar to those of abbots and local historians in places like Angthong and Kampaengphet. The proprietors of hundreds of small restaurants claim that Thelonious Monk or John Lennon ate at their establishments. They all benefit from that ephemeral whiff of presence.

Of all of these stories, the least-substantiated but most common oral claim is that To's father was King Rama I. The power of this claim is obvious, as are later royal connections to subsequent Chakri-dynasty monarchs. Besides the Buddha himself, there is no superior association to claim in Thailand than to that of a king. Even though there is no solid evidence that it is true and none of the major published biographies claim a royal bloodline for To, the rumor persists.[11] Not even Prince Damrong, who wrote about Somdet To, states that his relative was To's father. He simply states that his father was a *mae tap* (military general) fighting in the north. However, the story often told at monasteries and in the amulet markets is that he was the son of the king. The reason the rumor is cultivated is not because historians and devotees of Somdet To have labored to establish its truth but because very few biographers and the royal family itself have never denied its veracity. Phra Siri at Wat Rakhang told me in 2006 that since Somdet To never spoke about his father, there was no reason to believe it was not the king. A nun named Maechi Chaemchit was embarrassed to speak with me about the issue of Somdet To's paternity, because she believed his father was indeed the king and she was not sure if foreigners knew that in the past Thai kings could have many wives and sire many dozens of children. The Thai film dramatization about Somdet To does not have an actor playing his father, just one representing his mother. He is conspicuously absent. The mystery is left alone. The ordained and lay followers are happy to benefit from the suggestive power of silence. There is enough innuendo and circumstantial evidence to keep the rumor vaguely plausible. There is power in this ambiguity.

Many biographies simply do not mention the father, even though the mother is discussed. To's mother was most likely from the north, and King Rama I led thirteen separate military campaigns there between 1767 and 1782. By the time To was conceived in late 1787, however, most of his campaigns were in the east along the Cambodian frontier. The fact that Somdet To was sponsored by the king in his studies despite his probable refugee status, as well as his placement at a royal monastery, his later position as adviser to King Rama IV, and his devotion and titles from King Rama V, all suggest some royal genes.

Thipkosa's famous biography of 1930 is not vague about the paternal line. Thipkosa relates the story, similar to the one mentioned, of a thirsty General Chakri, who would later become King Rama I. He meets a beautiful and clever young village girl named Ngut in Kampaengphet and asks her to marry him (as a minor wife). Thipkosa spends a great deal of time emphasizing the class differences between the general and the young girl. In one scene, the young girl's mother, who is described as brash and direct, chastises the general for associating himself with a common girl born of farmers and foresters! The man who would soon be king is humbled; he raises his hands in a *wai* (a common Thai hand gesture showing respect and humility). He requests to be their son-in-law using the gentle and self-deprecating phrase "ma on nom yom tua pen luk khoi."[12] The parents of the young girl did not readily agree, though, and the general is made to beg for their approval, entreating them with an increasing lexicon of honorifics. He must sign a contract on a banana leaf, offer money, and bathe properly before he is allowed to take their daughter. Thipkosa, who was a low-ranking scholar in a world of much higher-ranking nobles, must have enjoyed relating this story of a nobleman bowing to a farm family. Thipkosa never claims that this is a true story but includes it regardless.

Many scholars and devotees simply will not state unequivocally that Somdet To was the son of King Rama I, but counterevidence is given only sparingly. For example, Phra Khru Kalyananukun's biography states that To's father was unknown and "from another place."[13] One documentary film starts off talking about Somdet To's mother, emphasizing the fact that she lived during Rama I's reign, and then juxtaposes a painting of his mother on a mural at Wat Indrawihan with a painting of Rama I in Wat Rakhang. Later the abbot of Wat Sateu is interviewed in the film. He mentions Somdet To's father as not being Rama I, but as he speaks scenes of Somdet To's statue is shown on the screen on an altar in Rama I's former bedroom, which is now the library building at Wat Rakhang.[14] One of the easiest biographies to find is one sold in the amulet market between Tha Maharat and Tha Phra Chan across the river from Wat Rakhang. It is a popular text advertising rare amulets made by Somdet To. Here Somdet To's father is not even mentioned, as if To's mother had conceived him immaculately. Every other detail down to the time of day he was born is provided. His mother, here named Khet, is mentioned. The absence of the father's name and birthplace is notable.[15] This is relatively typical, though, in the To biographical tradition. One small biography simply states that little is known about his father, but his name was believed to be simply La (no surname). La could have simply been married to Ngut (or Khet) later, though, because it is also not agreed upon if his mother was married when she left Kampaengphet or even if she was from there. However, since Somdet To visited Kampaengphet as an adult, there seems to be some connection with this small northern city. The mystery remains. Some connection is enough.

Two mural paintings at Wat Indrawihan refer to Somdet To's possible royal connection. On a new set of murals (painted in 1980) depicting the life of Somdet To at Wat Indrawihan there is a small painting of King Rama I on horseback with an inscription next to it stating, "Krung Kampaengphet" (City of Kampaeng-phet). This is very close by on the wall to another painting depicting a young commoner woman with a naked infant. The inscription there reads, "Mae Ngut," the name of Somdet To's mother. Even though it states that the child is the son of one Nai Phon, giving the artist a little license we can assume that the child is Somdet To and that there is a not-so-subtle suggestion being made that Rama I is the real father of the baby, since he supposedly met Mae Ngut in Kampaengphet and the inscription does not say the child isn't Mae Ngut's. Furthermore, she is leaning over the baby, while the supposed father is placed at a distance from the baby. In another area of Wat Indrawihan, there is more conflicting evidence of Somdet To's father. There are two statues partially hidden behind a small build-ing and obscured by another larger image. These two statues have signs in front of them that say, "Pitha Manda khong Somdet Phutthachan Phrohmarangsi To" (Father and Mother of Somdet To). These are the only two statues that I have seen in Thailand of a monk's parents. In many textbooks on Buddhism, monks are often described as mendicants without family attachments. They are, in a sense, children of the sangha, sons of the Buddha, not of some inconsequential lay family. However, Mr. Nikon, one of the directors of the Somdet To charitable foundation (which sponsors thirty elementary schools for poor children in rural Thailand), told me that these statues were established by Somdet To himself in the 1860s. Several other people claimed that they were made out of a strange ma-terial by Somdet To and were extremely heavy and no one in the history of the monastery had been able to move them.[16] Both parents are depicted in monastic robes with shaved heads.[17] Seeing a robed statue in Thailand with breasts is truly rare.[18] The statue of the father does not look anything like other images of King Rama I known in Thailand. The sign does not suggest that the father is King Rama I. However, there used to be a mural behind these two statues, but it was removed during renovation several years ago. I am very happy I photographed it before it was removed. The mural depicted a battle scene, Thai and Burmese armies arrayed against each other. Behind the statue of To's father is the Bur-mese army, directly behind his mother's statue is a small section of the mural with the Thai general, supposedly General Chakri (King Rama I), on horseback; his face is turned away from the viewer, but his body is next to the head of To's mother's statue. When looking at the face of Somdet To's mother, one could see the painting of King Rama I slightly to the left of her head. Could this have been a subtle suggestion by the painter? No one I have spoken with at Wat Indrawihan has said that the statue is of King Rama I. However, I have had four different devotees tell me that Somdet To's father was the king as they were standing in front of this statue supposedly claiming a different father. However, biological fathers and surrogate fathers do not cancel each other out. Jesus Christ's father was just a carpenter from Nazareth, right?

## COLD SHOWERS AND SECRET LAO INCANTATIONS: CUE THE TRAINING MONTAGE

The juxtaposition of a poor refugee mother from a distant northern province and a rakish king is the meat of romance and adventure stories worldwide. The young To was a child of the villages but was ideally sired by a warrior-king. He was an uneducated outsider who was accepted into the pavilions of the best royal monastic schools of the capital. The biographies of his training and adult life have two major themes: he was trained by powerful meditative and magically gifted monks in rural monasteries and thus understood the suffering and patois of the poor, and he was honored by the royal family and high-ranking monks as a textual scholar with an acerbic wit and unmatched intellectual acuity. This ability to operate in both the common and the noble worlds across sectarian and class lines is consistently emphasized in both the written and oral traditions. The double quality is found in the descriptions of many popular Thai saints and kings over the past two hundred years.[19]

After the young To was fully ordained as a monk in 1807, most likely at Wat Rakhang, under the tutelage of Phra Achan Kaeo, he quickly became well-known for his pithy and spontaneous sermons, his meditative ability, his ability to memorize and chant Pali texts, and, most important, for his protective magical powers. These powers were cultivated through years of training in the techniques for executing protective drawings, perfecting amulet recipes, and learning Pali incantations. Several biographies emphasize his connections to famous teachers, especially outside the inner sanctum of Bangkok royal monasteries. This connection was made more significant since the neighborhoods in Bangkok he grew up in were populated by Khmer and Lao refugees.[20]

One of the reasons Somdet To is perennially popular and powerful in central Thailand is because he is associated with these rural folk from the northeast and north. There is a common belief in Thailand that Khmer and Lao monks have secret knowledge of magic (*saiyasat*) and profound powers of concentration. These mysterious forested lands seem to percolate in the minds of many a Bangkok Buddhist with obscure symbols and sounds. Many magicians in Thailand claim that they learned their trade in Cambodia or Laos. This common stereotype, like the common American one that Native Americans are somehow more mystical because they are closer to nature, is reinforced by frequent newspaper articles about local magicians from the Khmer and Lao border regions covered in protective tattoos and holding protective amulets, bones, ivory phalluses, being able to swallow nails, exorcize ghosts, and produce love potions.[21] Amulet-trading magazines often relate miracles and publish photographs of these rural magicians. Even the former prime minister, Thaksin Shinawatra, was rumored to have a Khmer magician on his payroll.[22] The fact that most central Thai incantations, tattoos, and *yantras* are composed in Khom script (closely related to Khmer) fuels this association (although historically the Khom script and the supposed magical qualities of Khmer culture and the region have little to do with each other).[23]

Vague ideas about Khmer and Lao culture blend in the minds of many Buddhists in central Thailand. Whereas "Khmer" often has negative connotations connected to black magic, "Lao" seems to invoke a more benign, "naturalist" stereotype. Several people I interviewed seemed to make no distinction between these diverse linguistic, ethnic, and cultural groups. There are some historical precedents for this modern association of these distant rural peoples and powerful magic. In the late nineteenth and early twentieth centuries the Siamese royal government actively fought against rebel village armies in the northeast of Thailand led by millenarian, ethnically Lao *phu mi bun* (men possessing merit), who were said to be able to protect their bodies magically against bullets and knives, as well as curse Siamese soldiers.[24] One of these figures, Ya Chao Tham, operated on the border of Cambodia and Laos in the late 1800s and was feared and respected by both ethnic groups. As a member of the Champasak (southern Lao) royal family, he was said to have pacified the Brao ethnic group in southern Laos and in Stung Treng (northern Cambodia), as well as strike fear in the French because of his powerful magical skills. It was said that he had the power of invisibility and invulnerability because of his possession of powerful amulets, including two desiccated corpses of female and male aborted fetuses.[25] Stories about him and others circulate through the region. There is a rich oral tradition of Lao soldiers being able to levitate and create invisible shields around themselves.

This magically powerful force, represented by people like Ya Chao Tham in the distant forests outside the cultivated plains of Bangkok's Chao Phraya River valley, needed to be tamed by the central government. However, in the process of incorporation and neutralization, their powers became even more intriguing in popular Thai imaginings. Moreover, the area where Somdet To's mother was believed to be from was considered throughout the nineteenth century to be the borderlands of western Laos by the authorities in Bangkok.[26] Before the war with Lao vassal states in the late 1820s, many Lao were honored in Bangkok as prominent guests. For example, one of the princes of Luang Phrabang was ordained in Bangkok after the cremation of King Rama II. He remained in robes and studied in Bangkok for many months. A French observer noted that in general "it was remarkable . . . the great liberty given the subjects of the Laotian tongue: the court of Bangkok completely respected their customs, dress, and institutions."[27]

However, this attitude at the institutional level seemed to change. In 1902, around eighty thousand monks became subject to a law of the royal government of Siam that controlled their admission to monkhood, the right to ordain, the size and status of monastic ground, the ranking of monks. This was part of a massive reform movement that, as I have discussed in other studies, was only partially effective. There was certainly resistance in the form of renegade monks in the north like Khrupa Siwichai and rebellions of holy men in the northeast sporadically until 1924. In fact, in King Rama I's reign, an attempted coup d'état in 1802 by allies of the king's brother was assisted by "Lao" magicians who had been trained in northern Thailand (this was an area still called Lao by the Siamese). The king's brother had spent much time in Chiang Mai fighting against the Burmese and had been assisted by local magicians. Supposedly, he and his chief adviser, Thong-In, learned these techniques, which helped the usurpers become invincible.[28]

In many histories of Thai Buddhism the Thammayut sect (Pali Dhammayuttika, Thai Nikai) of monks, which was founded in Thailand by King Mongkut and Prince Wachirayan in the mid-nineteenth century, was seen as antithetical to these Lao magical practices. The Thammayut were originally initiated to serve as protectors of the royal ideal of pure Buddhism. However, the Thammayut monks changed over time from being representative of state or royal Buddhism or of Bangkok to a collective symbol of independent forest practice. Over time, many of these monks have gained popularity among magical amulet dealers, prognosticators, and spirit mediums, who invoke the names of these forest ascetics to draw on them for protection and power. The state's efforts to eradicate these practices failed, and the Thammayut has grown to be a potential independent source of charisma and power offering its members and followers an alternative resource in the modern practice of Buddhism.

The modern lineage of forest monks is seen as beginning with Phra Achan Man Bhuridatto and Phra Achan Sao Kantasilo. Thammayut monks like Phra Achan Man, Mahabua, and Phra Achan Cha are seen by scholars like Jack Kornfield as symbols of pure Buddhist simplicity; they are described as straight-talking monks for the people, who do not sully themselves with excessive textual scholarship, monastic examinations, the practice of protective magic, or elaborate rituals. They lead the ideal monastic life in the forest, meditating, preaching, and not harming trees. They are not interested in politics, modernization, or involved in the commercialization of Buddhist practice. However, this characterization the Thammayut is skewed. Hayashi Yukio has asserted that the beginnings of the forest tradition in the northeast were part of a state-sponsored program to pacify and incorporate the Lao populations of the region into the Thai polity. Phra Achan Man and Phra Achan Sao were agents of Thai nationalism sent by Prince Wachirayan, who believed that pure Buddhism was textual and canonical and that the local religious practice of the northeast was simply layers of superstition and ignorance.[29] He goes on to show that the first monastery of the forest tradition in the region, Wat Supatthararam, was built by the elite in 1853 with funds granted by King Mongkut. Soon six other royal monasteries were established in this region, which was considered a hot spot for Lao rebels and which was still neither formally nor practically under central Siamese control. In fact the local leader of the Buddhist sangha before this period was a Lao monk who possessed rank and insignia in the Lao royal government. King Mongkut had him replaced, upon his death, by a Bangkok-trained monk who spread the central elite Siamese interpretation of Buddhism—Thai Buddhism. He promoted the study of the Thai language, disparaged local religious practice, built monastic Pali libraries, and appointed other Bangkok-trained monks to take over the local ecclesia.[30]

By 1899 the word "Lao" was removed from administrative documents for the region. This centralization and nationalization was seen as urgent because of the millenarian rebellions of local holy men (*phu mi bun* or *mo wiset*) made powerful by their protective magic and ability to predict the future. Several rebellions in the north and the northeast were started by local monks and a *mo wiset* from Laos who claimed either that the future Buddha was coming or that they themselves were a future Buddha. They attracted followers by magically curing disease, teaching the *dhamma*, exhorting followers to follow the precepts, and refraining from eating meat. In 1924 in particular they claimed that the new Buddhist era under the power of Metteya (a future Buddha) would be centered in Vientiane, Laos, a particularly dangerous claim to make to the Siamese authorities. Using their supernatural powers and stolen rifles, they destroyed

Siamese governmental regional offices and refused to pay taxes. The Thammayut were part of the Siamese government's efforts to destroy this Lao resistance movement, which sought its strength from the popular belief in protective magic and prognostication.[31]

However, these efforts were not entirely successful. Three well-known Thammayut monks, Achan Thet, Achan Sing, and Achan Fan Acaro, accompanied seventy other monks to "eliminate spirit beliefs by spreading thamma and erecting forest temples."[32] But, their popularity grew because they were seen as

> beings feared by the guardian spirits and evil spirits who lurk in forests and caves. They enter natural graveyards, acquire wisdom (pannya law wicha), and have no fear of death; they conquer the forest world. They heal themselves with spiritual unity (thamma) when afflicted with illness during their ascetic practices. They subdue evil spirits and destroy the guardian spirit cults in every village they visit during their wanderings, converting them to Buddha's teachings . . . They hold religious services morning and night and can cure illness by chanting sutras.[33]

These wandering teachers were not only known as reforming teachers and purveyors of a rational, canonical Buddhism but also as popular because of their superior healing powers. They didn't destroy spirits, they converted them. Over time this is how these wandering monks have been valued in the northeast and throughout Thailand, as powerful healers and usurpers of the magical power previously associated with the Lao, Khmer, and Thai lay magicians. Included in the many published biographies of these Thammayut monks are stories of their practicing astral projection, visiting one another in dreams, using mind control to tame animals, and speaking with ghosts in the forest. Moreover, as a sign (nimitta) of their level of meditational achievement, their followers show that after they die often their bones crystallize.[34]

These monks were popular because they were active in solving local problems, not just because they were solitary meditators. Their amulets are valuable possessions for collectors and healers. Their statues, pictures, magical yantras, and relics are found in taxicabs, city bazaars, rural monasteries, and magicians altars throughout the country. Of course the history and controversies surrounding the wandering monastic Thammayut tradition of the northeast is not our central concern, but it is important to understand the complexity of how modern Buddhism is practiced and understood in Thailand. The lines between urban and forest monks, textual and popular Buddhism, precepts and magic, social activism and pure asceticism, central and periphery are always fluctuating. The state may have long arms, but its fingernails often get broken and dirty.

Somdet To did not grow up in the rural northeast, but his connection to the neighborhoods of Bangkhunphrom, Srapathum, and Wang Lang in Bangkok, combined with his mother's supposed northern blood, are often invoked as giving him an early dose of rural knowledge. In fact, it is his mother's status as a rural refugee that has given him as much stature as a powerful monk as his connections to King Rama I. In the nineteenth century, Bangkhunphrom, Srapathum, and Wang Lang were immigrant neighborhoods (they are still referred to as ban Lao, Lao neighborhoods, by many today). They were originally populated by refugees from the north who had fled there (especially so for Wang Lang) from the Burmese invaders, as well as by Lao and Khmer populations forcibly settled there by Siamese armies that had captured them during the frequent nineteenth-century wars along the Mekong. There is a large plaque posted at Wat Indrawihan in the Bangkhunphrom neighborhood that calls the area ban Lao. There is a painting of Somdet To surrounded by women with distinctive Lao-style skirts and hairstyles among the murals of Wat Indrawihan. In fact, Wat Indrawihan is named after a Lao prince, Chao Inthraram, who was one of the Lao forcibly settled in the neighborhood.[35] Phra Arannik, Somdet To's teacher there, was ethnic Lao. He was a famous meditation teacher and magician in Vientiane who had been resettled in Bangkhunphrom. He was made the abbot of Wat Bangkhunphrom Nok (now Wat Indrawihan). Today there is a large painting of Phra Arannik at Wat Indrawihan. It depicts him walking in the forest followed by a small group of lay supporters. In the background is the famous stupa and national symbol of Laos, That Luang, and a Lao-style monastery. The connection of Wat Indrawihan and Somdet To to Laos is not hidden. They are glorified by the purveyors of his lineage in modern Thailand. The prominent place of this painting at Wat Indrawihan seeks to reinforce Somdet To's connection to Laos and Lao secret teachings.

Somdet To often spent time at Wat Pathum Wanaram (Wat Srapathum) during the reign of King Rama IV. He stayed there, a Thammayut monastery, as the king's personal guest. Phra Ratchapandit, the senior secretary and assistant abbot of Wat Srapathum, well-known for his encyclopedic knowledge of Bangkok history, granted me an interview. He informed me that dozens of Lao Buddha images at Wat Srapathum (including the famous Luang Pho Soem, Luang Pho Saen, and Luang Pho Sai golden images) were taken from Vientiane after Siamese armies destroyed the city in 1827.[36] Indeed, every document I have been able to find about Wat Srapathum promotes these images as Lao originals and a mark of pride and prestige, defying the common stereotype that Lao ancestry is considered low class and shameful.[37] Somdet To was said to be quite fond of these images, further reinforcing his connection to the sacrality of the mystical Lao as well as to King Rama IV.[38]

When Somdet To was a student at Wat Rakhang (and later abbot) he had access to the largest collection of Lao and Thai manuscripts (composed in Tham and Khom scripts, respectively) in central Thailand. King Rama I had ordered manuscripts to be collected in the library of Wat Rakhang in order to edit, revise, and renew the Pali Tripiṭaka after the fall of Ayutthaya. One of Somdet To's teachers, Somdet Phra Ariyawongyan Sri, was the head of this project, and although from the south, he translated and transcribed Lao- and Khom-script manuscripts.[39] I spent many years studying these Lao, northern Thai, and northeastern Thai manuscript collections (many now held at the National Library), and an extremely large portion of them are protective and astrological texts.[40] One monk, Phra Maha Narongsak Sophanasithi, who granted me several long interviews and provided me with many books, stated that the Lao monks who resided at the monastery when To was a boy taught him "secret Lao meditation" techniques and gave him recipes for making amulets. Somdet To's amulet recipes often call for Lao herbs and flowers. Phra Maha Narongsak even believed that King Rama V's power came from Somdet To, because he was the king's Pali teacher when the king was a child. In these Pali lessons, Somdet To passed on Lao magical secrets! Phra Mahasomkiat at Wat Indrawihan has emphasized the power of Lao magic and stated that is why people came from all over the world to gain access to this protective power at Wat Indrawihan. Even the tallest Buddha image in Thailand, which Somdet To had commissioned, is rumored to be filled with Lao mystical drawings, herbs, and other mysterious "foreign" imports.[41]

Somdet To trained with not only Phra Arannik but also with several other rural magicians. These teachers are featured in several biographies and often in amulet trade magazines. Each connection Somdet To is said to have had to these individual teachers creates another lineage of prestige. The economies of entire monasteries and the careers of monks have been made thanks to their association with Somdet To. One of the most popular biographies is not a book or magazine, it is a feature film (more dramatization than documentary) of Somdet To's life. The VCD is easily found and sold at several monasteries associated with Somdet To as well as in the amulet markets and religious bookstores for approximately ninety baht (less than three dollars). It has had many pressings, and a recent edition comes with a free amulet. This film spends a great deal of time on Somdet To's teaching lineages and his magical training.[42] It is worth an in-depth description because it is one of the most common ways Thai Buddhists come to know a biography of To and is thus more important for our purposes than supposedly more reliable but less-popular sources.

The film opens in 1788 with the abbot of Wat Rakhang suddenly stopping on his morning alms rounds. A smile grows on his face because he has a strange sense that something wonderful has happened. When he is asked by one of his students why he has stopped, he states that a great teacher has been born somewhere in the kingdom. Like an angelic herald, he was correct; the scene shifts to rural Ayutthaya, where baby To is born. The infant, holding a flower, is brought to Wat Bangkhunphrom, where he is called a *bodhisatta* with *saksit* (sacredness). As he grows up, a dizzying array of monasteries and teachers are associated with his training. He studies at Wat Yai Muang in Pichit Province, where he is seen protecting insects and developing compassion, it is said, for the lowliest of creatures. He studies meditation and Pali grammar as well. He is told that he must be both a *phra kammatthan* and a *phra parian* (meditation master and scholar-monk). He studies the Abhidhamma with the abbot of Wat Chainatbuli and then eventually is brought to Bangkok to study with Phra Achan Kaeo of Wat Bangkhunphrom Nok. He is trained to read palm-leaf manuscripts and also in herbal medicine and sacred healing. The typical montage of training sequences is presented to dramatic music. Years pass and the actors playing To change until he is a fully ordained monk in his twenties.

Here the film shifts from his training to his relationship with the laity. The theme of this section is attractiveness. First there is a humorous scene of a *katoi* (transvestite) falling in love with the young To during alms rounds. The man in woman's clothing flirts with the young To every morning. To and another monk giggle a little but do not directly insult the transvestite. Instead it is a scene that promotes To's dedication to his celibate vocation and compassion for the young man. The next scene is similar, showing a beautiful young woman who begins to fall in love with To as he goes on alms rounds in the morning. Despite his robes, the young lady, who is depicted as proper and polite, cannot help herself. Her love makes her swoon. She cannot sleep at night. She decides that she must reveal her true feelings. She visits him at the monastery accompanied by her father and stares at him seemingly unable to speak. Her father approves of her love and tells To that he can marry her if he gives up his robes. In a society that permits temporary ordination, this is not a shocking suggestion; however, To remains stoic and silent despite the young woman's beauty and propriety. The girl leaves. That night, To is tempted by the woman. He takes a cold bath and then looks into a bowl of water (like a crystal ball). In the water he does not see his own reflection but that of the Buddha. He decides that he must remain a monk. The next morning the young woman gives him a jasmine flower and proclaims her love for him. He tells her that the only plant he desires is the bodhi tree of enlightenment. She cries and he chants Pali verses.

The film moves on to To's training in the magical arts and to the long list of teachers associated with him. One teacher, Khru Ta Saeng of Wat Manichonlakhan in Lopburi Province, is particularly adept in incantations and meditation.

His simple title, teacher, and the rural forested setting show that To is not simply a Bangkok monk trained in Pali but a student of the mysterious Lao and Khmer magical arts. Khru Ta Saeng teaches To to create a magical invisible and impenetrable cage around himself, his parents, his preceptor, and his teacher. In several scenes Khru Ta Saeng is depicted teaching the young To in the middle of the night surrounded by candles. In one instance, Khru Ta Saeng places four fresh human corpses on the floor in front of To.[43] To is told to meditate while looking at the dead bodies. This spooky scene is punctuated by Khru Ta Saeng's laughing maniacally like an evil genius (although he is never said to be teaching the "dark arts" or being anything but a Buddhist master). Then the young To is told to close his eyes and consider the nature of death. To's muscles do not even twitch when Khru Ta Saeng suddenly bangs large bells near his head while he meditates. His trance grows deeper, and then he is instructed to chant in vernacular Thai "Tai nae tai nae" (Surely I will die, surely I will die). Then he chants that he will be a ghost and he cannot escape death. Death will come soon. All the while, Khru Ta Saeng has an approving, but sinister, smile.

In the next scene, Khru Ta Saeng takes To deep into the forest, and as it grows darker To loses his way. All of a sudden, right before To's eyes Khru Ta Saeng vanishes! To is left alone at night in the forest, where he is tested for his ability to survive without fear. This fear of the forest at night is a common trope in Pali and Thai narratives. For example, in a story from the Pali *Dhammapada-atthakathā* monks are afraid and terrorized by tree spirits as they meditate at night in the forest. The Buddha gives them the incantation to chant to dispel their fears. The *Khandha, Mora, Vatta, Āṭānāṭiya paritta* texts, among others, are all used for physical protection.[44] The biographies of the monks Achan Man Phuridato and Phra Achan Thet, among many others, both have lengthy scenes of the monks' being afraid at night in the forest and overcoming those fears.[45] To successfully meditates in the forest alone and then finds his way back to the monastery in the morning. Then To must fast for three days. At night they meditate together and chant the incantation "Bot Phra Narai Paet Rup" (The Eight Indras) and then the "108 gāthā" (108 verses). These incantations have become well-known in Thailand among those interested in magic. They are often chanted in a shortened form made up of syllables, which makes them undecipherable to the lay or untrained audience. Then he prostrates seven times and is told that these incantations will make everyone have attraction and lust for him (Thai *saneha*, Pali *sineha*). However, these incantations will be effective only if he possesses compassion. As he chants, special effects in the film show the room spinning, and all of a sudden To opens his eyes to see that he and his teacher have magically switched places. They morph into each other and Khru Ta Saeng states, "Khru Ta Saeng pen Khru To Khru To pen Khru Ta

Saeng" (Saeng the teacher has become To the teacher, To the teacher has become Saeng the teacher). Then in an eerie moment, To laughs maniacally in Saeng's voice. They have become one![46]

Somdet To's training with others is now complete. He has become his teachers and embodies their knowledge. The scene shifts and To is alone in the forest. It is a foggy night and he wanders away. He has taken on a *dhutanga* (Thai *thudong*) ascetic life of wandering alone in the forest.[47] The next scene has To as an older man being called back to Bangkok from the forest by the new King Rama IV fifteen years later. King Rama IV (Mongkut), made famous in the West by the story of Anna and the king of Siam, had heard about To's power and knowledge and wanted him to come to help the kingdom. Rama IV had been born of a noble mother and had been a monk for twenty-eight years himself. Indeed, most sources, including one Western observer, state that Somdet To was indeed a favorite of the new king. Since many viewers of the film would probably believe Somdet To was of royal blood, it would be entirely plausible that he would be seen as a key adviser to the new, very Buddhist, king.[48]

The film shows Somdet To taking over the abbotship of Wat Rakhang and being given the royal title of *thepakawi* (literally, "poet to the gods") by King Rama IV, which is the third-highest rank a monk can receive. The abbotship of Wat Rakhang is significant. Wat Rakhang Ghositārāma is the site of the first palace in Bangkok history on the Thonburi side of the Chao Phraya River. It is directly opposite the present-day Grand Palace. Its manuscript library, which still stands and was recently renovated, was the original home of King Rama I before the Grand Palace was built and the capital moved across the river. This is a fact that many people nowadays offer as strong evidence that To was the king's son. He was made the abbot of the king's old house! It is also the home of the first collected Pali Tripiṭaka of the Bangkok era, the first manuscript library in the city, the first modern Abhidhamma College, and the home temple of Bangkok's first *sangharat* (the head of the entire Siamese Buddhist order). The simple monk who had wandered among the Lao and Khmer for three decades learning meditative and magical techniques had now, in the minds of many, returned home to take up his birthright as a prince among monks. His training was complete and he was now needed to protect his kingdom.

## REWARDING THIEVES AND INSULTING KINGS: LIFE IN THE CAPITAL

Now that Somdet To was the abbot of Wat Rakhang, he lived directly across from King Rama IV. There are numerous stories about their visits to each other, as well as about Somdet To's public life among the laity of Bangkok. Several of them are included in most major biographies and are depicted in the film dramatization about Somdet To's life. Four short stories should suffice to demonstrate how they emphasize To's ability to hobnob with royalty and still remain a common village monk.

One of the funniest stories is about theft. Somdet To is famous for helping thieves, drunkards, and abusive laity and monks reform themselves. One morning Somdet To was meditating in his small monastic cell (*kuṭi*). He was so silent and still for so many hours that a local thief thought that no one was in the cell. He sneaked under the small structure, and since it was old there were many gaps and small holes in the wooden floor planks. He reached his hand through a gap and started groping around for items to steal. Since Somdet To was a favorite monk of King Rama IV he had many royal gifts on the floor. Somdet To saw this seemingly bodiless hand coming up through the floorboards, and instead of grabbing it and capturing the thief, he felt compassion for the foolish man. He started to place valuable royal gifts like silver betel nut sets, gold utensils, brass drinking bowls, and so on into the thief's hand. The thief just figured that Somdet To had so many things that he was easily grabbing the best stuff. This continued for a while until the thief had filled his bags. He started to crawl out from under the monastic cell but was having a lot of trouble carrying all his loot. He started placing the items one by one into his small canoe that he had dragged up onto the banks of the river near Somdet To's cell. After he had loaded the canoe, it was so heavy that he could not drag it. He pulled and pulled but was getting nowhere when all of a sudden the canoe became much lighter and the thief found himself easily dragging it. He turned around and saw Somdet To himself pushing the canoe and helping the thief! The thief dropped his end of the canoe and screamed and started bowing and apologizing. Somdet To laughed and said, "If you need something, just come and ask me." The thief became his disciple and gave up his life of stealing. Somdet To did not care about royal gifts. It is said that he used one of the expensive ceremonial fans King Rama IV had given him as a paddle for an old canoe.

Somdet To refused to use his royal titles like Phra Thepkawi and Somdet Phutthachan. In fact, he openly mocked himself and his titles. Like many stories from the Pali *jātakas* or the *Dhammapada-atthakathā*, which begin with the Buddha's overhearing monks complaining, one story in the various Somdet To collections begins with To's overhearing several monks complaining about another monk who was lazy and never went out on morning alms rounds. This lazy monk expected, because he was older, that the other monks should serve him. Somdet To heard the monks complaining about ranks and titles. The next morning, Somdet To led the alms rounds as usual, and as he approached the cell of the lazy old monk, he started yelling, "I am the Great Royal Somdet Phra Phutthachan To" over and over again. The lazy monk was woken from his sleep and shocked and embarrassed. Somdet To looked surprised when the old monk emerged from his cell and said, "Oh, since you do not need to go on alms rounds for yourself, you must have a higher rank than me, the Great Somdet Phra Phutthachan To." The embarrassed monk bowed his head in shame. The next morning he stood at the back of the line near the young novices and went humbly on the alms rounds.

Eschewing royal gifts and titles was insubordinate, but Somdet To, it is said, was so respected and famous that he could directly insult a king in public. King Rama IV was crowned as absolute regent in 1851. He resided at the Grand Palace, and it is said that on his first day as king in his new house, he decided to throw a little lawn party on the banks of the river under the pavilion in front of his palace. Since he had been a monk for almost twenty-eight years, it is popularly told that he wanted to imbibe some fine spirits and spend time with a few of his consorts. The noise from this soiree bothered Somdet To across the river. Somdet To walked down to the bank of the river and climbed into a small canoe and started paddling to the Grand Palace. The king saw this and yelled out to him something to the effect of, "I gave you a high rank, you should not paddle your own small canoe, it is improper, where is your assistant and a proper vessel?" Somdet To precariously stood up in the center of his canoe in the middle of the river, and as the canoe rocked back and forth, he yelled back, "I figured since a king could act inappropriately and below his own rank, then all people in his kingdom could act any way they wanted to as well!" The king was so embarrassed by Somdet To's pithy and biting response that he went inside and stopped drinking and cavorting in public.

This was not an isolated public censure of the monarch. There are several stories of Somdet To's humiliating the king. It actually happened so frequently that many people believe that Somdet To must have been a blood relative of the king if he could speak so directly and acerbically in the presence of royalty, especially in a country famous for its lèse-majesté laws and the extreme deference shown to members of the royal family. I will relate only one other story to illustrate the great revelry that many followers of To take in telling these stories. It happened that one day, on the anniversary of King Rama IV's ascendancy to the throne, he ordered that every royal monastery in the city construct a decorative boat to float past the Grand Palace in a beautiful flotilla. However, the king did not provide any funds for building these massive flower-filled barges. On the day of the flotilla the king and his entourage watched as barges floated gently past the palace, each more beautiful and ostentatious than the last. Finally, the last boat floated past. It was a tiny wooden canoe without decoration. In the canoe was a monkey sitting with a sign tied around its neck that read, "It is better to lose face than to lose robes" (which rhymes in Thai: *taek na di kwa sia pa*). The king was furious and demanded to know which monastery had sponsored this boat. It was indeed Wat Rakhang and its abbot Somdet To right across the river. The king summoned Somdet To to the palace to explain this insult. He calmly explained that the king had required monks to build floats for a flotilla; however, he had not provided any funding, and the monks are not allowed to raise money for themselves. It is improper to ask the laity to give money for things unrelated to teaching the *dhamma* (*song tham*) and spreading the religion (*phoi phae sasana*). Since the flotilla was unrelated to teaching the *dhamma* and the monks had no money for frivolous events such as this, they had only one option for raising the money—sell their robes.[49] They decided that it would be better to lose face and be embarrassed in front of the king than to be naked! The king bowed his head and never again asked for monastic funds to be used for royal celebrations.

Somdet To dared to put himself not only above kings but also below drunkards, children, and hunters. One of the most popular stories about To comes from later in his life when he decided to take time off from being the abbot of Wat Rakhang and giving sermons in the royal court to wander in the forest and visit other monasteries. It is said that he went to Saraburi, Kampaengphet, Angthong, Kanchanaburi, Prachuab Khiri Khan, Singburi, and other provinces known for their farms and slow-flowing rivers. Many of these short trips were taken by To alone in his canoe. They are documented not only in stories but also by the images, amulets, and sermons he gave at monasteries. Today, many abbots and students claim that Somdet To visited their monasteries in the past and are excited to show off the images he left there. I went to several rural monasteries that To had supposedly visited. Somdet To is talked about by countless monks, nuns, and laypeople as if his footprints were still fresh. On one of these trips it is said he came across a small animal caught in a hunter's trap in the forest. He felt compassion for the animal and released it. However, he also felt compassion for the hunter, and so he placed himself in the trap and waited for the hunter to return. When the hunter saw that he had caught an old monk, he was dumbfounded. Somdet To tells the hunter that he is giving himself as food to the village because the greatest *dāna* (gift) a person can give is her or his own body.[50] The hunter puts down his rifle and releases Somdet To and vows to never hunt again, because he would rather kill himself than another sentient being.

In another story, a drunk man confronts Somdet To while the old monk is giving handwritten *phra yan* protective incantation cloths to villagers who are afraid of ghosts. The drunkard tells Somdet To that he is useless and tells him to leave the village. Before Somdet To can respond, the drunk throws a punch at his head (a terrible moral crime in Thailand). The fist magically passes through Somdet To's head as if it were ghostly itself. The man runs away. The next day Somdet To is summoned to help cure a man who has been seriously injured. Somdet To is surprised to see it is the same man who tried to punch him the day before. He realizes that the man was drunk and that after he had run away from him was accosted by followers of Somdet To, who beat him to a bloody pulp. Somdet To is ashamed that his followers would use violence to defend his honor. He bows down below the injured drunkard and holds him gently like a parent holding a sick child. The drunkard cries and vows to change his life.

Other stories, in which Somdet To breaks up fights with deprecating jokes or magically helps children find lost toys, are also common. Sometimes he is angry and yells at younger monks or even the king. In some stories he humorously teases women gossiping in the monastery courtyard. In others he embraces a sick man. These stories, more than elevating Somdet To to superhuman status, actually often depict him crying or caressing people. In fact, they depict him as quite human, emotional, humorous, and personable. In one scene, he holds and gently comforts a child (the future famous monk Somdet Phra Phutthak-hosachan Chaloen) because he is afraid of Mae Nak. Then Somdet To (whom the novice affectionately calls Grandfather) tells the novice that if he is afraid he can sleep next to him. They defy the image of the ideal Theravada Buddhist monk as distant, detached, calm, and either meditating alone in a cave or walking silently in a forest. However, Somdet To is not an anomaly. Famous Thai monks from the past and present, like Phra Phayom, Luang Pho Khun, Phra Wachiramethi, are often lauded for their ability to tell jokes, comfort followers, and cleverly trick and deflect detractors and naysayers.[51] Somdet To is not depicted as slowly detaching himself from society over time. He does not fade away into a nibbanic trance in a cave but becomes more and more invested in the future of his students and his nation.

## DEATH WITHOUT A BODY: PHOTOGRAPHS AND FUNERARY VOLUMES

Returning to the film biography of Somdet To's life we can see and hear how his followers imagine and come to know his emotional life in Technicolor and Dolby sound clarity. The final stages of his life begin in the film with a dramatic scene. Somdet To is sitting with young novice students and other followers in his cell and receives news that his dear teacher, Khru Ta Saeng, has passed away. He is handed the relic bones and his face wilts. The actor playing Somdet To, Udom Singmoli, demonstrates his range by sobbing uncontrollably. It is an emotionally draining scene in which between gasps of breath and through tears Somdet To has flashbacks to his training and youth and proclaims sadly that his teacher's "battles" (*rop*) are now over. Emotionally and physically drained, as if his teacher and he were truly bound together, Somdet To begins his own slow descent into death.

Soon Somdet To is seen gathering his students around him. He names Luang Pho That the new abbot of Wat Rakhang (which is extremely important for the history of Wat Rakhang and the amulet trade, as Luang Pho That supervised the making of some very valuable amulets and learned the magical technique from Somdet To) and tells them that he must leave the monastery for a while and prepare for death. Several scenes of him making amulets follow; a bird is filmed flying into a setting sun with gentle music playing in the background. The final scene has him giving an amulet to a young novice named Thammathawon (Samanen Chang), who would later become famous for making his own amulets because of his association with Somdet To. Next to the novice is Luang Pho That and another novice, most likely one named Chuang, who would also become well-known, an older, unnamed layman, and most likely an actor supposed to be representing Phra Achan Kham of Wat Amarin (a close friend of Somdet To's). There are five men in front of Somdet To as he lies down on a raised wooden platform with his head on a simple pillow. Behind him are five Buddha images. This is a subtle but important image. The historical Buddha is often depicted as surrounded by five disciples on his deathbed (although he is also occasionally depicted surrounded by crowds). Having five men kneeling in front of To invokes the death of the Buddha. Since five Buddha images also look down at To, it suggests that To will be a future Buddha. In Thailand, it is commonly believed that there are five Buddhas in this epoch, including the historical Buddha. The five are commonly depicted in cloth paintings, murals, and modern paper posters. Without claiming enlightenment for Somdet To, it suggests that either he is enlightened and will become a Buddha after death or that he will be reborn only one more time and walk in the next life as a living Buddha. His last word to the disciples is *anicchang* (Pali *aniccaṃ*, "impermanence").

The scene shifts to one that is not at all subtle. It is well-known to anyone who has ever lived in Thailand. The filmmakers attempt to closely replicate a scene taken from a combination of two of the most well-known and replicated photographs in Thai history. The photographs, which are also depicted in murals, in the National Wax Museum, and sold in poster form in every major

Buddhist bookstore and ritual implement shop in the country, are of Somdet
To. They are two of the oldest photographs in Thailand. They were most likely
taken by Robert Lenz, a German photographer who ran the largest studio in
Siam in the late nineteenth and early twentieth centuries.[52] In both, the eighty-
five-year-old Somdet To is photographed sitting on a raised dais. In one his eyes
are closed and he is meditating in a very distinct way—his hands are curled into
fists and he has them stacked one on top of the other as if he were holding a
sword against his chest. The first photograph was taken on June 24, 1872, at Wat
Indrawihan (which is strange because one brochure at Wat Rakhang states that
Somdet To died on June 22). He sits in a half-lotus position on top of a dais surrounded by flowers, candles, and incense sticks. In the first photograph there
are two novices standing erect as if guarding him from behind the dais. In front
of the dais are two laymen facing each other with two offering bowls in front
of them. In the bowls are huge mounds of amulets that To has just finished
making covered by a small cloth. The laymen are dressed in simple loincloths.
However, in the film depiction, the two novices are missing and the two laymen
are replaced with two senior monks in attendance. These monks are taken from
the second famous photograph. This photograph was taken in 1867 in the Thonburi district of Ban Chang Lo (about seven blocks from Wat Rakhang) when
Somdet To was giving a private sermon at a patron's home. However, in the second photograph Somdet To is seen with his eyes closed holding a palm-leaf
manuscript. In the first photograph are Phra Khru Platmit of Wat Rakhang and
Phra Achan Kham of Wat Amarin. But in the film, it is Luang Phu That (the
abbot at Wat Rakhang after Somdet To) and an unnamed monk. By combining
elements of these two famous photographs into one film image, the director is
able to invoke the reverence of a famous historical moment and add some documented fact into a film that has largely dramatized stories whose veracity could
be questioned.[53] It also helps to elevate the position of Luang Pho That and his
lineage. In the final scene of the film, viewers are reminded of these two famous
and genuine photographs of Somdet To and thus left with an impression that all
they have seen is simply a series of historical facts. Since the film has scenes
of the ghost Mae Nak, Somdet To performing miracles, magical shape-shifting
monks, and events not corroborated by physical proof, it is important to leave
the impression that the director has merely put history into the film. Since the
narrator never cites conflicting evidence or uses the Thai equivalent of phrases
like "some people believe" or "many doubt," it is implicitly suggested that everything the viewer has seen is as true as a photograph. The veracity of Somdet To's
history is rarely doubted even though there are dozens of conflicting accounts,
dates, and names. However, the historicity or historicalness of his life is important for the miracles attributed to him after death. Certainly many doubt, but in

general my interviews revealed a passive desire to believe, especially since these miracles involve personal and national protection. After all, many confided in me, "there is no harm in believing."

Just as there is mystery surrounding Somdet To's birth, there is also much mystery surrounding his cremation. This is not unheard of, but a bit strange. There are other famous monks, probably the best known being Achan Man Phuridato, whose death is a mystery. It is said that he simply disappeared near the end of his life into the forests of Laos.[54] Many believe that he became an enlightened arhat. However, most monks' cremations are well documented. In fact, they are the most documented events, because this is the occasion in Thailand for distributing memorial amulets, books, fans, and other items to those attending the cremation. One could argue that from the late nineteenth century until very recently most Buddhist texts published in Thailand were inspired by the cremation of a monk or layperson.[55] The National Library's Buddhist studies section is filled primarily with cremation volumes. The introductions to these volumes nearly always include photographs of the deceased, a four-to-five-page biography, a list of accomplishments (academic degrees, military ranks, and so on), and letters from important people (like members of the military, government, sangha, or royal family) eulogizing the particular person. These short biographies are a great, untapped source of Thai intellectual, social, and cultural history. The texts that follow these letters, biographies, litanies, and photographs can vary from reprintings of well-known poetry collections to secondary historical works, royal chronicles, novelettes, and the like. The families of most lower- and middle-class Thais cannot afford to produce, print, and distribute these funeral volumes for their deceased relatives; however, when a member of the Thai economic or social elite is cremated, distributing a cremation volume is de rigueur. High-ranking monks nearly always have cremation volumes produced in their honor. Often they are printed at the monasteries themselves. However, Somdet To, one of the highest-ranking monks of his day and the most famous monk in Bangkok history, does not have a cremation volume.

There are several cremation volumes that have been distributed at other people's funerals that reprint biographies of Somdet To or offer new studies of his life and works. They are compiled largely from other biographies but presented as a new work. The biography of Somdet To by Thipkosa has been reprinted numerous times. The one most commonly cited by scholars was supposedly written by Phra Khru Kalyananukun and was distributed at the cremation of Mrs. Thong Yu Hiranpradit in 1986.[56] In the introduction it states that Phra Khru Kalyananukun had long been a dedicated follower and had modeled his life after Somdet To's, although he does not state why. He was born in 1900, so he could not have met his idol. The author of this 1986 introduction never claims that Phra Khru Kalyananukun actually wrote this history of Somdet To, but he does claim that he spent years studying his work. He was so dedicated to Somdet To that he helped build a pavilion in his honor on the grounds of Wat Rangsri in northern Bangkok (one of the largest cremation centers in Thailand, with a large, modern incinerator, and still a popular place to bow down to a large image of Somdet To).[57] The introduction includes photographs of these various buildings and images of Somdet To.

This is a good example of how the Somdet To movement has grown in Thailand, one monk, one layperson at a time dedicating themselves to sponsoring buildings, texts, and images of a person they never met and who, they claim but never state definitively why, inspired them. This is not a top-down movement concocted by the elite to manipulate the masses. It is a participatory, rhizomatic movement that is sustained and fueled by many different entrepreneurs, fans, and students from various backgrounds and classes. Even though they are idiosyncratically produced in honor of laypeople, monks, and nuns, these cremation volumes, printed for free distribution, are not necessarily limited in their readership. There is great social capital produced, but not much actual, if any, economic capital. For example, the *Kittikhun lae Phra Barami Somdet Phra Phutthachan To Wat Rakhang lae Wat Indrawihan* was freely distributed at a funeral in 1986 and had 2,100 copies printed funded by three laymen and one laywoman and composed by a committee of local scholars led by Mr. Samat Khongsat. Such cremation volumes in addition to the hundreds of shorter biographies included in inexpensive amulet trade magazines or pamphlets distributed freely at monasteries allow great access to the many lives of Somdet To.

Despite their preponderance, it is not necessarily strange that Somdet To did not have a volume distributed at his own cremation. In fact, the oldest cremation volume I have been able to find is from 1894. Somdet To died in 1872. The first printing press in Thailand was started in 1836 by a Christian missionary, and it was not until the 1860s that books were being printed by Thais in the Thai script.[58] However, what is strange is that we have almost no information on his actual death and cremation. This is usually the one event in a monk's life, especially a royally supported, high-ranking one, that we have significant details about. Many scholars that I have interviewed have also been perplexed by the lack of information on Somdet To's cremation.[59] There are actually very few sources besides the film and a few biographies that mention his death (but not his cremation). It is said in one biography that he died of a kidney disease. A beautiful hardback biography of Somdet To contains one page about his death and states simply that he died of the "disease of old age" (*rok charaphap*).[60] Anand Amantai's large biography of 2000 provides details on nearly every aspect of Somdet To's life but conspicuously leaves out reference to his death and cremation.[61] Most biographies gloss over or fail to even mention the fact of this famous monk's death. The film merely has one monk stating, "We cannot figure out what this disease you have is." He died at Wat Indrawihan, where he supposedly was first a student as a child and where the statues of his mother and "father" are located. The abbot of Wat Indrawihan, Phra Ratcharatanaphon, told me that he had died in a small *sala* (pavilion) near the front of the monastery, but that *sala* was torn down in the 1980s to make room for a parking lot. That is about all we know. Why would every minor aspect of his life be recorded but the actual site of his deathbed be bulldozed to make way for a parking lot? This is strange because the value of Somdet To's bone, hair, fingernail, and so forth collected from the cremation ashes, as well as pieces of his robes, bowl, and walking stick would all be valuable in the religious paraphernalia markets of Thailand, as well as collected by museums and sold on eBay. For famous monks there are often records of cremations contained in royal chronicles, letters, and the like. Other important cremations have been recorded by the numerous foreign officials, teachers, and merchants living in Bangkok in the late nineteenth and early twentieth centuries. However, there is nothing about Somdet To that I have been able to find in any public or private record. Even scholar-monks, including the abbots, at Wat Rakhang and Wat Indrawihan claim that they do not know where Somdet To's relics (ashes, bones, hair) are kept. There are thousands of small reliquary boxes interred in the stupas and walls of both monasteries. Not one is the focus of worship as the remains of Somdet To.

Many writers, including Samat Khongsat, and I believe that the mystery surrounding his cremation is similar to that surrounding his conception. If we do not know where or by whom he was conceived and we do not know when his body was ignited, then no one can claim exclusive ownership of his lineage, his bloodline, or his physical relics. He has the possibility of being a teacher for all Buddhists in Thailand and beyond. Moreover, the mystery of his own relics creates a great deal of healthy speculation in the market for his amulets. The relics of Somdet To are something often in the back of the mind of many amulet dealers and consumers. Could they actually exist? If so, what would their value be, both economically and magically? It is also a common belief in Thailand that the bones of enlightened monks (or those who are nearing enlightenment) will turn into crystal when they are burned on a funeral pyre. I have seen many crystallized (or supposedly crystallized) bones, including those of the teacher of my teacher, who showed them to me in 1994 in rural northeastern Thailand. Thousands of examples can be seen in monastery museums and in display cases, and they are often held in small aluminum or acrylic containers by monks, who pull them out to show their friends, students, and families when they are sitting casually and recalling the lives of their mentors. If his followers had knowledge of

Somdet To's cremation, then they would certainly want to know if his bones had crystallized. The inability to check and the lack of eyewitnesses add to the sacredness of this monk. The power is in the not-knowing. Great monks do not die, they simply fade away.

## THE WHY OF SOMDET TO

The German traveler Adolf Bastian is the only known foreigner to provide an eyewitness description of Somdet To. He provides solid evidence that Somdet To has not merely become famous over time but was renowned throughout Bangkok before widespread printing, film, photography, and the Internet. In his 1863 account, he writes as follows:

> I was told [by the abbot of Wat Borworniwet, a well-known Pali grammarian and one of the highest-ranking monks of the Thammayut sect] that the very paragon of religious knowledge [in Siam] was the abbot of Vat Rakhang (monastery of the bells), one Achan To [Somdet To], and so I spent my first free time introducing myself to him. He received me with great reserve and I soon worked out from his rather unfriendly disposition that this old gentleman belonged to the strictly conservative school, which would very much like to boot foreigners and their reformist ideas out of the country. Even before we managed to end the first compliments, he had found an opportunity to disappear into one of the back private quarters of his house from which he did not emerge anymore. Instead, he sent his favorite pupil to work our discussion points with me . . . A few weeks later . . . Phra Klang, or Minister of Finance, had invited us to a celebration that would take place in the evening at his residence. There we found everything richly decorated, and a select company had gathered . . . Some famous preachers made an appearance one after the other to lecture the gathering, and among them was "my friend" from Rakhang monastery. In pompous language he celebrated the superiority of the true faith, the profound wisdom of the Buddha, and the unfathomable depth of Buddhism's learned secrets, and then he hacked into the foreign barbarians, who came into the country believing that this priceless source of wisdom would also be accessible to them. The fools! How could they hope that their blind eye and their hardened heart, unprepared by a monk's vows or by the silence of life in the monastery and meditation in solitude, could be receptive to an understanding of the highest and holiest! . . . In this celebration, as always on such occasions, the gifts offered to the priests

were encircled by a long robe, which was tied at one end to a Buddha statue, so as to be charged with magical power. During the lecture the Phra Klang knelt in front of the speaking abbot, pouring water from a golden bowl, and afterwards he handed over a new monk's robe, which was connected by white cloth to this consecrated circle . . . The first preachers at the celebration had limited themselves to reciting Pali sentences, to which they added Siamese translations . . . When his excellency (chao khun) from the monastery of the bells took to the pulpit a freely improvised speech in doggerel verses followed, and the Pali book that he held in his hand was not even opened. For the most part it was a real haranguing sermon, filled with crude fun and popular song, everything in the most easily grasped, popular dialect, which was also duly appreciated and laughed at by the audience. In his introduction he remarked that it was the custom at occasions like these to recite Pali prayers, but that this time he would like to stray away practice and speak—in such words that could also be clearly understood by the common man—about the evil of mankind's traditional enemies, constituted by these three basic vices: moha (stupidity or the error of one's ways) dosa (anger), and lobha (greed) . . . and insistently advised them to give up their hopeless attempts. He knew very well the priceless goods that they planned to load their ships with, but their wish would remain unfulfilled.[62]

I include Bastian's lengthy description of his meeting with Somdet To because it points out some important reasons Somdet To was considered the "very paragon of religious knowledge" and why he is held up as the greatest monk in central Thailand's history. It helps us begin to answer the question, Why is this monk so famous? with which I started the chapter. Bastian's account highlights four points that have been slowly made evident throughout this chapter.

## NATIONAL PROTECTION

Somdet To is often lauded, and from Bastian's words it seems justifiable, for being a defender of Siam (Thailand). In fact, it seems as if he was explicitly jingoistic. Somdet To gave sermons throughout central and northeastern Thailand over his sixty-six-year monastic career. We can imagine that the nationalistic rant Bastian heard was not the only time he addressed this issue. Furthermore, this attitude is reflected in the way his life has been told and the miracles that he is believed to have directly caused since his physical death in 1872. Indeed, one documentary film and the murals at Wat Indrawihan depict a scene in which Somdet To meets two Christian missionaries outside the gates of Wat Rakhang. He outwits them by asking them where the center of the world is. When they seem confused by the question, he states that since they believe the world is round the center is wherever a person decided it was. The *jai khlang* (heart, center) was "right here" (*ni lae*) because the center was simply a matter of perspective. In Somdet To's perspective, clearly the center of the world was Siam.[63]

Somdet To's association with national protection and national pride can best be seen in his association with defeating the French. Any student of Thai history knows the year 1893 and the famous Paknam Incident. This is when Siam experienced its first real threat of colonization. While Siam's neighbor countries had already succumbed to colonial power, Siam remained unoccupied by foreign military forces. However, in 1893 French gunboats trolled up the Chao Phraya River into the waters of Bangkok. The French retreated without a battle; the Siamese army was never fully mobilized. The reason that Siam was not attacked that day and the larger reason why it remained the only nonofficially colonized nation in Southeast Asia is generally attributed to the diplomatic efforts of King Rama V (Chulalongkorn) and the fact that the British and French found it more advantageous to keep a Siamese buffer state between them and simply exploit the country economically.

However, numerous fans of Somdet To told me a completely different reason why the French gunboats did not fire their deck canons that day in 1893. The story often told was most clearly related by Nat, a seller of religious books and amateur history buff in Bangkok. Although some details changed, his story was retold in largely similar ways by dozens of others, including several monks and laypeople especially at several monasteries along the river. Nat's story tells that in 1893 when the gunboats started approaching the Grand Palace several laypeople and monks rushed to Wat Rakhang and Wat Chayasongkhram on opposite sides of the river. They knew that before he died Somdet To had buried several valuable amulets underneath two large stupas. Somdet To, many believed, had commanded a certain group of followers to go to these large stone stupas (which can still be seen on the grounds of these monasteries) and chant a protective chant, the *Jinapañjara gāthā*, continuously. This chanting empowered by these buried amulets would create a powerful magical barrier across the river and defend the city. The French gunboats were supposedly magically repelled by the chanting and the amulets. Other versions of the story, and one depicted in the film about Somdet To's life, has him going out on a canoe alone right before his death and dumping thousands of amulets into the river in the area between Wat Rakhang and Wat Indrawihan. In the film he stands up after he has dumped the amulets and chants the *Jinapañjara gāthā* four times while facing north, south, east, and west, in order.[64]

This is not the only story in which Somdet To is said to protect the country after his death. Parts of central Thailand were occupied by Japanese military garrisons between 1942 and 1945. Although there was never a massive Japanese presence in Thailand, many Thais were forced into slave labor for the Japanese war machine. The fact that Bangkok was never massively bombed by Japanese or Allied forces and the major palaces and monasteries remained largely undamaged is held by many Thais as lucky, but by others, especially fans of Somdet To and other famous monks, as a direct result of their protective magical practices. In particular, I was told by a monk named Sirisak and a layperson named Pat that during the bombing of Bangkok in 1943, Somdet To was seen levitating in the sky above the city and that his presence deflected bombs away from important monasteries and the palace. This story, which was not corroborated by many others, is similar to stories about two other famous Thai monks, Luang Pho Chat and Luang Pho Chong, who are also said to have magically protected the city from falling bombs.

The Thai historian Chalong Soontravanich has noted that amulets, those of Somdet To being the most famous, in general have been connected with national protection in the twentieth century. Well before the Japanese threat, in 1902 soldiers from Bangkok stopped at Wat Tha Maprang in Phitsanulok in north-central Thailand to search for amulets buried under a famous reliquary. They found old amulets, it is said, and wore them around their necks to protect themselves in a battle with Shan rebels near the border of Burma and northern Thailand. These amulets, called *ngiao thong puen*, like Somdet To's amulets, have become sought after in the present-day amulet trade and are still believed to be able to protect the borders of the country.[65] Sika Ang (pseud.) and Soraphon Sophitkun, two writers of popular amulet histories, often recount stories of national protection in weekly columns in newspapers like *Thai rath* and in amulet trade magazines. During the American war in Vietnam, many American soldiers stationed at bases in Thailand actively sought amulets from their fellow Thai soldiers. Richard Ruth notes in a number of interviews he conducted with these former Thai soldiers, for example, that American soldiers were interested in a particular amulet, the Phra Chinarat Indochine, originally pressed in 1942 to protect Thailand from Japanese attack. This amulet, depicting one of the most famous Buddha images in the country, the Phra Phuttha Chinarat image from Phisanulok in northern Thailand, was consecrated by the *sangharat* at Wat Suthat in Bangkok and given to military officers for the explicit purpose of protecting them and their troops. By the time of the American war in Vietnam, possessing one of these amulets was considering especially auspicious, as it provided invulnerability from bullets, mortar shells, and the like. One of Richard Ruth's interviewees recalled the following:

There were some *farangs* [foreigners] who came and asked me for amulets. They said, "Thailand number one Buddha!" So I gave them some . . . When we had nothing to do we would sit around and drink beer together. We'd meet in the PX and shake hands, and they'd ask for Buddha amulets.[66]

The association of amulets and physical and national protection was not a mere pastime and cultural oddity. It was and is an intensely detailed practice. It is a practice of which Somdet To is considered the greatest master in Thai history. In fact, the only known copy of Somdet To's own handwriting comes from a mulberry-paper manuscript that was found in 1953 by Lamun Sutakhamo, an assistant to the abbot of Wat Rakhang, in an old pile of books. It is an amulet recipe book. Regardless of the effectiveness or origins of these incantations, drawings, recipes, and rituals, we can easily see that Somdet To and the *Jinapañjara* defend the country and cures illnesses.

In the 1970s, Somdet To was elevated again to a protector of the country by one of the most politically influential military leaders in the country. Suchat Kosonkittiwong, a spirit medium working in Bangkok, started the Pusawan (or sometimes known as Hupphasawan) movement. He claimed to be the medium for the consciousnesses (*luk winyan*) of three *bodhisattas*, Luang Phu Tuat (the most famous monk from southern Thailand, who lived in the late Ayutthayan period and whose following in southern Thailand is comparable to Somdet To's in central Thailand), Mahaphrom Chinapanchon (Mahābrahma Jinapañjara, an Indian Brahman who lived at the time of the historical Buddha), and Somdet To.[67] The significance of the name Jinapañjara will become evident in chapter 2. Suchat believed that Somdet To was the reliever of the psychological suffering of the Thai people (while Luang Phu Tuat relieved their physical suffering and Jinapañjara protected Thai rituals and made amulets and other objects powerful). He started a foundation called the Munithi Chinnaphuto and said that these three powerful beings had called on him to save Thailand from communism and renew Buddhism during this age of decline. He even claimed that Somdet To and Luang Phu Tuat were actually twenty-five-hundred-year-old *bodhisattas* who had lived at the time of the Buddha! His teachings were taken up in the late 1970s by military generals who were eager to combat the left-leaning democratic movements that had been successful in overturning dictatorial military rule between 1973 and 1976. Prominent generals, a former deputy prime minister, high-ranking businessmen, the army commander in chief, and many other members of the conservative elements of the Bangkok elite were regular visitors to Suchat's headquarters in Ratchaburi Province. Many of these elites had lost their power with the rise of the left, and Peter

Jackson argues that Suchat's movement was seen as an avenue to a possible re-gaining of their power. Suchat's influence had started to wane by 1981 as his practices became increasingly bizarre. He started building statues of Jesus Christ, the Virgin Mary, the future Buddha Metteya, Shiva, Ganesh, Kuan Im (Chinese Guanyin, Sanskrit Avalokiteśvara, a bodhisattva generally associated with Tibetan and East Asian Buddhist traditions), and the former Thai kings Taksin and Rama I. He even visited the former Soviet Union and the United States to meet politicians interested in contributing to what he saw as his universal peace mission. These bold moves were all trumped by his claim that Somdet To and Luang Phu Tuat had told him that the king of Thailand (Rama IX) should abdicate the throne and form his own political party and become prime minister. This was the last straw, and he was discredited and a warrant was issued for his arrest. He fled the police for several years before being found in 1987. Although Suchat was discredited, the fame of Somdet To, his signature protective chant, which in many ways Mahābrahma Jinapañjara embodied, and Luang Phu Tuat retained their status.[68]

In 2002 Wat Indrawihan built a new pavilion dedicated to Somdet To. Its supervisor, Nikorn, told me that the pavilion had been built for the sake of national well-being. At one end is a statue of Somdet To, in the middle is a replica of the famed Emerald Buddha, facing Somdet To, and on the west side of the room is a twenty-five-foot-high painting of Somdet To overlooking the Emerald Buddha (this is the reverse of the practice at most Thai shrines, where the statues or photographs of monks are always smaller and sit below the main Buddha image). When one kneels in front of the Buddha, which is the first thing a Buddhist does upon entering the pavilion, one sees Somdet To peering down on the Buddha and oneself. Surrounding the room are a series of six twelve-foot-high plaques with the *Jinapañjara gāthā* painted on them in different scripts—Khmer, Lao, northern Thai (Lanna), Devanagari (Indian), Roman, and Burmese. These scripts represent the scripts of the nations surrounding Thailand (Malaysia's national script is Roman). Somdet To's signature incantation is projected out to Thailand's neighbors and creates a magical barrier around the room and the nation.

For a nation, a religion, and a people famous for being friendly and wel-coming, modern Thai Buddhism often does not represent the stereotype of the Land of Smiles. Somdet To is not famous for being a promoter of the unity of humankind or the equality of all religions. He saw his practice of Buddhism as a superior technology and became a hero to many Thai people after the Asian financial crisis in 1997, the Thai embassy burning in Cambodia in 2004, the military coup of 2006, and during the continuing Islamic insurgency that has claimed thousands of lives. As Bastian showed, he warned in 1863 against the Siamese becoming slaves to foreign gold and creeds. His message still reaches a captive audience today.

Buddhism linked with national protection is not entirely new, though. Siam changed its name to Thailand in 1939, several years after the change from an absolute monarchy to a constitutional monarchy in 1932. Since that time the state has sought to gain more direct control over the sangha than had been the case during the absolute monarchy. In 1934 an independent government committee was established to examine sangha finances, and in 1941 the new Sangha Act effectively gave the government control over internal sangha organization and executive offices. The various military and elected governments over the past sixty years have generally asserted that the sangha should play a more "practical" role in modern Thai society and become more "socially engaged." This social engagement promoted by many Thammayut monks, the government, Christian missionaries, and Western critics of the sangha led the two major monastic universities to institute programs in which urban, educated monks would provide social services for the poor, especially in the north, northeast, and south. The role of the monastery in health and education was seen as part of the original vision of the Buddha, even though there were no monasteries at the time of the Buddha and textually it could be argued that nuns and monks in early Buddhism were encouraged not to be socially engaged. In 1966 Mahachulalongkorn Monastic University stated that its students should provide "voluntary social services, both material and spiritual, for the welfare of the community, such as giving advice and help in the event of family problems and misfortunes." Monks from these universities were assigned to be teachers in rural areas, volunteers in hospitals, and to assist in community economic development. They also established numerous new monastic schools that were designed to prepare rural students for future training at the monastic universities in the city and disseminated textbooks printed for urban monastic students. The universities provided training courses to prepare their "volunteer" students. The monks sent out were also part of the nation-building process aimed at including the rural areas in the north, northeast, and south. This became an anticommunist movement when the Department of Religious Affairs sent *thammadut* (envoys of the *dhamma*) to the northeast to spread Buddhist teachings and help with rural development. Most monks were sent to the northeast, the place of most communist activity and ethnic Lao residents. A report of their progress in 1969 confirmed their role in combating communist activity, which they believed "caused the people great suffering." These monks were working side by side with anticommunist government policies and the U.S. military, which had thousands of troops stationed in the region. Monks were also involved in helping the government pacify and incorporate hill tribes and Muslim populations in the north and south of the country.

In fact, it could be argued that Thai Buddhism is becoming less open today than it was in Bastian's time in the mid-1860s. In June 2007, I attended a rally and hunger strike in front of the national parliament building, where five monks were sitting in coffins fasting in order to demand that the new constitution include a provision naming Buddhism as the national religion.[69] This movement has gained mass popularity, especially in response to the growing Islamic insurgency in southern Thailand. Perhaps the most popular living monk in Thailand is Luang Pho Khun in Nakhon Ratchasima Province in northeastern Thailand. He is renowned for blessing Thai Royal Air Force fighter jets and Royal Army tanks with holy water and incantations. There are often rituals of blessing soldiers and handing them amulets in Thailand today.

Indeed, Somdet To himself was a child of border wars. Many biographers/hagiographers agree that he was born either in Ayutthaya to a refugee mother who had fled Thai-Burmese battlegrounds in the border area of Kampaengphet or during the conflict in Kampaengphet. These scholars firmly locate the young To in battle zones. Many believe that he was sired by a general fighting along the border. Somdet To fled to Ayutthaya and then to Bangkhunphrom (Bangkok), and it is suggested that he also spent some time in Samut Sakhon on the coast south of Bangkok as a refugee. The Bangkhunphrom neighborhood he grew up in in Bangkok from at least the age of fourteen was populated by Lao refugees. He was a student of the Wat Rakhang monastic school in the Lao and Khmer refugee neighborhood of Wang Lang. He most likely died among the then well-established Lao community of Bangkhunphrom. He grew up seeing the effects of wars. Furthermore, his life is told in many ways as a parallel to the life of Bangkok and the Chakri dynasty. Even if he was not actually the biological son of King Rama I, his biography starts in that reign soon after the burning of the previous Siamese capital of Ayutthaya. He was involved in the lives of King Ramas I, II, IV, and V. He was the son of a liberator, the adviser to a modernizer, and teacher to a defender. He was considered the paragon of religious knowledge as Bangkok grew from a small refugee settlement to a huge capital city. Reading Somdet To's biographies reminds people of the early struggle and eventual glory of Siam. Somdet To is depicted as having contributed to and protected that glory. This is often contrasted to the demise and eventual colonization of neighboring Burma, Laos, Malaysia, and Cambodia. Thanks to Somdet To, Thailand alone remained free. The love and respect fans show to Somdet To is partly, I believe, rooted in nostalgia for an imagined time when Bangkok was regal, free, new, and wealthy, before tourists, the IMF, the World Bank, the Vietnam War, military coups, and Islamic insurgencies.

## *A MONK FOR ALL PERSUASIONS: PARTICIPATORY NATIONALISM AND ASSOCIATIVE FAME*

Another reason that Somdet To was so famous when alive and grows more famous as years pass is because he represents the everyman in Thailand. His qualities are respected by all classes, Buddhist lineages, women and men, and liberals and conservatives. Bastian noted, like most Thai Somdet To biographers, that he was a Pali scholar. In fact, Bastian was recommended to meet with Somdet To by a Thammayut Nikai lineage (Somdet To was in the Mahanikai lineage) Pali grammarian.[70] Somdet To studied with well-known Pali scholars like Phra Achan Kaeo and Phra Achan Horathibodhi at Wat Rakhang and at Wat Mahathat, two of the oldest monastic schools in Bangkok. He is continually lauded, as we will see more fully in chapter 3, for his skills not only in reading and chanting in Pali but also in composing Pali texts, the highest mark of a Pali scholar. Today his photograph hangs in the monastic university library of Mahachulalongkorn Monastic University. All the biographies agree that he was a special child. He was known to have great mnemonic powers and could chant thousands of verses in Thai and Pali without textual aid. In other stories it is said that he was the favorite monk of King Rama IV, the great Westernizer and centralizer of Thai Buddhism, founder of the Thammayut lineage, who called for a return to the canon and to strict interpretations of the *Paṭimokkha* (a book of precepts for monks). He was, supposedly, the only monk who openly debated King Rama IV on doctrine and practice. He was called to chant Pali at royal funerals and was put in charge of the royal Pali library. His laudatory epigraphs speak to his intellectual acumen, scholarly skills, and liturgical expertise. In a recent documentary on his life, he is referred to as "ariyasong phu pen brach haeng paendin siam" (the noble and erudite sage of Siam), and he is described in Pali as "mahāsañño mahāpañño mahālābho mahāyaso" (one possessed of great perception, great wisdom, great fortune, and great fame).[71]

In addition to his Pali skills, which were generally held only by the elite in Siam in the nineteenth century and are still rare among monks today, he was also associated with royalty. He was not simply a hired hand for royalty when they needed a skilled liturgist and scholar; he was a royally sponsored novice and later recipient of the very high royal titles *phra maha khun, thepakawi,* and *somdet phra phutthachan.* Most monks would never dream of obtaining even one of these titles in their lifetime. As mentioned, he is believed to have been the son of King Rama I (and sometimes of King Rama II), he was the Pali instructor to Thailand's most beloved king, Rama V.[72]

However, Somdet To is not characterized as bookish, elite, or aloof in most Thai biographies. He is referred to as "khru To" (simple teacher To). Bastian noted that he spoke in the crude vernacular of the commoners and that he joked and acted without proper deference in front of high-ranking officials. In the few sermons we have, he employs a coarse lexicon and peppers his homilies with somewhat abrasive and loutish jokes. Popular legends promote his acting downright bristly and obnoxiously to the king himself! He eschewed royal titles, is often depicted sitting in a simple wooden monastic cell or wandering among rural villages. In the film version of his life he openly jokes around with women in the market and puts is head below that of a drunkard. He does not simply stoically meditate on a raised dais but paddles his own dilapidated canoe and sits on the floor weeping among his novice students. Some of his photographs show him in a formal setting on a high seat, but others show a monk in wrinkled robes leaning against a wooden table next to a poor man's bed. He spoke of his poor refugee mother but not of his mysterious royal father. He chose to move to the less-prestigious monastery of Wat Indrawihan in a Lao neighborhood near the end of his life and made amulets for free distribution to the poor and sick. One of the foundations named in his honor has funded the building of over thirty schools in poor villages.

Somdet To remains popular in part because he is a mystery. It is difficult to know about not only his paternity, hometown, and cremation but also what type of monk he was—was he a member of the bookish elite or of the busy marketplace refugee communities? His biographers do not try to define him and simply refer to his many and various qualities that defy class and even ethnic rubrics. He has also attracted biographers from different classes and different schools of Buddhism. For example, he has been the subject of three major hardback biographies published by serious academic presses like the National Library Press, the Mahamakut Monastic University Press (a Thammayut university), and the wealthy Saeng Dao Sroi Thong Press. But he is also one of the most commonly imaged monks on the covers of lower-class pulp amulet magazine covers. Some of these magazines, like *Saksit*, include short biographies in simple vernacular Thai for the reader who has not studied in elite secondary schools and universities. His amulets are collected by the present-day royal family and owned by university professors, as well as selling for ten cents a piece at roadside stands. The elite and traditional Wat Rakhang produces amulet catalogs and biographies, as does the popular Wat Indrawihan. Both groups have stories about Somdet To. These amateur storytellers and historians paint similar pictures of

To—he had the qualities of both the elite and the common. In many ways, this is quite similar to the hagiographical traditions of King Rama V and the present King Rama IX, as well as of the Thai national poet Sunthorn Phu and the famous monk Buddhadasa Bhikkhu. They are all depicted as elites who work(ed) among the poor, as brilliant minds who can communicate in the simple vernacular. They have access to the regalia and accoutrements of the powerful and sacred but often choose to walk the streets among the people. Famous photographs of King Rama V have him cooking his own simple dinner, smoking a hand-rolled cigarette, and sitting shirtless in his *pakama* (casual male skirt). Photographs of King Rama IX include him sweating while helping a farmer in a rice paddy, touching a poor old woman, playing his saxophone, sitting next to Elvis Presley, and shopping in a crowded bazaar. Americans like to call this a down-to-earth quality. This quality is valued, though, only if the person does not have to be humble and simple. The real poor are never called down-to-earth. Somdet To is lauded for his coarse speech and openness to all people specifically because he did not have to act like that. He could have sat back with his titles and fame and been served by others.

Despite this class-crossing quality, I had assumed at first that liberal, Westernized Thai Buddhists who emphasized socially engaged Buddhism, Vipassana meditation, and criticized superstition, magic, the amulet trade, and the commercialization of Buddhism in general would be critical of Somdet To, or at least not pay him any attention, but I was mistaken. I was shocked when I learned that one of the most liberal scholar-monks in modern Thai Buddhism, Thanissaro Bhikkhu, an Ohio-born Caucasian man named Geoffrey DeGraff who has been a monk for thirty years and who writes books that discuss the demise of Thai Buddhism, the purity of the Thammayut dispensation, and the central place of the canonical *Dhammapada* and the Vinaya, collected amulets of Somdet To. He had actually collected some of the popular stories of Somdet To to tell to his mostly Western students in Southern California as well. Another scholar, Suchitra Chongstitvatthana, the chair of the Thai Literature Department of the elite Chulalongkorn University, who has advanced degrees from the University of London and the University of Edinburgh, speaks English fluently, and is a friend to the royal family, has a rare amulet of Somdet To's and has great respect for him. Rangsit Chongchansitto, from rural Phangnga Province in southern Thailand, was one of the student revolutionaries who had to flee to the jungles of northeastern Thailand for five years after the violent government crackdowns of 1976. Now he is a professional musician and one of the most respected historians of religion in Bangkok. Even though he is a former member of the Thai Communist Party and considers many stories about Somdet To the product of superstition (*khwam cheua thi ngom ngai*), he still wears many amulets connected with Somdet To and chants the *Jinapañjara*. Elites and commoners as well as liberal, conservative, scholarly, and commercially minded people collect, research, worship, and discuss Somdet To.[73]

Somdet To has certainly not been "frozen" by his hagiographers, and if Somdet To has become the image of true spirituality for Thai Buddhists, then their image of true spirituality is strikingly different from what many readers might consider true Buddhist ethics! The image and story of Somdet To are neither clear nor consistent. There are not any conflicting documents, hidden manuscripts, compromising photographs, textual variants of his that have been buried for posterity. In fact, the National Library's major biography actually includes photographs of some of his handwritten notebooks, replete with misspellings, corrections, and marginalia. Some of Somdet To's biographers openly note when there is controversy surrounding where he was born and even occasionally who his father was. Fans of his in the marketplace and in monasteries openly talk about the vagaries of his life and seem comfortable with not knowing certain parts of his biography. The mystery allows his legend to grow, it allows him to be the everyman for Thai Buddhists. He is famous in large part due to the fact that his image exists in different shapes in different people's minds. Biographers have not created a single, stereotyped ideal out of his life.

There is no propaganda machine that has attempted to craft a particular narrow hagiography of Somdet To for its own political ends. There is not a single factory making his amulets, or a single committee writing his biographies. There is no smoky backroom filled with corrupt politicians or capitalist exploiters. The money from his amulet sales, his book sales, his posters does not go into one, untraceable offshore bank account. There is no royal commission or monastic council secretly planning how it is going to convince the masses of Somdet To's power. No political party has made a concerted effort to invoke Somdet To's name for its own benefit, and no military dictator has created stories of Somdet To's ability to magically protect the nation. Somdet To fans are from every class, spread among many disconnected places in Thailand. A person reproducing photographs of him in one house generally has no connection to a person creating *phra yan* cloth of Somdet To in another. They are generating and regenerating his biographies and images separately without any concerted effort to create one ideal. The diversity in Somdet To's hagiographical tradition shows that the purveyors of his story are neither being unconsciously controlled by the parameters of a particular biographical genre nor consciously manipulating a genre. This is an open and participatory hagiographical tradition with many people profiting. There has been some subtle competition over his image between monks at Wat Rakhang and those at Wat Indrawihan, and many individuals, as pointed out, have claimed to be inspired by To, have claimed that they were saved or cured by him, and the like. However, every fan base has a variety of stories about its hero in this way. The difference with Somdet To is that there is not one powerful group, like an advertiser or political party, behind the cultivation of his image. It has evolved through the efforts and worship, and sometimes greed, of thousands of willing participants. People profit from their associated fame that comes with the most tenuous connections to Somdet To. People are protected by knowing one of his short incantations or holding one of his small clay amulets.

## PROTECTIVE MAGIC

In many ways it is Somdet To's talent as a magician and healer that makes him famous. There are dozens of oral and written accounts of his ability to cure the sick, close soldiers' wounds, cast away ghostly denizens, and vanish at will. Since his death, there have been hundreds of stories of people claiming his amulets have saved their lives, helped them get promotions, win the lottery, or pass difficult examinations. His famous incantations have been credited with miracles of many and varied types. He "cured" Mae Nak. Bastian noted that he claimed that he possessed the "unfathomable depth of Buddhism's learned secrets" and participated in the production of protective power using a sacred string and a Buddha image at a royally sponsored sermon. These practices and stories are so essential to understanding Somdet To's fame that they are the focus of chapters 2 and 4.

## TEACHINGS

The last and certainly the least-important reason Somdet To has historically been the most famous monk in Bangkok, if not central Thai history, is based on his teachings. The actual Buddhist doctrine or ethical lessons he conveyed in his sermons are the smallest part of any of his biographies. In fact, I have come across only one short, twenty-two-page collection of his sermons. They are relatively simplistic descriptions of basic Buddhist teachings. There are hundreds of editions of his famous Pali incantations (which he did not compose himself but made famous through his use of them in magical protective rituals), at least three thousand amulets he made himself, pools of holy water, and yards of *phra yan* protective cloth. There are countless numbers of statues of him, from one inch to one hundred twenty feet tall, in brass, copper, plastic, gold, silver, wood, glass, and stone. There are many biographies in a variety of publications. Why do we know so much about his life, have so many photographs and statues, have so much of his stuff, and have so few of his own words?

There are two reasons. First, Somdet To was simply more famous for his actions. People sought him while he was alive not necessarily to hear the profound import of his insight but to have him protect or cure them. Learning basic ethics is relatively easy. Most good monks can convey the nature of the Four Noble Truths, the obvious truths of impermanence and suffering, and the clear value of nonattachment. Every good monk can explain the Vinaya monastic code and relate a good Buddhist *sutta*. The ability to chant Pali well is certainly difficult, and this is why monks in Thailand are often lauded for this ability more than for the contents of their sermons. The few sermons we have, along with Bastian's description, suggest that he was known for simple, straightforward, bombastic, and vernacular lectures. He held manuscripts and was often photographed next to manuscripts, but the contents of these texts is almost never discussed.

Most of the writings we do have in Somdet To's own hand are astrological charts, detailed amulet recipes, esoteric *phra yan* cloth drawings and formulas in Khom script, and Pali incantations.[74] Most of these writings are indecipherable to most of the monks and laypeople I have met. Even monastic students in Somdet To's own lineage at the scholarly Wat Rakhang have trouble understanding them. I have worked for several years translating these pieces, and they are not ethically profound, they do not contain any philosophical or psychological ruminations; rather, they are technical manuals for performing rituals. These are texts that *do* things, yet they *say* very little.

This is not strange. There are many monks who are famous as great teachers, and we have little or none of their actual teachings. The famous teacher of Achan Man, Luang Phu Sao Kantasilo, was the teacher of my own abbot's teacher. As a monk, I was never taught any of his own teachings. I saw his wooden monastic cell, I held one of his bone relics, and I touched a piece of his robe. I heard stories of his ability to meditate among tigers in the jungle and walk hundreds of miles in a week, but I knew nothing of his insights into interpersonal psychology, soteriology, or ethics. Achan Man's biography, famously translated into English in part or whole by Than Achan Mahabua, Stanley Tambiah, and Thanissaro Bhikkhu, also contains many stories about Achan Man's wanderings, the people he met, the bravery he had meditating in charnel grounds and among wild animals but actually little about his sermons or meditative techniques. Luang Pho Tuat, Luang Phu Chaem, Khrupa Sriwichai, among many others, are famous for the things they did more than what they taught.

This may come as a surprise to readers who have grown up in the Protestant Christian, Sunni Islamic, Advaita Vedanta, or Reformed Jewish traditions, where preachers, imams, swami, and rabbis are famous for their words more than for their deeds. Protestant preachers in particular use teachings as a mark of superiority. Famous American preachers like Chuck Smith, Greg Laurie, and T. D. Jakes emphasize that they do not participate in "empty" ritual or the worship of graven images but convey the moral truths and just laws of the New Testament. The like has generally been quite rare in Thai Buddhism, where the ability to chant in Pali (a language that 99 percent of laity and even monks do not understand), produce amulets, bless buildings and images, interpret dreams, perform acts of compassion and charity, physically soothe and comfort the suffering, and predict the future are virtues. The ability to explicate texts, make social commentary, or solve ethical debates is certainly valued, especially if the monk, like Phra Phayom, Phra Payutto, or Achan Cha, has a good sense of humor and knows how to turn a clever phrase. There are popular books in Thai that are "dhammic guides to business," tell "how to lower daily stress through a study of the *dhamma*," and the like. However, the most famous monks in Thailand build a widespread fan base because of the former skills rather than the latter. Of course, these skill sets are not mutually exclusive; Somdet To, from the few sermons that were collected, was popular for his humor, and he was often, as most biographies mention, called by wealthy families and royalty to give private sermons in their homes.

Virtue in Thai society is often determined by actions, not words. Therefore, the hundreds of stories about Somdet To, apocryphal or not, are "teachings." Followers or fans do not need to hear what Somdet To had to say. They just need to know what he did. The stories in general tell us much about the values that he inculcated. First, the thousands of amulets he made and largely freely distributed (as well as the dozens of very large Buddha images he had cast) reflect the Thai value of abundance (*udom sombun*). In English, "abundance" is a noun rather than an adjective, but in Thai, a place and a person can be described as possessing "*udom sombun*." Generally, in Thai Buddhism "more is more." Shrines, as we will see in chapter 4, are sites of accretion. At most monastic rituals or sermons there are fake trees with cash for leaves placed on the altar by families who let it publicly be known who has given the money. The names of donors are written or painted on the walls of every monastery. Altars themselves are crowded with gifts, flowers, bowls, clocks, incense, and small images. Colorful and intricate murals often fill nearly every open space on the walls. The doors are carved from top to bottom with inlaid mother-of-pearl or gold filigree. One gets the sense of overflowing wealth. The best examples are Wat

Suthat, Wat Phra Kaeo, Wat Sommanat, Wat Suwannaram, and Wat Traimit. The main *ubosot* (Pali *uposatha*) and *wihan* (*vihāra*) halls are crowded with gifts, images, smoke, candles, and murals. There are over five hundred eight-foot-tall Buddha images surrounding the courtyards of Wat Suthat alone. One does not get the obvious impression of a religion that promotes nonattachment, impermanence, simplicity, and asceticism. There are no silent and sparse Zen rock gardens in Thailand.

Somdet To was famous for overwhelming his patrons with amulets, chanting, and *phra yan* cloth. In turn he received overwhelming gifts, so much so that he did not mind when thieves absconded with them. Certainly, he was honored for his wanderings in the forest and for his forgoing of the delights of sex and gluttony. It is often mentioned that he could sit in quiet meditation for hours. However, when one visits monasteries associated with him (or indeed almost any non-Westernized, Thai monastery), the image of the simple forest monk carrying his worldly possessions lightly on his back or the monk sitting alone in a distant, undecorated cave is not often found. Lifelong forest-meditating monks make up only 3 to 4 percent of the total number of the ordained class in Thailand, and that number has grown in the twentieth century. It certainly was an anomaly in Somdet To's time.

The stories about Somdet To also convey the value of graciousness (*khwam sawatdiphap*). Graciousness is not simply an open and welcoming quality in Thai but also has an aesthetic sense. Just as the "virtue" of abundance is sensual, a gracious person is a beautiful person with a beautiful warm smile (*yim yam cham sai*) who welcomes strangers to their home with gifts, food, and drink. Somdet To is described as handsome and physically impressive. However, he is also gentle, kind, and disarming. The stories often speak of him helping drunkards, poor children, wounded soldiers, disgraced monks, and the generally crestfallen and destitute. He is kind even to ghosts. In fact, the only people he is generally depicted chastising and offending are royalty and, in at least one case, Westerners. It is easy to be gracious to the wealthy and powerful; Somdet To is described as being gracious to the masses, not the elite.

In addition to these qualities, the stories demonstrate that Somdet To is valued for having given people a sense of physical security (*khwam blot phai*). Amulets, images, and incantations are believed to create protective armor. This will be evident in chapter 2. Right now, let me briefly mention two recent Thai films that reflect the virtues of security and heritage. The first is by the same director who made *Nang Nak*, Nonzee Nimibutr. In an interview with the director, he told me that since I was interested in Buddhism, I should see his new film *Baytong*.[75] Named after a village on the Malaysian–southern Thai border, the film starts with a young monk learning that his innocent sister has been killed by a bomb planted on a train by the Islamic insurgency. He travels to the south as a monk to see his family. Soon, he realizes that he must give up his robes and become his five-year-old niece's caregiver. As he readjusts to lay life he learns that despite his monastic training some desires do not lead to suffering. He cares for his niece as if she were his own daughter and falls in love with a local village woman. Nonzee, like many other viewers I met, sees this as a perfectly appropriate "Buddhist" film. The qualities of a monk are not necessarily reserve, discipline, indifference, and concentration but also affection, warmth, protection, and duty toward others even if it means giving up the robes. Somdet To did not give up his robes but is depicted as a caring father more than as a reverent being reaching for emptiness. He guides and protects. He is a lantern held in the hand, not a beacon on a hill.

Finally, the stories, which take up the bulk of the pages in most biographies, emphasize the value of heritage (*moradok*). As mentioned, Somdet To was born out of war but grew up in a new city and what many Thais consider the golden age of the latter nineteenth century. This was a time when Siamese kings were regular visitors in European capitals and their children were students at elite British and French finishing schools. Siamese silk, pewter, and spices were popular with foreign merchants. Siamese armies were easily winning new territories in the Malay, Khmer, and Lao regions while their neighbors were falling under the yoke of colonialism. The forests were still healthy and filled with tigers and tropical birds. Slaves were being freed. Railroad tracks were being laid. Rebellions were being squashed. Many present-day Thai people are obsessed with the nineteenth century. There are reenactments, museums, photographs, statues, and coffee-table books devoted to the theme. Somdet To's stories are set in this glorious time. They invoke a time when generosity and magic were still possible in the city.[76] This is the world that, for many Thais, Somdet To inhabited. Understanding the importance of Thai nostalgia for this period is essential to understanding why Somdet To is famous for simply representing an ideal past and a truly Thai heritage.

## CONCLUSION

On March 12, 2009, there was a great commotion in the fields near Wat Tan Jet Yot in rural Prachuap Khiri Khan Province. Devotees and television news crews had gathered in a field to prostrate, chant, and take photographs of a strange outcropping of *ton tan* (sugar-palm trees). These trees had grown in a particular way. When viewed from a distance they looked like Somdet To seated in meditation.[77] To me, this story sounded extremely similar to the common stories of

Catholics seeing images of the Virgin Mary in rock formations, water stains on church walls, or in blood spatter. From the photographs of the trees, anyone who knows the iconic way Somdet To is depicted in seated meditation can see the similarity. However, what is telling is that photographs of these trees were already being produced after the event to sell as amulets. In this way, anyone with a camera could participate in Somdet To worship and the Somdet To economy. One could say that even nature, the very land of Siam, was celebrating the life and work of Somdet To.

Somdet To is arguably the most famous monk in Thai history, but his approaches to texts, rituals, ghosts, and sermons is certainly not unique. In fact, one of his own teachers is lauded for having similar qualities. Phra Somdet Ariyawongsayan (Suk) of Wat Mahathat (better known as Luang Pho Suk Kai Tuan of Wat Ratchasittharam) was one of Somdet To's Pali and meditation teachers. He was also elevated to the highest rank in the country, *sangharat*, in 1819, a rank Somdet To himself never achieved, and was famous for producing amulets, as well as his own signature Pali chant, the *Phra gāthā ya kai thuan*. He drew protective *yantra*, was friends with the royal family, and taught a whole generation of elite monks in early Bangkok. He was patronized by King Rama I, advised King Rama II, and ordained Kings Rama III and IV. He was also both a *vipassanādhura* (a monk who focuses on meditation practice) famous for his meditation techniques developed at Wat Ratchasittharam and a *ganthadhura* (scholar-monk) who taught Pali at Wat Mahathat.[78] This is a very similar résumé to Somdet To's, and his heritage is claimed by monks at different monasteries. The reasons why Somdet To became so famous when other powerful monks like Somdet Suk and his peers faded into the obscurities of history is a combination of royal lineage, teachings, magical power, hagiographic force, and nationalism. The fact that Somdet To lived slightly later than his teacher is also important, because Somdet To had the opportunity to be photographed. These photographs became extremely important to the cultivation of Somdet To's image in subsequent generations of fans. Moreover, although Somdet Suk made amulets, which can be found in private collections today, he did not produce the large numbers of amulets that Somdet To did. However, despite these differences, the reasons why certain monks stand out cannot be simplified to one or two reasons. Their biographies, before, during, and after their biological lives, must be examined in their total context. No general ideal of what makes a good Buddhist can be applied to Thai monks, nuns, or laity. In fact, it could be argued that according to translocal Buddhist ideals and ethics, Somdet To could be seen as a particularly bad monk—ritualistic, xenophobic, emotional, and involved with the social lives of the laity around him. It is difficult to determine what makes a good Thai Buddhist monk. However, this close examination of Somdet To's life has highlighted some of the most common qualities, actions, and experiences that are valued by Thai Buddhist practitioners and fans. The difficulty of determining what makes a good Thai monk is also found in determining what makes a good Thai Buddhist text. It is to this topic I now turn.

Visitors to Wat Rakhang Ghositaram (Bangkok/Thonburi) offer gifts to one of the oldest known images of Somdet To. Behind Somdet To the *Jinapañjara gāthā* is inscribed in gold. This image has a number of miraculous stories connected with it, and often more people visit it than the main Buddha image at Wat Rakhang.

A monk sits behind a counter that has several different Somdet To statues (in a variety of sizes and materials) for "rent" (*chao*).

The largest statue of Somdet To in the world inside a shrine (presently still under construction) in rural Nakhon Ratchasima Province. Visitors affix leaves of gold to the statue's legs and feet and chant the *Jinapañjara gāthā*. The white strings stretching out from the statue's hands lead to around the building and into surrounding ponds, thus creating holy water (*nam mon*). This statue's construction was funded in large part by one of Thailand's most famous film actors and philanthropists, Sorapong Chartree.

Statue of Somdet To's mother (dressed as a nun) at Wat Indrawihan (Bangkok). Behind the statue is a mural depicting, perhaps, King Rama I meeting Somdet To's mother in the late eighteenth century in rural Kampaengphet Province.

Lifelike resin and wax statue of Somdet To at Wat Indrawihan (Bangkok). The string from the statue's hand leads into a small pool on the bottom of which the *Jinapañjara gāthā* is inscribed in Khom script. An audio recording of the chant is projected from speakers in the shrine room.

Statue of the ghost Mae Nak Phrakhanong and her infant(s) at Wat Mahabut (Bangkok). Visitors offer her dresses, cosmetics, cash, jewelry, and gold (among many other gifts). Her shrine is very popular, especially for soldiers and women, to visit.

Special reclining chair with audio speakers used to project recordings of the *Jinapañjara gāthā* into the ears of patients at the Arogyasathan Health Clinic run by Dr. Supachai Charusombun in Bangkok.

Monks and laypeople chant in front of a large Buddha image surrounded by Chinese-style murals and mirrors at Wat Ratchaorot (Thonburi).

## 2. Texts and Magic

There is a health club in a wealthy residential district of Bangkok where anyone can make an appointment with one of Somdet To's biggest fans. In one of the office suites on the fourth floor of the nondescript modern building is the Arogyasathan Health Clinic run by Dr. Supachai Charusombun.[1] In July 2006 I made an appointment, walked through the glass doors, filled out the medical-history form given to me by one of the six friendly nurses and technicians on staff, sat down to browse through the coffee-table books. There were books on cancer treatments, healthy lifestyles, and stress relief alongside a bookshelf laden with a nice collection of Buddhist chanting books and meditation guides. There was even a short anthology of *traipidok* (Tripiṭaka) *suttas* and an edition of Somdet To's signature chant, the *Jinapañjara*, which caught my eye. As I sat in the waiting room, I examined brochures for oxygen therapy and admired a mannequin displaying a special set of undergarments designed to maximize lung expansion and diaphragm lifting. There was Buddhist chanting being played softly in the background, and names were being called followed by "The doctor will see you now" in Thai.

As I waited, I chatted with some other patients. Most were a bit coy, as you might expect, about the reasons they were in a medical office. However, one forty-two-year-old woman was quite open. She explained that she was a mother of two (seven and five years old) and was a successful businesswoman. She had been having stomach problems for years, and the physicians she had seen attributed it to acute ulcers. Then she found out that she had the early stages of stomach cancer. Some physicians thought it was her diet, some family history, some stress, and some environmental factors. She had tried different treatments and was considering chemotherapy. She had heard about this clinic a few months previously, and this was her sixth visit. She was skeptical. She was not a person open to alternative or "Buddhist" medicine. She had not been to a monastery for personal spiritual reasons in years. She had been at a few funerals but had not participated in any of the chanting and had left after giving a card to the family of the deceased. She was busy. She had to pick up her children from school, attend meetings, hire and fire employees, and the like. She had a graduate degree from one of Thailand's best universities. She wondered, "Why me?" She simply "didn't have time" (*mai mi wela!*) to get sick. So I asked her, "Then why are you clearly spending a lot of your time in this clinic, waiting for your appointment, talking to a nosey foreigner?" She said that she did not necessarily believe in these alternative treatments and questioned the science behind them, but the treatments seemed to be working. The chanting made her feel better and her stomach seemed to be getting better, and her energy level was returning. She did not know if she would keep coming, but she might give it a few more tries. She was called in. I went back to reading about the Buddhist science behind the Dr. Supachai's treatment regime.

In his book on the subject, *Montra bambat: Mahasachan satphaet tang luat* (*Mantra Remedy: The Miracle Circulatory System Treatment*) Dr. Supachai claimed to unleash the power of the *Jinapañjara* and use its sound not only to soothe the mind but also to cure physical ailments including cancer, diabetes, and related long-term illnesses. When my name was called, I met the doctor, and he explained the treatment I had read about in his book and seen in his video, *Montra bambat ton Phra Gatha Chinabanchon chabap chamrachai* (*The "Jinapañjara gāthā" Heart-Clearing Mantra Remedy*). We started the session by my telling him my interests in Somdet To. He said that it did not matter if I had faith in Somdet To or not, or even if I was interested in Buddhism. To him, this was purely science. He had received degrees from holistic colleges in Nanjing and Shanghai and had studied acupuncture, aroma therapy, music therapy, qi gong, and tai chi. He claimed to have mastered fifty-seven methods of treatment. In addition, he had studied the theories of Einstein, the Big Bang, and was the adviser to the Be Well Foundation in Thailand. He had traveled to India and was trying to bring the science of music and chanting to the Thai public.

In his travels, he had realized that the Thai already had a powerful tradition of mantra therapy, but its true purpose had been lost. The chanting, especially of the *Jinapañjara*, was an extremely effective method if combined with mudras (deliberate hand movements) and the proper posture and teacher. He led me through these hand movements and explained how the chanting from the CD (or from a teacher) would enter the fingertips (if placed in the correct way) and travel through the heart and then throughout the circulatory system. The chanting had certain rhythmic features that could balance the blood flow, open up energy channels (like *nadi* in yoga or *xian* in acupuncture) and cure diseases. The person would walk more swiftly, breathe more fully, and sleep more deeply.

He answered my questions openly and vivaciously. I summarize his points here. The science behind this was obvious, he claimed. Ninety-five percent of people "practice Buddhism because of the culture they were born in" (*watthanatham ton tua eng*), but only five percent knew the science behind Buddhism. The foundation of true Buddhism was nature (*thammachat*). Even the Five Precepts were natural, not moral. For example, (1) "Do not participate in sexual misconduct" means that one needs to be worried about sexually transmitted diseases; (2) "Do not take intoxicants" means that you should watch what you eat and drink; (3) "Do not lie" means you should respect your body, and so on. The Buddha was a doctor and therefore he was concerned with *dhamma*, meaning he was concerned with your health and well-being. *Dhamma* means health. In the past, he continued, monks were the physicians of society as well as the teachers. Since many monks had given up this aspect of their work, laypeople like him needed to fill a need for society.

The primary method the monks used in the past was the mantra. Pali was a special language, he asserted, because when chanting it certain vibrations were generated and these cured diseases. The Vedic *ṛṣi* (seers) before the Buddha knew this science and passed it down. The sounds needed to be generated in the navel and projected through the stomach, through the lungs, and out the mouth. The various *chak* (Sanskrit *cakra*, "disk of energy") were coordinated in this way, like in most forms of yoga. There was no need to think about the meaning of the words; the power came from the particular vibrations they created. Vibrations are what make up the universe; Einstein knew this, and the Big Bang had sent out waves of vibrations throughout the universe. The *Jinapañjara*, Somdet To had discovered, was particularly good for this blood harmonizing. It could be chanted in three ways (all contained on CDs he had in his office, of which he gave me copies). The first was the *mon* (Sanskrit *mantra*, Pali *manta*), which was an abbreviated chanting using syllables, *tua hua chai* (heart syllables) or *yo* (abbreviated syllables). In his opinion, this was not very useful for sonic mantra therapy. The second was the *mon gatha* (Pali *manta gāthā*), which were the full verses of a mantra, and these were designed for chanting and curing. The last was the *wet mon* (Vedic mantra), which was drawn by magicians on *yantras*. This method was also useful for protecting the body's health but not for sonic mantra therapy. He demonstrated his method by standing up and chanting while moving his body in quite striking and violent ways, throwing his chest in and out and breathing heavily. He then began to move his hands in complicated ways, intertwining his fingers and raising his hands up and down. He also emphasized that the Vedic drawings as well as the heart syllables worked the same way as the mantra verses (*wet* is a Thai derivative of this Sanskrit word, but it has little connection to the Sanskrit Vedas and connotes a vague notion of "mystical ancient science" or "traditional medicine"; *wet mon* can also be translated as "magical incantation"). The sound of the mantras are recorded on a computer and then projected on the computer screen as electronic algorithmic shapes. These shapes when viewed on a computer screen looked like old Khom letters, which he told me "were the original script in which Sanskrit and Pali were composed." The *Jinapañjara* made some particularly striking shapes when the sound was transferred to shapes by the computer. He was not able to show me on the computer, but he drew me some examples on a piece of paper that looked like Khom letters. Although the semantic meaning of the words in the *Jinapañjara* did not matter, he thought that it was interesting that the text was about protection. He also noted that *Jina* was a name both for the Buddha and for other Indian teachers, including the god Brahma himself. This was no coincidence, he stressed. The Buddha and Somdet To and Brahma were all conquerors of pain and suffering. *Pañjara*, although meaning "cage" or "armor," he translated as "aura." *Pañjara* was something that enveloped a person and protected them, like an aura does.

I thanked Dr. Supachai for his help and his openness. He gave me some more reading material, and I was escorted to the hallway by his assistant. He was gracious, kind, and focused. I was, like the woman I had met in the waiting room, skeptical and did not make all the connections between the Big Bang, blood flow, Vedic mantras, Brahma, Somdet To, Khom letters, and the *Jinapañjara* that he did, and, I assume, never will. He seemed to care about his patients and had a passion for his craft. He also earned quite a nice income through his clinic, his weekend retreats, and his lotions, books, vitamins, and DVDs. Certainly, only the wealthy could go through a series of treatments with him, especially while seated in the high-tech padded reclining massage lounge chair he had in the therapy room. The chair even has built-in speakers that play the *Jinapañjara* on a continuous loop. The *Jinapañjara* has come a long way.

This chapter is about texts. I show how the method of textual anthropology or anthrophilology helps scholars question (1) the nature of Pali "prestige" and supposed superiority of canonical texts to Southeast Asian apocryphal Pali and vernacular texts; (2) the entire study of the so-called Theravada tantra, *yogāvac-arin* Buddhism, or esoteric southern Buddhism; and (3) the use of the words "magic" and "esoteric" when describing Buddhist practices. Overall I hope to show that a study of Thai Buddhist texts is suspect if their multiple mediums (including electronic) and written and oral transmission traditions are ignored.

Dr. Supachai is just one of the many Thai Buddhists who use texts in innovative ways. So often, scholars of Buddhism study texts as isolated entities. They have words, they mean something, that meaning is in the words, the words are on the leaf of the manuscript. Even when multiple versions of a text are studied, it is usually to compare semantic meaning to semantic meaning, tracing the morphological and phonological evolution of words in order to gain some insight into their possible ethical, linguistic, literary, or historical importance. Furthermore, the original text often remains paramount in scholarly studies. So questions of change are often asked in reference to the original: How has the original been changed? How has it become at worst corrupted or at best "imbued with local wisdom"? The textual mediums, performative contexts, the audience reception, the pedagogical or homiletic uses are rarely examined. As Paul Mus has warned scholars, "working at a great distance from the object of study, one sometimes risks confusing a library with a country."[2] This chapter, therefore, is not about how original Pali canonical texts have changed in the modern Thai context but about the processes of textual circulation and the quite remarkable things Thai Buddhists do with words and texts.

To this end, I look specifically at one text, the *Jinapañjara*, and trace the ways it has been used in multiple mediums, by multiple types of Buddhist practitioners, over the past two hundred years. The *Jinapañjara* is compared in this chapter and in chapter 3 with a variety of other popular Thai vernacular and Pali Buddhist texts used in rituals, liturgies, and performances. Although I briefly mention them, I am not concerned with its origins, its lexical, morphological, and historical integrity. I do not mournfully lament the loss of its original meaning or the martial ethics of its content. I do not see it as a product or victim of modernity. Instead, the television programs, popular anthologies, handbooks, Web sites, blockbuster films, CDs, and avant-garde dramas, the text and others like it, are compared along with their various contexts. Regardless of its original intent or even occasionally the text's semantic meanings, I show how its versions and mediums reflect pervasive Thai attitudes toward security, heritage, graciousness, and abundance. They form part of the repertoire of a Thai Buddhist and are used in different ways and for different reasons by each practitioner. This is not simply a study of "texts in context" but of how texts can create contexts and how shifting contexts create new possibilities for old texts.

# THE *JINAPAÑJARA GĀTHĀ*: THE MOST POWERFUL TEXT IN THAILAND

The *Jinapañjara gāthā* (Thai *Phra gatha chinabanchon, Verses on the Victor's Armor*) is a protective text composed in Pali that is arguably the most widely recognized Buddhist text in modern Thailand.[3] It is studied by elite monastic university students as well as used in folk rituals in the rural areas of the north and the northeast. The present *sangharat* (ecclesiastical leader of all Thai Buddhists) has named it one of the seven essential Buddhist texts that all Buddhists, lay and ordained, should memorize and chant. Although it should be chanted every morning (and often by many monks), it is the designated chant for Thursday, which is "teacher's day" and an extremely important day of the week in Thailand.[4] It is so pervasive that it (or syllabic representations or abbreviations of it) is printed on color posters, wallet-sized laminated cards, at the bottom of pools of holy water, in modern textbooks, and chanted on television and radio frequently. It is featured in films, sold on CD and audio tape, and has its own chanting club of dedicated fans who promote it throughout the country.

For anyone who spends time in Thailand and can read Thai script, the *Jinapañjara* is the most public and best-known Pali text in the entire country (especially in central Thailand). I have asked dozens of monks and nuns to chant it for me from memory, and all of them could without a problem. In fact, many laypeople, especially men who had been monks previously, could chant it from memory as well (or at least the first few verses). It could be chanted by elite university professors as well as poor by rural monks. Most often, the people who could chant it did not know the Pali language. They have a good idea of what the text means because they have read or heard a Thai translation, but they have had no formal training in Pali grammar and could not judge the quality of the translation. It is not easy to memorize this text, as it has phonetically complex sounds and very little repetition. I remember having to memorize this chant as a monk in the early 1990s. I was assigned this chant in my first few days as a monk since it was common at liturgical occasions and for rituals protecting homes and property. I found it much harder than other, repetitive Pali chants but used it very often and therefore it became easy to recall on demand.

There are many different Thai translations. These Thai translations, although somewhat less ubiquitous, are also well-known and easily found in student anthologies, on posters and small prayer cards alongside pictures of Somdet To. They are usually not chanted, though, and so not committed to memory. The Pali text is ubiquitous in taxicabs, home shrines, on the bases of images, and on the radio. However, outside liturgical collections in Malaysia and Sri Lanka, this text has been mentioned only twice, as far as I know, in Western-language texts, both times by scholars influenced by the French school of Southeast Asian Buddhist studies, John Strong (from Sulak Sivaraksa) and Donald Swearer.[5] In both instances there is less than a paragraph of commentary and no serious interpretation.

The reasons why this text has been largely ignored by Western scholars of Buddhism are discussed later in the book. Here I am concerned with why is it so popular in Thailand. There are many ways to answer this question. First, let's look at its content.

My translation of the *Jinapañjara* reads as follows:

### Phra gāthā jinapañjara

1. Jayāsanākatā[6]-buddhā jetvā māraṃ savāhanaṃ[7]-catusaccāsabhaṃ rasaṃ ye pivimsu[8] narāsabhā[9]
   *The Buddhas, those bulls of men, having defeated Māra and his elephant, [each] having established [his own] victory seat, they drank the ambrosia of the Four Noble Truths.[10]*

2. Taṇhaṅkarādayo[11] buddhā aṭṭhavīsati[12] nāyakā sabbe patiṭṭhitā mayhaṃ matthake te munissarā
   *The Buddhas, the sonorous teachers, the twenty-eight guides beginning with Taṇhaṅkara, they are all fixed on my head.*

3. Sīse patiṭṭhito mayhaṃ buddho dhammo davilocane saṅgho patiṭṭhito mayhaṃ ure sabbaguṇākaro[13]
   *The Buddha is fixed on my head. The dhamma is in my eyes. The sangha, the holder of every virtue, is fixed on my chest.[14]*

4. Hadaye me anuruddho sārīputto ca dakkhiṇe koṇḍañño piṭṭhibhāgasmiṃ moggallāno ca vāmake
   *Anuruddha is in my heart and Sāriputta is on my right side. Koṇḍañña is on my back and Moggalāna is on my left side.*

5. Dakkhiṇe savane mayhaṃ āsuṃ[15] ānandarāhulo kassapo ca mahānāmo ubhāsuṃ vāmasotake[16]
   *Ānanda and Rāhula are in my right ear. Kassapa and Mahānāma are both in my left ear.*

6. Kesato piṭṭhibhāgasmiṃ suriyo va pabhaṃkaro nisinno sirisampanno sobhito munipuṃgavo
   *Sobhita, the bull of teachers, [he is] the sun seated in full glory, the light bringer to the hair on the back [of my] head.*

7. Kumārakassapo thero[17] mahesī cittavādako so mayhaṃ vadane niccaṃ patiṭṭhāsi guṇākaro

*Kumārakassapa, the elder, the holder of virtues, the famous orator, the great seer, he is fixed forever in my mouth.*

8. Puṇṇo aṅgulimālo ca upālinandasīvalī therā pañca ime jātā nalāṭhe[18] tilakā mama

   *The five elders, Puṇṇa, Aṅgulimāla, Upāli, Nanda, and Sīvalī, they are born on my forehead as auspicious signs.*

9. Sesāsīti mahātherā vijitā[19] jinasāvakā etesīti mahāthera jitavanto jinorasā[20] jalantā sīlatejena aṅgamaṅgesu saṇṭitā

   *The remaining eighty great elders, the disciples of the Jina, the victors, these eighty great elders, triumphant, pacified by the breast of the victorious one, burning with the fire of morality, are marked on each and every one of my limbs.*

10. Ratanaṃ purato āsi dakkhiṇe mettasuttakaṃ dhajaggaṃ pacchato āsi vāme aṅgulimālakaṃ

    *The Ratana [sutta] is in front of me. The Metta sutta is on my right side. The Dhajagga [paritta] is behind me. The Aṅgulimāla [paritta] is on my left.*

11. Khandhamoraparittañca[21] āṭānāṭiya suttakaṃ ākāse chadanaṃ āsi sesā[22] pākārasaṇṭitā[23]

    *The Khandha and Mora parittas and the Āṭānāṭiya sutta are the sheltering sky [above me]. The remaining [parittas and suttas] are a fortress [around me].*

12. Jinānānāvarasaṃyuttā sattappākārasaṃkatā[24] vātapittādisañjātā[25] bāhirajjhattupaddavā asesā vinayaṃ yantu anantajinatejasā[26] vasato me sakiccena sadā sambuddhapañjare[27]

    *Enclosed in the seven fortresses, infused with the power of the manifold Jinas. The external and internal misfortunes, caused by weather and disease, let them go completely to destruction because of the heat of the eternal Jina. No matter what I do, I dwell in the cage of the fully enlightened one.*

13. Jinapañjaramajjhamahi[28] viharantaṃ mahītale sadā pālentu maṃ sabbe te mahāpurisāsabhā

    *Living on the ground in the middle of the cage of the Jina, always let all the great men guard me.*

14. Iccevam anto[29] sugutto surakkho jinānubhavena jitūpaddavo dhammānubhavena jitārisaṅgho saṅghānubhavena jitantarāyo saddhammānubhāvapālito carāmi jinapañcareti[30]

    *Verily, in the end, I am completely well sheltered, well protected. Whatever [misfortune] arises is conquered by the power of the Jina. The horde of unworthy ones is conquered by the power of the dhamma. Danger is*

*conquered by the power of the sangha. I move about freely in the armor
of the Jina guarded by the power of the true* dhamma.

While it is obvious that the content of this set of verses is about protection, it is
the particular way a person chanting is protected and what they are protected by
that is important for understanding why Thai Buddhists repeat and print this
chant. If there could be a signature Thai chant, then this would be it. However, the content says nothing about the five, eight, ten, or two hundred twenty-
seven lay and monastic precepts, nor about the bedrock Theravada virtues
(*brahmavihāras*) of compassion, loving-kindness, equanimity, and sympathetic
joy. It provides little philosophical insight. The only texts mentioned by name
are other *paritta* protective chants. The Tripiṭaka is not invoked. It states nothing about giving (*dāna*) or meditation (although meditation may be implied).
Words like "victor" "conqueror," "armor," "destruction," "protection," "horde,"
"fortress," "wall," "power," "disease," and "cage" dominate the text. The ritual
use of protective marks (tattoos or auspicious protective signs) is mentioned but
not canonically designated rituals like ordination or alms rounds. Nirvana is
not mentioned.

This poem is defensive, even martial, in its import. For example, this martial
rhetoric is constantly emphasized through the choice of the epithet *jina* (conqueror) for the Buddha. The author even replaces the standard "triple gem" in
Buddhism (Buddha, *dhamma*, sangha) in the last verse with the tripartite Jina,
*dhamma*, sangha. Moreover, there are a number of parallelisms in this poem.
They each work to set up a conflict between the inner and the outer, the good
and the bad. In the twelfth verse the author states that the external and internal
misfortunes (weather and disease) are destroyed or subdued by the power of the
ascetic heat of the conqueror. He specifically chooses the word *vinaya* for destruction or submission here. Here the author offers a clever wordplay. "Vinaya,"
of course, is usually associated with the codes of monastic discipline. Vinaya is
a good thing. It is that which protects the monastic community from internal
division and unethical conduct. However, here the author uses it in its more
literal sense of "submission" or "destruction." In the tenth, eleventh, and twelfth
verses the seven of the most common liturgical texts in all of Theravada Buddhism (the *Ratana sutta*, the *Metta sutta*, the *Dhajagga paritta*, the *Aṅgulimāla
paritta*, the *Khandha* and *Mora parittas*, and the *Āṭānāṭiya sutta*) are not simply
texts but "fortresses" or "enclosing walls." The disciples of the Buddha, all the
Buddhas in fact are guards or protective tattoos. They are not teachers of compassion or wise sages. In the last verse, the author uses the word *saṅgha* in two
different and oppositional ways—a good community (the community of nuns
and monks) and a bad community (*ari* + *saṅgha*). In this way, the sangha is not

an open and inclusive community that embraces all sentient beings and welcomes them into the dispensation of the Buddha but a defensive group that protects itself from "hordes" or "gangs" (also perfectly legitimate translations of the word *saṅgha*) of enemies (*ari*). In the very last line, the true *dhamma* (*saddhamma*) is that which creates a "cage" or "armor" and protects the practitioner. This poem does not depict the pluralist, gentle, and passive Buddhism so often presented in Western textbooks and classrooms.[31]

So why is this chant so prevalent, so important? The answers to these questions tell us much about Thai Buddhist values and ratiocinations. There are several overlapping reasons why the *Jinapañjara* is so prevalent in Thailand, ranging from the history of the text, its connection to Somdet To, the text's power to make holy water and amulets, miraculous stories of its healing energy, national protection, and ghost taming. I discuss these reasons in the following section before turning to a reflection at the end of the chapter on the uses of the terms "tantra," "esoteric," and "magic."

## HISTORY OF THE *JINAPAÑJARA GĀTHĀ* IN AND OUTSIDE OF THAILAND

Although a student of religion may assume that the oldest canonical texts in a religious tradition are the most important, age and canonicity may be the least-important reasons for the popularity of the *Jinapañjara*. The *Jinapañjara* is not a canonical text. It is not Buddhavacana (a text believed to have been spoken by the Buddha himself twenty-five hundred years ago). It should not be assumed that a ritual text like the *Jinapañjara* is less important to a Thai Buddhist than an ethical or philosophical text. Ritual chants don't inspire, they order. They don't explicate, they inculcate. Too often in the past they have been passed over by students and scholars of Buddhism looking to find out what Buddhism means — what wisdom the Buddha has for us, how his words can be applied to our lives, and so on. These assumptions and approaches, many of which I held myself when I first encountered Buddhism, must be shelved in order to understand the value of the *Jinapañjara* to millions of Thai and non-Thai Buddhists.

Although the text is ubiquitous in Thailand and lauded by the elite, royalty, as well as by the average monk and layperson, its semantic meaning has not been the subject of much inquiry. The text's history has been studied, but when it has been investigated, it has been lauded not for being a Pali text composed by the Buddha in India and passed down by sages in Sri Lanka but as a text composed (or at least adapted) in Thailand by a Thai monk. In fact, the two major Thai scholars who have written on the text have stated directly that the text as it is chanted in Thailand is not South Asian, is not necessarily the authentic words of the Buddha. These facts are not necessarily negative attributes. Thailand is honored as a place where Buddhist texts are being composed. Thailand, not India or Sri Lanka, is becoming the center of Theravada Buddhism.

The first scholarly study of the *Jinapañjara* was compiled by the *sangharat* himself, Somdet Phra Ñāṇasaṃvara (Suvaḍḍhano) in 1986 and published at the central university for the Thammayut lineage, Mahamakut Monastic University.[32] Although scholars tell us constantly that the Thammayut is the most "orthodox" lineage and supposedly promotes the study of the canon and a classical supralocal understanding of Buddhism, the Thammayut's most senior monk and the head of all Thai Buddhists has written an entire book on this Thai "unorthodox" and noncanonical text. The first thirty-one pages of the history, which I summarize here, emphasize the text's Thai origin. However, he (well, he and his team of researchers, which included several senior professors at Mahamakut) points out that there is a controversy over the origin, but most of the evidence points to its origin in the northern Thai (Lan Na) city of Chiang Mai in the late fifteenth or early sixteenth century. He states that he researched manuscript archives in Sri Lanka and Burma and that there are no old manuscripts found there.[33] Moreover, he states, quite correctly, that the *Jinapañjara* today in Sri Lanka is not very popular and not part of the regular ritual chanting. It is not even a separate text; instead it is part of a larger text known as the *Buddhanavamavinicchaya*. In Burma, the verses are found in one edition of the commentary, the *Vinayasamūhavinicchaya*. The way the Chiang Mai text got from northern Thailand to Burma and then to Sri Lanka, he speculates, was at the time of the first phase of the Burmese occupation of Chiang Mai between 1558 and 1685. He offers an extensive and accurate account (corroborated by manuscript and epigraphic sources) of the Burmese period and states that the text, like many northern Thai Pali and vernacular Buddhist texts, was brought to Burma at that time. This is all confirmed by evidence from manuscript archives in Burma. There was a great collecting of northern Thai Buddhist texts by the Burmese at this time. I have written about this history and so omit it here, but suffice it to say, the *sangharat* is certainly correct in stating that a scholar should not assume that the texts found in Burma or Sri Lanka are always older than northern Thai and Siamese texts, because many texts were exchanged.[34] Thai Buddhists learned Buddhism largely from Sri Lankan and Burmese emissaries and texts, but the Sri Lankans and Burmese also learned occasionally from Thai texts.[35]

The *sangharat* interviewed the famous scholar-monk Phra Dhammananda of Wat Tham Ma-O in Lampang Province in northern Thailand. Phra Dhammananda is a Burmese national who has spent most of his life in Thailand and researches in Pali grammatical texts in Burma and Thailand.[36] He states that the *Jinapañjara* is from Chiang Mai, but it is unknown who composed it. He lists sixteen possible northern Thai Pali scholars living in Chiang Mai in the sixteenth century who would have had the skills to undertake the task and believes that the writing style looks like that of Phra Silawong, who also composed the *Uppātasanti*. The oldest edition of the text is found in a manuscript titled *Kamphi saṅkhayāpakāsakaṭīkā*. There are two editions of this manuscript in Khom and Burmese script in the National Library of Thailand. The *sangharat* and Phra Dhammananda believe they are from an earlier northern Thai manuscript. The Khom-script manuscript refers to the *Jinapañjara* as the *Ratanapañjara gāthā*. There is also a Sinhala-script edition called the *Jinapañjara paritta* written on central Thai mulberry-paper manuscript (Thai *samut khoi*) found at Wat Mahathat (Bangkok) in 1976, but the original date of composition in unknown. This could indicate that the text came from an earlier Sri Lankan edition and was copied in Bangkok. It is believed, though, that the *Kamphi saṅkha yāpakāsakaṭīkā* was composed by the well-known northern Thai Pali scholar Sirimaṅgala in 1520, and this, the *sangharat* claims, could be the original text as well; however, he believes that many monks in Laos and northern Thailand at that time were inspired by Sirimaṅgala, and this text could have been originally composed in Vientiane or Sukhothai by one of his students. There are similar literary qualities found in other Pali texts composed in northern Thailand like the *Uppātasanti*, the *Buddho me nātho*, the *Aṭṭhārasahatthubbedho*, and the *Buddho majjhime*. These texts invoke the protection of twenty-eight Buddhas, the *arahants* (enlightened disciples) of the eight directions, as well as of Brahmanic deities, and even female disciples (*ariyasāvikas*). The invoking of crowds of beings to protect the chanter seem to have been a common theme in texts in northern Thailand in the fifteenth and sixteenth centuries. This combined with the fact that there are two inscriptions from the 1460s in Chiang Mai Province (one in Amphoe Phrao and one on the Tha Pae Gate) ordered by King Tilokarat of Chiang Mai that invoke the protection of twenty-eight Buddhas like the *Jinapañjara* lead the *sangharat* to lean toward a northern Thai origin for the text.

The *sangharat* admits that another edition, which casts some doubt on the northern Thai origin of the *Jinapañjara*, is listed in the 1921 edition of the manuscript catalog of the Prince Wachirayan Royal Library in Bangkok. Although the manuscript is missing, the catalog states that this manuscript is in Sinhala script. He states that this text was composed in ink, though, and could have been a late edition. However, when I examined the 1916 edition of this catalog, this Sinhala-script edition of the *Jinapañjara* was not listed, and the details of whether the text was composed in ink or inscribed on different types of manuscript was not provided. Since the *Jinapañjara* is not listed in the ninety-seven texts brought from Bangkok to Sri Lanka in 1798, the *sangharat* and his team believe that the text was brought to Sri Lanka earlier, perhaps through Burma, where it was expanded in a twenty-two-verse edition included in an anthology of chanting texts in Roman script published in 1961 by one Narada Thera (Mirror of the Dhamma). There was also a Burmese edition with an English translation published in 1979 called the *Ratanapañjara*, which is very close to the fifteen-verse edition common in Thailand.

Although, the *sangharat* admits, these editions give conflicting evidence, it seems that there was an early fourteen-verse edition that was either a shortened version of a Sri Lankan twenty-two-verse original, or vice versa. The edition most commonly associated with Somdet To has fifteen verses, although there are numerous fourteen-verse printed editions. A hint of nationalism may have made the *sangharat* lean toward the later "Thai original" thesis, but he gives some convincing evidence that supports his preference. A scholar named Phunphon Asanachinda from Chiang Mai was interviewed by the *sangharat* and stated that the northern Thai people have great respect for the *Jinapañjara* and locally refer to it as the *Sut jayabanchon*. There are *yantra* editions, local chanting traditions, and even several Lan Na–script (Yuan/Tua Kham Muang) manuscripts called the *Sut jayabanchon* and the *Jaya anisong*. Phunphon's statements have been confirmed by my time working in northern Thailand and Laos, where the *Jinapañjara* is popular and part of the common repertoire of local monastics. Moreover, a protective ritual in the north uses two *yantra* drawings based on the *Jinapañjara* in Yuan script that are different, and apparently older, than the *yantras* composed by Somdet To in central Thailand. One *yantra* has thirty-two squares with thirty-two numbers, and the second has eight sets of nine squares each with syllables from the *Jinapañjara* in them. There is an 1851 manuscript of these *yantras*, as well as the whole text, composed on mulberry paper (northern Thai *pap sa*) found at Wat Chayamonkhon Wiang Tai in Nan Province. There is also a composition of the *Jinapañjara* in "heart syllables" (*tua hua chai*), and a local incantation using three words drawn from the text, *ratanaṃ purato āsi*, which is a *gāthā tan hian* (a text that helps the chanter be well fed and wealthy even in difficult times). There are four manuscripts of the *Jinapañjara* in the library of Phra Dhammananda's Wat Tham Ma-O included in longer anthologies of liturgical texts. Even though a manuscript of the *Jinapañjara* from Nan states that the text was composed by Buddhaghosa of Sri Lanka, this is a common appellation given by Thai writers when they do not know the original author. Moreover, the story that accompanies this appellation is strange. It states that Buddhaghosa locked the text in a *hip* (a northern Thai word for "manuscript chest") and locked it with two locks and instructed no one to sell it. Then Buddhaghosa, it is claimed, chanted the twenty-nine verses (a very long version) while walking with his hands raised in respect and traveled around

Sri Lanka with it. This story is doubted by the *sangharat*, and he believes that since the *Jinapañjara* is so intimately involved in the ritual, artistic, and intellectual life of northern Thais, it seems to be a local text. However, since it has similar qualities to other texts, like the *Bāhum* and the *Jayamaṅgala kātha*, the Thai *Jinapañjara* could have been part of a larger Theravada tradition of protective texts invoking the Jina.[37]

While there have been very few editions of the text produced in Sri Lanka and Burma, there have been dozens produced in Thailand, each following the "standard" fifteen Pali verses. One of the older print editions was published at Wat Rakhang based on the 1932 edition by Phra Maha Heng Itthacaro. Phra Phatmuni edited a very popular edition at Wat Thongnopakhun in 1972, and Nai Chani Krasaesin published an edition under the auspices of the Ministry of Education in 1986. Phra Dhammananda published an edition based on a 1956 Burmese edition at Wat Tham Ma-O with fifteen verses.[38] Pungkham Tuikhiao produced a Lan Na–script edition based on the 1851 Nan manuscript from Wat Chayamongkhon Wiang Tai. Pha Sasanalophana (Niran Nirantaro), of Wat Thepsirintharat in Bangkok, produced one of the earliest Thai translations, and the novice Chamrun Thammada of Wat Mahathat in Bangkok produced another. There are hundreds of different printings of the *Jinapañjara* (mostly short books and pamphlets but some as laminated pocket-size booklets and others as large posters) and at least sixteen recorded versions available on audio tape, CD, VCD, and DVD. There is a downloadable version for MP3 players. It is also available as a ring-tone downloaded to cell phones. Besides these popular versions, the manuscript research involved in searching for copies of the *Jinapañjara* has involved some of the most prominent and skilled scholars in Thailand, including Somchai Nopchaloenkun, Songsri Praphatthong, Praphat Surasen, Wirat Unnathawarangkan, Wichira Thammamethin, Saman Wongphraikon, Lamduan Thiankhanthikun, among many others. Rarely has so much scholarly talent been expended on such a small text. Rarely has there been this much scholarly work done on canonical texts in Thailand! The scholarly energy spent by Thais on this text stands in stark contrast to the almost complete lack of work on the text outside of Thailand. This is just one example of a much wider problem in Thai Buddhist studies. There is a major incongruence between Thai and non-Thai scholars regarding the subjects deemed worthy of research.

## RECENTERING THERAVADA BUDDHISM

What is striking here is that many of these Thai scholars, including the *sangharat* himself, all seem to see the possible Thai origin as a good thing. Even though this would indicate that the Buddha did not utter this text himself, nor that it was composed or compiled by the great Sri Lankan and Indian commentators like Buddhaghosa or Dhammapala, the Thai origin has trumped them in terms of the prestige that foreign and some royal Thai scholars used to accord to South Asian commentators and the Buddha and his direct disciples.

Sri Lanka and India, and to some extent even Burma, are still honored as places where Buddhism is older and where monastics are well educated; however, there is a slow movement away from seeing Buddhism as a religion that came from South Asia to viewing Thailand as a place where Buddhism is centered and spreading out to the rest of South and Southeast Asia. This decentering of Buddhism from Sri Lanka to Thailand is a massive process involving texts, images, ecclesiastical organizations, patrons, kings, and students. While I cannot comment on it at length here, let me simply state that because of the economic strength and vigor of Thai patrons, Sri Lankan, Nepalese, Cambodian, Lao, Burmese, and even Vietnamese monks are now coming to study at Mahachulalongkorn and Mahamakut universities in Bangkok. One Sri Lankan monk I met, Koman, told me that there was no "temporary" ordination in Sri Lanka and he wanted ordination only for a few years to get an education. He was planning on going into either professional English translation or business. He thought a Buddhist degree in Thailand would help him understand his religion better and better prepare him for the lay life after he disrobed. Other Sri Lankan monks are attracted to the monasteries in Thailand because they are not controlled by powerful families, which often exclude certain castes and families from their cloisters. The International Association of Buddhist Universities is now run out of Thailand, and Thai monastic printing presses are producing more and more textual material in Thai, English, and Pali.[39] One Sri Lankan monk, Soratha, joked with me that the food on alms rounds was even better in Thailand! Thailand has also moved from bringing famous Buddha images into Thailand to exporting them. Beginning in the nineteenth century (and occasionally before that), Thai monarchs and wealthy patrons started donating large Thai-style (usually seated Ayutthayan-style) images to Japan, Laos, Sri Lanka, Nepal, and Cambodia (as well as, today, to Australia, the United States, and Europe). One of the main images at the famous Temple of the Tooth Relic in Kandy, Sri Lanka, is a donated Thai image. Many of the images at smaller Sri Lankan monasteries are also newly cast Thai ones. In turn, places like Wat Benchamamophit in Bangkok have started small image galleries displaying images the abbot and his patrons have gathered in Japan, India, Sri Lanka, and China. If they do not collect images, often Thai artists copy foreign-style images and place them below the central Thai ones in monasteries. There is an International Tipiṭaka Hall at Chulalongkorn University that has on display printed editions of the Pali canon from all over Asia, with the oldest Thai edition, of course, in a rotating electric display case in the center of the room. Even naming the new international airport in Bangkok Suvarnabhumi can be seen as a subtle way of telling the rest of the Theravada world that Bangkok has now become the center of the Land of Gold.

I could go on and on with examples, but for my purpose here, it can be seen that Thai scholars as well as devotees promote the theory that the *Jinapañjara* was originally composed in Thailand. They see the text as equal to canonical Pali texts from South Asia. I have discussed the problems with using the terms "Tipiṭaka" and "canon" in Thailand extensively before. Let me simply point out that although some less-scholarly descriptions of the *Jinapañjara* in popular magazines and in Somdet To hagiographies mention that the text is an ancient (*boran*) text composed in Sri Lanka (rarely is it ever stated, though, that the Buddha himself composed it), but Somdet To "corrected" (*tam hai thuk tong*) it.[40] Moreover, they state that Somdet To's fifteen verses are superior in terms of their sound and power to make amulets and holy water. Popularly among amulet dealers and many monks and laypeople I have been told that Somdet To "found" an ancient manuscript of the *Jinapañjara* hidden in the cracks of an old stupa in Kampaengphet in north-central Thailand. This story occasionally appears in amulet magazines as well. Remember, Kampaengphet is one of the places many believe Somdet To, or at least his mother, was born. After finding this ancient manuscript, Somdet To adapted it, or "corrected" it, for use in Thailand. This is a striking statement. Most often stories of monks' finding hidden manuscripts, like the stories of the *gter ma* texts found by Tibetan monks or the scrolls found by Chinese monks in caves, are important because they show that the Buddha's actual words were preserved and discovered untouched by monks centuries after his death. They are important because they are claimed to be the words of the Buddha. However, in the Thai case, fans of Somdet To and elite scholars emphasize that the text was composed in Thailand, or that even if it was composed in South Asia sometime in ancient times, it needed to be "corrected" by a Thai monk. Buddhist legitimacy, which for so long has been associated in Thailand with Sri Lanka or the Indic world, is slowly being remade by a self-legitimizing Thai Buddhist pride. This is promoted by the sangha, the Royal dynasty, and the people themselves, who are proud of the success their country has had compared with the horrible natural disasters, colonization, genocide, political oppression, and poverty of their Theravada neighbors in Burma, Cambodia, Laos, and even Sri Lanka.

# HIDDEN POOLS AND HOLY WATER MACHINES

Despite local scholarly interest and some popular stories, the origins of the *Ji-napañjara* are not extremely important to most Thai Buddhists or even to dedicated fans of Somdet To. Surprisingly, even Dr. Supachai, who uses the *Jinapañjara* to cure cancer, was neither interested in nor particularly knowledgeable about the origins of the text. The same can be said for most monks, novices, and dedicated Somdet To and Mae Nak fans I spoke with throughout Thailand. The origins of the chant are much less important reasons for its power than its association with the person of Somdet To and his use of it to make amulets and holy water.

Although I do not believe there is solid evidence that the *Jinapañjara* was composed in northern Thailand originally, and though I think that the evidence the *sangharat* employs, although quite extensive and impressive (only a small portion of which I could describe here), does not definitively prove the text was not brought in some form (perhaps a longer twenty-two-verse form) from Sri Lanka through Burma in the fifteenth century, it does not really matter. What matters is that most fans of the text today believe that Somdet To either composed it himself or adapted it from a secret manuscript he found in Kampaengphet, northern Thailand.[41] It is this "origin" for the text that is much more important for assessing what makes a text valuable in Thailand than the philological, codicological, and epigraphical research by great scholars like the *sangharat*. No matter what scholars write, even by respected monks like the *sangharat*, Somdet To is seen by most as the author, and therein lies a much more important source of power.

Somdet To's power to heal, give sermons, help the poor, make amulets, and his association with the royal family all contribute to raising the status of the *Jinapañjara*. We do not know why Somdet To thought this particular text was so important. He could have picked a chant from the canonical *suttas* or even an Abhidhamma text. There is not a clear reason why he simply did not elevate a well-known protective (*paritta*) incantation like the *Rattana*, *Mora*, or *Mangala suttas*. It could have been that the *Jinapañjara* mentions the seven most famous *paritta* texts. It could have been seen by him as superior because it invokes these texts, as well as the power of the Buddha, his eighty major disciples, and the total power of the *dhamma* and the sangha. Here we certainly see the Thai values of abundance, security, and heritage. Perhaps he saw the *Jinapañjara* as powerful because of its all-encompassing message.

Regardless of why he chose this set of protective verses, most fans are more concerned with how Somdet To used the *Jinapañjara* to make holy water, infuse amulets, and protect the kingdom. Dozens of oral stories, printed biographies, and the popular biographical film dramatization referenced in chapter 1 describe the way Somdet To would stand in a canoe in the middle of the Chao Phraya River in Bangkok and chant the *Jinapañjara* in all directions while throwing amulets into the river. He would write the *Jinapañjara*'s "heart syllables" in Khom script in white powder (*pong*) and use the dust created by the act of writing it to spread over food, make medicine, and use as the base of clay amulets. He would write the text on cloth to be worn as shirts for warriors (replicas of these warrior shirts with photographs of Somdet To can be seen in the Tha Phra Chan amulet market in Bangkok; they cost approximately four dollars and can be worn under uniforms by soldiers or simply by civilians in need of protection). Many would assert that Somdet To would inscribe the *Jinapañjara* on brass and gold plates and give them to people to place on the wall above the doors of their homes and businesses. These stories are peppered throughout popular magazines and newspapers. For example, on the cover of one magazine, emblazoned with a photograph of one of Somdet To's images, is the headline "Abhinihan pha yan anuphap krua To!" (The Supernatural Power of the Protective Cloth and Aura of Somdet To!). The long subtitle on the cover tells of a man named Suchip Kaeoma who escaped unharmed despite being hit by a "ten-wheeled truck" (*sip lo*) while riding his motorcycle because of his wearing of a *yantra* cloth made by Somdet To. The actual article describes this incident as well as the good fortunes of three men, Phairot Chatraphon, Chanaphon Chinapancaphon, and Khampan Mulakham, who were all avid collectors of Somdet To amulets (*phra Somdet*), *yantras*, and images. Of course, this magazine, like dozens of others, advertises Somdet To's and other amulets for purchase. These amulets are empowered, in part, through the chanting of the *Jinapañjara*.[42]

Over time, the *Jinapañjara*, just like the legend of Somdet To, has taken on a life of its own. It has been used to heal the sick, protect soldiers, ensure favorable results on examinations, and the like. There are numerous examples, but a few will suffice. Each of them contributes to the reason the text remains relevant not only among the rural poor but also among a highly cosmopolitan, urban Southeast Asian population.

Perhaps the first time I fully understood the power of the *Jinapañjara* was at a shrine on the grounds of Wat Indrawihan in Bangkok. This monastery is located in one of the busiest sections of old Bangkok. It is a large monastery with a school, ceremonial halls, a shrine dedicated to Kuan Im, a library, a bell tower, and one of the tallest Buddha images in the world (measuring almost fifteen stories high). A small shrine near the back edge of the monastery holds a chanting station for the *Jinapañjara*. This shrine is an anomaly of Thai Buddhist construction. It is unique because it is in the shape of a hexagon, has a low roof and door, is brick red, and has a dome the likes of which are not seen anywhere else in the country. Central Thai shrines are usually characterized by open-air pavilions with the ubiquitous orange and blue–tiled, three-tiered roofs. The doorway of this particular shrine, although in the middle of the city, is hidden by several shade trees and a curved pathway. It gives the impression that you are entering a cave. In fact, it is called the Tham Bo Nam Mon Somdet (Cave of the Holy Water Pool of Somdet To).

Inside, a seasoned patron of Thai Buddhist shrines is surprised. First, there is a second door that you must pass through after entering the cavelike structure. This door is made of dark-tinted glass and is sealed because the shrine is air-conditioned, again, relatively uncommon for a small shrine, even one in hyper-modern Bangkok. Beyond the glass door the room is almost completely dark, unlike the standard, well-lit open-air shrines. What little light there is comes from a small skylight in the dome that reflects off of glass vials filled with holy water with the names of wealthy patrons etched into them. These vials line the walls of the man-made cave. Besides being bathed in this flickering hue, the visitor is also enveloped by the steady sound of the *Jinapañjara* being chanted through a speaker.

The image in the center of the room is the source of the recorded *Jinapañjara*. Here sits a resin-and-plastic, life-size replica of Somdet To in his determined and intense meditative pose. The speaker is placed behind his head to give the impression that he is chanting. However, outside the shrine there is an expensive stereo system that plays CDs of the *Jinapañjara* on a continuous loop. On a small plaque in front of the image it states that the chanting and the holy water produced by its power will ensure a clear mind, cool heart, and a long life and success. The water, which must be placed on the front and back of the body every day while chanting the *Jinapañjara gāthā*, can be obtained at this small shrine. This is because the resin image of Somdet To is holding a long white string, called a *sai siñcana*, that trails from his wax hand into a large pool of water in front of the image. On the bottom of the black pool the *Jinapañjara* is inscribed in gold in a pattern of increasingly smaller concentric squares. In South and Southeast Asia these incantations (often abbreviated or composed in code with small drawings) are called *yantra*, or *yan* in Thai. The verses in *yan* form are inscribed in the magically and culturally powerful, but incomprehensible to the vast majority of Thai people (including monks), Khom script. Patrons, including every monk at the monastery with whom I spoke, cannot read it. Moreover, since the chanted verses are in the classical Theravada language of Pali, most patrons, including the monks, cannot understand it. As is often the case with magical incantations throughout the world, the power of the verses comes not from its semantics but from its sounds, shapes, the situation in which it is chanted, the ethical and ritual purity, as well as the meditative power of the chanter, and the intention and dedication of its listener. The patron seated on the floor of the cave shrine is instructed through small signs to listen to or read the chant (the transliteration in Thai script of the Pali verses is provided on small handouts, wallet sized, as well on as A4-size photocopies). It is understood that one should listen to or read along with Somdet To with a clear mind and respect. Many sit in meditative postures with their eyes shut; no one speaks, and the cave is so small that you can often hear the breathing of the people on either side of you. A formulized dialogue is created between the image and the audience. This dialogue is reinforced by the copies of the text inscribed on the bottom of the pool, on gold plaques, on paper handouts, and played over the loudspeaker.

After listening or reading, then one should meditate, and then take a small plastic bag of the holy water home (plastic bags are provided and recently plastic bottles with a picture of To on them have become available for a small donation). There is also a water fountain outside the building with paper cups next to it. If a patron does not have time to go into the shrine, they can simply get a paper cup and drink the holy water (which comes from the pool through a series of pipes) while standing outside. Patrons drink a sip and place some more on their heads. There is a sign next to the water fountain that tells patrons, in English, "Holy water for drinking only" and, in Thai, "Ham lang meu" (do not wash hands). I was told this had to be put up because sweaty tourists were sticking their face and hands in the water, not for the purpose of being blessed but to get some respite from the humid and hot Bangkok air. To ensure the efficacy of the water, whether drunk outside or touched inside, one should place some water on one's head every day and chant the *Jinapañjara* every day.[43] This process should be initiated on a Thursday because that was Somdet To's birthday and is the day of the week dedicated to teachers in Thai culture. The well-known relationship between images, abbreviated *yantras*, the Khom script, the Pali language, and meditative poses is not surprising here. These are common features in the ritualization and deification of forest and urban monks.

The location of the cave shrine in a busy part of town next to a place with rare convenient parking spaces, several bus lines, and off one of the main thoroughfares of the city makes obtaining the water, visiting, and listening to Somdet To convenient and fast. The shrine is also a cool, dark respite from the heat and noise of the city. This convenience and coolness are inviting. Even though the verses and *yantra* are in Pali and written in Khom script, people do not turn away in confusion or apprehension.[44] Thai Buddhists grow up hearing but largely not understanding Pali chanting. The words have efficacy whether they are understood or not. Since monks do not monitor the comings and goings of patrons, there is no one checking, except if you count Somdet To's resin image, if you choose to leave a donation or not.[45] Although this shrine's architecture, lighting, and use of technology are unique, shrines to Somdet To, as we will see in chapter 4, are certainly not.[46]

Somdet To's images, the *Jinapañjara*, and amulets are increasing in popularity over time. Even though he died in 1882, his life has never been so popular. In fact, a new bronze image of him is being constructed in Saraburi (central Thailand) and will be over sixty-five feet tall. Colossal and tiny images of Somdet To are mass-produced and line the religious markets (*talat phra*) near Wat Suthat, Wat Mahathat (both in Bangkok), Thai Town in Hollywood, the Little India market in Singapore, and various markets in Thailand, like the ones near Wat Sothon in Chachoengsao and at Wat Ban Rai in Nakhon Ratchasima.[47]

## CHANTING CLUBS AND HORROR FILMS

One of the most informed people I have met in Thailand studying the *Jinapañjara gāthā* is a popular radio disc jockey. Her name is Rassamee Maneenin and she is the host of a weekend show that focuses on new books, music, and events in Bangkok on FM 99.1. She also has another radio show, on FM 92 from 7:30 to 10 P.M. Monday to Friday on family issues, as well as one AM 1107 on general Thai cultural news and events. Since she often talks about hot topics in Bangkok, she decided to start a master's degree in Thai studies and write a thesis about Somdet To since he is one of the most talked about monks in the city. She requested an interview with me because she heard through the grapevine that I was studying Somdet To myself. Although she wanted to interview me, I think I learned more from her than she did from me. I had been working on manuscripts of the *Jinapañjara* and interviewing historians, but she told me about her work with members of the Jinapañjara Chanting Club (Chomrom Suat Phra Gatha Chinabanchon) and with a popular film actor who had dedicated himself to Somdet To.

The chanting club, a number of whose members I met later that year, is based in the outskirts of western Bangkok, had been formed around 2002 but had only grown in large numbers after it had helped organize a group chanting by laypeople and monks at the Siriraj Hospital on July 23, 2006. Siriraj Hospital is the oldest hospital in Thailand, about four blocks from Somdet To's home monastery of Wat Rakhang. It is where the royal family receives its medical treatment. The group was chanting important protective incantations, like the *Bahum*, *Jinapañjara*, and *Bojangha paritta*, in order to help King Rama IX

(Bhumibol Adunyadej) recover from his stomach ailments and a recent injury he had received to his spine and ribs (sustained while walking his dogs). This group believes that the *Jinapañjara* especially is the most powerful protective incantation in the realm, and it meets regularly to chant the text to protect the kingdom. The director of the club, Dr. Pichai Towiwich, a former professor of chemistry at Chulalongkorn University, retired early to dedicate himself to Somdet To. The club meets not only to chant the *Jinapañjara* but also to invoke the spirit of Somdet To through a medium. They receive instructions from Somdet To through the medium. Their motivation comes from long-term interests in the state of the nation. Many are former members of the Thai Communist Party, which was banned in the 1970s. They work to help the country, but now by invoking the teachings (and ethereal body) of a Buddhist monk instead of the teachings of Marx and Lenin. These efforts to contact Somdet To in the spirit world (which is never clearly defined by the practitioners) are also pursued by Dr. Bunchai Ghosonthanakun, who runs an English as a Second Language school at the Central Shopping Mall in the Ladphrao district of Bangkok. He believes that Somdet To is secretly still alive (he would be over two hundred twenty years old now) because he is a *bodhisatta*. The Jinapañjara Chanting Club, like the alternative medicine doctor and sonic therapist Dr. Supachai, is keeping this chant relevant even to Buddhists who do not have much time to go to a monastery regularly. These efforts are being helped by a new pop song by the singer Kanakama Piradee, who remixed the *Jinapañjara* for a popular-music audience. The music was composed in collaboration with the self-professed Somdet To scholar and modern Buddhist lay intellectual Satienpong Wannaphok, who has also written a popular book about Somdet To.[48]

Getting back to my interview with Rassamee, she kindly talked about her many interviews with people who were dedicated to the *Jinapañjara*. She interviewed an engineering student at Chulalongkorn University who had been hit by a car and was lying on the street gripping his thigh in pain. He began chanting the *Jinapañjara* and miraculously was not injured. One student I met at Wat Rakhang told me she was prostrating to an image of Somdet To and chanting the *Jinapañjara* because she wanted to do well on upcoming examinations. Another student played a CD of the *Jinapañjara* in her car to protect her from accidents. Another student was hoping to gain confidence for a job interview and believed that the *Jinapañjara* helped her not only keep her composure but also get the job. Another student was hoping to study in the United States and chanted the *Jinapañjara* before her TOEFL examination. Her goal was a 677 on the exam, and she chanted the *Jinapañjara* and received a 667. Close enough.

Some people I interviewed took this dedication to the *Jinapañjara* very far. For example, the popular movie star Sorapong Chartree, the award-winning star of the blockbuster hit films *Suriyothai* and *Naresuan*, was so indebted to Somdet To for helping his career that in 2004 he commissioned a huge sixty-five-foot tall statue of Somdet To as well as an entire *vihāra* and garden built along a highway in Si Khiu District in the rural northeastern province of Nakhon Ratchasima. The *Jinapañjara* is played on a giant stereo system at this complex. Sorapong is the self-designated president of the Somdet To Fan Club (called by that name in English) and has spent several million dollars on this site. When I visited the site for the first time in February 2008 I was struck not only by the immense size of the statue of Somdet To and the ornate mixed Thai and European–style building that was built specifically to house this image but also by the over fifty acres of gardens, reflection pools, waterfalls, and fountains. The entire complex is served by several restaurants, shops selling Somdet To T-shirts, umbrellas, CDs of the *Jinapañjara*, amulets, and the like. I spoke with one of the tour guides, Somchit, who kindly gave me two amulets and a book describing the *Jinapañjara*, and he explained that the entire building, which was still under construction, would be covered in Italian marble. He also showed me a large glass panel inscribed with the *Jinapañjara* in gold leaf and lists of the thousands of people, besides Sorapong, who had donated hundreds of thousands of baht to help build the building and forge the image (which is claimed to be the largest in the world).[49] Besides building the image of Somdet To, the foundation started by Sorapong had donated over a hundred computers to a local rural elementary school, several cars to an orphanage, and supported other charity projects. For the ground-breaking ceremony, a stadium was rented out and marching bands entertained the crowd of several thousand.

In another interview in July 2006 I had a chance to speak with the director of the hugely popular film *Nang Nak*. Nonzee Nimibutr, who graciously invited me to his home (which is also his studio, film company, and creative space), was extremely generous with his time, especially considering that he is the director of a number of important Thai films, like *Baytong*, *Jan Dara*, and the upcoming *Queen of Langkasuka*. He is one of the best-known filmmakers in Asia. He is particularly famous for being provocative. For example, *Jan Dara*, which has graphic scenes of abortions, lesbian sexual intercourse, and incest, was censored in Thailand. In *Nang Nak*, he told me, he was trying to emphasize the attachment and love between Mae Nak and her husband Mak instead of simply depicting Mae Nak as a bloodthirsty killer-ghost. He was successful; many scenes between Nak and Mak are emotionally touching, and even in the final sequence in which Nak is subdued by Somdet To, the audience sympathizes with her longing for her husband and her child instead of remembering her murderous rampages. The film has recently been extensively written about, in very innovative ways, by Arnika Fuhrman, Adam Knee, and Alan Klima.[50]

Whereas they look at the film through the lenses of gender theory, psychology, and cultural studies, I look at the way the film depicts Somdet To and highlights the importance of the *Jinapañjara*.

Nonzee wrote and directed this film (and even wrote a book about the making of the film) because he had grown up hearing stories about Mae Nak from his parents and friends. He had often gone to see popular versions of the Mae Nak story at local movie theaters (indeed, there have been over twenty-two Thai films about Mae Nak made since 1936). There was also a 3-D film version, *Ya Nak*, made after Nonzee's supposedly definitive version, in 2003. As I mentioned in the introduction, in 2008 a sumptuous, high-production-value animated version was released in which a buxom, red-headed Nang Nak protects Thailand from foreign ghosts like Dracula, the Grim Reeper, a Jack-o'-Lantern-headed flying ghost, a Western-style red devil, and even the long-haired young girl ghost (Sadako) from the internationally popular Japanese film *The Ring*.[51] Nonzee's version, though, outshone them all financially. It is the third-highest grossing Thai film ever made. Part of the popularity was because of the high quality of the screenplay, cinematography, directing, and acting; however, Nonzee told me that it might also be connected, although he smirked to himself while saying this, to the fact that he and members of his film crew paid obeisance at the shrine of Mae Nak at Wat Mahabut, as well as at shrines to Somdet To and Mae Nak throughout central Thailand. Every morning before filming he hung flowers and amulets over the cameras and chanted the *Jinapañjara*. He had a mixture of fear of the ghost herself and hope for the success of the film critically and commercially.

Before making the film he wondered to himself why these two characters, Nak and Mak, would capture the imagination of the Thai people. I imagine the same question can be asked about Dracula and the way Euro-American culture keeps returning to that story. Nonzee believes that his characters struggle with what all Thai people have struggled with, the threat of war, the commonality of dying in childbirth, and the poverty of farmers and fishers. He also told me that he was always bothered by Mak in the story—why didn't he listen to the advice of Somdet To? Why was he so attached? These questions, while he never fully answered them for himself, drove him to research the period and the story for two years and interview hundreds of people about the legend. He learned how people chanted the *Jinapañjara* to protect themselves not only from Mae Nak and other ghosts but also from the Japanese during World War II and the Vietnamese during the American war in Vietnam. Although he is not a firm believer in the power of amulets, he did say that the stories of Mae Nak and Somdet To both reflected the struggle between attachment and the Buddhist teachings of nonattachment. Somdet To, in the story, teaches Mae

Nak the dangers of attachment, but people are attached to his amulets and her memory.

Briefly, let me retell the plot of Nonzee's film (which is largely similar to all the versions). Nak and Mak are introduced standing on a dock along a small jungle stream (nowadays the Phrakanong Canal in southern Bangkok).[52] They are both crying, because Mak has been drafted into the military (this is one of the reasons the ghost of Nak is described as "hating" [krot] military conscription) and has been called to fight the Burmese.[53] Nak is pregnant, and subsequent scenes show Mak being injured in battles and watching his friends die while Nak suffers from cramps and constant anxiety. She somehow feels the pain Mak does, and when he gets injured, she feels sharp pains in her stomach. She speaks to a local monk, and he tells her not to worry. However, he does not realize that Mak and Nak are somehow magically bound together. They are so in love that they feel each other's pain even though they are separated by hundreds of miles. This mutual pain comes to a crescendo when Mak is shot and taken, unconscious, into the care of Somdet To and Nak is giving birth at her home. Two ritual technologies are juxtaposed here. In quickly shifting scenes, the audience sees Somdet To healing Mak's wounds using a combination of herbs, amulets, and, most important, by chanting the Jinapañjara and then sees Mak suffering in labor while an old midwife uses folk remedies and warns of bad omens associated with an owl, a violent storm, and a spider. The old woman's remedies do not work and Nak dies in childbirth along with her unborn fetus. Mak is saved by Somdet To, but he does not realize his wife and child have died. Somdet To tells Mak that he should become a monk and give up his attachment to the world of families and war. From the expression on his face, Somdet To seems to know that Mak is headed for suffering if he returns home. Mak does not heed Somdet To's advice and returns to his home to embrace his wife and child. When he returns home he sees them waiting for him on the dock. However, this is an illusion he is seeing. The ghost of Nak has created the impression that she and their son are alive.[54] Mak is the only person who can see them, though.[55] He is thoroughly fooled. He lives with his wife and child, he has sex with her, they kiss and laugh. His neighbors think he is crazy and attempt to warn him that he is living with a ghost. Any neighbor who attempts to tell him the truth, however, dies. Nak visits them at night and kills them. She also kills the old woman (who had stolen the ring off her dead hand) and threatens the local monk. The village is rightfully angry at Mak and afraid of his ghost wife. They summon the local monk to chant and protect them with sacred string and Buddha images. However, he does not chant the Jinapañjara, and therefore the chanting has limited effect. Nak still terrorizes them, and in a violent scene she attacks dozens of men that try to burn down her house. Viewers watch (or turn away!) graphic scenes of flesh burning and men screaming in pain. Another group of villagers summon a local Brahman priest, who chants in Sanskrit and attempts to dig up Nak's corpse (most Thais cremate corpses, but in cases of unnatural death, bodies are bound with sacred string and buried). As he is attempting to crush Nak's corpse's skull with a rock, the spirit of Nak enters his body and possesses him. Then Nak uses the Brahman's own hand to kill himself.

Finally, Somdet To appears in the forest. The storm dies down immediately, the rain and wind stop. Somdet To's novice approaches the local monk and Mak and rudely tells them to stand back while Somdet To "takes care of business" (*tura*). The way this young novice treats an older monk is telling, because it shows how Somdet To's students were superior to other monks. In also reflects the powerful ritual technology for which Somdet To was known—it was superior to that of Brahmans, village monks, local folk rituals, and even the world of ghosts. Somdet To calmly sits down on the ground in front of the open grave of Nak. He summons her in a direct and laconic tone. She appears, rising out of the grave. While everyone goes into shock and is afraid of the ghost, Somdet To is not affected. He simply chants the *Jinapañjara* for hours. The night passes and the sun rises. This mimics the night of enlightenment of the Buddha, when he started meditating at midnight and gained enlightenment after nine hours (three watches). Somdet To subdues Nak through the chanting and then explains to her in simple Thai that she must give up her attachment to Mak and to this world. He instructs Mak to come and embrace his wife for the last time. They cry and proclaim their love for each other. Then Somdet To chants a final incantation and states, "Gatha mun it" (which is Lao for "these are the foundational verses"). Her corpse desiccates in front of his eyes, and the ghost disappears. His novice walks over to the corpse and, using a hammer and chisel, removes a large piece of her forehead bone. He gives it to Somdet To, and Somdet To tells the local monk that he has Nak's spirit captured in the bone and that she cannot bother his village anymore. He walks away. Later Somdet To is seen inscribing a *yantra* on the bone, writing the Khom letters that represent the *Jinapañjara* and whispering to himself, "Ma, a, ua." "Ma, a, ua" is the well-known Sanskrit mantra "aum" (or properly known in the West as "om") spelled backwards.[56] "Aum" is the sound believed by magicians in the region to represent the entire Pali Buddhist canon (Tripiṭaka), just as the *Jinapañjara* invokes the all of the Buddha, the gods, the *arahants*, and all the major protective chants (*sattaparitta* or *cet tamnan*). After drawing the *yantra*, Mak is then seen cremating his wife's corpse as an ordained monk. As Mak is seen paddling his canoe into the distance, the narrator states that the forehead bone was used by Somdet To as a belt buckle for years and then handed down to his novice and then to a

Thai prince and then lost. The mystery remains, and many Thai amulet dealers think that the royal family may possess the forehead bone, which certainly adds to the family's mystique and prestige.

Besides the obvious gender and class issues evident in Nonzee's rendition, for my purpose, the importance of this rendition of the Mae Nak story is that it helps explain why the *Jinapañjara* is still relevant in modern Thailand. Nonzee went to great efforts to include the *Jinapañjara* twice in this film, and the chanting in the film is extremely accurate. He consulted Brahmans, monks (at Wat Rakhang and Wat Mahabut), as well as historians like Satienpong Wannaphok and Anake Nawigamune.[57] There were no changes to the text for dramatic effect. Moreover, both times he has the *Jinapañjara* being chanted by Somdet To himself, further reinforcing the idea that he was the original author. It is also important because the local abbot and his students chant canonical texts, but they have no effect. However, this distinction means little in Thailand, and the vast majority of viewers would not even consider the *Jinapañjara* as being a noncanonical text. Nonzee told me that he wanted everything in the film to be authentic, from the hairstyles, to the clothes, to the rituals. The authenticity is one of the reasons, Nonzee believes, his version of the film resonated with audiences and was discussed more than any other version. Audiences are more often familiar with these chants and practices than with the canonical texts. Many in the audience undoubtedly can recognize the sounds of the *Jinapañjara* even if they do not understand the semantic meaning. The *Jinapañjara*, therefore, is relevant for what it does, not for what it means. Somdet To and others did and can use it to protect themselves from menacing ghosts and even from heartbreak. The *Jinapañjara* released Nak from this world (*manusyaloka*) and freed Mak from his attachment, even though the text itself mentions nothing about attachment.

Not all versions of the film are as overtly Buddhist or include Pali chanting like Nonzee's. In fact, there was a humorous version made in 1953 and a 3-D version in 2003. The latter, although it is rather gory, with poor acting and simplistic special effects, is worth describing briefly as it postmodernizes the story in telling ways. First, the film is set in 2003 on the set of the filming of another version of Mae Nak (there are direct references to Nonzee's version). If this is not confusing enough, the actress who plays Mae Nak in the film within the film falls in love with the actor who plays Mak in the film within the film. However, he rejects her because she is "clingy." Then she is drugged and raped by the director of the film within the film. During the rape scene she has flashbacks of her stepfather raping her when she was a child. Distraught, she goes to the shrine of Mae Nak at Wat Mahabut and asks Mae Nak for power over the men who have hurt her. She becomes possessed by Mae Nak and subsequently starts killing the other actors and members of the film crew, all in an effort to win back the actor playing Mak. In the end, she kills him and literally rips his beating heart out of his chest (in 3-D!). The last scene finds her in a mental hospital giving a soliloquy about the power Mae Nak gave her to seek revenge on the men who wronged her. This version does not retell the nineteenth-century version of the story. It is a commentary on the very popularity of the Mae Nak genre of films. It is also a commentary on the belief people have in the shrine of Mae Nak at Wat Mahabut. In this version, the very real statue of Mae Nak at the very real shrine in Bangkok (it is filmed on location) becomes an actress in the film. This is important when I discuss the power of statues in Thailand in chapter 4. Here, though, I should note that unlike other versions of the story, here Mae Nak survives by possessing other women. She is a hero not because she eventually gives up her murderous ways through the power of Somdet To and the *Jinapañjara*. She is a hero because she continues to protect women who are attached to their loved ones.[58]

These films and the many renditions of the Mae Nak story are also important for what they tell us about Thai Buddhism in general. Although Mae Nak was a murderous ghost, her shrine is a popular site of devotion. She is offered gifts so that she will intervene on behalf of women whose fathers, brothers, and husbands have been called to serve in the military. She is invoked by soldiers to help them be released from military duty. She is also entreated for a variety of reasons connected to things as vague as good luck to specific protection from stabbing or wining a particular day's lottery. Moreover, she is treated sympathetically by novelists, filmmakers, and playwrights as a person who was a dedicated wife, a loving mother, and a protector of her household. Mae Nak and many occupants of the spirit world in Thai Buddhism are not seen as simply evil but as powerful figures who can be employed in the service of protection and profit. Somdet To, as Nonzee so powerfully depicts, did not fear ghosts nor deny their existence but respected them and used the Buddhist technology he had at his disposal to mitigate their power. While many liberal, modern, or socially engaged Buddhist thinkers in Thailand and the West might discount the existence of ghosts or proclaim belief in them as superstitious or non-Buddhist, the most famous monk and the third-highest grossing film in Thai History show that they are certainly in the minority.[59] Elite intellectuals, avant-garde filmmakers, members of the royal family, and millions of monks, novices, nuns, and laypeople in urban and rural areas respect the power of ghosts and the ritual efficacy of protective chants such as the *Jinapañjara*; moreover, they sympathize with the desire for permanence and the power of love and attachment. Case in point: in the spring of 2010, for the first time in the history of the Thai film industry, a Thai film, *Uncle Boonmee Who Can Recall His Past Lives*, directed by

Apichatpong Weerasethakul, won the Cannes Film Festival Palme d'Or. Of course it was a film about ghosts! In an interview with the BBC after he won the prize, the director stated, "I would like to thank all the spirits and all the ghosts in Thailand who made it possible for me to be here."[60]

As a last side note, any good student of the Pali canon will tell you that immediately after his enlightenment the Buddha himself was mistaken for a tree spirit. A young woman of a wealthy family, named Sujata, gave him his first offering after his enlightenment. She was intending to present food to a tree spirit and pray for a husband of proper caste. Even after chanting a mantra at the feet of the Buddha, she did not realize that the Buddha was not a tree spirit until after some time. The story of Sujata is not uncommon. Ghosts and spirits are frequently mentioned in Pali canonical and commentarial texts. Certainly in present-day Thailand, the ghost of Mae Nak, tree spirits, and other beings are not mistaken for the Buddha; however, they are seen, alongside the Buddha, as they were twenty-five hundred years ago, as legitimate receivers of gifts with powers to hear and grant wishes.

## THE THERAVADA TANTRA OR THE ESOTERIC MAINSTREAM

Ghosts, incantations, and apotropaic ritual are common in Thai Buddhism. However, these specters and practices have generally been labeled as animistic, Brahmanic leftovers, or part of the belief system of folk Buddhism. However, there has been a small but growing number of scholars who have not seen these protective magical practices as being a lesser form of religiosity or even as non-Buddhist. Instead, these practices have been labeled by some as tantric or esoteric. While these scholars correctly point out that these practices and the texts that guide them have been present in the region for centuries, some also argue, inaccurately, that they have been suppressed by the elite royal reformers of central Thailand over the past one hundred fifty years. As we have seen, texts like the *Jinapañjara* and practices associated with invoking ghosts, deities, Buddhas, and arhats of the past, as well as the lingering presences of famous dead monks, are not only common but perhaps also the dominant form of daily liturgy and practice in most of Thailand. In this section, I compare the descriptions of this Theravada tantra or esoteric southern Buddhism to the practices associated with the *Jinapañjara*. I argue that the terms "tantra" and "esoteric" are misleading, because they suggest that these practices are not in the mainstream. I argue that the rituals associated with Somdet To are central to the way many Thais express and interpret Buddhism.

An entire field, albeit quite small, so-called tantric Theravada, has grown up around the work of François Bizot. Bizot has published thirteen books or articles on the so-called esoteric texts of Laos and Cambodia. His French colleagues François Lagirarde, Olivier de Bernon, and Catherine Becchetti have also produced in-depth and philologically and historically impressive studies on these texts.[61] These texts include versions of the *Ratanamālā*, the *Saddavimala*, the *Gavampati sutta*, a group of texts known as the *Mūl kammaṭṭhāna*, the *Dhammaviṅsun*, the *Paṅsukūl* genre, the *Dhammakāya*, and a series of important *yantras*. French scholars have also been the primary researchers on so-called tantric Buddhist practices in Burma. Duroiselle and Finot were the first to sketch out the history (which later turned out to be largely a myth promoted by later Buddhist reformers) of the Ari sect of monks in Burma, who placed fermented wheat liquor on their altars alongside meat. Ari monks kept the policy of *ius primae noctis* for all newly married virgins and put on public displays of boxing, sold amulets, predicted the future, practiced alchemy and astrology, kept their hair two inches long, wore cylindrical hats, and engaged in ritual fornication. While these less-savory practices should not be labeled simply esoteric, they are set in contrast to the seemingly orthodox Mahāvihāra brand of the Theravada.

These esoteric texts and many of these protective and transformative practices are pervasive in the ritual life of Cambodians, Burmese, and Laos, but many scholars use the modifiers "esoteric," "tantric," "folk," "mystical," "obscure," "Vedic," "Brahmanistic," or connect their origins to "an Abhāyagiri substrate," "a pre-Aryan Austro-Asiatic cult," "a Mūlasarvāstivādin" leftover, or associated with the amorphous animistic traditions of rural Laos, Burma, and Cambodia. While there has been some effort to look at these types of texts or practices in Thailand, no effort has been made to look at their use among the Bangkok elite at monastic universities and at urban royal monasteries.[62] These are not just rural practices of the unlettered masses. The few scholars who have studied these texts further lament their obscurity because of the growing globalization and rationalization of Southeast Asian (especially Thai) Buddhism. These texts and practices are presented as strange remnants of the past and of the countryside and set in contrast to the royal and Western reforms of the nineteenth century, which returned the pure Sinhala ordination line and practices in accordance with the Pali canon.

From the studies it would seem that bodily protection and these texts of the so-called Theravada tantra are a product of a slowly dying generation of rural ritualists in the mountains and hidden valleys of Greater Laos (parts of northern and northeastern Thailand and southern China), the Shan states, and Cambodia. Central Thai Theravada is instead characterized by a well-administered

Vinaya-based orthodoxy that barely tolerates the practice of protective rites in the northeast and north. Modern Thai Buddhism as studied by Rory MacKenzie, Jim Taylor, Suwanna Satha-Anand, Saichon Sattayanurak, among others, is often presented as the struggle between two camps.[63] The first is the hyperrational, socially engaged Buddhism of Buddhadasa Bhikkhu, Sulak Sivaraksa, Phra Payutto that has been inspired by the forest simplicity of Achan Man, Luang Phu Mahabua, or Achan Cha. The second is the seemingly oppressive and Vatican-like ecclesiastical hierarchy and dogmatism of the royal Buddhist council (Mahatherasamakom). The discourses of both groups are based on the idea that there was a pure and practical Indic Buddhism that was propagated and preserved in Pali by monks strictly following the Vinaya rules of the *Pāṭimokkha*. Buddhism over time became corrupt and complicated due to globalization and the social upheavals of the twentieth century. Each group wants to return to the imagined purity of the distant past either by preaching the simplified basic message of the Buddha as they see it—defining the core principles in a straightforward way—or by purifying ordination lines, assessing the correctness of the *sīmā* boundaries of monasteries, and centralizing education, textual production, and administration. They are both positivist discourses of corruption and renewal. They both promote a rationalized approach to the Theravada that seemingly stands in stark contrast to the ritually preoccupied and tantrically inclined lay practitioners of the hinterlands. Most English-language writing on Thai Buddhism suggests that the Buddhism of Buddhadasa, Achan Cha, Achan Man, Sulak Sivaraksa, Bodhirak, Phra Pajak, and the royal reformers is normative, modern, and accessible. The only difference is that the first group supposedly holds the liberal values of women's rights, pluralism, environmental protection, village-based democracy, and spiritual equality, while the second group conservatively protects tradition, centralization, state support, and male-only ordination. To both groups, the *Jinapañjara*, the practice of Somdet To, and worship of ghosts like Mae Nak are esoteric, rural, and old-fashioned.[64] The beliefs and practices of Thai Buddhists can best be approached and research agendas and questions can better be formulated if we see the primary unifying feature of elite and folk Thai Buddhism as the so-called esoteric traditions and texts rather than as "Pali," "the Theravada canon," "social engagement," or "Vinaya-based orthodoxy." The institutionally well-organized, centralized, Vinaya-based Theravada orthodoxy that Western books describe as being the hallmark of Thai Buddhism is secondary in many ways to the mainstream esoteric practices and texts pervasive in urban and rural, elite, and common Thai practice.[65] Seeing these esoteric traditions as mainstream may help us listen to what questions and concerns the vast majority of Thais have about their own ritual and religious life.[66]

The primary technical foundation of Thai Buddhist practice is the connection between the human body, the body of the Buddha, certain Pali texts, the alphabet, and the basic divisions of time. It is an algebraic system that seeks to manipulate a series of knowns in order to control or uncover a wide array of unknowns. The *Jinapañjara*, the *yantra* drawings associated with it, as well as many other similar ritual texts reveal a profoundly "mathematical" view of the universe, in which there are always equations between the micro- and macrocosmic worlds. This practice is certainly seen in the complex Thai astrological systems. While it would take an entire book to begin to explain these astrological practices, let me just say here that the equivalencies seen between dates, days, planets, colors, letters, and parts of the body in Thai astrology are very similar to those evident in the protective texts and drawings associated with Somdet To and elite, well-known monks like him still practicing throughout Thailand today.[67] Of course, Tambiah has alluded to this system "symbolically" in his study of Thai architecture, urban planning, and cosmology.[68] However, this is not simply a symbolic system but a technical system. The letters, numbers, and drawings used in the formulas are indices, not symbols. They are believed to directly cause events or protect objects if chanted, drawn, or tattooed correctly and with the right focus. These equations do things. They solve problems.

Before I get too far afield, let me state how I am using the terms "esoteric" and "tantric." The *Jinapañjara*'s content can be associated with what François Bizot has called the *yogāvacarin* traditions of Southeast Asia, meaning "practitioner of a spiritual discipline," or what Crosby, Swearer, Finot, Ray, Lagirarde, and Strong have called, with much reservation, the "tantric" Theravada, or what Lance Cousins calls the "esoteric traditions of southern Buddhism."[69] All agree on the general parameters of these texts and practices, even though they might not agree on their general rubric. Swearer defines the parameters of the esoteric or tantric Theravada as (1) identifying one's physical body with the qualities of the Buddha, (2) the use of esoteric syllables and words (*mantra, yantra*) to represent the identity of the microcosm and macrocosm, (3) the "dharmic potency" of sounds and letters, (4) esoteric initiation for the "realization of soteriological and mundane ends." Crosby adds the interpretation of texts esoterically in ways seemingly unconnected with their purported semantic meaning and the use of texts to protect the body and mind from danger.[70] These four aspects generally describe practices that involve manipulating letters, sounds, and movements (like the names of the Buddhas of the past, the days of the week, the names of the years, the parts of the body, and the five *khandhas*) in an algebraic logic to achieve desired ends. These names, letters, sounds, and so on are all possible Xs and Ys that can be shifted around and used to replace unknowns.

Knowing when and where these primary numbers can be used to replace unknowns is one of the powers of the monk or lay ritualist.

Let me offer an example; one of the most common protective incantations and *yantras* used by Somdet To and many others is the "Nā-mo bu-ddhā-ya." These five syllables can invoke powerful protective forces. Of course, *nāmo buddhāya* simply means "praise to the Buddha." However, skilled ritualists read it as five separate syllables: "Nā" is connected to the Buddha Kakusandha, the color white, the nose, the *krita* era (*yuga*) of Indian time, and the five guttural letters of the Pali alphabet. "Mo" is connected to the Buddha Konagamana, the color blue, the epiglottis, the left eye, the *tretā* era, and the palatal sounds and letters. "Bu" is connected to the Buddha Kassapa, the color yellow, the base of the throat, the ears, the *dvāpara* era, the nasal sounds and letters. "Ddhā" is connected to the Buddha Gotama, the color red, the sternum and the navel, the *kali* era, and the dentals. "Ya" is connected to the future Buddha Metteyya, the color white, the forehead, the future era, and it is considered the gate to *nibbana*. Sometimes the *nāmo buddhāya* is drawn in the shape of the island of Sri Lanka.[71]

These equivalencies are found in other common incantations. For example, in the *Itipiso* incantation, the number of syllables in the verses are said to correspond to the dimensions of the first human being (56, 38, 14). These equations often correspond to which colors of flowers, which types of images, how many sticks of incense and candles, and which gestures and which shapes are drawn during a protective ritual. The *Jinapañjara* is supposed to be chanted on a Thursday and offerings made to the image of Gotama Buddha (and now Somdet To); also required are nine white candles, nine sticks of incense, the forehead is supposed to be touched with holy water while chanting, and the like. The times of chanting, bodily equivalents, and ritual implements for various Abhidhamma texts are even more intricate, since they are often connected to preparing a corpse for cremation or burial.[72]

This type of detailed coordination of physical actions, colors, implements, syllables, times of day, and days of the week is similar to many magical traditions and mainstream religious practices, like Vedic fire rituals, Catholic novenas and octaves, Hindu *pūjas*, and La Regla Lukumi healing rites. However, Thai practitioners are often very flexible in their practices and do not maintain a fixed ritual system. In fact, many of these days, body parts, eras, Buddhas, colors, and syllables are interchangeable. Instead, these signs can be moved around and adapted to different rituals. This is not a static structure but one in which new events and new knowledge are negotiated and arranged in a system based on what Sahlins would call the "relation between happening and structure."[73] Cultural structures, or what I would prefer to call repertoires, do not predefine how a person embedded in a certain culture will act but shape the way she or he interprets, recounts, and manipulates the events they take part in in creating, as well as shaping the way new information is processed and articulated.

This is one of the reasons I refrain from referring to these Thai practices as tantra. It is a term that is not part of the repertoire of most Thai practitioners, and by using it, scholars are condemned to interpret the new information they learn from Thai experts into a wholly different repertoire that is all their own. Scholars use the term "tantra" for a wide array of practices and texts among Indian, Tibetan, and East Asian Saivites and Buddhists. Geoffrey Samuel defines "tantra" in Indian and Tibetan contexts as a "relatively coherent set of techniques and practices" that includes "elaborate deity visualizations, in which the practitioner identifies with a divine figure at the centre of a *maṇḍala* or geometrical array of deities; the use of transgressive Kāpālika'-style practices associated with cremation-grounds and polluting substances linked to sex and death, and internal yogic practices, including sexual techniques, which are intended to achieve health and long life as well as liberating insight."[74] Ronald Davidson's highly detailed study of the origins of esoteric Buddhism in India discusses the prominence of the Yoginī-tantric texts and the *Hevajra tantra*, the story of the twenty-four Bhairavas, the Cakrasaṃvara system, Maheśvara's battles with Vajrapāṇi or Heruka, *vetāla* ghosts, the *aghori* ascetics, and other prominent South Asian and Tibetan tantric features, rituals, and professionals. None of these terms or their close equivalents are part of Thai or broader Southeast Asian practices to any serious extent (outside of Java and Angkorian-period Cambodia). Almost none of these practices can be associated with Somdet To's practices nor with most other protective practices in Southeast Asia. Visualization of deities is rare (although some Southeast Asian mediums "invite" deities into their bodies). Sexual practices are extremely rare. For example, there are texts like the ninth-century Indian *Buddhakapāla-yoginī-tantra-rāja*, in which the Buddha passes away in a vagina, or the *Śrī guhyasamājatantra-nidāna-gurūpadeśana-vyākhyāna*, in which the Buddha is depicted as residing in the vaginas of women of "adamantine body, speech, mind, and heart."[75] We find nothing of this kind in Southeast Asian texts as far as I have seen. Some incantations popular in Thailand are designed to attract the opposite sex, but sexual acts as a part of rituals, especially by monks, are largely unknown and are scandalous when even rumored. Even among lay practitioners like *mo wiset*, these sexual rituals are rare, but there are some *yantras* that depict naked couples embracing. Certainly monks like Somdet To meditate on cremation grounds and, as mentioned in chapter 4, the collection of "corpse oil" is known in some circles, but skull cups, the consumption of liquor, fish, meat, blood, and other polluting substances is hardly known. However, the larger point is that the tantric system

and texts in South Asia and Tibet are diverse, and despite the institutionaliza-
tion of many tantric practices in medieval India, Japan, China, Mongolia, and
Tibet, there is certainly no official set of practices and stories that delimits a
generally accepted tantra. Scholars define "tantra" along similar, but certainly
not identical, lines to Samuel, but even he admits that the term even in Indian
and Tibetan studies is highly contested. Since the term "tantra" has yet to be
defined adequately by experts in those fields, it is misleading to use it when
discussing practices in Southeast Asia. It is misleading on the one hand because
it is too narrow. In Buddhist studies, "tantra" invokes thoughts of Kashmir and
Tibet, or perhaps the Chinese term *mijiao*, or the Japanese term *mitsu* generally
associated with Shingon Buddhism. It has become a regional term associated
with northern Buddhism. On the other hand, it is too broad. Some scholars use
it as an umbrella term that covers a wide range of diverse Hindu and Buddhist
practices. This lack of specificity is not useful. One tantra cannot be used to
represent another tantra. Until we define at least one tantra, it may be wise not
to apply the term to every antinomian Buddhist practice involving liquor, fish,
and meat or sexual practice, deity visualization, and the use of *dhāraṇī*, *rakṣā*
or *paritta* protective texts or human body parts. Skilling emphasizes this point:

> Neither Thai nor Khmer Buddhism . . . represents itself as "Theravadin"—
> let alone "Tantric." In India itself the Tantra is a contested term—there is
> no agreement as to what the long-lived, diverse, multicultural, multireli-
> gious term "Tantra" means . . . The word Tantra is not used in South-East
> Asian Buddhism to describe either texts or practices (and the adjective
> *tantrika* is equally unknown).[76]

"Esoteric" is also not an adjective used generally in Thailand. Lance Cousins calls the texts and practices of this tradition "Esoteric Southern Buddhism"
to connect it to the well-known tantric/esoteric traditions of Tibet and northeastern Asia. There are certainly connections that lead to productive comparative exercises. However, "esoteric" has other connotations; when scholars use
this term for these texts and practices, it conveys the impression given by these
scholars implicitly as well as explicitly that these practices are secretive, magical, practiced only by the initiated ritual experts, and limited in their societal,
cultural, and historical influences. "Esoteric" has another meaning in Buddhist
studies, that texts and practices are difficult to understand, mysterious, and hidden.[77] The practices involved with the *Jinapañjara* and other protective texts
used in Thailand are not secretive or reserved for the initiated or ordained.
There are no caches of secret *suttas* that are kept in caves by nefarious monks or
lay practitioners. There are no elaborate initiation ceremonies into the "eso-

teric" training. Certainly there is one-on-one training in drawing certain *yan-tras* or memorizing certain mantras, but this training is open to nearly any monk, nun, or layperson who expresses a desire to learn them. There are also relatively easy-to-read Thai texts describing these methods. For example, I was trained in how to draw a *yantra* to protect a motorcycle on my fourth day as a monk. Within my first month in the robes, I was trained in how to measure a lay couple's arms in order to create the right length of braided candles used for burning and empowering water during a wedding ceremony. Certainly, if an Irish Catholic kid from the United States can be trained in these practices as a freshman monk, then most Thai practitioners are not attempting to hide these practices!

*Yogāvacarin* is an equally vague and broad term that is generally not found in texts or stated explicitly by most Thai practitioners. Bizot uses it because of these Khmer references and also because he has tried to establish connections with Sri Lankan practices evinced in the *Yogāvacara Manual*, translated as the *Manual of a Mystic* in 1916.[78] It makes little sense in describing Thai practices. However, despite my reservations about this term, Bizot's work is important. Bizot shows in several books that texts were chanted alongside *yantra* drawings and combined with the use of sacred white string (*sai siñcana*). Moreover, these texts identify parts of the ritualist's body with particular Buddhas of the past (Taṅhaṃkāra, Koṇḍana, among others), particular protective texts such as the seven *parittas*. These features combined with the chanting of ritually powerful words like *arahaṃ*, as well as the *Itipiso* and *Nāmo buddhāya* incantations connect South and Southeast Asian esoteric practices. He also notes that these practices are connected to protective tattoos and meditation practices.

Bizot seems to be on to something here. He has identified a major episte-mological and technical stratum of South and Southeast Asian Buddhism that has largely been ignored by scholars of Theravada Buddhism. However, is this stratum esoteric, tantric, or *yogāvacarin*? The *Jinapañjara* clearly identifies the body of the five previous Buddhas (as well as of disciples) and the seven *parittas* with the ritualist's body and suggests practices of tattooing (or marking the body) and meditation. While the word *arahaṃ* is not mentioned, it is well-known by those who respect Somdet To, and the incantation *Nāmo buddhāya* is inscribed in stone on shrines dedicated to Somdet To.[79] Biographies and litur-gical books in the Somdet To lineage include the *Itipiso* and *yantra* drawings of it. The *Jinapañjara* is also associated with Thursday (other ritual and protective texts like the *Bahuṃ* and *Jayamaṅgala*, which are also used to invoke Buddhas of the past, are associated in Thailand with other days of the week), and when amulets are made and infused with the chanting of the *Jinapañjara*, they are made from different colors (in the forms of different flowers), soil from different parts of the country, and other specific formulas. There is little doubt that the *Jinapañjara* and other texts and practices in the Somdet To ritual sphere are what some other scholars have named esoteric or tantric.

Texts and practices called esoteric, tantric or *yogāvacarin* in Southeast Asia are disappearing, according to François Bizot. He associates this loss with the destructive onslaught on religion by the Khmer Rouge regime in Cambodia (1975–1979) and the negligence of practitioners and manuscript archive keepers in northern Thailand and Laos.[80] Therefore, he states that rural folk traditions are slowly dying because of modernity. Bizot himself laments their imminent disappearance because of the destruction of the Khmer Rouge in Cambodia, communist reform in Laos, and modernization and canonization in Thailand. With the modern penchant to preserve, reprint, retranslate, and distribute canonical texts in Thailand and Burma, as well as the massive loss of texts and traditions in Laos and Cambodia, this is a major concern of practitioners and of the field. However, this is certainly not the case in modern Bangkok or Thailand in general when it comes to the *Jinapañjara* and other esoteric texts. I am arguing that these texts and practices are widespread and often better known than canonical texts and teachings. They are clear and logical. They are memorized, chanted, and employed in ritual by laypeople, monks, and nuns alike. They are pervasive in cities and in the countryside. They are used by Thammayut and Mahanikai monks. They are part of royal and common rituals and are as pervasive in modern periods as they were in premodern periods. Seeing these practices as mainstays of Thai religion may lead to a rethinking of what it means to be Theravadan and Thai. Anyone can go to the amulet markets of Bangkok and surrounding provinces and see copies of Somdet To's amulets, read literally thousands of articles in popular amulet collector's magazines purchased throughout the country about the value, miraculous powers, and beauty of these small stone objects. He is one of the least-esoteric monks in Thai history. Therefore, can we call the *Jinapañjara* and the amulets and practices associated with it esoteric, as Cousins, Bizot, Lagirarde, and Swearer have done for extremely similar texts and practices?

The *Jinapañjara* and related texts show the pervasiveness of "esoterism" in everyday Thai Buddhism.[81] They also show that the image of a stagnant, pristine, Mahāvihāra-type Theravada Buddhism as a counterpoint to a diverse and syncretic local Thai Buddhism is suspect. The Sri Lankan brand of Theravada, whether we associate it with the Abhāyagiri or Mahāvihāra, the exegetical work of Buddhaghosa or the reforms of the twelfth century, the reforms of King Rama IV or Prince Wachirayan, is also internally diverse and infused with texts that can be defined as esoteric but that are part of mainstream, noninitiated monastic and lay practice in Sri Lanka, Laos, Burma, Cambodia, as well as in

Thailand. The modern urban Thai Theravada, if there is even such a thing, cannot be associated simply with the canon, or major monastic universities, or strict adherence to the Vinaya, and furthermore, royal monks, monastic Pali scholars, and royal patrons are as esoteric in their practices as any rural monk or lay practitioner. This does not mean that most Thai Buddhists are not aware of the various teachings of socially engaged Buddhists like Buddhadasa Bhikkhu, Achan Cha, Achan Lee, and others; indeed, these are quite popular teachers in modern Thai history. Many canonical *suttas* and the Vinaya (in abbreviated form) are also familiar. However, if we do not recognize the overwhelming interests many Thai Buddhists have in Somdet To, in the *Jinapañjara*, in Mae Nak, and in protective rituals in general, if we reduce these texts and practices to the level of curious oddities, then we are missing a great deal about Thai religion.

## SPEAKING MAGICALLY

The *Jinapañjara* and protective texts like it are certainly not esoteric in Thailand. Chanting them, understanding them, using them, holding them do not require any special initiation or ordination. They are public and participatory texts. While skills in meditation (*jhāna*, *vipassanā*, or other) are valued, they are not required to wield these texts. In fact, in terms of popularity and access, most canonical texts are more "esoteric." They are lesser known and harder to access. For reasons given, I would hesitate to refer to the *Jinapañjara* and related texts and practices as tantric or *yogāvacarin*. These terms are simply not used often by Thai Buddhists. In fact, Thai Buddhists do not refer to these texts and practices under any general rubric besides simply "Buddhist" (*kamphi khong phra phutthasasana*). They are part of standard, everyday Buddhist study and practice.

From an outsider's or etic perspective, these texts could generally be called magical. Emicly, the Thai word that most Thai-English dictionaries give for magic is *saiyasat*. However, in Thai the *Jinapañjara* and other protective texts are not considered part of *saiyasat*. *Saiyasat* may come from the Sanskrit word *sāyaśāstra* (which could mean "dark science" or "science of the evening hours"). *Saiyasat* texts and practices can be used for nefarious, aggressive, or malicious purposes, but *saiyasat* is not an exclusive or firm category.[82] There is a dizzying number of different opinions on what *saiyasat* connotes in Thailand. Some people I spoke with considered it dangerous, some irrational, some necessary for protection, a product of a materialistic society, a traditional science that should be preserved, the reason Thailand was a successful and free nation. Some see it as a skill reserved only for advanced monks that can be used for protective (good) or aggressive (bad) ends. A good friend of mine from rural Phisanulok Province, Phimjan Muenram, said that her family preferred inviting *mo phi* (ghost doctors or experts) to the house for ceremonies over monks. When I asked why, she stated that even though monks are more prestigious to many, sometimes *saiyasat* used by *mo phi* was more effective in solving basic domestic problems and specific periods of bad luck. *Saiyasat* in her opinion is neither good nor bad; however, sometimes it is necessary.[83] Monks can perform *saiyasat* too, of course, she said, but sometimes inviting monks is more trouble than it is worth because of their eating, time, and ritual restrictions. Her opinion, like that of many, is relatively neutral. Some opinions of *saiyasat* I encountered were certainly negative, though. *Yantras*, tattoos, incantations associated with *saiyasat* are designed to cause harm, invoke lust, or psychologically and economically punish. For example, on November 23, 2009, Dion Peoples called my attention to a "cursing" (*khut*) ritual being performed over seven days at Wat Daeng in Ayutthaya Province by people seeking revenge on bandits who had cut off the heads of several important Buddha images at their monastery and at the nearby Wat Dong Wai. With the ritual, referred to in the Thai newspapers as *saiyasat*, the sponsors declared they hoped the bandits would die after performance of the curse. Seeking murderous revenge in the name of the Buddha is generally considered unsavory!

No matter how one might judge the "good" and "bad" goals of magic, the system generally works on the same algebraic logic. There are certain symbols, like the tiger, the phallus, and naked men and women, that are directly associated with nefarious goals; however, microcosmically, certain words, certain objects, certain intentions performed by certain people at certain times of the day or week can produce specific macrocosmic affects. It is not always a difference in intention. The technology can also be slightly different. For example, tattoos below the waist have sinister power, while those above the waist do not. Certain days of the week, especially Saturday mornings and Wednesday afternoons, are astrologically particularly dangerous times and thus good times for *saiyasat*. Some monks, nuns, and novices stay away from *saiyasat*. They say that it is the province of lay (mostly) men called *mo wiset* (doctor of wizardry). Somdet To was not a *mo wiset*. Yet some biographers and followers describe his practices as *saiyasat*, as long as *saiyasat* is understood as "protective magic." As we saw in the previous chapter, the only known extant text in Somdet To's handwriting uses the term *saiyasat* to describe his use of amulet recipes and protective incantations. Somdet To did not attack others, and the *Jinapañjara* is not used aggressively or maliciously. Although he used incantations, holy water, *yantras*, and the like, he did not claim to be a magician; he was a man, ideally, on the path to enlightenment.[84] The jury seems to still be out among many Thai Buddhists whether *saiyasat* is good or bad, but perhaps the question is the problem. Perhaps it is not a case of being good or bad but of being effective or not.

Often times, though, as Jacob Neusner has stated, "one's group holy man is another group's magician."[85] Marcel Mauss has seen magic as a way to separate certain practices socially from "religion." Magic, in his view, is secret, mystical, and prohibited compared to the public rites of religion.[86] Michael Bailey has called attention to the fact that in the West, magic has generally been used to define the "other." In Greece,

> *mageia* referred quite precisely to foreign cultic rites, specifically those of Persian priests or *magoi*. In its etymological origins, the Western term "magic" was defined first by simple geography. Because the foreignness of *mageia* carried dark and sinister connotations, the term gradually became extended to include many illicit, covert, or private rites performed by Greeks themselves.[87]

In Thai, there are terms that distinguish good (protective) and sinister magic. However, there is little consistency in how Thai practitioners and enthusiasts use these terms. There seems to be a lack of specificity in the ways terms refer to practices and intentions. Many Thais are comfortable with the ambiguity. These terms are drawn creatively from Sanskrit and Pali. *Itthirit* (protective power) or *wetmon* (the use of magical words), as well as local terms for magically "blessing" something (*bao sek* and *pluk sek*), are more commonly used by monks than *saiyasat*.[88] However, Pali terms like *iddhipāṭihāriya* (referring to wondrous psychic powers like clairvoyance, levitation, psychokinesis) or *abhiñña* (supercognitive powers used to see the future and past lives, read minds, and the like) are generally not used when discussing the protective power of the *Jinapañjara* or *paritta* practices more broadly. As we will see in the next chapter, what is generally referred to as Thai Buddhist ritual and liturgy often employ the same logic, implements, aesthetics, lexicon, and officiants as *saiyasat*. Magic is in the eye of the beholder.

Despite this emic incongruence and ambiguity, can scholars talk about protective practices as being "magic," or more specifically as "white or protective magic"? Can we even speak generally about Thai Buddhism at all? The term "magic," like the terms "culture," "religion," "secular" must be qualified when speaking of everyday protective practices in Thailand. Neuroscientists and psychologists associate magic with trickery and mentalism. Instead of defining magic in comparison with the metacategories of science and religion, they define it by methods, stratagems, performance, and effects (i.e., conjuring, misdirection, and sleight of hand).[89] These tricks are generally not associated with practices connected to *yantras*, Pali and vernacular incantations, holy water, and amulets. Monks like Somdet To did not try to make objects disappear, practice psychokinesis, levitate, or cleverly shuffle a deck of cards.

Magic has been described in the field of religious studies along two general lines, one linguistic and the other sociological. Cassirer, Weber, Annette Werner, and Frits Staal have associated magic (East and West) as an "inordinate belief in the efficacy of mere words," or as "thinking that fails to recognize the essential differences between representation and reality," or as "a basic confusion of linguistic and physical relationships . . . [It] disregards the distinction between physical and psychological causes, the difference between energy and information."[90] Tambiah, following J. L. Austen and John Searle, has viewed magicians as employing "performative utterances." These utterances inherently confuse the relationship between metonymic language and metaphoric language.[91] In short, magicians wrongly assume that words can "do things" in the physical world. Sociologically, magic has been described as a tool of the powerless. In this way, magic has been associated with the oppressed, the nonindustrial, "configured as the province of women, children, foreigners, primitives, and other deviants."[92] Magic is not central to ecclesiastical religion and it is not quite science. It is the tool of those who do not have access to real laboratories or state-sanctioned colleges, churches, and vestments.

Randall Styers criticizes both of these approaches to the study of magic. He argues that the scholarly association of magic with a false belief in the kinetic efficacy of language repeatedly affirms that "language is inert and powerless." It also, more broadly, "configures a sharp and impermeable boundary between nature and culture, a natural world subject to nonhuman causality and the artificial, transitory world of human language, meaning, desire, and value." Therefore, magicians are always seen as premodern leftovers, as quaint cultural asides, because "to be modern is to recognize this essential binary" between nature and culture. Language, as part of culture, functions only as "a medium of passive representation," and therefore "the construction of meaning and assertion of desire are portrayed as lacking all causal efficacy."[93] According to most scholars, then, "any sense that human desire or behavior can influence other human beings or the natural world [through magical techniques] . . . that human techniques can exert control over other persons, powers, or events—any such sense falls into magic."[94] Scholars like Cassirer, Stark, Keller, and others see magic as separate from religion. This limits proper religion to the seeking of objectives that are "transcendent or supraempirical," without any "attention to materiality or pragmatic worldly ends."[95] Magicians are thus not quite religious. They are base, selfish, emotional, and concerned only with power in this world.

Styers's observations are particularly important for understanding how Buddhism in Thailand and throughout Southeast Asia has been defined. One of the most well-known binaries in Theravada Buddhist studies is worldly/ nonworldly (or mundane/supramundane). This is a translation of the Pali words *lokiya* (worldly) and *lokottara* (above the world). *Lokiya* practices have worldly objectives, such as wealth, fame, beauty, and love. They also include the aims of celestial beings, like heavenly denizens, goddesses, and gods, as well as hell beings. *Lokottara* practices are focused on achieving enlightenment. Western scholars have been particularly enamored with this binary. Peter Jackson, Stanley Tambiah, J. L. Taylor, Geoffrey Samuel, among others, have all described good monks as concentrating on *lokottara* objectives.[96] Samuel goes as far as to make the uninformed comment that "the Buddhist monk does not interfere with the rituals of everyday life [in Burma and Thailand], except to be present as a way of generating merit."[97] Monica Lindberg Falk has stated that there is a firm boundary between *lokiya* and *lokottara* activities in Thailand and laments that *maechi* (nuns) are reduced to being associated with the former.[98] She writes that the "lokottara person is economically unproductive, and thus completely dependent on productive members of the lokiya for material support. The assembly of monks [which she calls *lokottara*] provides a religious field of merit for ordinary people."[99] Melford Spiro, in his classic study of Burmese village Buddhism, divides Theravada practice into three realms: nibbanic, kammanic, and apotropiac. The first is *lokottara*, and the second and third fall under *lokiya*.[100] In another study he writes: "World-renunciation is the message of the Dhamma, it was practiced by the Buddha, and is exemplified by the Saṅgha . . . The world and its works are vanity."[101] Tambiah bases an entire book on this subject, *World Conqueror and World Renouncer*, in which he writes, "Those forms of earthly existence belong to *laukika* [*lokiya*], this world of sensation, and are to be distinguished from the *lokottara*, the *true* 'otherworld' of *nibbana* at the very top of the pilgrim's progress."[102] He continues, emphasizing that although the *Aggañña sutta* emphasizes that both worldly leaders (kings who rule according to the *dhamma*) and enlightened beings (Buddhas) are seen as important in Buddhist notions of world order, in fact, drawing from the *sutta*, the bhikkhu "who breaks all worldly norm goes from home to a homeless life . . . who breaks through the bonds of society, is chief among them all . . . There are two foremost of superior beings, the bhikkhu and the king, but the former is superior."[103] So, even though Tambiah purports to write a straightforward historical account of Buddhism and worldly political activity, he actually establishes from the very beginning that he is writing about bad, nonideal, less than superior monks who work in the world by colluding with politically powerful men and institutions. Those monks who work in communities either as healers, fortune-tellers, administrators, ritual performers (at funerals, weddings, house blessings, and the like), counselors, or community activists are seen as lesser monks relative to those few who live a reclusive life in the forest or as cloistered scholars. While this hierarchy of religious roles is clear in Taoism and Brahmanism (and to some extent in Catholicism, where a scholar or ascetic monk is given a higher status than a parish priest), it is not so clear in Thai Buddhism. As I mentioned briefly in my previous study of Buddhist monastic education, it is more accurate to see Thai monastic life as a process in which a person can play many different roles, often simultaneously. Scholars of Thai Buddhism often discuss the differences between the Thammayut Nikai, the supposedly more scholarly and ascetic lineage, and the Mahanikai, the community-oriented or more "worldly" lineage. This distinction is not as prevalent in everyday monastic life. Many members of both lineages work with the community, and members of both are closely involved with political and royal leaders. Some members of both concentrate on meditation and ascetic practices, but this is usually for a short time. Some members of both sects work with community groups on ecological, health, economic, and social issues. They are both "worldly" at some points and "otherworldly" at others. These changes in emphasis can happen over the course of one year or even one day. In addition to this distinction, there is a traditional distinction in South Asia between monks across sectarian lines known as *ganthadhura* (those who carry the burden of textual study) and *vipassanādhura* (those who carry the burden of meditation practice). This distinction was never significant in northern Thailand or Laos, and today these are terms rarely used by monks and nuns in either place. They have become relatively common in central Thailand, but it is rare to find a nun or monk who only studies texts and never meditates or vice versa. It would be more accurate to say that any particular student leans toward one tendency or the other. No matter how we judge which lineage or approach to practice is more ethical, closer to the Buddha's intentions, or soteriologically efficacious, in terms of monastic education, in the premodern and modern periods, sectarian divisions have been less prominent. The broader categories, such as *araññavāsī/pupphārāmavāsī* (forest/flower garden monastery dwellers) and *gāmavāsī/nagaravāsī* (village/city dwellers), to describe monks are taken too seriously by scholars who see them as lifelong choices with a strict hierarchy. This is not the case. There are periods of asceticism in most monks' lives interspersed with periods of administration, social work, ritual activity, and so on. Rarely do monks choose to live one type of life strictly over their entire careers; in fact, very few monks actually stay ordained for their whole lives.

Looking at the story of Mae Nak and Somdet To, we can see that this worldly/otherworldly binary is clearly inadequate. Moreover, the rural/urban dichotomy is also inadequate. It is common in everyday Thai speech and in many anthropological and historical studies of Thailand (in Thai and Western languages) to talk about Thai "traditional" culture (alternatively labeled *thamniam* [customs], *watthanatham* [culture], *prabeni thong thin* [folk rituals], *watthanatham ban nok* [culture of the "outer villages," i.e., nonurban], *watthanatham chonabot* [rural culture]) versus Buddhism (*sasana phut*). This traditional culture is often referred to as animistic, pre-Buddhist, and ancient (*boran*). This dichotomy is questioned at the shrine to Mae Nak at Wat Mahabut, a place that is now in Bangkok proper but that in the nineteenth century was a suburban village. It was relatively easily accessible by canal boat but not in the city grid yet. The film versions of the Mae Nak story play off that suburban location by showing a "village" on the edge of a city. Today Wat Mahabut (discussed more extensively in chapter 4) is an urban monastery with a large parking lot, elementary school, convenience stories, and the like. However, it can still be reached by canal boat, and on its edges are overgrown stands of jungle trees. The story is still extremely popular, as seen in Nonzee's film, in the new animated version, among many others.[104] Mae Nak straddles and perhaps even collapses these two worlds. The problem is that most scholars and social critics have associated the story of Mae Nak with only the "outer villages" (*ban nok*) or pre-Buddhist/animistic/premodern folk culture, without seeing the complicated nature of the story as a negotiation and even negation in some ways of a rural/urban, premodern/modern dichotomy.

Somdet To is a perfect example of a monk who changed roles and whose biography questions facile dichotomies. He was a community monk, then a forest meditator, then a magician, then a political voice, then a social worker fighting for the poor, then a forest meditator again, and then a healer. Often he is depicted in intense isolated meditation in the morning, then giving a house blessing in the afternoon. In fact, many refer to Somdet To as an *arhat* (enlightened one). According to Tambiah, he was the type of monk who had apparently reached the end of the "pilgrim's progress." However, at the end, on his deathbed, he is photographed with amulets and holy water. He played many roles up until the end of his life. One role was not necessarily more important than another. He was honored for being able to play many roles. He was not unique. Many Thai monks are "multitaskers." The *lokiya/lokottara* distinction is not very useful in describing Thai monastic life.

These Western scholars are not alone; elite Thai Buddhist social commentators and scholars have also discussed this binary. Phra Dhammapiṭaka (also known as Phra Payutto), Phra Phayom, Buddhadasa Bhikkhu, Suwanna Satha-Anand, and Sulak Sivaraksa, all who have either trained in the West or worked with Western scholars, chastise monks who deal in *lokiya* matters. Furthermore, this distinction is certainly found in canonical Pali texts (although perhaps not as prominently as it would seem from modern writing on the subject). Moreover, Thai, Burmese, Cambodian, and Lao monarchs and powerful monks have conveniently used it as a tool for attacking practices they deem threatening to their power to define religion. Pattana Kitiarsa, following Davisakd Puaksom, has noted that for Sulak Sivaraksa, the Thai scholar and activist nominated for the Nobel Peace Prize, "the notable dichotomy lying behind [his] reasoning is the Buddhist-based distinction between the 'secular' and 'spiritual/religious' (*lokuttara*) matters. Siamese rulers and intellectuals have for centuries maintained that while *farang* are superior in mundane/secular matters (*thang lok*), Siam is far stronger in the spiritual or moral (*thang tham*) realm."[105] Sulak uses this reasoning to emphasize an anti-Western and antiglobalization self-sufficiency model for Thailand. This self-sufficiency in terms of economics is in line with what Sulak sees as core Buddhist values. There is a major incongruence here, though. Sulak and others who lament the worldliness of modern Buddhism want monks to remain above the world and thus quiet, rational, and powerless. However, they also want them to work in the world, be socially engaged, in order to return it to a bucolic, utopian paradise.[106]

However, this distinction is seemingly not applied to monks who have "socially engaged" *lokiya* objectives. "Socially engaged" monks (meaning monks who promote environmental programs, support AIDS hospices and drug rehabilitation centers, and the like), despite the fact that they certainly have *lokiya* objectives, are not seen as areligious, nonideal, or non-Buddhist. Why are these worldly practices good and worldly protective magic bad? Why is one type of worldliness good and another type bad? Why does opening an orphanage or ordaining a tree count as a healthy Buddhist practice but drawing a *yantra* to protect a home from fire, blessing holy water to protect a car from an accident, holding an amulet to help study for an examination, or chanting the *Jinapañjara* to ward off menacing ghosts not? Certainly, the former practices demand what Steven Collins has correctly described as "epistemological respect," meaning that they have proven and direct causes and effects.[107] Opening an AIDS clinic clearly helps treat HIV/AIDS; chanting a protective incantation over a person with AIDS may have nothing more than a placebo effect. These are different technologies for dealing with disease, fire, flooding, hunger, poverty, and the like. Their efficacy can be judged epistemologically; however, can they be judged ethically? Magic might be bad science. It might be inefficient health care. However, does that make it bad religion?

By associating magic with the worldly, it is effectively removed from the realm of religion and ethics. It is a "cultural" practice, a psychological coping mechanism, a superstition. It is relegated to the economic and the simplistic. It is not noble or supramundane.[108] Even though these monks who supposedly deal in the worldly realms of magic soothe people's anxieties, respond to their requests for protection, visit their homes and businesses, cremate their dead, hold festivals, help them maintain decorative, dance, musical, and literary traditions, build community involvement in their local monastery, and generate funds for social services, schools, building projects, and create jobs, they are somehow not included in the realm of social engagement as it has been defined by scholars. This effectively removes agency from the thousands of cultivators of pervasive protective textual and meditative traditions. It removes agency from the millions who chant the *Jinapañjara* or hold an amulet. The Protestant ideal of religion as quiet, reserved, individualistic, service oriented, textual, and focused upward has placed Buddhist ritual and "magic" on the outside looking in.

This commentary is not designed as an apology for Thai protective rituals. I am not concerned with which practice is considered *lokottara* or *lokiya*. However, by relegating the practice of protective rituals (whether they are referred to as esoteric, tantric, or magical) to something outside religion or something non-Buddhist or even something worldly, then they cannot be studied or understood as something integral to Thai Buddhist life. It forgets that many monks become highly skilled, like Somdet To, in Pali recitation, adhere to the precepts, and develop high levels of meditative concentration specifically as a precondition for the development of magical powers. Moreover, it suggests that millions of Buddhists, including the royal family, intellectuals, and thousands of nuns, novices, monks are somehow ignorant or are simply going through the motions for the sake of tradition. They have mistaken culture for religion, the mundane for the supramundane. Unless Buddhist studies scholars start reading the Theravada through the practice of protection and abundance, security, graciousness, and heritage as values on par with *lokottara* values like selflessness, indifference, and compassion, most Thai Buddhists will remain a cultural curiosity with nothing to teach the field of religious studies.

The problem may be that scholars of Buddhist studies are often trained by and swap stories among folks in the field of religious studies. Before I end this section, let me suggest briefly one possible line of research that may be fruitful if we want to integrate the study of Theravada tantra or Thai magic into the study and teaching of Buddhism. The late Henry Ginsberg, the doyen of the study of Thai painting, wrote a fascinating master's thesis at the University of Hawaii in 1967.[109] His was a study of the Thai literary tales derived from Sanskrit tales known as the *Tantropākhyāna*, especially the collection of ghost stories called the *Piśācapakaraṇam*. This vernacular Thai text, unlike the rest of the *Tantropākhyāna*, has little connection to any known Sanskrit text. It seems to be the creative work of Thai authors. It was quite popular in the mid-nineteenth century in Bangkok; there were several manuscript copies, and it was actively studied by both Thai and foreign scholars in the late nineteenth century. Bishop Pallegoix included it in his list of important vernacular Thai "secular" texts in his 1850 Thai grammar. There were some English and German translations made of the stories in 1872 and 1894, respectively (this was a time in which there were very few translations of any Thai texts available). Adolf Bastian, who was the only foreigner we know of who actually attended a sermon of Somdet To's, hand copied these ghost stories in 1864 (one year after meeting Somdet To). It was certainly seen as an important collection. However, you would be hard-pressed to find any foreign or Thai Buddhist studies scholar who knows of this narrative collection today.

Why is this important? Reading these stories one sees how stories of ghosts and protective incantations to cope with them were commonplace in Thai literature. However, in the twentieth century, with the rise of distinct academic fields such as religious studies and Buddhist studies, scholars in these fields have almost universally ignored the study of vernacular Thai literature and, like Pallegoix, have regulated it to secular culture. It was also ignored by Thai scholars of Buddhism after the nineteenth century. Vernacular Thai literature, especially if it could not be traced to Pali narratives or did not have clear Buddhist (i.e., monks, *bodhisattas*, Buddhas) characters, was considered outside the purview of the modern fields of religious and Buddhist studies. Moreover, often times palm-leaf manuscripts (*bai lan*) are studied, while the study of *khoi* and mulberry-paper manuscripts have been neglected because these were often vernacular rather than Pali texts. However, these texts were copied and circulated among monks as well as among laypeople and clearly influenced modern Thai understandings of ghosts and the ritual need to protect against them. They are also the precursor to modern Thai films and novels that depict ghosts and the practice of protective magic so popular among Buddhists. The manuscripts include both "common" *samut thai dam* (blackened *khoi*-tree bark paper) and expensive and elite *samut thai khao* (unblackened, white *khoi* paper).[110] From the colophons we can see that these manuscripts were copied by monks and have Pali blessings written at the end. These manuscripts are not found just in rural homes; they are kept in royal libraries and museums. For example, on one *Piśācapakaraṇam* manuscript, a monk named Phra Phimontham pays homage to the triple gem (Buddha, *dhamma*, sangha) in his colophon.[111] Over the course of the twentieth century these *khoi*-paper manuscripts and supposedly secular stories became the object of study of art historians and comparative literature specialists (and very few of them as well), while Pali and/or palm-leaf manuscripts became the focus of local and foreign Buddhist and religious studies scholars working in Thailand. The *Piśācapakaraṇam* is one of many vernacular narrative collections (not to mention the vernacular ritual and astrological manuals) that have not been studied by scholars working in Buddhist and religious studies. Perhaps one of the reasons the pervasiveness of magical practices and ghost belief in Thai Buddhism seems as if it is an anomaly, a strange localism, an animistic leftover, or a dying tantric substrate is not because these practices and beliefs are rare or dying but because they are rarely studied in the fields in which most scholars belong. These stories resonate with Thai Buddhists but often are not registered by Buddhist studies scholars. Scholars of Thai literature today, both local and foreign, are often not trained in Buddhist studies, Pali literature, or monastic history. Scholars of Buddhist studies rarely take courses in Thai vernacular literature or art history. We have much to learn from one another, for what is normal to one field may be strange to another and vice versa. Ginsberg, who was one of those rare scholars who felt comfortable in both fields, realized this as a very young man in 1967 when he translated this colophon in one of the manuscripts he was studying: "You who have heard these tales, honor them well and make your hearts pure and clear from vice and in the future you will have happiness in the heavenly city of Nirvana."[112]

## CONCLUSION

One can see that the so-called esoteric texts of Theravada Buddhism are not a remnant of the past barely surviving in small rural communities on the Lao and Cambodian borders of Thailand. They are part of a common logic at the very foundation of Thai Buddhism that links the body of the Buddha and the body of each human being in a universal algebraic net. This body-centric practice is based on created ephemeral bodies at the time of danger, anxiety, or death for protection through the use of nonsemantic and syllabic interpretations of Pali words and the mapping of those words onto the physical body and the physical world. In this way the phases of the moon, the days of the week, the parts of the body, the names of Buddhist texts, previous Buddhas, famous teachers are seen as existing in their own syllabic, mathematical, temporal, and spatial relationships. The *Jinapañjara* invokes these relationships and uses them for protection. Those adept in this Buddhist algebra of replacing unknowns with knowns and transforming signs into symbols and back into signs are able to reveal a network of power in this world that is accessible to everyone provided they know the access codes. Somdet To did. This logic values permanence over impermanence, reincarnation over transmigration, the investigation and manipulation of these signs in the network over ethical and speculative philosophical rumination, abundance over simplicity, heritage and security over nonattachment, graciousness and protection over indifference, and syntax over semantics. Seeing this logic as one of the major ways that Thais interpret and articulate Buddhism will, it is hoped, encourage scholars to expand the parameters of their research questions and agendas, as well as question the monolithic nature of the Theravada or the quick association of the Theravada with the Thai. Seeing abundance, heritage, security, and graciousness as Thai Buddhist values will help expand the way scholars understand the ethical import of the Theravada and Buddhism in general. Can we see the use of protective magic as compassionate? Can we see social events such as ritual and liturgies as building a sense of loving-kindness? Can we see the attempt to figure out the algebraic and magical logic of the world as building awareness? Can we simply respect these practices as technologies in themselves without recourse to supposedly more noble values?

These orthodox and esoteric, local and Indic, Vinaya-based and "tantric" practices, premodern and modern exist in a false dichotomy in descriptions from the francophone and anglophone traditions of recent Buddhist studies scholarship. However, this dichotomy is rarely articulated by Thai, Cambodian, or Lao Buddhist studies scholars or practitioners. Seeing the pervasiveness and influence of texts like the *Jinapañjara* as well as of Somdet To over time will, I hope, lead to a more-intensive study of so-called Pali and vernacular esoteric texts in modern Thai Buddhism, and eventually to new ways of defining what is esoteric and tantric, as well as normative and canonical in Thai Buddhism.

# 3. Rituals and Liturgies

In the Rietberg Museum in Zürich there is a bronze sculpture depicting half-human, half-chicken creatures and a saw cutting off a man's head. This small statue tells us much about ritual and liturgy in Thai Buddhism.[1] The small, cube-shaped piece is missing its top, which originally depicted the powerful, enlightened *arhat* Phra Malai looking over various scenes of various hells. Circular saws cut off people's heads in one hell, the metal beaks and talons of humanoid chickens tear the flesh off of other sinners. In another, emaciated, naked men beg for their lives before hot irons stab and brand them. In Buddhist legends, Phra Malai, at the behest of the Buddha, traveled to various hells and heavens to give a report to the Buddha. He saw the horrible fates of those who lived lives of selfishness, anger, hatred, and delusion.

This Dantean Pali story, composed either in Sri Lanka or northern Thailand sometime in the fifteenth or sixteenth century, known as the *Māleyyathera-sutta*, is better known in its eighteenth-century verse form, "Phra Malai."[2] It is a very popular story in Thailand. These scenes are part of the repertoire in Thai murals, illuminated manuscripts, and statuary. Large Phra Malai mulberry-paper manuscripts depict scenes from hell.[3] Murals in dozens of monasteries show half-human creatures impaling emaciated men and women while flames lick at their feet. Today there are popular and quite garish comic books describing different hells.[4]

One of the most public and graphic depictions of hell is found in the hell theme park on the outskirts of southern Bangkok near the resort town of Bang Saen. Visitors to the park are greeted with a sign in English and Thai, "Welcome to Hell," and in the park there are life-size Styrofoam and plastic dioramas depicting each level of hell. In one, a woman is being ripped limb from limb by ogres, and in another a saw is separating a man's legs from his torso. Giant worms devour sinners in a vat of molten lava, and iron tongs pry open a man's throat. All these scenes are in a garden on the grounds of a Buddhist monastery, Wat Sang Saen Suk. Perhaps the strangest thing to a non-Thai visitor is that this park is not strange to a Thai Buddhist. Just like Southern Baptists, Mexican Catholics, or Pentecostal Christians in the United States, for Thais constantly imbibing scenes and listening to sermons about hell are part of daily religiosity. The serene and compassionate Buddhism depicted in most Western textbooks and documentaries is hard to find while watching chicken and goat men feasting on human entrails. There are similar parks to this hell theme park at Wat Thawet in Sukhothai, Wat Phairongwua in Suphanburi, the massive hell sculpture garden in the forested grounds behind Wat Bha Rak Roi in Nakhon Ratchasima (northeastern Thailand), Wat Aham in Luang Phrabang (Laos), the Taoist-Buddhist Jade Emperor (Ngoc Hoang) Pagoda in Saigon (Vietnam), Aluvihāra Monastery in Matale (Sri Lanka), among many other places. Between 2001 and 2006, I had the chance to visit each one of these hell theme parks and was struck not only by the garishness of the sites but also by the number of children and families who visit them. In northeastern Asia, descriptions of hell are popular in Japanese and Korean literature about the bodhisattva Jizo (Sanskrit Kṣitigarbha), who vows to empty various hell realms of all sentient beings before reaching enlightenment. This is not a new phenomenon. The Pali collection *Petavatthu* (*Stories of Hungry Ghosts*) dates from as old as the first century B.C.E. and are as gruesome in their descriptions of suffering and death as any modern horror film. The famous fourteenth-century Thai cosmological text *Three Worlds of King Ruang* (*Traibhūmikathā*) offers descriptions that overlap with those of Phra Malai, the *Petavatthu*, and popular *jātakas* like the *Nimi* and *Lohakumbhī*. In China and Japan, the *Xuepen jing* (Japanese *Ketsubonkyō*), or *Blood-Bowl Sutra*, tells the story of Mulian (Mokuren), a disciple of the Buddha's famous for his supernatural or magical powers, who descended to hell to save his mother.[5] Phra Malai is not the only witness to hell in Buddhist literature and art. The bronze piece in Zürich is particularly beautiful, but it is certainly not unique.

This chapter questions one of the most prevalent theses in the study of modern Thai Buddhism, and indeed Theravada Buddhism in general. There have been many studies that posit that starting in the late eighteenth century and continuing until today, there has been a standardization of Buddhist practice, texts, and administration. Many have argued that because of the introduction of printing presses, a growth in "canonical fundamentalism," greater administrative capabilities and social control methods assisted by improved roads, communication, tax collection, as well as the ossification of national languages, borders, symbols, and shared histories, there has been a concomitant homogenization of Buddhist belief and practice. This increased ecclesiastical administration has been welcomed and promoted by the state, as seen in modernist movements in Cambodia, Laos, Thailand, Burma, and Sri Lanka. In these studies, scholars argue that this growing orthodoxy and centralization has, for better or for worse, been founded on the notion that royal reformers, colonial officials, and elite monks all wanted to return to an original Buddhism that would connect them to the larger "Theravada" world, as well display a sense of modernness to European colonials and missionaries, who had regularly lambasted the sangha and the royal family for excessive ritualism, unfounded superstition, and ecclesiastical foot-dragging.[6]

Often the heterodox aspects of Buddhism in Thailand are seen as a product of modernity, consumerism, globalization, the Internet, economic anxiety, or as caused by corrupt monks and the "unlettered masses," who simply follow fads and trends rather than study Pali and Buddhist philosophy. In the effort to define the parameters of Thai Buddhism, hell theme parks and flying saints are just some of the heterodox elements left out or described as new and strange. For example, despite the ubiquity of death and hell scenes on the walls, in the books, in museums, and in the gardens of Thai monasteries (old and new), the famous Thai historian and high-ranking member of the royal family, Prince Damrong, "after reading 'as much of it as he could stand' found the Story of Phra Malai equally worthless as dogma and as poetry."[7] Prince Damrong's comments found in a letter to Prince Narisa of February 6, 1939, are part of a long reform of Buddhism by the royal family that had begun in earnest during the life of Somdet To in the 1830s. This story of reform has been repeated, for good reason, many times by scholars. Peleggi, Wyatt, Thongchai, Loos, among others, describe the obsession with modernization, centralization, and demystification during the reigns of King Mongkut (Rama IV) and King Chulalongkorn (Rama V) (1843–1910). They all state, quite correctly, that these monarchs and their sisters, brothers, sons, cousins, wives, and noble friends became quite interested in Western (and Japanese, I should add) secular and religious forms of administration, education, ecclesia, and jurisprudence. In the early twentieth century, Kings Rama VI and VII went on to either reform the military and medical systems, inspired by Japanese and Western models, or create new national institutions, like the national theater, national museum, national cultural board, and the like. They also became enamored of foreign stuff. In their travels and schooling in England, France, the United States, Japan, India, Indonesia, and other places, they collected books, art, furniture, cameras, and clothing.[8] This trend continues today. The royal family, especially Princess Sirindorn and her father, King Bhumibol (Rama IX), have produced dozens of photograph albums and travel diaries available in any major bookstore in Thailand. They have filled galleries with pieces collected while abroad or presented to them as gifts from foreign dignitaries and religious leaders.

Scholars have emphasized that all these travels and reforms have been part of an overall effort to create a nation centered on the central authorities in Bangkok. Southeast Asian studies in general has been particularly focused on nationalism and nation building over the past forty years.[9] These studies have been foundational to the way we understand the connections between culture and power and the creation of things like national languages, national flags, national holidays, anthems, and ministries. These are designed to create in the population a sense of being Thai, a love of country and religion, a willingness to pay taxes, an active participation in civic events and historical commemorations, a respect for leaders, and a general acceptance of civil obedience. These reforms, institutions, and policies have created benign citizens.[10]

Despite the historical accuracy, solid research, and critical nature of these studies, there is often an assumption that these royal and state policies and reforms work, are coordinated, and are all encompassing. Research data used by Thai as well as foreign scholars is often limited to documents produced by the elite. Members of the Thai elite like King Chulalongkorn, Prince Damrong, Prince Wachirayan, Prince Narit, King Mongkut, and others are often reduced to single-minded autocrats and ideologues and used as examples of the chauvinism of a nation-building machine. Reading these studies from afar, one would assume that states in Southeast Asia have near-total power in controlling the cultural, economic, and political lives of their citizens. States loom, citizens kneel. There has been a tendency until recently to see modernity as singular and Western. However, recent work has shown that the religious lives of people in Vietnam, Cambodia, and Malaysia are heterodox and idiosyncratic.[11] I look to contribute to these conversations.

The ecclesiastical, political, and military elite (both royal and nonroyal) have not been particularly repressive or concerned with the fact that most Thai Buddhists have not participated actively in these reforms or national institutions. In fact, there are whole areas where the elite have not attempted to create a national standard. In this chapter I discuss two of these areas, ritual and liturgy. I hope to show that dynamism and debate are alive and well in Thai Buddhism contra the large number of studies that lament the deleterious centralizing effects of state control of Buddhism. This chapter argues that there is not one way of defining a Thai Buddhist ritual or liturgy. There is no national, standardized Buddhist ritual calendar (although there are bank holidays for certain Buddhist celebratory days), and there is no standard national Buddhist liturgy. However, if one looks closely at these rituals and liturgies, then certain nonprescriptive cultural repertoires emerge. These shared repertoires have a way of self-corralling and pacifying diversity. There is a common etiquette, familiar gestures, and broad aesthetic norms. Organizers of rituals and liturgies at various monasteries do not need to follow state-sanctioned regiments, but there are cultural and religious expectations. These expectations, these repertoires, are known but rarely systematically described or even explicitly articulated. However, tracing them in specific contexts helps give shape to the contours of Thai Buddhism.

## RITUALS, TEMPLE FESTIVALS, DECOMPOSING CORPSES, AND THE NATIONALIZING OF DIVERSITY

Images of death and suffering are part of the repertoires of Mae Nak and Somdet To. Popular posters advertising graphic novels and films about Mae Nak in the 1950s and 1960s depict her rising out of a grave with blood dripping from her tongue or as a half-skeleton, half-beautiful woman gazing wistfully at her clueless husband.[12] In Nonzee Nimibutr's popular 1999 film, Mak has a dream of soldiers burning in hell. The 2005 3-D version of the film is revolting in its excessive gore. The story of Mae Nak is one of death and subsequent attachment to earth. Mae Nak avoids going to the next life but creates a hell on earth. Some of the most gruesome depictions of death and hell are found at two monasteries connected to Somdet To, Wat Rakhang and Wat Sommanat in Bangkok. The walls of the main *vihāra* of Wat Rakhang are covered with some of the most intricate and evocative murals in the city. Besides depicting scenes from the Thai version of the *Rāmāyaṇa* (*Ramakian*) and daily-life scenes from eighteenth- and nineteenth-century Bangkok, there are two extremely graphic and disturbing depictions of hell. They both depict the different levels of hell and are situated below the upper registers, which depict palaces, heavenly creatures, and floating Brahmanic realms drawn from the *Traiphum phra ruang* (a famous fourteenth-century Thai cosmological text). The main section covers nearly the entire rear wall of the *vihāra*, measuring thirty-five feet wide by twelve feet high. In this large panel one sees half-animal, half-human creatures (with chicken, boar, vulture, and horse heads) using spears to pierce the flesh of naked and scared human women and men as they climb trees covered in thorns, swim in molten pools, and stand on razor blades. Along the bottom is a field of skulls and bones. Vultures tear flesh, guards laugh, and rapacious worms burrow into arms and legs. These are very typical scenes taken from various descriptions of hell well-known throughout Buddhist literature and described in the *Traiphum phra ruang*, *Phra Malai*, *Nimi jātaka*, and the *Petavatthu-atthakathā*. However, one scene is seemingly taken from Thai historical sources. There is a Thai palace in which a group of naked men, with their hands and necks bound with ropes, being led out of the front gate by human soldiers. There are no hell creatures in this scene, and it may be drawn from scenes from the Siamese war with the Burmese. The entire set of Wat Rakhang murals mixes fantastic mythological scenes taken from Indian and Thai Hindu and Buddhist literature with scenes from Thai daily life and history.[13] Actual Siamese kings are depicted near Rama and Indra. Palaces and monasteries modeled on actual Bangkok architecture are situated in fantastic gardens and landscapes drawn from classical Indic literature. This works to ground the literary, Buddhist, and cosmological tales in the lives of the audience. In terms of the scenes of hell, they are much more of an effective ethical device when the victims have Thai faces and are being led in shackles out of Thai-style palaces. Hell is much more visceral when it is made familiar and imminently possible.

The murals in the *wihan* (*vihāra*) of Wat Sommanat depicting the *Inao* story (inspired by a Javanese epic) have received considerable scholarly attention in Thailand and have been the subject of a major preservation project.[14] However, the murals in the ordination hall (*ubosot*) have been largely ignored by scholars, even though they are popular with Thai devotees and monks. The *ubosot's* murals were most likely painted in 1860.[15] The lower register of the walls in the *uposatha* hall have murals painted with scenes of death meditation. Unlike most mural paintings from this period, the scenes are not filled with dozens of characters, temples, palaces, and animals. Instead, panels on the lower north and south walls and eight corner panels depict a single monk standing or sitting next to a corpse in different levels of decay.[16] First the corpse is pinkish and bloody, next it is bound with sacred string. In another panel the corpse is gray with lifeless eyes; in another the corpse's torso has separated from its legs and arms; next the corpse is being picked apart by vultures with its intestines being pulled from its now headless body. Finally, a monk sits staring at a skeleton and eventually a pile of scattered bones.[17]

It is difficult to interpret whether these scenes are meant to depict hell realms or earthly charnel grounds. The former interpretation is supported by the fact that above the lower register there are extensive murals of quotidian earthly scenes. Usually the upper register of monastery murals in Thailand depict heavenly realms and the lower registers depict earthly scenes. Therefore, if the earthly realm is in the upper register, one could assume that the lower register represents hell. However, usually hell scenes are phantasmagoric. In Wat Sommanat they are simplistic and realistic. Death is cold and imminent. The intestines, the blood, the bones are visceral and at eye level. There are no leaves on the trees. The sky is gray. Here the monk is without implements and sitting or standing. The first panel and the back wall offer clues on how to read the entire set. On the back wall one sees a funeral and perhaps the *pansakul* ritual. A monk is depicted chanting over a corpse, and people dressed in white are entering the temple. There are multiple corpses lying on the ground and a monk meditating in front of them. Perhaps the rest of the scenes depict the body after it has been taken to the charnel ground, not to be cremated but to be left exposed for monks to use as an object for *asubhakammaṭṭhāna* meditation.

Somdet To was famous for meditating while staring at naked corpses. This is still a practice at some monasteries, like Wat Khao Yai in Pichit and Wat Hualompong in Bangkok. The first panel on the northern corner of the hall panel seems to confirm this. Here the monk depicted in meditation on the dismembered corpse surrounded by vultures has an uncanny likeness to Somdet To.[18] Somdet To is one of the most easily recognized monks in Thailand. His face is seen on images, in photographs, in books, on magazine covers. The artist could have painted the face of any monk. He painted a face nearly identical to that of Somdet To. This is further supported by the fact that this monastery is a Thammayut monastery, which was built in honor of Queen Sommanat, King Mongkut's chief queen. Somdet To was a friend, close adviser, and maybe even a blood relative to King Mongkut. He was one of the Pali teachers and protectors of King Chulalongkorn. King Mongkut sponsored the initial construction, and it was continued in earnest by King Chulalongkorn. These supposedly rationalistic, Western-influenced monarchs, who wanted to purify Thai Buddhism of superstition and noncanonical practices and beliefs, sponsored murals that depicted decomposing corpses. These kings (and the first Thammayut abbot, Phra Ariyamuni Phuttha Siri Thera-Thap) did not simply tolerate these practices, they actively advertised Somdet To on the walls of the monastery built in honor of King Mongkut's chief queen.

These practices were merely depicted on one royal temple's murals. Indeed, about a fifteen-minute walk from Wat Sommanat, along the Lot Canal, the bodies of prisoners (who died unnatural deaths, of course) from the nearby prison along Mahachai Road were left out for vultures to consume and for the public to watch. The bodies were deposited at Wat Sraket. This monastery is one of the most important royal monasteries of Bangkok. Today it is home to one of the premier Pali-language schools, and for several decades it was home to one of the largest Pali-language printing houses of the city (Bhumiphol Press). Directly behind the monastery is one of the main centers for the production of monk's alms bowls and decorative caskets for funerals. Wat Sraket and its former corpse depository were not hidden. In the late nineteenth century they were in the center of the city along the "royal way" (Thanon Ratchadamnoen). They are situated at the corner of two large canals that were major commercial arteries and still are very busy today. The former national library was three hundred feet away. Within a quarter mile are the royal-sponsored monasteries Wat Boworniwet, Wat Loha Prasat, among several others, as well as Somdet To's last monastery of residence, Wat Indrawihan. Wat Sraket was so central to the Buddhist and royal life of Bangkok, that it became the base of the Phu Khao Thong (Golden Mountain) in 1899. Here a relic of the Buddha was presented by monks from Sri Lanka. King Rama V had a man-made "mountain" constructed so that the relic could be held in a stupa high above the city. This was actually the highest point in the city until the Dusit Thani Hotel was built in 1970. Both before and after this relic was in place, the monks at Wat Sraket and other surrounding temples came to watch the consumption and decomposition of corpses. The closure of the prison and city health codes eventually stopped the practice. However, during Somdet To's life it was an active corpse depository and meditation center. After 1888, a relic of the Buddha and the relics of prisoners were present at the same monastery. The royal reformers certainly did not disapprove of these supposedly esoteric practices.[19]

In general, most Thai elite reformers have actually not attempted to actively "cleanse" Thai liturgy and ritual.[20] Just as there is a great diversity in Thai mural depictions, there has been little effort to standardize or centralize ritual structure, dates, implements, vestments, and liturgical texts. Moreover, the supposedly lessnoble motivations and objectives of ritual and liturgical practices (fear, love, revenge, wealth, long life, protection) have not been actively purged from formal performances, literature, or homilies describing and informing daily ritual practice. The "rational" and modern ideas promoted by socially engaged monks and lay scholars and activists have also not generally affected the practice and diversity of liturgies and rituals.

Although there were few efforts to create a national standard, there have been significant efforts to document and elevate certain rituals on the national scale. For example, King Chulalongkorn produced a study of twelve major Thai royal celebrations in 1888.[21] Descriptions of these rituals, including the plowing festival, Triyampavai-Tripavai ("Hindu" New Year), and others, have been reprinted many times. They are also depicted in a series of worn but stunning murals on the walls of the *uposatha* hall of the small monastery Wat Ratchapra-dit, near the Grand Palace along the Lot Canal. Most of these national monthly rituals are connected in some way to religion, and Brahman priests and Bud-dhist monks participate. Many of these celebrations are now national holidays, like Songkhran Day, Visakha Puja Day, and Loi Kratong (only two of which are "Buddhist"). One panel shows the king observing the solar eclipse of 1868. They are advertised by the Tourism Authority of Thailand and advertised in the Thai Airways International magazine *Kinnaree*. However, King Chulalong-korn's descriptions are not prescriptive. The rituals and liturgies that accom-pany these celebrations are performed differently in different regions of the coun-try and even within different monasteries in one city. For example, on Khao Pansa Day there are regional versions of the celebration, most of which find no justification in early Buddhist literature. For example, in Ubon Ratchathani, contests are held to build and carve massive (some fifty feet high) candles to be paraded around the provincial capital.

The oft-cited 1888 *Royal Rituals of the Twelve Months* (*Ruang phraratchaphithi sipsong duan*) composed by King Chulalongkorn does not attempt to create a national standard. In fact, his documenting of the annual rituals performed in Thailand reveals his acceptance, if not outright promotion, of diversity in Thai ritual. Moreover, it shows that what was considered proper Thai ritual was not and should not be equated with Theravada Buddhism. In fact, in each month, the rituals described are a mixture of Chinese, Brahmanic, Theravadan, and local. Local rituals with no clear connection to Indic or Sinitic roots are not rele-gated to "folk" status or listed as curious anomalies. For example, in the chapter on the rituals of the fourth month, he describes rituals of presenting golden trees, the chanting of the Buddhist Āṭānāṭiya sutta, a ritual to suppress the haunting of ghosts, New Year celebrations (*trut* or *sampaccharachin*), a curative ritual (*aphathaphinat*), a Brahmanic fire ritual (*phithi phrahm hom kun*), a ritual of offering gifts to members of the Buddhist sangha (*phithi song*), a ritual entreat-ing the gods in the morning (*prakat thewada wela chao*), a healing ritual involv-ing the shooting of guns (*ying beun athana*), and various other rituals involving holy water, a bodhi tree, and the invocation of dreams.[22] The divisions and hier-archies between Buddhism, Brahmanism, local, and Chinese religions are vir-tually erased in this presentation.[23] Rituals associated with Theravada Buddhism are not elevated. It is more of an encyclopedic project than a standardization or reform effort. Even regional variations of rituals are described. While the simple fact of calling rituals in the southern city of Nakhon Sri Thammarat or north-eastern Thailand Siamese could and should certainly be seen as a subtle form of Siamese hegemony, the text does not present these noncentral Siamese ritu-als as lesser or anomalous forms. Finally, in the descriptions of each ritual, one can see that Pali chants and Brahmanic ritual implements are brought into local protective and healing rites (and vice versa). For example, in a description of a ritual for New Year's Day (originally a Khmer Brahmanic celebration), there is mention of the repetitive chanting by members of the sangha of a canonical Buddhist Pali *Āṭānāṭiya sutta* as well as of the firing of guns in the air for the purpose of protecting the populous from danger and for allaying their fears.[24] Other prominent Thai scholars and royal family members have written descriptions of Thai Buddhist rituals without attempting to define the superior form of the ritual. Prince Anuman Rajadhon's *Life and Ritual in Old Siam* documents many ghost-protection rituals and land-spirit rites without explicitly condemning them as superstitious or non-Buddhist. More recently, Phoensri Duk and others have produced a large survey of Thai rituals that is not limited to defining Buddhist, national, secular, Hindu, or animistic rites.[25] They are all grouped together as Thai, which could be interpreted as a hegemonic rhetorical move.

King Mongkut was a great reformer and a man interested in Western notions of rationality and the scientific method. Dozens of books about King Mongkut in Thai and English emphasize this modern, rational attitude toward religion and the reforms that led to his founding of the Thammayut lineage.[26] However, as we saw in chapter 1, King Mongkut's "favorite" monk and adviser was Somdet To, who made amulets, chanted protective incantations, tamed ghosts, hated foreigners, and drew *yantras*. He also believed that certain powerful Buddha images, like the Emerald Buddha and the Phra Bang, contained *phi* (ghosts) and had the power to end droughts.[27] Moreover, King Chulalongkorn's Pali teacher, many believe, was Somdet To. King Chulalongkorn himself went on a short pilgrimage to Kanchanaburi and Angthong looking for a famous and ritually powerful image of Somdet To after the monk's death.[28] Each of these elite reformers did not want simply to remove the protective, magical, and local aspects of Thai Buddhism. They were not antisuperstitious zealots, maniacal centralizers, or unabashed modernists aping the West. If anything, their writing on religious subjects reveals a curious speculative attitude and ethnographic character.[29] There is no doubt that they saw central Thailand as the rightful center of political power and themselves as virtuous and absolute rulers; however, this political control did not carry over into a need to control or mitigate the diversity of ritual and liturgical practices in the realm(s) they aimed to tax and administer. They made no great effort to create one guidebook for proper celebrations, rituals, and liturgies. A great diversity remains.

In some ways, in the twentieth and twenty-first centuries, the Thai government and sangha have actually attempted consciously and unconsciously to create even greater diversity in Thai ritual. The rise of various "cults" to the memories of past kings like King Naresuan and King Chulalongkorn, or local heroes like Thao Suranari and Chao Thippachak, over the past hundred years have been actively promoted by the royal family and politicians in various provinces.[30] Under the reigns of Kings Rama VI and VII several national committees were established to raise and provide state resources for Thai cultural expressions. King Rama VI started the national theater in 1911, which was later taken over by the newly established Fine Arts Department in 1932. The Fine Arts Department (Krom Silapakhon) also established the National Academy of Dance and Music (1934), the Royal Entertainment Department (1935). The National Museum grew at its present location in Sanam Luang Park in the 1940s.[31] These organizations have not attempted to strictly control what counts as Thai art, culture, or religion but have employed a number of talented and creative people who have taken Thai art in new directions. Indeed, the national censor board has attempted to control the depiction of sex in films, freedom of the press has been limited, and criticism of the royal family is quickly condemned. However, in terms of cultural and religious expression, instead of corralling and directing Thai cultural expression, these national organizations have actually provided resources to foster creativity. For example, the Fine Arts Department has named five artists national artists. These five, Vanida Puengsunthorn, Pinyo Suwannakiri, Ruethai Chaichingrak, Prawet Limpparangsri, and Arvuth Ngoenchuklin, have not created a national style or a handbook for what makes good Thai art.[32] Instead, they are each renowned for their innovative work in new designs for pagodas in India, novel interpretations of traditional Thai teak homes, and modern Thai architecture. Arvuth Ngoenchuklin was recently assigned to design the funeral pyre for Princess Kalyani, who passed away in December 2007. He combined numerous mythological tropes from Sanskrit classical literature. Like the murals of Phra Malai at Wat Rakhang or on the piece at the Rietberg Museum, the funeral pyre includes sculptures of half-human, half-animal creatures. Instead of representing hell beings, they represent heavenly creatures on the mythological mountain Mount Meru at the center of the world. Although he considers himself a traditional Thai artist steeped in history, he actually combines elements well-known in Indic and Southeast Asian Hindu and Buddhist art in creative new ways. He has mastered a certain repertoire but is not controlled by it.[33]

This creativity is not only evident at the national, elite level but also promoted by minor officials and abbots at the provincial level. At various monasteries throughout the country many abbots and monastery patrons promote worship ceremonies in honor of deceased and living abbots, scholar-monks, soothsayers, and meditation masters. These local rituals are promoted by wealthy patrons and politicians seeking to bring in tourist and pilgrimage money. In the past ten years there has been a push for local, provincial governments, in conjunction with the Tourism Authority of Thailand and hotel and tour-group operators, to create new light-and-sound rituals. These events attempt to "anthologize" numerous diverse rituals, dramas, dances, and historical reenactments with highly choreographed music, dance, and laser-light shows. These are now standard shows at the Angkorian ruins of Phimai and Khao Phanom Rung in northeastern Thailand and are semiannual events on the banks of the Chao Phraya River near the Grand Palace in Bangkok. They also have been arranged for holidays in Lopburi, Sukhothai, Ayutthaya, and other monument-rich Thai cities. There is even a hill tribe "Akha Mountain People" light-and-sound show sponsored by the Tourism Authority of Thailand. They combine impressive uses of smoke machines, sound systems, Thai- and English-language narrators, hundreds of actors dressed in period costumes, elephants, and fake palaces and monasteries made out of Styrofoam and plastic. Instead of offering a sterilized or standardized version of Thai myths, historical events, or rituals, they actually create new rituals, myths, and offer rereadings of historical battles or love stories. Each producer reinterprets history and myth to create a new show that she or he hopes will be of interest to tourists and school groups (both Thai and non-Thai).

A good example of this kind of show was the Wimaya Nattakan Light-and-Sound Show that ran from 2001 to 2004 at Phimai Historical Park in Nakhon Ratchasima (Khorat) Province. There were English, French, and Japanese guides and narrators. The Tourism Authority of Thailand, Web sites, and posters promoted the show as honoring the history of "the city of brave women." It promised to highlight "a rich legacy of ancient, awe-inspiring Khmer archaeological treasures, majestic historical sites, and charming traditions." For the show, a new ritual and liturgy were developed called the Bai Sri Su Khwan, which was described in English as "a traditional welcome and well-wishing ceremony" followed by a guided tour of "the awesome architecture of the ancient Khmer empire within Phimai Historical Park" and a "delicious dinner of northeastern cuisine amid the archaeological wonders while being entertained by traditional folk performances of northeastern Thailand." After the ritual, tour, and dances, the organizers put on a series of what they called vignettes of Buddhist religious processions, the ancient ritual dance of the boxers and the Phimaipura or Vimayapura dance, as well folk and traditional dances such as the "Bai Sri Su Kwan dance, Manohra Len Nam dance, the Dung Krok and Dung Sak mortar and pestle dance." The combination of these "folk dances," new ritual, "Buddhist" processions, and technology set to the backdrop of the Angkorian temples was wholly new in Thailand. The Isan, or Lao, folk dances were unknown, as were the Thai Theravada Buddhist processions, in the Angkorian period when the temples of Phimai were first built. Tai-speaking peoples were not even living in the region when Phimai was built and active as a Brahmanic ritual center. These rituals, liturgies, and dances had never been performed together at any time in history, and most had been developed simply for this light-and-sound festival.

A less high-tech way in which the state, in this case the Bangkok Metropolitan Administration and the Fine Arts Department, diversifies ritual in Thailand was seen in September 2007. That month the Sao Ching Cha (Giant Swing) next to Wat Suthat was repaired. This section of the city is known for its Buddhist paraphernalia stores and artisans who supply monasteries, office buildings, and private homes with bronze, resin, wooden, and plastic images of the Buddha, Shiva, Vishnu, Brahma, Somdet To, kings and queens past and present, and the like. Here is also where many people purchase robes, bowls, umbrellas, toiletries, and other items to donate to local monasteries. The Giant Swing is a sixty-foot-tall wooden and red lacquer swing consisting of two teak pillars and a decorative crossbar that was used from 1784 to 1931 as a ritual site to celebrate Triyampawai. Because of the expense in keeping up the swing, the ritual was discontinued until September 13, 2007. The first record we have of the ritual is found in Jeremias Van Vliet's diary. In 1633, he wrote that this was a ritual in Ayutthaya as well. He was told that two Brahman priests had brought the swing from Benares (India) in 1491 as a gift to King Ramathibodhi.[34] King Rama I reestablished the swing in Bangkok. The culmination of the ritual was four Brahmans swinging back and forth on a wooden board suspended from the sixty-foot-high crossbar. They rose over seventy-five feet in the air in long sweeping arcs trying to grab a bag of gold coins hanging from the teak pillars. This ritual was not only popular with crowds but was, in addition, established as one of the "twelve royal ceremonies" in 1888. King Mongkut is said to have promoted the ritual by inviting important monks, Brahman priests, and royal family members. He combined the Brahman ritual with royal processions and alms offerings to Buddhist monks. Fireworks were added in the mid-nineteenth century as well.[35] At the September 2007 festival, Bangkok governor Apirak Kosayodhin, with the king and queen ceremonially presiding, welcomed over eight thousand spectators to the renewal of the Giant Swing festival. Combined with the Sanskrit chanting by Brahmans, there were pavilions with classical Thai dancing, pop music, Buddhist monks chanting in Pali, and speeches by organizers and politicians. This megaceremony brings together many things common to the cultural and religious repertoires of modern Thai citizens: (1) royal blessings, (2) "Brahmanic" chanting, (3) Pali chanting, (4) secular political supervision and hundreds of police officers, (5) tourists taking photographs, (6) hundreds of food vendors, the Wall's Ice Cream jingle played repetitively on rolling handcarts, pop music, classical Khmer-style dancing, and the like in a section of the city flanked by a Brahman temple, the massive Buddhist monastery of Wat Suthat, a small Vishnu shrine, a major city government building, and dozens of small shops selling civil servant uniforms, Buddha images, ritual items and monk's robes and bowls. This ritual was promoted as a "renewal," but nothing like it had been seen before.

Today, Thai Buddhist rituals can be classified in many ways. There is no list that could hope to be exhaustive. There are the everyday offerings to land-spirit "houses" (*san phra phum*) seen throughout the country, as well as domestic rites honoring the rice mother (Mae Phosop), and many rituals dedicated to matrilineal and ancestor lineages. Often studies divide these rituals between "monastic" and "lay" rituals. This is not always a helpful or accurate division. For example, in northeastern Thailand and Laos, the Baisi Su Khwan protective ritual that involves inviting spirits to protect all those in attendance is a part of nearly every monastic and home celebration. It is even an essential part of the monastic and novice ordination rites in this region, this despite that the ritual cannot be performed by monks because it often involves offering a small glass of rice whiskey to the spirits (monks can do just about every ritual as long as it does not require them to break a monastic precept—handling liquor or killing an animal would break these precepts). However, the rituals often take place on monastic grounds, and monks observe and encourage them. I have even seen monks correct laypeople on the proper way to perform the offering and chant the mixture of Pali and Thai or Lao involved. Monks even participate in the tying of sacred strings around the wrists of all in attendance, even though this is the crescendo of the Baisi Su Khwan, a supposedly lay ritual.

In monasteries, there are ecclesiastical rituals often guided by texts called *kammavācā* that are part of the daily and yearly schedules of monks. These calendrical rituals include daily morning and evening prayers (*tham wat chao, tham wat yen*). The *uposatha* observance is held every two weeks, and the *Pāṭimokkha* (the monastic code) is chanted in full. Often monks are judged as "trained" in Thai Buddhism when they can chant the whole text from memory. For many this is a de facto examination that is expected of any monk who has been in the robes more than two or three years, if not sooner. Some monasteries are famous for having monks who can chant the *Pāṭimokkha* very quickly and others whose monks can chant it very beautifully.

Besides these biweekly ceremonies, South and Southeast Asian Buddhists added the quarter days in the lunar cycle to the list of monthly days of observance, establishing four Sabbath-like days each month (known as *wan phra* in Thailand). *Uposatha* days are times in which devout (or even casually observant) lay Buddhists often voluntarily vow to keep the Eight Precepts (i.e., refraining from consuming intoxicants, speaking untruths, slander, rumors, sexual activity, killing living beings, stealing or hoarding property, eating after noon, excessively decorating oneself, sleeping on luxurious beds). In practice, this means that many lay Buddhists, especially elderly women, dress in white, do not wear cosmetics or jewelry, and sleep in open-air pavilions on monastic grounds. They spend their time meditating, talking casually, listening to chanting, reading, making decorations, cleaning and polishing ritual implements, and cooking. Novices, nuns, and monks often use these days to chant for the public, offer sermons, and counsel visitors who may be having personal problems.[36]

On every *uposatha* day, whether it is a major public and monastic holiday like Wan Wisakha Pucha, Wan Khao Phansa, Wan Ook Phansa (also called Pavāranā), Anāpānasati Day, Wan Magha Pucha, Wan Asanha Pucha, or just a weekly day of observance, many people bring food to the monastery, offer candles, incense sticks, flowers, and money (and sometimes statues, bowls, robes, books, among other items used by monastery occupants).[37] Some stay all day taking on the Five or Eight Precepts, while others simply present their offerings, meditate or chant for a few minutes, and stroll around the grounds. Children can play in the courtyards of most monasteries and mothers can nurse their infants. There are occasionally even some laymen playing card games or repairing a broken faucet or window. Usually labor at a monastery (unless it involves major construction or digging holes, which monks are forbidden to do) is done by nuns, novices, and monks. However, on *uposatha* days, many laypeople do volunteer work. Therefore, *uposatha* days are usually lively and busy times at a monastery. Monasteries are also busy on widely celebrated public holidays connected to Hindu, animistic, and royal festivities like Songkhran Day, Loi Kratong, the King's Birthday (Father's Day). There has never been a sustained or vocal protest by members of the Thai sangha to raise the profile of Buddhist celebrations over Hindu, national, or royal holidays. Some rituals are performed on demand and not according to prearranged lunar dates or major holidays. These include house blessings, vehicle blessings, acceptance of gifts, honoring the taking of the Five or Eight Precepts by laypeople, among others. Some of these life-cycle rituals include funerals and cremations (*pithi ngan sop lae phao sop*).[38] There is also a tradition of playing music at many of these rituals and having classical Thai dancers perform. There are troops of dancers and musicians contracted to monasteries that have large crematoriums. Songs for funerals in particular include "Nang hong," "Thepnimit," "Thepbantom," "Phiromsrang," "Kalya yiam hong," among others.

Offering ceremonies and alms rounds (*piṇḍapāta*) are probably the simplest and most frequent ritual activities of nuns, novices, and monks.[39] Every morning, most monastics leave their monasteries at dawn (if not earlier) and walk slowly through their local villages or city neighborhoods. Besides the daily morning alms rounds, nuns, novices, and monks can also receive alms at their monasteries (especially on an *uposatha* day) or attend a special event where they receive alms. These special events are called *tak bat* and can take place at a private residence or at a business. They are common on anniversaries of the founding of schools, grand openings of supermarkets, the first day of a clearance sale at a furniture store, and the like. These ceremonies ensure the business or school year will be successful. There are famous *tak bat* ceremonies in various provinces. For example, the Bun Bang Fai (rocket festival in Yasothorn Province in which villagers launch homemade rockets to ensure a good planting season) has a very large *tak bat* for the sangha. Bun Phra Wet rituals (three-day rituals of chanting of the *Vessantara jātaka*) held in various provinces at a number of famous monasteries start and end with a *tak bat* offering. In Saraburi Province, the Tak Bat Dok Mai is an offering of flowers called *dok hong thong* at Wat Phutthabat. At this monastery and many others the *tak bat* is followed by boat races, carnival games, beauty contests, and elephant expositions. Ceremonies in Surat, Loei, Nakhon Sri Thammarat, and Phisanulok are particularly famous and draw visitors from all over the country.

On any given day at monasteries across the country one can witness individuals, couples, small groups of students, friends, or families kneeling in front of a single monk listening to a short sermon or receiving the Five Precepts. These encounters intersperse formal gestures and chanting with jokes, the voicing of personal problems, or chatting about current events. Sometimes a monk will show visitors relics, amulets, images or take them on a tour of the monastery. Wealthy donors pride themselves on getting this one-on-one "face time" with particularly famous monks, but in actuality, there are no restrictions, and any person, rich or poor, woman or man, can make an appointment with even the highest-ranking monk in the country. For example, there are several homeless people who sleep in the open-air pavilions of Wat Rakhang. They not only use the pavilions for shelter but also contribute to the ritual life of the monastery. They volunteer their time to make flower arrangements, sweep the grounds, and feed the wandering cats and dogs that are ubiquitous at most Thai monasteries. In this way, the monastery acts as a nonjudgmental homeless shelter and temporary mental-health facility.

The last ritual I briefly mention is the "annual monastery festival" (*ngan wat bracham pi*). Many monasteries hold an annual, often seven- to ten-day-long festival or carnival. These are raucous and fun events. Usually there are Ferris wheels, carnival games, beauty contests, several stages with bands and small dramas playing (often these are amateur Chinese-style romance operas or Thai puppet shows), magicians, Pali and vernacular chanting being played on loudspeakers, variety shows with comedians, dancers, and short humorous skits, and the like. Children run around, monks shout out winning lottery or raffle numbers, there are food vendors everywhere, fireworks are launched, and the entire monastery is lit up with multicolored fluorescent light tubes hanging from trees, gates, and eaves.

I have been to dozens of these festivals. I always, like everyone else, eat too much and stay up too late. Much money is generated for the monastery at these festivals, and it is a good way for children and families to get together. Although besides the Pali chanting and the fact that most people who go to the festivals purchase amulets, prostrate to Buddha, monk, and deity images at various shrines on the monastic grounds, there is very little of the religious involved. Still, these festivals are part of the repertoire of many Thai Buddhists. I recently (February 2008) took a drive from Bangkok to Kanchanaburi. I decided to simply count the number of billboards I saw advertising monastic festivals in this ninety-mile drive from hyperurban Bangkok to very rural Kanchanaburi (we were going to villages along the Burmese border). I counted 149 billboards advertising monastic festivals. Most were dated 2007 or 2008. There was even an advertisement for an annual festival at a local Muslim mosque in Nakhon Pathom Province. Festivals were taking place at monasteries like Wat Sawang Arom, Wat Sao Hong, and many others.[40] Many of these signs depicted crystal balls to tell people that there would be fortune-tellers (or monks skilled at astrological prognostication) and amulet sales. Several signs mentioned the name of the abbot of the monastery, and some had emblazoned in bold print, "Ruai ruai" (Rich, rich) to assure drivers that attending the festival would help them learn auspicious lottery numbers (*boe huai*) and gain merit to become rich in the near future. One of the first signs we saw was for one of Somdet To's monasteries, Wat Indrawihan, which holds its very large festival for ten days every March.

My son and I spent a nice afternoon at Wat Indrawihan during this annual festival on March 3, 2008. Besides being able to buy ice cream, ride a merry-go-round, play carnival games (including a shooting game with very loud pistols), and buy home healing remedies, we were able to "rent" amulets (a person cannot "purchase" a Buddha, nun, or monk image; they must be "rented"; however, in practical terms, a person actually owns the image for life), bow down to Somdet To, listen to a recorded sermon, play a lottery game (an electronic game of chance, like a slot machine, in the shape of a Buddha image), acquire holy water and sacred string from two monks, and prostrate to the statues of Jivaka, Indra, Brahma, Kuan Im, King Taksin, Phra Arannik, Somdet To's mother, King Chulalongkorn, Phra Sankhachai, Jatukham Ramathep, and Somdet To. My son released birds to make merit while I rented a *yantra* cloth (*pha yan*) I had never seen before. We could even have gotten tattoos. My four-year-old and I had a superfun time. Somdet To's image was encountered everywhere at the festival as if he were a master of ceremonies gazing at children eating squid-flavored chips and winning plastic guns in games of chance. This festival drew more visitors (including local Muslim and Christian families) to Wat Indrawi-han than any other ritual that year. Usually, annual monastery festivals draw larger crowds to their respective monasteries than any of the major Buddhist holidays or life-cycle rituals. Although these festivals are clearly the place where many very young Thai Buddhists acquire their first impressions of monastic life, I think one would have trouble fitting this monastic festival neatly into any previous description of Theravada Buddhist belief and practice.

All these rituals, whether calendrical or life-cycle oriented, are governed by the idea that giving (*than*) is a way of making merit (*bun*) to ensure a good next life or good fortune in this life. While ordaining as a monk is the best offering a person can make, offering a scoop of rice to a novice in the morning is also considered very meritorious. Some wealthy donors offer the funding to build entire monasteries or libraries, while others make an effort to undertake pilgrimages to important monasteries throughout Thailand and the world to bear witness to the relics of the Buddha, *bodhisattas*, and famous *arhats* and teachers. Taking on the Five or Eight Precepts once a week is also considered meritorious, because one is giving her or his time and giving up desires. Monks are considered the most meritorious of receivers of alms. There are some cultural associations with certain gifts. For example, if you give a Buddha statue to a monastery, then you will be beautiful. If you give candles, your eyesight will improve. If you give texts, you will be intelligent. Most Thai Buddhists believe that these benefits will come only in the next life, but some see these benefits as affecting the quality of a person's present life.

No matter how many rituals I list and briefly describe here, Thai Buddhist ritual cannot be defined comprehensively because it is highly idiosyncratic in its forms and the motivations of its participants. I conclude this section with two examples. On February 9, 2008, my family and I accidentally happened upon the ordination of a middle-aged professional man. The ritual was very casual: children played inside and outside the *uposatha* hall; there were bottles of Coca-Cola and Fanta offered to the two dozen or so family members and friends; each member of the family took turns cutting a piece of his hair off, bowing, and circumambulating. This was all done amid the din of traffic and laughter. My children, wife, and I were immediately invited to partake in the fun. At the beginning of the ceremony, white envelopes of money were offered to the monastery along with robes, bowls, candles, toiletries, and other ritual and practical items. Certainly the actual chanting was precise and formal, but in general this was a relaxed and festive time. We circumambulated the *uposatha* hall; we collected the coins that were ceremoniously tossed in the air by the ordinand; and we kept taking on and off our shoes as we moved between inner and outer ritual spaces. The monastery earned much-needed funds, and the family earned merit, took hundreds of photographs, and made time to sit in the shade and get reacquainted. This ordination could be understood only by getting to know this family. Why was this clearly successful and busy man, surrounded by friends and family, joining the monkhood in his late forties? Did his mother pass away and was he honoring her memory by becoming ordained? Was he going through a midlife crisis? Did he land a big promotion and decide to become temporarily ordained as a way of thanking his ancestors for their support and protection? I found out bits and pieces about his life chatting with family members but did not want to pry into their affairs. It was also more fun to just joke around and watch the children play.

On the same day as this ordination, we were taking a stroll through another monastery across the street from the one holding the ordination. In this monastery we were invited to another ritual, this time a *tak bat* ceremony. A large family had gotten together to feed the monks their morning meal. They hired two cooks, a waiter, and a dishwasher. They double-parked so they could unload pots, utensils, plates, and the like. They saw us taking pictures and corralling our son. They gave us bowls of noodles, Cokes, and ice cream. Monks came over to tickle the kids and ask us where we were from. Chanting took place after the monks had eaten; there were impromptu tours of the monastery and general chitchat. The reason this family happened to be holding this food offering on that day was related partly to Chinese New Year, which had just passed, and partly to the fact that one of the monks at the monastery was the nephew of the organizer. This was not a Chinese temple, no one spoke Chinese, the nephew was not of high rank. This event could not be predicted, but something similar to it was taking place at hundreds of monasteries throughout the country at that very moment. Although there was much familiar and predictable about the structure of both the ordination ritual and the *tak bat* food offering, there was little predictable about the personalities and motivations of the participants. They shared a common repertoire with overlapping, but not prescribed, moods, aesthetics, tropes, and liturgies.

## LITURGIES AND CACOPHONIES

Liturgy is a place where the tension between orthodox standardization efforts and the independent will of local intellectual agents is seen. Liturgies are public and often published. However, the needs and desires of local teachers and students are indeed just that—local. It is not that local practitioners actively

resist the central sangha authority, embodied in the *sangharat* and the Mahatherasamakhom. Individual teachers, whether in Bangkok or in rural areas, often
ignore or adapt the ritual and liturgical practices of the country's most senior
elite and royally sponsored monks. But, since the Mahatherasamakhom has not
dictated that only one type of liturgy be used in each ritual or homiletic occasion, the use of local liturgies is not a particularly deviant or dangerous practice.
Local teachers continue to practice their own traditional liturgies or creatively
combine new and old practices based on the availability of texts and the requests
of their own students and lay audiences. Liturgy is where these local contingen-
cies and agendas are most clearly expressed.

Liturgical studies in general are also important because they force the scholar
to juxtapose otherwise disparate texts. Therefore, they break down dubious divisions between canon and commentary, vernacular and classical literature, and
oral and written presentations of a text. They give scholars an opportunity to
study texts in different mediums—from palm leaf, to mulberry paper, to codex,
to online text, to CD and DVD. Studying texts in isolation and not seeing how
they fit into ritual and performance limit our understanding of not only what a
text means but also what it means to an audience in a specific time and place.
Looking at liturgies enables us to see texts in different contexts. Such examination gives attention to both audience reception and authorial intention.
Liturgical studies therefore allow us to focus on the physicality, the kines-
thetic encounters of bodies in ritual settings, and the orality of a performance
rather than simply see the value of a text in its semantic meaning or its place in
a canon.[41]

"Liturgy" is a term referring to a regulated form of public worship. It is most
commonly associated with the Roman Catholic tradition. The most ubiquitous
form of public worship in Catholicism is the mass. Herein there is a standard
liturgy of the word (*Ad liturgiam verbi*) followed by the liturgy of the Eucharist
(*Liturgica eucharistica*). The Roman Catholic liturgy (mass, *Ordine missae*),
which can accompany funerals, last rites, weddings, baptisms, and other sacra-
mental rites, is flexible in form, but the texts used in the liturgy remain relatively
static. They are readings that change in a regulated sequential manner depending on the date (these include the Epistles of St. Paul, the psalms, antiphons,
and readings from the Four Gospels of the New Testament and readings from
the Old Testament). This body of texts is considered canonical. There is a standard liturgy and canticle that marks date and liturgical passage by which Roman Catholic priests abide. There is some creative expression and commentary
in the homily section of the liturgy of the word. There are also aesthetic differences (in music, dress, processionals, recessionals, and ritual implements), but,
overall, the Roman Catholic liturgy of the word is performed in strikingly simi-

lar ways around the world in various vernaculars.[42] Similar sets of Catholic prayers drawn from the canticle are used in other sacraments, like confession, nuptials, last rites, and so forth. Certain prayers, certain vestments, and certain ritual implements and gestures (oil, water, sign of the cross, scapula, and so on) are like movable bridges that link the entire Catholic liturgical system inter- and intranationally.

Like their Catholic counterparts, Thai Buddhist public rituals vary in form and in content, but they do not have standard bridges linking them. They change depending on the occasion—a house blessing, a funeral, a wedding, a consecration, and so forth.[43] However, unlike in Catholicism, there is no canonical set of liturgical texts from which they are drawn. There is no standard Thai canticle. Despite the administrative, educational, and monastic disciplinary reforms of the nineteenth and twentieth centuries, Thai Buddhist liturgical texts are expansive and idiosyncratic. Centralization and nationalism have reached only so far. New prayers are rarely introduced into the Catholic liturgy, but this is common in Thai Buddhism. This liturgical flexibility has allowed practice to remain sophisticated and adaptive in the face of centuries of Christian and Islamic missionary activity, secularism, scientific materialism, and modern urban malaise. However, one of the reasons missionaries have been so unsuccessful in Thailand is the ability of Thai ritualists to make their practices and texts relevant on the one hand and timeless on the other. The basis of stability of sacrality and idiosyncratic growth and maneuverability is the combination of Pali and the vernacular in a flexible and evolving liturgical canon.[44]

Rituals generally have liturgical texts associated with them. Despite the fact that liturgical texts are the most commonly memorized, chanted, and heard in Thailand, they have received very little scholarly attention.[45] Thai public liturgies draw from a wide corpus of texts that, despite their differences in age, author, provenance, "canonical status," and even ethical message, are considered equally powerful. This could not happen in Roman Catholicism or Islam or in many cases Judaism, where there is a stable set of canonical text(s) that are designated as such in public liturgies. A Roman Catholic priest cannot insert a fifteenth-century Latin chant or a seventeenth-century French commentary or a twentieth-century English missal into his liturgy. A Sunni Muslim imam cannot treat thirteenth-century Persian Sufi poems or nineteenth-century Malay commentaries as canonical and equal vehicles of sacred recitation. In Thai liturgies, Pali and the vernacular play off each other, and the sources of the prayers range from canonical to noncanonical, from classical to contemporary.

## PREMODERN LITURGICAL CHANTING
## BOOKS IN THAILAND

The oldest manuscript liturgies in the region are found in northern and northeastern Thailand. This region was independent from Siamese or Thai control until the early twentieth century, but its Buddhist thinkers influenced and were influenced by the liturgies, translation methods, and ritual technologies of Siam over time. Early liturgical prayer books most often contain sets of *paritta*. *Paritta* are protective texts that keep the chanter safe from evil spells, menacing otherworldly creatures, and the very real dangers of knives, disease, betrayal, fire, and poison. They are some of the most popular and widely known texts in Buddhist Asia. For example, Mabel Bode has written, "To this day, [the *paritta* is] more widely known by the Burmese laity of all classes than any other Pāli book."[46] Malalasekara has written: "the Pirit Pota [Sri Lankan *paritta* collection] . . . forms part of the meagre library of every Singhalese household."[47] Any Buddhist who regularly attends temple ceremonies or requests monks to bless her or his property or endeavors is familiar with these chants and their modern vernacular translations, which often serve as subjects for sermons. *Paritta* literature has long been associated with ritual action and protective implements such as string, holy water, candles, amulets, incense, engraved metal mantra texts worn around the neck, and the like. Primary textual sources abound for these *paritta*. The earliest Pali chronicles and commentaries (fourth to fifth century c.e.) mention the use of *parittas* in protective rites in several places. Older canonical texts also mention the use of *parittas* in ceremonies; for example, the *Vinayapiṭaka* (Vin II 109–110), where the Buddha is said to have permitted the use of a protective chant to cure a snakebite. The canonical *Āṭānāṭiyasutta* is a protective *paritta*.[48] Indeed, it provides a list of protective spirits who can be invoked to protect the four great kings. The *Milindapañha* states the Buddha himself sanctioned the use of these protective texts (Mil 150, 27). In the *Devadhamma jātaka* there is a story of a *yakkha* (a type of spirit) that inhabits a pond. In the *Dhammapada-Aṭṭhakathā* there is a story in which the Buddha recommends the use of a protective mantra for monks who are afraid of tree spirits residing in the forest (DhpA III 6). In the *Palāsa*, *Gagga*, and *Ayakūṭa jātakas*, as DeCaroli notes, there are tree-dwelling spirits, a spirit whom a king employs as an efficient tax collector, and spirits who crave blood and alcohol offerings.[49] He also points out that in the *Aṅguttara nikāya* the Buddha recommends that people worried about the loss of political power offer gifts to the shrines of spirits.[50] In northern and northeastern Thailand manuscripts containing liturgies of protective chants were composed with much frequency for over four hundred years. Even in times of warfare and heavy taxation there were Pali and vernacular manuscripts being made when many other genres of Buddhist literature declined in production.[51]

The number of *parittas* in various collections varies widely, but they most often include the *Ratana, Mora, Khandha, Dhajagga,* and *Āṭānāṭiya suttas.* Palm-leaf manuscript collections often have Pali and vernacular sections, creative translations, and homiletic cues and asides. For example, I came across a manuscript from Wat Kumbhapradit in northeastern Thailand, most probably composed in the early nineteenth century, called the *Suat mon nissai (Bilingual Chanting Book)* written in Tham Isan script that is an anthology of protective *paritta* texts.[52] It contains nearly complete vernacular and Pali versions of the *Maṅgalasutta, Ratanasutta, Karaṇīyamettasutta, Khandhasutta, Morasutta,* and the *Dhajaggasutta.* Although the colophon does not provide much information on the provenance and dating of the manuscript, the scribe states that these *parittas* are useful for combating giants and other menacing denizens from nonhuman worlds.[53] The manuscript does not contain complete vernacular translations of the Pali *parittas* but simply vernacular verbal cues or trigger words to guide a preacher when leading the liturgy or giving a vernacular sermon explaining the *parittas* after the recitation. There are frequent reorderings of the Pali words and verses to fit the needs of the preacher and repetition of certain key terms that the preacher wanted to emphasize when explaining the text. These vernacular cues do not stick closely to the Pali text and demonstrate that the preacher felt he could creatively interpret and explain the Pali prayers. The Pali prayers served as a font of important and sacred terms that could be manipulated in a sermon and commentary.[54]*Parittas,* including these six, have been the subject of dozens of vernacular translations and commentaries produced in modern Thailand and Laos and are central to liturgical practice because they are often parts of funeral and other life-cycle ritual liturgies. The recitation of these *parittas* often begins with the chanting of the *Bot krap phra, Bot namo,* and *Itipiso,* as well as the *Tisaraṇa.* The process of anthologization, liturgicalization, and vernacular translation and commentary was idiosyncratic. In this manuscript, for example, the author emphasizes the power of the *Khandhasutta* to protect against poison and wild animals in the forest. While this is connected to the Pali commentarial tradition of the *Khandhasutta,* this local northeastern Thai manuscript makes particular reference to the ability of this *sutta* to protect wandering *Dhutaṅga* monks in the region.

Another early collection of protective liturgical prayers is found in an 1830 mulberry-paper manuscript composed in Chiang Mai (SRI manuscript #7902401E068). This manuscript, also entitled *Suat mon nissai,* varies significantly from the Wat Khumbhapradit manuscript. For example, it starts off with a long section praising the qualities of *arhats* who have crossed the "great ocean" and reached enlightenment, as well as the honoring of Indra (Sakka). Then begins the story of how the gods, Brahmans, and giants circling the world asked the Buddha about the nature of auspiciousness (as in the opening of the *Maṅgalasutta*) and listened to the *munivaravacanam* (the speech of the most excellent of wise men). Following that, there is an emphasis on how the words of the *paritta* protect the chanter from fire, poison, thieves, demons, drowning, ghosts, and the "diseases of the countryside." There are also long lists of animals, insects, and diseases that this *paritta* is effective against, rather like an advertisement printed on the side of a bottle of vitamins or headache medicine. The chanter should also concentrate on the qualities of the Buddha, *dhamma*, and sangha and the groups of Ten and Thirty perfections. It is not until the eighth page of the manuscript that the *Maṅgalasutta* is mentioned as a *paritta*. From here the author creatively translates selected words of the Pali *Maṅgalasutta* (often out of order, with vernacular synonyms and cognates, in an extremely repetitive fashion). These texts were also expanded upon orally in performance. This manuscript contains a different collection of *parittas* from the Wat Khumbhapradit *Suat mon nissai*, even though they have the same title. For example, the *Khandhasutta* is not included, but the *Aṅgulimālaparitta*, the *Bhojjhaṅga sutta*, and a chant containing "various verses" (*Pakiṇṇakagāthā*) are included. A local vernacular chant is included at the end of the manuscript that has no Pali equivalent (and may have been of the author's own creation).

None of this is strange given that there was very little regional standardization of chanting books before the rise of the printing press in the mid-nineteenth century. In fact, not only are there widely different collections of chants to be used at various public liturgies but collections of chants were often bound with other, medical (*tamra ya*), astrological (*horasat*), grammatical (*waiyakon*), and reward (*anisong*) manuscripts as well.[55] These lists of chants were a font of material that each ritualist could independently draw upon when conducting a liturgy.

## MODERN CHANTING BOOKS: FROM INTERNATIONALIZATION TO PARTICULARISM

There have been efforts to standardize modern liturgies. The first was an effort to internationalize or universalize the Thai liturgy and thereby create a pan-Theravadin liturgy. This began not with the meaning of the chants but with the actual letters used to write them. King Mongkut wanted to produce not only a standard Siamese/Thai liturgy but also a universal script for Pali.[56]

In approximately 1841 Mongkut invented the Ariyaka script. From my comparisons, it seems to be a radical adaptation of two scripts: Mon and Greek, which are two languages that the polyglot king studied as a monk and as a king with foreign missionary and with Thai experts.[57] Since King Mongkut was intensely interested in other forms of Theravada Buddhism in Sri Lanka, Burma (including the Mon), and Cambodia and was attempting to reform monastic discipline along what he believed were universal and "original" standards, he may have developed the script because the one factor that ties the Buddhisms of South and Southeast Asia is the Pali language. He spoke Pali. He invited Sri Lankan, Khmer, Mon, and Burmese monks to study at Wat Bovaranives (which even today has a large number of international monks in residence). The one factor inhibiting universal Theravada communication in Pali was the fact that each Theravada group used its own script for writing Pali. He devised the Ariyaka script to solve this problem. The monastery's own annals state that he wanted to spread the teachings of Buddhism and so he had "monastic codes of conduct" (pāṭimokkha), "some chanting books" (nangsue suat mon bang), and "other texts" printed in the Ariyaka script (akson ariyaka) in order to replace manuscripts. Actually, only four texts were ever printed in this script: Suat mon, Bhikkhu pāṭimokkha, Bhikkhunī pāṭimokkha, and the Dhammapada. What I want to emphasize here is that the first text printed in Ariyaka was a liturgical prayer book. This edition of the prayer book differs from many royal editions that were produced later, including the Royal Chanting Book (Nangsue suat mon chabap luang). First, there are only eight prayers in Mongkut's edition: Maṅgala, Ratana, Metta, Khandhaparitta, Dhajagga, Āṭānāṭiya, Āṭānāṭiya-parittaṃ-niṭṭhitaṃ, Bhojjhaṅga-parittaṃ-niṭṭhitaṃ. These are often called the Chet tamnān (Pali Sattaparitta, English Seven Protective Prayers) even though there are rarely exactly seven in the set. Second, King Mongkut did not include the widely popular Mora and Aṅgulimāla parittas, even though he included the other major parittas. Third, nearly every liturgical prayer book after Mongkut's is much longer and includes vernacular introductions, facing-page translations, and ritual guides. It seems that King Mongkut was trying to avoid the vernacular in his Ariyaka-script edition and include only parittas that were universally accepted (i.e., in Burma, Cambodia, and Sri Lanka) in order to create a standard Pali liturgy for the Theravāda Buddhist world. The Thai historian Prince Damrong, a grandson, admirer, and disseminator of King Mongkut's scholarship, also promoted this emerging Thai internationalism.[58] He wrote a short history of the paritta genre and consistently emphasized that the Thai practice of chanting protective paritta prayers was part of the larger Buddhist religion practiced in Sri Lanka, India, Cambodia, Laos, and Burma. He attempted to trace the origins of the Thai practice.[59]

This royally inspired trend did not continue. Later editions of liturgical chanting books abandoned this universalizing mission. They include, for example, a wide range of chants that are particular in many ways to the Thai liturgical tradition and not found in Sri Lanka, Laos, or Burma.[60] Moreover, they are in Thai script with Thai vernacular introductions, they were published on the occasion of funerals of important figures in Thai society, and they make no overtures to the idea of an international Theravada movement or school. Dozens of different Thai chanting books published in the twentieth and twenty-first centuries speak to a consistent diversity of approaches rather than a modern standardization and nationalization of religion. A few examples should suffice.

The first is from a satin-covered book called *Suat mon plae (Chanting Book Translated)*, a liturgy produced in honor of Khem Thanonkhon for his funeral in 1912. It was compiled by Phra Chaem Ariyamuni, who declares in his introduction that these chants are suitable for a wide range of "auspicious occasions" in "a home or at a monastery." This prelude, unlike the main *sutta*, has not remained consistent in Thailand. The prelude to this 1912 chanting book not only includes the *Chet tamnan* with the *Mora* and *Aṅgulimāla parittas* but also mentions the benefits of the *Maṅgalasutta* for blessing the worlds of humans, giants, gods, and Brahmans. Later editions of the *Maṅgalasutta*, like that included in the *Royal Chanting Book Translated (Suat mon chabap luang plae)* in 1991, remove this prelude and mention only the twelve-year argument between the gods concerning the nature of auspicious actions. This prelude is not included in the *Complete Edition of the Northern Thai Chanting Book (Suat mon muang nuea chabap sombun)*.

## FURTHER LITURGICAL CHANGES AND CONTINUITIES

In the second half of the twentieth century there was a great growth in idiosyncratic liturgical chanting books, for the most part editions published for funerals or temple festivals and amulet-production ceremonies. There are too many to list here. Some of these independent chanting books have seen multiple reprintings and are still widely available.[61] In any religious bookstore in Bangkok, Khon Kaen, Chiang Mai, or elsewhere one is struck by the variety. What is most notable about these modern books is their comprehensive approach. They include, of course, the expanded *Chet tamnan parittas*, the *Bot namo* and *Tisarana*, but this is just the beginning. They also include other prayers for a variety of occasions—funerals, for lighting and extinguishing candles, for granting the Five Precepts, and so on. One of the most popular ones is the 1999 (third) edition of the *Mon phithi samrap phra bhiksusamanen lae phutthasasanikachon thua pai* compiled by Phra Khru Arunthammarangsri (Iam Siriwanno) of Wat Arun Rachawararam in Bangkok (based on an earlier edition published at Wat Ratabamrung in Chonburi Province in 1991). It comes in two sizes and two versions, a pocket size and shelf size and a Pali version and a vernacular version. Novices are often seen holding the pocket-size edition during liturgies trying to memorize the Pali. Even though it is small in size, its eight-point font allows it to include 174 additional chants. Arathana (Pali *ārādhanā*) are a genre of "requests" from the sangha and announce ritual or liturgical acts. Dozens of these additions are modeled in many ways on the *anisong* blessing collections, which are short Pali and vernacular texts praising acts of merit like giving books, food, images to the sangha.

The manner in which these "catchall" liturgical books expanded is relatively easy to identify. Like the *Kham arathana phra parit* most expansions of chants are not completely original local additions but subtle extensions. Verses in the *parittas* are expanded, terms are elaborated, and titles of *suttas* are extended into multiple verses. One type of expansion in liturgical books published in the past forty years is the use of the terms *tham wat chao* and *tham wat yen* (morning and evening liturgies). This an attempt to standardize the daily liturgy of monks throughout the country, comparable to what Roman and Orthodox Catholics refer to as "matins" and "vespers." Well-known recitations are now grouped into these two ceremonies. There is a variety in these morning liturgies as well, though. Most often they include *Bot krap phra*, the *Bot namo*, and the *Itipiso*, but some books, like the *Nangsue suat mon* published at the famous Suan Mokkhaphalaram meditation center in Suratthani Province, southern Thailand, include the *Ratanattayapanāma gāthā* and *Saṁvegaparikittanapāṭha*. Others, like the mentioned *Mon phithi*, do not include these last two prayers but do have the *Gāthā phra moggallāna dap fai narok*, the *Taṅkhaṇikapaccavekkhaṇvithī*, and others. The variety is even greater in the evening liturgies. Some authors have efficiency and consistency as objectives, while others have comprehensiveness.

New liturgical books do not offer the novice, monk, nun, and layperson only a very large collection of Pali and vernacular chants (sometimes with facing-page translations, sometimes in two separate volumes). They also differ from their premodern antecedents by offering physical instructions, such as when and how to kneel upright or with one's legs folded to the side (*nang phap phiap*), when to genuflect (*wai*), to respond, to bow the head, to light candles, and to offer flowers. Some books go as far as to offer drawings of Buddhists bowing or kneeling in ideal positions.

Not only do new liturgical books provide physical instructions on how to sit, but some ritual manuals, which are related to chanting books in many ways, give detailed instructions on how to draw protective diagrams, tie sacred cord, make holy water, and so forth. The most comprehensive guide to these "magical" protective practices, often called *saiyasat* in Thai, is Thep Sarikabut's *Tamra phrawet phisadan*, a massive tome that provides a detailed liturgical guide to magical ceremonies replete with diagrams, instructions on making ritual implements, notes on the pronunciation of incantations, instructions for calling rain, magically unlock doors, invoke spirits, and so on. Here we see Sanskrit as well as Pali recitations mixed together and notes to the practitioner about the dangers of this dark science.[62] There are also many liturgical books connected to magically obtaining wealth. For example, Thotsaphon Changphanitkun has recently published *Kruang rang mahasetthi: Pucha laeo ruai* (*The Millionaire Amulets and Sacred Objects: Worship Them and Get Rich!*), a guide to chanting and the production of amulets, and *Katha mahasetthi: Suat laeo ruai* (*The Millionaire Incantations: Chant Them and Get Rich!*). The latter contains over one hundred Pali and Thai chants (including the *Jinapañjara*) that are designed to bring wealth.[63]

While many of these liturgical books present themselves as "standard"— namely, not emphasizing the specific monastery at which the liturgy was designed to be performed or the creative compilation efforts of a specific monk— some modern books are explicitly idiosyncratic. Premodern *paritta, pithi, chalong,* and other manuscripts used in liturgies were often highly specific to a particular monastery, teacher, or regional lineage. Printing presses and efficient distribution have partly muffled this cacophony of liturgical traditions, but certainly not silenced it. Not only are individual books published but also chanting books explicitly connected to particular monks and monasteries. The liturgical tradition connected to Somdet To illuminates this well. As we saw in chapter 2, these liturgies range from pocket-size laminated cards with the single signature protective *paritta* connected to him, the *Jinapañjara gāthā*, to large chanting books replete with his photographs, short biographies, *phra yan* (*yantra*) drawings, and CD/VCD/audio-tape inserts. The *Jinapañjara gāthā* (Thai *Phra khatha chinapanchon*) is commonly printed in central Thailand but is not included in published liturgies as part of a liturgical sequence or set (and not in the northern Thai editions or, as far as I have seen, in premodern manuscripts). Although it is easily found in many books, there are some idiosyncrasies unique to the Somdet To liturgical tradition. For example, the short chanting book *Yot phra kan traipidok ton chabap doem lae phra khatha chinapanchon* (*The Standard Edition of the Pinnacle of the Tripitaka and the Jinapañjara gāthā*) includes the chant to Kuan Im. This is directly connected to the elaborate Kuan Im shrine built at Wat Indrawihan in the late 1990s and to the fact that this monastery is patronized by a large number of Sino-Thai Buddhists (as are many central Thai monasteries). *The Explanation to the Chanting for Kuan Im* (*Kham chichaeng suat khatha phra mae Kuan Im*) is also included in this liturgy. It states that Kuan Im is a very important bodhisattva and that each chanter must first wash their hands (not a common request or custom in Thai liturgies), mentally invoke thoughts of gratitude for their mother and father (an explicit reference to filial piety), and move lit incense sticks in a circular motion (not a Thai Buddhist custom). The chant itself is a mixture of vernacular Thai, Pali, and Chinese. Following these recitations are additional ones not seen in other Thai liturgies but popular among the Sino-Thai population, like *Khatha bucha ngoen* (*Verses in Praise of Money*), *Khatha mahalap* (*Verses to Gain Great Luck*), *Khatha soem sap* (*Verses to Increase Wealth*), *Khatha to ayu* (*Verses to Increase Lifespan*), and the like. Other parts of the liturgy include minor recitations to accompany ritual actions, like *Khatha sek nam lang na pracham wan* (*Verses to Chant for Consecrating Water for Daily Face Washing*). Specific recitations, such as this last example, are directly attributed to certain Thai monks, like Luang Phu Suk, and another to Luang Pho Pan. Other editions are too numerous to mention.

Returning to Somdet To's signature prayer, the *Jinapañjara gāthā*, not only does this particular book include it but so also does every other book in Somdet To's liturgical book genre. Most include the Pali recitation, and many now also have the vernacular Thai translation. In addition to this, some liturgical books include instructions on how to chant the text with nine sticks of incense, nine lotus flowers, and so on. They emphasize that this prayer should be chanted on Thursdays (often associated with Somdet To). Other chants in numerous books include *Anisong* (Pali *Ānisaṃsa*) *Chinapanchon* (*Benefits That Come to the Person Who Chants the "Jinapañjara gāthā"*) and 121 *khatha khong Somdet To brahmarangsi* (121 *Verses Composed by Somdet To*). The latter is a protective *yantra* drawing. There are also accompanying Pali and vernacular prayers in praise of Somdet To himself—*Khatha bucha phra Somdet* (*Verses for Worshipping Somdet To*). In fact, not only is Somdet To made the object of recitations but two books in this genre that are commonly available in Bangkok also include recitations in praise of two other famous and now deceased Thai monks: Luang Pho Sot and Luang Pho Thuat. Although the *Chet tamnan*, *Bot namo*, and *Itipiso* are included in these liturgical books, modern Bangkok is not witness to a growing standardization and streamlining of liturgical chants, but exponential variety.

If liturgical books from central Thailand show a wide variation, an even greater diversity can be seen by traveling to monasteries throughout the country, since individual monasteries or small groups of monasteries produce their own versions of liturgical books. Some of these liturgical guides are printed and bound in a professional manner; others are handwritten and photocopied for consumption by students in the monasteries or regular local patrons. My abbot, Luang Pho Sombun, used one of these handwritten prayer books when he was teaching me in rural northeastern Thailand how to chant. He continued to use his notebook after new, printed chanting books were donated to the monastery. He was an avid proponent of chanting in the vernacular (in his case, southern Lao) as well as in Pali in order that the laity would understand some of the recitations. He also drew *phra yan* on homes, motorcycles, water buffalo, and married couples. He also blessed amulets. In these ceremonies, he chanted only in Pali. Other northeastern Thai and Lao monks I have resided with or interviewed have similar attitudes—vernacular and Pali prayers were equally acceptable for performance in morning and evening chanting sessions and for public rites such as funerals and weddings, but protective rituals were to be conducted solely in Pali. These Pali recitations are varied and may be either canonical or noncanonical.

There are published regional liturgical prayer books as well. The 1994 *Suat mon mueang nuea chabap sombun* (and the earlier version, 1976, *Suat mon mueang nuea*)[64] by Bunkhit Wacharasat, for example, is shorter than the expanded central Thai books but includes numerous chants not found in other regions.[65] For example, the ordination ceremonies (*kammavācā upasampadā* and *pabbajā*) are not included in many central Thai liturgical books and are found bound separately; however, they are the first sections of northern liturgical collections. Furthermore, the central Thai liturgies often do not include the *Ārādhanā* and *Kham thawai* series, which are found under separate title. The *Chet tamnan* and *Sipsong tamnan* (*paritta*) sections are much longer in the 1976 northern edition than in most central Thai editions. There are numerous chants specific to the northern tradition as well; for example, chants like the *Wantha luang*, the *Wantha luang baep haripunchai*, *Sagge luang*, the *Ahirājasuttapātho*, and the *Khatha kho fon* (*Verses for Calling the Rain*). Some of these are certainly known in central Thailand but do not have a prominent place in central liturgies or liturgical books.

In southern Thailand there are a series of regional liturgical prayer books linked to the lineage and following of Luang Pho Thuat. Like Somdet To in Bangkok, Thuat in the south, especially around Nakhon Sri Thammarat and Songkhla, has developed a great following after his death. Luang Pho Thuat has a special recitation, but there hasn't developed a set of particular chants or liturgical sequence directly associated with him. There is an *anisong* dedicated to him that speaks of the merit accrued when offering his image gifts. This is a region whose local liturgical traditions have yet to be explored. In recent interviews with monastic leaders in southern Thailand, Michael Jerryson has learned that there are local liturgical anthologies composed in the southern dialect. These are individually produced and handed down from teacher to teacher. The south has also seen a recent flurry of liturgical ceremonies and amulet distribution festivals at funerals for high-ranking government officials and monks. At these funerals, the extremely popular Jatukham Ramathep amulets are sold or distributed alongside liturgical guides and funerary volumes.[66]

In northeastern Thailand, there are the cults of Achan Man, Luang Phu Sao Kanthasilo, Luang Pho Faen Ancaro, and others. Moreover, the two lineages of Achan Mahabua in Sakon Nakhon and Luang Pho Khun in Nakhon Ratchasima have thousands of followers. However, while several monasteries like Wat Hin Mak Peng in Nongkhai have printed their own liturgical books, as far as I have seen there has not been the promotion of a specifically northeastern liturgy. It seems that many liturgies are taught the way my abbot taught me near the town of Khong Chiam (in the northeast)—through rote memory and handwritten notes specific to a teacher and lineage.[67]

There is also a diasporic liturgical tradition among Thai communities in the United States. I have visited dozens of Thai monasteries in Southern California, Ohio, Pennsylvania, Massachusetts, Washington, and Oregon. Many of these monasteries have produced their own editions of liturgical books in Thai and in English. These books are most often quite short, pamphlet-style books. The most common one is the *Pali Chanting with Translations* published and distributed by the Thammayut lineage at Wat Bovaranives in Bangkok beginning in 1993. I have seen this used at both Mahanikai and Thammayut lineage monasteries in the United States. It was translated into English from the Pali by Phra Khantipalo, who was guided by a number of Pali Text Society English translations. This set of chants is identical to the *Royal Chanting Book*; therefore, we may see the elite standardization envisioned (unsuccessfully) in Thailand actually taking root in the diaspora. However, if the Thai Buddhist immigrant follows in the path of the Vietnamese or Japanese, then there will soon develop an American form of Thai Buddhist liturgy replete with its own chanting styles, sequencing, and additions.

## BEYOND MANUSCRIPT AND BOOK: TECHNOLOGY AND AESTHETICS

There may be even more variety in Thai liturgies today than in the period before the printing press because of the large influx of refugees after the regional communist revolutions and American wars, especially Chinese, Lao, Khmer, and Vietnamese. This growth in liturgical prayers and lineages has recently been fueled by the use of audio and video recording and distribution, television, and the Internet. There are even chanting podcasts that can be downloaded to personal computers, MP3 players, and cell phones. In some CDs and VCDs there are shorter sets of chants (perhaps due to the 750 MB storage capacity of many CDs), like the audio recording of the *Banteuk sot suat phra parit*, which is limited to the *Chet tamnan*.[68] Another CD popular in Bangkok is the *Bot suat mon samrap chai nai ngan mongkhon tang tang*, which also has an English title printed on the cover, *Buddhist Auspicious Ceremony Prayer*.[69] In the introduction, a stern voice declares in Thai that this CD includes the "most auspicious mantras that are used at the most important rituals." This CD includes audio recordings of seventeen popular prayers, most found in the *Royal Chanting Book*, like the 12 *parittas*, the *Bot namo*, *Chumnum thewada*, but without the *Abhidhamma chet kamphi*, *Anumodanawithi*, and *Pakirnaka khatha*. The office of the *sangharat* of Thailand (officially the ecclesiastical head of all Thai monks) produces a CD called *Phra sut*, which has recordings of twenty-two well-known texts in a different order than in most chanting books. The limited data-storage capability of CD technology is not seen with the Internet. There a person can listen to and see a wide array of Thai liturgical traditions through streaming video, like those of the Dhammakaya lineage and at Khammathanna.com (sponsored by the Thammayut Nikai). There are dozens of other independent sites from Australia, the Unites States, and Thailand.

Even though there does not seem to be a growing standardization of liturgies with the use of electronic and digital cyber media, these changes in technology have brought other changes. With podcasting, CDs, and Internet access, largely urban, wealthy Buddhists in Thailand can accrue the perceived or actual benefits of protective chanting while sitting in traffic listening to a CD of chants with a *phra yan* hanging from their rearview mirror and a protective bumper sticker, or at home at their desks at 2:00 A.M. This may lead to a growing individualism and isolationism in practice. However, perhaps the online funeral homes and meditation chat rooms developed in South Korea will soon appear in Thailand. This may lead to new liturgical communities connected not by geography, blood, and language but by economic class and technical skill. It is too soon to tell.[70] Regardless, the competing forces of modernity and globalization cannot be said to lead to trends only in standardization in liturgical practice, as one may predict and the state-sponsored Thai sangha may plan. Individual agency, regional identity politics, self-reflection and self-improvement, cultural cross-fertilization, printing, and technological advancement balance the centralizing forces of modern nationalism and institutional efficiency.

Aesthetically, the look of a prayer book can also create a sense of traditional continuity or modern adaptation. Aesthetically, CDs, VCDs, DVDs, iPods, and so on look modern. They allow a modern practitioner to pray on the go and display her or his wealth and cosmopolitan lifestyle. However, there is also an aesthetic movement backward. Perhaps because of every religious tradition's obsession with authenticity, another change that has risen in the past twenty years is the publishing of chanting books in the style of premodern palm-leaf manuscripts or mulberry libretto manuscripts. These faux manuscripts are made out of cardboard and are shaped, folded, and open like old manuscripts. These are particularly popular in northern Thailand, where the use of old palm-leaf manuscripts by preachers is still common. One example is the *Suat thon muang neua*, which states in the introduction that it is particularly suited for house blessings (*pluk ban*), removing obstacles and curses (*thon khuet*), and removing parasites (*thon phayat*). It is an accordion or libretto book made with stiff yellow cardboard but printed using a computer. It copies the exact dimensions of a traditional palm-leaf manuscript, about twenty-two inches long and about three inches high, with twelve bi-folios (the exact size of most premodern single-fascicle manuscripts). There are many other northern and northeastern Thai texts like this. Here the form of a traditional text is used, but it is printed and distributed for mass consumption.

Aesthetically, despite the lack of standardization, there are familiar triggers and preludes in most Thai liturgies, like the *Bot namo* or the *Three Refuges*. Furthermore, most Thai liturgical spaces are similar. There is the ubiquitous red carpet in most modern *vihāras* (central image and liturgical halls); the windows, doors, color schemes, altar, not to mention the donation boxes, fans, and clocks, are all predictable. Moreover, the ritual implements, preaching chairs, yellow candles, incense sticks, and lotus flowers are amazingly consistent, often with just a few subtle changes to the untrained eye. All the monks must fold the robes in a certain manner, no one may wear shoes, and so on. Of course, art historians and ritual experts will always note the differences in the style of the images, the murals, the carvings, the mother-of-pearl, but for most audience members, liturgical spaces in Thailand are standardized spaces. These spaces and these well-known liturgical preludes subtly reinforce the value of tradition and the safety of consistency, but within this safe space, teachers can just as subtly add their own favorite chants and their own creative explanations and translations of those liturgical choices.[71]

## EXPANDING THE THAI BUDDHIST REPERTOIRE

Any visitor to Thailand will undoubtedly pass dozens of shrines on street corners, at bus stations, and on monastic grounds to supposedly non-Buddhist deities.

Besides the shrines to Thai royalty and national heroes, there are shrines to Hindu deities like Ganesha, Brahma, Shiva, Indra, and the uniquely Thai Jatukham Ramathep. This is not a new phenomenon; there are shrines and images dedicated to these deities found in the earliest Thai kingdoms. Perhaps the most popular shrine is that of the famous Than Thao Mahaphrom (referred to in English as the Erawan Shrine, a shrine around a golden statue of a four-faced Brahma image cast in 1956 on one of the busiest corners in Bangkok in front of what is now the Grand Hyatt Erawan Hotel and across from the Central World Plaza Mall, national police headquarters, and Gaysorn Plaza Mall).[72] This shrine to a Hindu god is so beloved by the people of Thailand that the foundation that administers it took in 1.5 million dollars in 2004 alone from donations. A mentally disturbed man (or at least that is one of the rumors) was beaten to death by a crowd when he attacked the image with a sledgehammer in 2006. The former prime minister Thaksin Shinawatra was rumored to have prayed to the image and performed secret magical rituals to ensure his shaky political fortunes in 2006 right before he was forcibly removed from office by a political movement led in part by Sondhi Limthongkul. This shrine competes with prestige in the country with royally consecrated Buddha images and receives more visitors daily than nearly any other ritual site in the country. This is not a mere aberration or passing fancy. Unique rituals and liturgies, including the frequent performance of classical female dancers, Sanskritized Thai chants, and the offering of yellow carnations and wooden elephants, have sprung up at the shrine.

This shrine connected to the Thai tradition of building *san phra phum* (spirit houses) on the grounds of homes and businesses to provide domiciles for land spirits displaced by human structures has spawned the creation of dozens of copycat shrines throughout the country. Clearly, these ceremonies have not "worked" in most cases, because politicians like Thaksin have lost power and Sondhi has been targeted for assassination (although the fact that he survived a daring assassination attempt might actually "prove," for many, the power of his magic).[73] The reasons these different political groups and leaders keep performing the rituals are numerous. They involve increasing their social prestige, their cultural capital, and outperforming one another in front of television camera crews. However, the reason these performances are so effective (they attract and enthrall thousands of their respective supporters) is that they draw on common features of the Thai religious repertoire. Politicians need to perform these rituals, because they are expected to. It would be like a U.S. presidential candidate not having the pancake breakfast during the Iowa primaries, or a president not throwing the first pitch for the annual Washington Nationals baseball team's home opener. It comes with the job.

The use of ritual to ensure political good fortune is not limited, of course, to Thaksin. His political opponents, represented beginning in 2007 by the PAD (People's Alliance for Democracy) party led by Sondhi Limthongkul, have performed rituals to guarantee their political goals. After a series of bloody street battles between PAD supporters and the government in Bangkok in the fall of 2008, Sondhi led two rituals. The first was a circumambulation of the government house grounds with him dressed in white sprinkling holy water and chanting. He called this a *dhamma* walk.[74] On the second occasion he stated that

> for many years in the past, the powers of many sacred things including the spirit of the City Pillar, the Equestrian Statue of King Rama V, Phra Sayam Thewathirat, and the Emerald Buddha, have been suppressed by evil people using magic. "Suppress" does not mean destroy, because sacred objects cannot be destroyed, as they have too much power. But "suppress" means not allowing them to emit their power, by encircling them. This is true . . . Like at the statue of the Emerald Buddha . . . Behind it there is a stone. Evil-minded people had allied with some in the Royal Household Bureau to allow a Khmer adept to go behind the Emerald Buddha and take the stone away, because that stone is the important thing for emitting power . . . Tacks had been inserted at the six corners [of the statue of King Rama V] so that the statue of the revered king could not emit its power. We drew out the tacks from all six places.[75]

A well-known historian and journalist noted that Sondhi openly accused Thaksin of being behind the destruction of the Erawan Brahma statue in March 2006. Sondhi said Thaksin "wished to thwart political forces rising up against him."

Five of the most blatant attempts to cash in on the popularity of the Erawan Shrine are shrines to the god Narayana (riding the mythical bird Garuda), the green goddess Laksmi, whose statue is on the fourth floor of the ultramodern high-end Gaysorn Plaza shopping complex, the elephant-headed god Ganesha, the triple god Trimurti, and the god (also green) Indra, all built within a fifteen-hundred-foot circumference. In front of the Intercontinental Hotel, the Central World Plaza Mall and Cinema Complex, the Amarin Plaza, and the Gaysorn Plaza, respectively. One is a shrine to the Hindu deity Trimurti (a statue that represents three major deities in Hinduism, Brahma, Shiva, and Vishnu, apparently competing with the Erawan Shrine representing only Brahma across the street and the nearby shrine to the god Indra). It was established in front of the Zen Department Store in the Central World Plaza originally but then moved because of construction a thousand feet down the sidewalk and now sits next to the Ganesha image. The Trimurti platform and image measures over twenty-five feet high and is surrounded by a moat as well as by incense and flower holders and donation boxes.

The Narayana, Indra, Lakshmi, Erawan, and Ganesha shrines are particularly popular with those aspiring to become wealthy, which would make them particularly appropriate, since they are in front of Thailand's most expensive shopping malls and hotels. The Trimurti has a unique following, because it is popular with women especially on St. Valentine's Day. St. Valentine's Day, like Christmas, has become widely celebrated in Thailand despite its "Christian" origins. On February 14, 2008, I visited the shrine to make an offering and observed hundreds of young Thai women offering long-stemmed red roses (another imported tradition), red incense sticks, and red candles (the traditional three offerings to a Buddha image, colored red in honor of St. Valentine) to the shrine. There was even a newly composed liturgy that the women read from handouts as they knelt in front of the shrine holding their roses and hoping to find love. The liturgy consists of one short Pali benediction (*Sādhu sādhu sādhu ukāsa*, "Praise, praise, praise exaltation!") and then a short Thai verse, which mentions only the fact that the Trimurti is a great deity but states nothing about his powers to help worshippers find love or companionship.[76] Despite the intention and the meaning of the chant having no relation, clearly this shrine drew a very specific group, young women. One woman I spoke with said she was confident that despite not having a boyfriend, her offering would ensure she met the love of her life that very evening. Even though the Trimurti image is actually based on a statue from the sixteenth century in Ayutthaya, it has not been a particularly popular image in the history of Thai religions. Since a few urban legends claim that young women who knelt down to the shrine when it was cast in 2004 met the men of their dreams, it has become to be associated with luck in love. The Trimurti in South Asia and in Ayutthaya were never associated with this specific type of blessing as far as I have been able to find.

Next to the Trimurti is the Ganesha shrine. Ganesha (Thai Phra Phi Kanet) has long been a deity known throughout Southeast Asia, generally associated with the arts and learning. However, there has been a recent massive growth in the popularity of Ganesha images, shrines, amulets, and liturgies. Ganesha amulets and images are sold ("rented") throughout the country, especially at Wat Phra That Cho Hae in Phrae Province, Wat Trimit in Bangkok, and at Somdet To's former monastery, Wat Indrawihan. There are shrines at the Brahmanic training school (Thewasathan Bot Phrahm) in Bangkok, Phraratcha Wang Sanam Chan Palace in Nakhon Pathom Province, murals of Ganesha at Wat Suthat in Bangkok, and an entire museum dedicated to Ganesha images and history in Chiang Mai. A very specific liturgy and ritual have been developed for Ganesha recently thanks primarily to the work of a Brahman ritualist named Thotsaphon Changphanitkun, who is associated with Wat Umathewi (popularly known as Wat Khaek), a Hindu temple on Silom Road in downtown Bangkok. Every year (since 2004) he has held a massive festival in honor of Ganesha and sells amulets, images, posters, plastic dolls, umbrellas, bumper stickers, and the like.[77] The appropriate times to worship Ganesha, Thotsaphon claims, are on the ninth or fourteenth of the month, between February and July, but never on Tuesdays. On those days, the worshipper should not eat meat and offer fruit of various sorts (especially bananas), milk, oyster sauce, and steamed rice sweets. While offering these gifts to an image of Ganesha, one should chant a Sanskritized Pali (with some vernacular Thai words as well) chant that begins with the word "om" but otherwise follows the vocabulary and phrases common in Buddhist Pali chants in Thailand, with the insertion of the name Ganesha in the middle of a chant that could easily be in honor of the Buddha. The chant is only three verses long and is a very simplistic series of honorifics. For example, the last verse reads in Pali phrasing using some vernacular Thai phonetic conventions "Tatiyampi phra phi ghanesavara sabbasiddhi bra siddhi me mahālābho bhavantu me" (For the third time, O venerable Ganesha, you are forever powerful, may you grant me success, great wealth, and possessions). After chanting this one should light an oil lamp and a stick of incense, think of the wish to be granted, concentrate deeply, and place the incense with the right hand along with a bottle of lamp oil and other gifts at the feet of the shrine. Other chants to Ganesha have also been composed by Thotsaphon that have similar syntax and meaning. They are all very short and easy to read or memorize by visitors to various shrines. Ganesha has also gained notoriety because of celebrity endorsements and stories of the great success and wealth that have followed their worship of Ganesha. These include the famous singer and actress Aphaphon Nakhonsawan, as well as the action-movie actors Anucha Tosawat and Pokon Phonphisut.

Like Somdet To and Mae Nak, Ganesha, Trimurti, Jatukham Ramathep, and others have become important due partially to testimonials of famous and successful celebrities who have been saved, enriched, or fallen in love because of being associated with them, performing their liturgies, holding their amulets, performing rituals in front of their shrines, and the like. The power of Somdet To (and in some cases Mae Nak) is seemingly more authentic to some because they were actual historical figures who lived in Thailand. However, what does not seem important to most people is whether they are associated with Hinduism or Buddhism. In fact, the casting of Ganesha images and amulets is ritually supervised and performed by Buddhist monks at Buddhist monasteries like Wat Phikhunthong in Singburi Province, Wat Mahathat in Nakhon Sri Thammarat, as well as at other monasteries in Phukhet, Lad Phrao (Bangkok), and Chonburi. One of the largest casting and consecrations (*phithi pluk sek*) of Ganesha images in Thai history took place at Wat Pak Nam under the supervision of the popular Buddhist monk Luang Pho Ke on December 13, 2007.[78] The large shrine in front of the Central World Plaza and next to the Trimurti "love" shrine has begun to develop its own following and has its own liturgy.[79] This is not necessarily a sign of the decline of Buddhism or the rise in Hinduism in Thailand; it simply reflects a general lack of concern with religious boundaries and a valuing of abundance and security. Ganesha is said to protect those with money and help those without it get it.[80]

As this book was going to press, the massive Red Shirt protests of spring 2010 were taking over a number of intersections in Bangkok. The center of these protests was at the Ratchaprasong intersection in front of the Central World Plaza, Gaysorn Plaza, and the Ganesha, Erawan, Trimurti, and other Hindu shrines just mentioned. These protests shut down the main high-end shopping district of Bangkok. When the government forces made their final push to expel the protesters, many took refuge in Wat Pathumwanaram, one of the monasteries most closely associated with Somdet To and discussed in the next chapter. Six of these protesters were shot, supposedly by government snipers stationed on the elevated train platform above the monastery. The monastery itself did not, however, physically suffer any damage. Other protestors torched the Central World Plaza and nearly burned down the entire complex. Photographs of these protests were displayed in newspapers, blogs, and televisions across the globe.[81] What is important for our purposes here is that only the building in front of which there were no Hindu shrines burned down. The neighboring shopping complexes and high-rises were spared from the fire. Rumors in blogs, chat rooms, and on the streets have abounded that the reason these buildings were protected was because of the shrines. In front of the Central World Plaza was simply a garish statue recently erected representing Thai-Indian friendship. It had not garnered a following of worshippers and was not consecrated as a sacred space.[82] Without protection by the deities, the building was destroyed. Stories like this increase the associative fame of these images even in the middle of tragedy.

## CONCLUSION

Most Thai Buddhists have never, it seems, had a problem developing their own novel liturgies or rituals, nor have they stopped questioning the efficacy of liturgy, meditation, ritual, and analysis. These idiosyncratic repertoires incorporate a number of wider cultural tools, tropes, lexicons, and images but are not corralled by an orthodoxic or orthopraxic standard. Indeed, Thai Buddhism could be classified as a religion highly, although not explicitly, resistant to orthodoxic and centralizing tendencies, even though it presents itself (and has been so designated by foreign scholars) as normative, traditional, and exceedingly well behaved.

The competing forces of standardization and expansion in Thai liturgical and ritual practice have not been pacified because of modern state institutional reform of Buddhism. In fact, the central authorities themselves are diverse. When we scholars talk about the state in relation to Thai Buddhism, to what are we referring? Do we mean the Department of Religious Affairs, the *sangharat's* office, the Mahatherasamakhom (the ecclesiastical council of the entire Thai sangha), the royal family and the Privy Council, the liberal Buddhist Foundation of Thailand, the higher ecclesia of the Mahanikai or Thammayut Nikai lineages, the prime minister's office, or the military? Before we begin a major study of liturgy and ritual in Thai Buddhism, we need to ask whether anyone gains economically or politically from having a particular liturgy or ritual organized in a particular way. However, we do not need to be narrowly deterministic. Orthodoxy is a process. Every time it is established, the unorthodox exceptions are highlighted. If one Thai author asserts that his liturgical text or ritual sequence is standard or one king declares the reform of a particular ritual sequence, then other authors rise up to suggest alternatives, or the heterodox liturgies are shown in high relief. The introductions to numerous liturgical books in modern Thailand contain statements emphasizing their correctness and comprehensiveness. The more technology allows for the production of new liturgies and rituals, the more people will claim that their liturgy is original, authentic, and orthodox in the economy of cultural authenticity. There is rarely one overarching agenda in the process of creating or maintaining a ritual or liturgy. Most histories of Thai Buddhism have been written either as histories of reform or as histories of resistance. To document the history of liturgies and rituals is to investigate a history of ambivalence—it is to study the texts and textual practices that document the anxieties persisting between tradition and modernity, reform and resistance, the vernacular and classical.

These competing forces in modern Thailand—centralization and standardization versus expansion and creativity—are not necessarily something that needs to be resolved by the scholar. Indeed, I do not believe that they can be. They show that it is not possible to classify elite reformers as interested only in predictability, modernization, efficiency, and control and local teachers as idiosyncratic, haphazard, and rebellious. People have the ability to negotiate different concepts and simultaneously keep contradictory thoughts in their heads.

Michael Foster has seen the acceptance of this combination of heterogeneous discourses and practices as returning agency to the people that the historian studies.[83] Liturgies and rituals are the place where these heterogeneous "tactics" are witnessed in modern Thai Buddhism. This is where each teacher can creatively combine and deploy the classical and the vernacular, the translocal and the local, the esoteric and familiar to impress, instruct, pacify, or manipulate his or her audience. As for the audience members, they can alternatively use the liturgies and rituals to protect their bank accounts, settle their anxious minds, fulfill familial obligations, realize enlightenment, impress their neighbors, assuage their guilt, relax, or protect themselves from being hit by a bus.

One of the statues of the fifty-three *bhikkhuni* (fully ordained nuns) at Wat Thepdhitaram (Bangkok). These are the only known statues of *bhikkhuni* in Thailand.

Sticker of Somdet To on a motorcycle. It serves as both decoration and, the owner hopes, protection.

Man examining a small Buddhist amulet with a jeweler's loop in an amulet market.

Large statue of the Buddha (named Phra Phuttha Mahamuni Srimaharat), originally built under the instructions of Somdet To in the 1850s at Wat Kutithong (rural Ayutthaya Province). Children enjoy visiting this statue because of the machine that shoots water from two small canons onto the statue. The *Jinapañjara gāthā* is inscribed at the base of the statue.

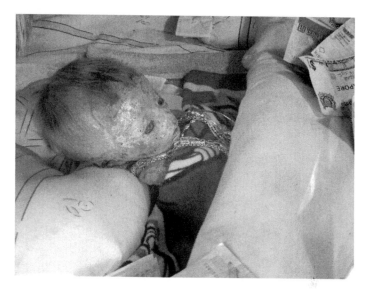

Desiccated corpse of Baby Ae (Dek Sirirot) in a glass coffin at Wat Mahabut (Bangkok). The corpse is dressed in pajamas and receives offerings of toys, candy, and cash.

Small, plastic statues of female spirits, including a Mattel Barbie doll dressed in traditional Thai clothing, on a shrine in front of a tree. A powerful female tree spirit is said to reside in the tree, which is found on the grounds of Wat Kaeo Fa (Nonthaburi Province).

A monk presents a protective female image soaked in corpse oil (*nam man phrai*) used to both repel bad luck and sexually attract women to the possessor.

Section of a mural painting from Wat Rakhang Ghositaram depicting a scene from one of the Buddhist hells. While many other mural paintings of various realms of hell depict mythological creatures and extremely gruesome torture techniques, this scene is more realistic and depicts both hell and the Siamese enslavement by the Burmese after the burning of Ayutthaya in 1767. Wat Rakhang was built soon after the fall of Ayutthaya and was the location of the first post-Ayutthayan Siamese royal residence in the Thonburi/Bangkok area. Most of the murals at Wat Rakhang contain a mixture of the cosmological and the historical.

A monk reading an amulet-collector's magazine in an amulet market.

An artist inscribes a dedicatory name and date on a newly made Buddha statue. New images like this are made to order by the hundreds every day in Thailand. Although one image might look identical to hundreds of others, the inscription, the relics placed inside it, and the relationships it has with other images it is arranged with are often quite different from any other image.

A group of novices from Pichit Province visit Wat Rong Khun in Chiang Rai Province. They walk over a pit representing hell into a heavenly, new monastery. This monastery was recently constructed and is the creation of the modern artist Chalermchai Kositpipat.

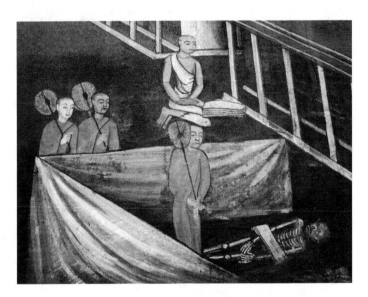

Mural in the *ubosot* of Wat Sommanat in Bangkok depicting monks performing a funerary rite. A manuscript, most likely of the *Abhidhamma chet kamphi*, is placed on a skeleton.

The best fixative is "Bedacryl 122 x" made by the Imperial Chemical Industries Ltd. of London represented in Thailand by the East Asiatic Co. Ltd.

—SILPA BHIRASRI, "Art and Religion" (1963)

# 4. Art and Objects

Silpa Bhirasri was born Corrado Feroci in Florence in 1892. He moved to Thailand in 1923. This Italian national ended up becoming a Thai citizen in 1944, adopting a Thai name, and having a state funeral in 1962. He is a national hero in Thailand. He founded and directed the first professional art school and eventually the first university dedicated to the arts in Thailand. He is considered the father of Thai art. He designed many of the prominent statues of the royal family and a number of important Buddhist and national monuments. He believed that traditional Buddhist arts in Thailand, like murals and images, must be preserved with Imperial Chemical's Bedacryl 122 x and other solutions, as well as being protected from rain, rubbing, adhesives, and touching. He wanted to ensure that the love of traditional art be, as he stated, "imparted to our young people," because "the old Thai living a simple natural life had a pure, naïve mind, spiritually supported by Buddhism . . . Nowadays the wants of material life are coupled with dominating dynamism . . . the old kind of spiritual work is no longer possible. In our days the making of images of the Buddha has become of commercial enterprise . . . in such cases the word 'art' becomes meaningless."[1]

Silpa Bhirasri's comments certainly can be considered condescending and positivist, and as products of the time. The field of art history has changed quite dramatically over the past twenty years. Many have moved beyond studies of stylistic development and an obsession with dating and identifying influences. Still, outdated as his sentiments seem, they appear to reflect much current thinking of scholars and social critics. On the one hand, curators and art historians like Stratton, Gosling, Ringis see art as something "traditional," "timeless," and "sublime."[2] It needs to be preserved and documented because of its beauty or because it corroborates something a scholar is trying to fix historically. These studies are informative and documentary. On the other hand, art at best is seen by many modern Thai (and many Western liberal Buddhist) ethicists and social critics as something symbolic but ultimately unnecessary for Buddhist practice. At worst, it causes attachment and is a product of elite propaganda, commercialism, and materialism. Art is valued as something beautiful and as evidence of a great tradition, or it is an arbitrary tool of the spiritually weak. I want to move beyond this dichotomy, draw on new developments in the study of art history, and look at less commonly studied art in Thai Buddhism.

Until this chapter, I have avoided any discussion of the objects that reside at Thai Buddhist monasteries. This has been difficult because Thai Buddhist repertoires are, in large part, material and sensual. The followers (or perhaps fan base) of Somdet To and Mae Nak, like many other Thai Buddhist fan bases, are sustained and characterized by their collection, production, and trading of stuff—amulets, images, posters, protective drawings, CDs, calendars, films, comic books, and even pillow cases, umbrellas, and coffee mugs. Aspirations are interconnected with objects. Beliefs are articulated through objects. Objects are not empty signifiers onto which meaning is placed. The fan base and the objects, the collectors and their stuff are overlooked in the study of religion, even in many studies in the growing field of material culture and religion.

What is striking is that these objects of everyday religiosity are often overlooked by art historians as well.[3] Certainly it can be argued that images of the Buddha, Brahmanic deities, ghosts, and other altar occupants in Thailand are not objets d'art. They are, as Pattaratorn Chirapravati has stated, sacred objects (*khong saksit* or *khong namasakhan*). Moreover, the dolls, clothes, small statues of Nang Kwaek, and various *kuman thong* are gifts for the main image (*krung bon* or *krung sen*). They are to be enjoyed by the Buddha, Somdet To, Mae Nak, or whatever is considered the main image. They are for the images, not for us.[4] The problem is that these images are often removed (through photography or physical movement to museums or shops) from this ritual context and are seen as objets d'art. Moreover, the gifts in front of the images have rarely been documented by art historians of Thailand. Photographs of images of the Buddha and others are alone on pedestals in exhibition catalogs. This problem is exacerbated in the case of amulets because of the traditional mobility of the amulet's ritual context. Amulets are often worn around a person's neck but are also often put on display in galleries and in catalogs. They are appreciated for their craftsmanship as well as for their protective power. They are objects of beauty, talismans, and commodities, depending on whose hands they are in at a particular time and place. Many Western art historians are not adequately trained in either Pali or even the Thai language. On the other hand, students of Buddhist studies are generally woefully trained in art history and material culture. While art historians influenced by Alfred Gell, Arjun Appadurai, and Daniel Miller have brought the study of ritual objects into the forefront of art historical studies, in terms of methodologies of studying Buddhist art, art historians have generally relegated themselves to the study of either the old and valuable or the static and the curated.[5] Southeast Asian Buddhist studies specialists have rarely made more than a passing reference to the art that resides in monasteries, treating it as mere window dressing distracting one's attention away from more important matters such as ethics, history, rituals, and texts. It is about time that scholars of Southeast Asian Buddhist studies pay attention to what Kaja McGowen has called the "fluid interstices of time-worn activities" and the "propinquity of things."[6] How have human activities in monasteries been constituted by the centripetal and centrifugal pulls of the things that accumulate around them? We need to bring art into the study of Buddhist practice and start practicing a new study of art.

First, I look to bring a discussion of art into the study of living Thai Buddhism. Art historians who work in Southeast Asia have concentrated primarily on the study of images, stupas, manuscripts, and murals produced by the elite and made mainly before the twentieth century. The field of Southeast Asian Buddhist art is changing, with greater attention being paid to art produced outside elite courts, but these changes are coming slowly. Therefore, I concentrate here on vernacular art made in the past one hundred fifty years. However, I want to move beyond this simple "filling-in-the-gaps" approach. I can lament what most art historians have ignored, but that is of limited use. I am attempting instead to alter the frame in which amulets and "religious" art are conceived and concentrating on the manifold relationships and associations objects have. In this study, it is more productive to avoid any dichotomy of folk/popular/low/vernacular art versus high/sophisticated/classical art. While certain images in Thai Buddhism are lauded for their age or precious materials, most are honored for their connection to certain powerful monks, their relics, their power to heal, or their power to protect. Many of these highly revered and powerful images are made of resin or wood, crudely and mass-produced bronze, plastic, copper, resin, or clay. Moreover, these images demand response and reaction. Patrons do not merely look at or prostrate before images; they affix gold, insert relics, draw holy water, request audiences, as well as comfort images with robes, pillows, food, and flowers. The accretion that takes place on altars or on walls is often moved to the side by art historians to get a better look at the original murals, images, and lintels underneath. I emphasize that sifting through the pile of stuff that accumulates around or on major images and murals reveals a history of response that can tell one more about a piece of art than the name of the artist or the style of the period. The main images have been studied and the ancillary images have been generally looked over, but the main images have become magnets that attract other images, and these other images may take on value of their own over time. However, the value is in their association with other images and with the people who both gave them and who over time give to them. I am particularly interested in these objects that have grown dense with associations.

Second, I, like Gregory Levine, write "against nostalgia and its art historical inflections, including fixation on moments of production and praise of masterpieces frozen, like wooly mammoths, in the past."[7] Instead of concentrating on the origins of pieces of art (which in some cases I mention), I want to study art as it exists and operates in dynamic ritual activities and highly complex synchronic relationships. Each piece is studied not in isolation for stylistic features, age, flaws, and material composition but in relationship with other objects in the room or on the monastic campus. As in Martin Holbraad's recent work on Cuban ritual objects, I want to move beyond aesthetic and iconographic analyses of individual objects and focus on recipients, rituals, and agents, as well as on the agency of the things themselves.[8] In a monastic setting objects take on increased agency in a sense because they are not owned by any one person. They are a possession of the sangha in general but are made and presented by the laity. Moreover, they are often believed to be inhabited by different spirits. There are no official curators, docents, conservators, patrons, trustees, consulting scholars, and the like assigned to monastic objects. Indeed, often there are stories of particular Thai Buddha images that state that the image chose a particular monastery in which to reside, or that a particular monastery was built specifically to house an image.[9] As is often the case with images of Hindu deities, Buddha images are often given particular personal names, bathed, and dressed. Other images are supposedly happy with only particular kinds of gifts. For example, a Buddha image in Chonburi Province is said to like boiled duck eggs, while others are fond of flowers of a particular color. There are relationships between certain murals, images, amulets, ritual implements, and architectural forms. Moreover, there are relationships between pieces of art and the community of traders, merchants, fans, nuns, monks, astrologers, and children in the monastic neighborhood. For example, at Wat Mahabut, the folding tables of the astrologers, the images of Kuan Im (Avalokiteśvara), the amulet collections, the local high school soccer mascot, smiling Buddha images, and the images of Mae Nak all depend on one another. While a museum display might accentuate the beauty, material, and craftsmanship of a single image, the image is ritually powerful only when lost among a forest of other images from which it draws concomitant associative power. Certainly a person might not be able to see a single image as well when it shares space with many other images, incense sticks, candles, and the like. However, as Daniel Miller has noted, some images are important for the simple fact that they are not isolated and seen individually. They are important because we "do not 'see' them. The less we are aware of them, the more powerfully they can determine our expectations by setting the scene and ensuring normative behavior, without being open to challenge. They determine what takes place to the extent that we are unconscious of their capacity to do so."[10] Therefore, instead of studying images individually as symbols of Buddhist virtues, as vehicles of meaning, or representative of certain stylistic developments, I am interested in how images participate in the social construction of reality—how they, in a sense, encourage certain behaviors. I look at the way objects promote new developments in practice, create new lineages, and cultivate new histories.

Third, I argue that images, photographs, murals, amulets, and buildings do not exist only in synchronic relationships but also diachronically. Images can produce other images, amulets, and holy water. Indeed, many images and amulets can be called offspring of older images. New images, sometimes mass-produced by the thousands, are consecrated through a ritual in which they are all tied together by a white string that is bound to both the older main image in a monastery and to monks and laypeople chanting. According to many people I interviewed at these ceremonies, the collective energy in the room enables the "birthing rites" of new images or amulets.[11] Photographs can produce murals and murals can produce photographs. Images can create, legitimize, and even usurp monastic lineages through uses of material, decoration, and positioning or staging. These shrines, images, and amulets are connected to certain highly local agendas that operate independently of state control, manipulation, or support. Somdet To and Mae Nak are two particularly good but certainly not unique examples. Images, monasteries, and amulets are not stable places. Monasteries and amulet markets are constantly changing and expanding. Images and shrines are always changing. This morphology tells us much about the ways Thai Buddhism stays relevant in the lives of an increasingly cosmopolitan and urbanized society.

It is striking that the monks in the Theravada school of Buddhism, known for their orthodox attention to the Vinaya, eschewal of material luxury, and austerity of monastic practice, dress, and comportment, are also the purveyors and stewards of some of the most lavish (if not gaudy) monasteries in the Buddhist world. There is hardly a monastery, even a forest monastery, in Thailand that could be called aesthetically austere. There are gold images, flowers, incense, posters, amulets, intricate murals, packed altars, signs nailed to trees with ethical maxims and advertisements, and large amounts of food, reading material, and paraphernalia found at thousands of Thai monasteries. Monks are neither hapless victims of the crude materialism of modern Thai society nor the overwhelmed recipients of the arbitrary gifts of overzealous merit makers too lazy or ignorant to meditate or read ethical and philosophical texts. Monks often promote, encourage, and explicitly advertise occasions to not only give gifts to their monasteries but also distribute objects to their fans. This chapter therefore attempts to talk about Buddhist material and artistic culture without simply lamenting modern Thai commercializing of religion, the creation of an "occult economy," or the materialistic corruption of spirituality.[12]

Finally, I show that there needs to be a historical and material turn in the study of images, amulets, and murals in Thai monasteries and shrines. So often the turn toward history in the study of Thai art is the turn toward Indic and Buddhist/Hindu history over local history. "Such a view," as Donald Lopez has noted, "could be construed as a transhistorical and self-identified essence that had benevolently descended on various cultures over the course of history, its instantiations, however, always imperfect."[13] Certainly, one must be grounded in Indology when studying Thai art (a solid knowledge of Chinese art would help as well). However, it is local history that is valued over Indian connections. Especially when studying amulets, the histories that contribute to our understanding are those that explain why certain amulets are valuable and others worthless, why some are believed to cure diseases and protect businesses and some are merely decoration; these are the histories of local lineages, local techniques, and local rituals. Indology and Indian history are of little help when admiring an amulet hanging around the neck of a Thai Buddhist. However, local historical study is required to understand local value.

Documenting the way people see Buddhist art in monasteries and monastery museums is impossible in a textual description or in a book of photographic images of statues and murals. Monastic art exists in a social and ritual atmosphere. Monasteries are places where one sees the way ritual, leisure, and an appreciation of heritage and abundance interact. Buddhist monasteries, and local Buddhist museums, are places where there is little effort made to control visitors or control the flow of information. There are usually no entrance fees (except occasional fees for foreigners), no guides, multiple entries and exits, and very few plaques or signs. Shrines and objects are scattered throughout the monastic grounds; there are occasionally places to sit and eat, play cards, buy lottery tickets, and so forth. Most monasteries and monastery museums are not somber places where monks strictly enforce particular ways of performing rituals. Even during sermons and liturgical chanting, people can be seen chatting in the corner, wandering around the grounds, talking on cell phones, eating, and flirting. Children are rarely corralled, and commerce abounds. Some certainly go to meditate (if they can find the space and silence), offer gifts, listen to sermons, or get advice from monks; however, there is much more "going on," and people are largely free to ignore rituals and images, or see them and prostrate to them on their own schedule. These are not places of forced spirituality, ethical directives, or detached repose.[14]

## MISPLACED PIETY: IMAGES AT WAT MAHABUT, WAT SRAPATHUM, AND BEYOND[15]

The first formal Thai taxonomy of images was most likely written by Paramanuchit Chinorot, who described and represented forty different postures of the Buddha in an illustrated companion manuscript to the well-known biography of the Buddha, the *Pathama sambodhikathā*.[16] These forty *pang* have formed a type of template for artists since the 1830s; however, they are not a prescription, and artists have certainly expressed individual creativity since. These poses, like "walking," "subduing Mara," "calling for rain," "great departure," and the lesser-known "floating the platter on the river," "stopping disease," "accepting an offering of a mango," and "pointing to a corpse," have been the subject of a number of studies.[17]

Thai scholars in particular have also traced the movement, relics, and politics of famous Buddha images like the Emerald Buddha, the Phra Phuttha Chinarat, Phra Khanthanrat, Phra Phuttha Nimitwichitmaramoli, Phra Phuttha Sihing, and Phra Sasada. Local abbots, devotees, kings, and scholars have written "biographies" of these Buddha images. On plaques at individual monasteries and in amulet magazines and popular histories, there are legends told about them and miracles associated with them. Some images even have their own travel tales that describe how they mysteriously traveled on the backs of wandering elephants, floated down rivers, magically avoided being burned in fires, deflected bullets and bombs, and disappeared from one place to reappear in another. Furthermore, people are so dedicated to certain images that they actually sacrifice themselves or harm themselves to honor the image. A noncanonical *jātaka* story popular in Thailand, Laos, Burma, and Cambodia known as the *Viriyapaṇḍita jātaka* describes a spirit that entered a famous Buddha image and possessed it. The image shook and emanated multicolored rays of light and spoke to the main character, Viriyapaṇḍita. The hero is praised by the animated Buddha statue because he sold his wife and children in order to buy gold to cover the image. The funds from the sale of his family were not enough to completely cover the statue. Therefore, he sliced off his own flesh in order to finish the job. The act of slicing off his own flesh led to a great loss of blood, and he passed out at the feet of the statue.[18] This story is not seen as a form of extreme or misplaced piety but is used to amaze others. The story ends with a short sermon telling the reader or audience to erect Buddha images out of anything they can find—clay, bronze, stone, gold, or wood.

There are more recent examples of human beings developing extreme relationships with Buddha images. In 1803, a high-ranking Siamese prince, King Rama I's brother and commander of the Siamese army, attempted to commit suicide in front of his favorite Buddha image in Bangkok, claiming that he was "offering up his own body as sacrifice to the Lord Buddha." Weak with cancer, he was easily stopped by his attendents.[19] Luang Pho Ban Laem, a locally famous standing Buddha image at Wat Phetsamutworawihan in Samut Sakhon Province, has a number of stories connected to it. Many claim that when they prostrate to the image, "he" speaks to them. Like some images of the Virgin Mary, he also reputedly weeps. These stories are called *itthiritpatihan* (miraculous).[20] Even one of the most famous modern novels of Thailand features a Buddha image as a character, Kukrit Pramoj's *Phai daeng*, in which a Buddha image serves as the conversation partner with the protagonist about the nature of communism, modernity, and war. While these stories are often glossed over or mentioned as humorous asides by art historians, they are extremely important to practitioners. This is not to say that every person who prostrates in front of these images believes all these stories. Many devout Buddhists have told me stories with a touch of humor and skepticism themselves; however, these stories are often much more important markers of the value of the image than the age, style, and material.

Buddhist statuary in Thailand does not include only statues of the Buddha, though. The small workshops in Bangkok (centered mostly near the intersection of Thanon Phran Nok and Thanon Arun Amarin and in the tight network of lanes and allies near Wat Suthat) produce more images of Buddhas, monks, Hindu deities, spirits, Taoist immortals, ṛṣi, Jade Emperors (made of resin, bronze, wood, copper, or plastic) than perhaps any other place in the world. Artisans churn out hundreds of images a month, some made-to-order and some for mass consumption. In my many interviews in these workshops, I have learned that images of famous monks rival the sales of Buddha images, and Ganesha images in particular have become extremely popular. Among images of monks,

Somdet To has long been the best seller. However, images of past kings, Kuan Im, and Nang Kwaek (a popular female image used for bringing profit to small businesses) are also big sellers. Occasionally, although this is not as popular as it was in the early 1990s, Greek and Roman deities or dolphins are also seen. These Hindu, Buddhist, Taoist, animistic, and Greco-Roman creations all compete for space in the shop fronts on these streets with other items for sale like robes, umbrellas, toiletry kits, and pillows offered to monks. One would assume that the gaggle of images found in these shops would not be replicated in more sacred environs. However, many monasteries in Thailand possess the same variety of objects.

Wat Mahabut, home of the country's largest Mae Nak shrine, is just such a monastery. Mae Nak is not alone. About six hundred feet from the shrine to the ghost Mae Nak is another important node of worship. One hundred nine years after Mae Nak was supposedly pacified by Somdet To and buried under a tree at the monastery, an infant named Sirirot Phibunsin (affectionately known as Ae or Dek Chai Sirirot) died when he was only thirty-nine days old. Since he died an unnatural death, like Mae Nak, he was buried instead of cremated. Not long after he was buried there was a terrible flood in Phrakhanong District, and the coffin of the infant resurfaced. His distressed parents, Pramot (a local police officer) and Sirilak (a nurse), brought his skeletal remains, which still had dried, leathery flesh clinging to them, to the abbot of Wat Mahabut. The abbot agreed to take care of the infant (*du lae luk*) in order to avoid upsetting Baby Ae's ghost. He ordered a glass coffin made, placed the coffin in a small wooden, freestanding house built specifically for the coffin, and opened the doors to the public. Although not given a monthly funeral like Mae Nak, Baby Ae nevertheless receives a lot of visitors.

Baby Ae's coffin is filled with toy airplanes, spacecraft, trucks, boats, several teddy bears, a giant stuffed Hello Kitty doll, a cell phone (supposedly if he wakes up and needs to make a call), and lots of cash. In fact, Baby Ae's entire skeletal corpse (dressed in children's pajamas) is covered in a blanket of cash that drops down on him from donors who slip twenty-, fifty-, and hundred-baht bills into a small slot on top of the coffin (as well as U.S. and Singapore dollars occasionally). Only Baby Ae's eyeless head, covered with a thin layer of grayish, leathery skin with blondish hair on top, is clearly visible through the glass. Next to the coffin is a place to give more offerings. One of the more popular gifts, besides toys, is excessively sugary children's fruit punch. A seventy-six-year-old woman named Khun Somwong, who keeps the shrine clean and generally manages the place, sat with me for a long time on several occasions talking with me about visitors and activities at Baby Ae's house. She and her son would even unlock the doors in the evenings for me (as I could often not get there before 6:00 P.M.).

Khun Somwong clearly was very attached to Baby Ae, and I suspected it was not just for the cash he generated for the shrine and her family. She spoke of him as her own child. She spoke of Baby Ae's parents, who would come once a year to the shrine, about the troop of about twelve to sixteen *kae bon* (a traditional type of dancer) who would dance in front of Baby Ae for a fee upon request, and the schoolchildren and mothers who would visit the coffin. Baby Ae was said to give people who visited him dreams, and in those dreams winning lottery numbers would be revealed. Most of Baby Ae's visitors are sports teams, though. Local high school and technical school teams would visit Baby Ae to give offerings before or after big soccer, *takraw*, or volleyball matches. They either asked Baby Ae to help them win the game or thanked him when they won. I only observed this twice, but Khun Somwong and the assistant abbot assured me that this was the most common activity. I asked several people, including most of the monks in residence at Wat Mahabut, how an infant corpse could help sports teams. I was told by people like Achan Sirisak, Achan Yai, Khun Patthana, Khun Som-chai, and many others that Baby Ae had "won" by not being destroyed by the flood. The assistant abbot (*phu chuai chao awat*), Phra Khru Withankitchathon, who is officially the monk in charge of the Mae Nak shrine and most day-to-day activity at the monastery, said that there was also some "proof." The small school connected to the monastery had one of the best *takraw* (a type of volleyball played with the feet and a rattan ball) teams in the city, even though they were a tiny school. Moreover, the local technical college had won the city-wide soc-cer championship after offering gifts to Baby Ae. However, he was skeptical. Even though the sports teams had won, he thought that the belief in the power of Baby Ae was not based in reality. Regardless, he thought the presence of the child was good for the parents, who were comforted that their child had in-spired so many people. He admitted that the three hundred thousand baht that the shrine brought in annually was also helpful to the monastery, as it was help-ing build a new dormitory for monastic students.

The display of infant corpses is a well-known practice in Thailand. The dis-play of Baby Ae is loosely related to the honoring of *kuman thong* and the col-lection of corpse oil. There are several groups that employ a staff of "corpse gatherers" throughout the country. The most well-known of these societies is the Poh Teck Tung, also called the Potek Xiangteng. It is a Teochiu-speaking Chinese group originally from Guangdong founded in Thailand in 1909. Many of the members who moved to Bangkok in the early twentieth century obtained permission from King Rama V to practice "second burials" for those who had died without relatives. This practice would ensure that these people who didn't have ancestors and children to honor them would not turn into menacing ghosts. The ones performing the second burial—involving digging up corpses, drying their bones, and rearranging them in a mass grave after cleaning them and chanting over them—would become their adopted ancestors. Originally there is not much evidence that corpse oil was gathered from the corpses. However, Francis Giles observed the practice as early as 1937, and the Teochiu word for a corpse that is mummified when dug up is *kim thong*, which is translated in Thai as *kuman thong* (a combination of Chinese and Sanskrit). There is a high likelihood that corpse oil was part of the early ceremonies in Bangkok and seems to be a custom added locally, since it is not found in mainland Chinese second-burial practices. Today this group runs a large temple in Bangkok, a 109-acre cemetery in the Bangkok suburbs, and a large number of private ambulances, whose drivers listen to radio and police bands and show up suddenly at the scene of motorcycle and car accidents to collect any dead body. They also visit hospitals requesting that the family members of a newly deceased child, sister, or husband donate the corpse to their society.[21] Some families donate the corpse of a relative; other corpses are given to the society if no family member claims them. Sometimes these corpses are used for *asubhakammaṭṭhāna* meditation, as discussed in chapter 3. Sometimes they are buried, as the Poh Teck Tung Foundation does, in mass graves, only to be dug up as a group once a year to gather corpse oil (*nam man phrai*) and bone relics from them. Then they are cremated en masse. This mass cremation not only creates merit for the foundation and those who attend but also allows for the easy, centralized collection of auspicious and protective ashes, bones, and oils. At one of these mass cremations, Marlane Guelden witnessed a large ceremony in which an infant corpse covered in gold, like Baby Ae, was entreated and worshipped.[22]

All these practices may have originated with the practice of creating and preserving another type of image, the *kuman thong* (golden boy). *Kuman thong* are the mummified corpses of stillborn children, aborted fetuses, and some are children who die in their first few days or even years of life. These corpses are mummified (bled, desiccated, and stored in camphor oil) and then usually covered in gold or blackened by roasting them slowly.[23] These practices are mentioned in the most famous premodern Thai adventure and romantic poem, *Khun Chang Khun Paen*. Here, the clever but devious and lecherous warrior Khun Paen is mentioned as cutting the fetus out of a woman and roasting it while chanting secret verses. Wat Tham Mongkhon in Kanchanuburi Province has a gruesome mural of this scene from the epic poem. He uses the corpse to give him invulnerability in battle.[24] One of the more famous monks of the twentieth century, Luang Pho Te Khongthong (1892–1981) of Wat Samngan in Nakhon Pathom Province, produced a great number of these *kuman thong*.[25] He had audiences with the present king, was put in charge of five monasteries in central Thailand, took on the task of restoring abandoned monasteries, and is much loved among dog owners today because of his care for and training of a little white poodle named Chao Nuat. He is often pictured with this dog, which supposedly went to the post office and picked up letters for his master and accompanied him on alms rounds. He was well-known for encouraging his followers to share their wealth with the poor, and he famously refused to live in a brand-new monastic cell built especially for him. He gave it to one of the youngest novice students in the monastery instead. Another monk famous for making *kuman thong* was Luang Pho Tim (1879–1951) of Wat Lahanlai in Chonburi. He supposedly mixed powder (*pong*) made of ground aborted fetus bones with powder produced from other amulets (including those made by Somdet To) to create protective talismans. There are a number of miracles associated with these monks' amulets and *kuman thong* that would take much too long to relate here. These stories and his *kuman thong* are still popular today in Thailand. However, these extreme practices are quite rare, and I have met only a few monks who have seen them performed. However, sensational cases do make the news. In June 2010 a woman was arrested who had fourteen fetuses in her home supposedly used for these rituals. The woman, Naengnoi Kaan, received the fetuses from an amateur abortionist in Ubon Ratchathani Province, held them at her home, and received phone orders to send them to potential customers looking to make *luk krok* (ghost children) or *kuman thong*.[26] Moreover, most *kuman thong* held by monks and lay magicians are not actual aborted fetuses but ceramic dolls covered in gold. However, no matter the reality, there are many stories. These come in the form of rumors heard in amulet markets and fantastic stories in popular magazines. They speak of certain ritualists who go to cemeteries at night to collect corpse oil or husbands who rip fetuses out of their wives' bodies. These stories are popular. I even heard them in Philadelphia. On October 9, 2009, I walked into a small Thai convenience store near the corner of Locust and Forty-third Streets in West Philadelphia down the street from my house. The only piece of reading material for sale in the entire store was prominently displayed above the cash register—a copy of *Mahapho* magazine with Luang Pho Te surrounded by pictures of *kuman thong* on the cover. The text below the cover photograph declared in bright red ink, "Aphinihan! [an English exclamation point followed the Thai text on the original], kuman thong, Luang Pho Te, thuk ruai ruai ranao" (Miraculous! The *kuman thong* of Luang Pho Te brings great luck and fabulous wealth!). I asked Jaeng, the owner of the shop for over twenty years and an actively practicing Buddhist, about the magazine, and she happily told me about the great luck Luang Pho Te's *kuman thong* brings. I sat on the stone wall outside my son's school across the street and read through the magazine, which contained (like many I had seen in Bangkok) hundreds of photographs of different types of *kuman thong*, many produced by Luang Pho Te and his students, as well as an article about Somdet To and a discovery of one of his old statues.[27] I picked up my son at school with a bigger than usual smile on my face. It is nice to "research" in your own neighborhood.[28]

Corpse oil is the prized substance in these ceremonies. Unlike statues of saints, Buddha images, or bas-reliefs, the importance of a mummified person is less in its aesthetic beauty or calming meditative affect than in its ability to be harvested for oil, bones, ash, and wax. *Nam man phrai* is an oily and fatty substance that is obtained by magicians, including monks, who either dig up corpses, or, in the case of Baby Ae, find corpses, to melt. The magician holds a candle or magnifying glass up to the chin, elbows, forehead of the corpse and melts the dried skin. The drippings are collected and are believed to have the power to be transformed through incantations into a love potion, protective oil, or even diluted into tattooing ink.[29]

In Singburi Province there is another type of corpse display. Luang Pho Charan is the abbot of the large *vipassanā* meditation center at Wat Ampawan. He is well-known in central Thailand as a person with the power to grant wishes. He has put on display two corpses of "fruit maidens" at the nearby Wat Prangmuni. These fruit maidens are about eight inches long, have grayish, leathering skin, and he claims that they were given to him by an ascetic in Sri Lanka in 1972. Fruit maidens, or *makkaliphon* or *nariphon*, are a well-known part of Thai folklore. The source undoubtedly comes from a scene in the Thai version of the *Vessantara jātaka* (Thai *Wessandon chadok*) in which, while in exile in the Himavanta Forest, Prince Vessantara's wife, Maddī, finds sixteen *makkali* trees on which, instead of fruit, hang small, beautiful women (*makkaliphala*). Scenes from the Himavanta Forest are popular in Thai mural painting, and many people I have spoken with seem to know this story disconnected from the *Wessandon chadok*. These trees were miraculously planted by Indra (Sakka) to distract men so that Maddī would be safe in the forest gathering water and food for her family. If a man, usually depicted in murals as a Brahman ascetic, picked and had sex with a fruit maiden, he would lose all his magical and virile powers.[30] Maddī is protected by the trees since she does not desire the female fruit. Luang Pho Charan claims that these fruit maidens are real and that when they fall to the earth and shrivel up, they can be collected by human beings. He luckily was given two while on pilgrimage in Sri Lanka. Only ascetics of certain powers are able to enter the Himavanta Forest where the *makkali* trees grow. Today at Wat Prangmuni visitors can hold the dried corpses, which do indeed look like young girls with stems coming out of their heads; however, they certainly look like carved pieces rather than organic. They are kept on a small pillow and surrounded by gifts of flowers. Holding these corpses of mythical beings is believed to grant a person good luck, especially in love.

Displaying corpses for auspicious purposes, even though according to most books on Thai culture corpses are generally considered inauspicious, is not limited to infant corpses; in fact, the display of mummified corpses of monks is spread throughout central and southern Thailand, perhaps the most famous being that of Luang Pho Daeng on the island of Koh Samui. Wat Nang Chi, a historically important monastery in Thonburi, has a small, relatively unkempt shrine with the mummified corpse of a *maechi* (nun) lying in a glass coffin next to the mummified corpse of a young child. The nun, Maechi Nopparat, died in 1944 when she was only nineteen years old after being ordained and serving for three years with the famous Luang Pho Sot of Wat Phak Nam. Even though she came from a family of poor salt farmers, she was born with great merit and compassion (*chai bun mi mettatham*), and this preserved her body.[31] Luang Pho Poon and Luang Pho Din, of Nakhon Pathom and Chainat provinces, respectively, have also been mummified.[32] These mummies are held in glass coffins for people to view and offer gifts. In front of Luang Pho Din's mummy is a life-size bronze image of him that even depicts him wearing his glasses. In front of Luang Pho Pun's mummy is a resin image made in similar ways to that of Somdet To from Wat Indrawihan discussed extensively in chapter 2. The images were made by the Thai National Artist Duangkaeo Phityakornsilp. Duangkaeo has invented a method of creating resin and fiberglass images with actual human hair. He became famous with the opening of the Thai Human Imagery Museum (i.e., National Wax Museum, Phiphitaphan Hun Khi Pheung Haeng Chat) in Nakhon Pathom. I first visited this museum in 1993 when I took a group of Thai high school students on a field trip. On July 23, 2006, I had a chance to visit again after seeing Duangkaeo's work on the Somdet To image. Here I saw the original wax statue of Somdet To. This statue was the model for the one at Wat Indrawihan. Unlike the one at Wat Indrawihan, the original also has statues of the kneeling, poor, and shirtless *yom* (lay assistants) and a soldier and novice standing behind Somdet To. The original was finished in 1982 and is one of the centerpieces of the National Wax Museum. The copy was installed at Wat Indrawihan in 1988. For many Thais, the wax statue is seen as the true image of Somdet To, even though the sculptor made Somdet To look healthier, stronger, and more intimidating. The actual photograph that the image is based on is of a rather small and frail elderly monk.[33] These resin images of Luang Pho Cha, Luang Phu Waen, Luang Pho Khun, Krupa Siwichai, and many others first displayed at the museum have now moved out into the monasteries. Even though they cannot produce corpse oil or be harvested for relics, they work like mummies in a way that freezes the ritual efficacy of monks. Indeed, the resin images do even more; they freeze, or hypostatize, ritual moments in time.

It can be said that hypostatization has been a regular practice of central Thai Buddhist image makers over the past century.[34] For example, occasionally when famous monks die, they are not cremated as with normal Thais. Instead, the corpses of the highest-ranking monks are propped up in a seated position (I have been told that a surgically inserted metal or wooden rod is sometimes used). The seated body is encased in thin gold leaf and plaster so that the wrinkles of the skin, the facial features, and muscle tone are frozen. The corpse is made into a living statue to freeze the body in time. These are not old, lifeless statues or artificial representations. A dedicated patron or person seeking protection and guidance can visit and prostrate to the image at any time. This was not done to Somdet To's body. In fact, we know precious little about his last days. Photographs, wax and bronze images have been preserved and placed in shrines throughout central Thailand. The resin image and faux cave shrine at Wat Indrawihan in Bangkok, discussed in chapter 2, take this hypostatization too its furthest extent by animating the image with sound and having the image hold a string that empowers the continually refilled pool of water.

One does not necessarily have to spend a great deal of money commissioning a resin image from Duangkaeo. Indeed, the idea of making an image of a powerful person for the purpose of asking that image to act ritually as if alive is an old Thai practice. The making of *hun phi* (ghost dolls) by sculpting clay into small human figures to contain their spirits (so that their ghosts don't move on to the next life) is mentioned in *Khun Chang Khun Paen*.[35] These images are found in many amulet markets today and are usually black, terra-cotta, or yellowish gray. They can be placed inside glass or clear-plastic lockets and worn around the neck, serving as a type of guardian angel. Indeed, the statue of Mae Nak at Wat Mahabut (and all her statues throughout the country) could be seen as a type of *hun phi* holding her in this life. These images are not representations, symbols, or simulacra, then; they are tools in an individual protective arsenal. They are powerful despite the fact that they are copies of copies of copies of the supposed original. They are to be held, honored, and respected as powerful in themselves. The normative Buddhist values of nonattachment and impermanence are forgotten in this process of hypostatization. Indeed, even the mummies of Luang Pho Pun, Maechi Nopparat, Baby Ae, and *kuman thong* are not less powerful because they are lifeless. They are not empty shells or mnemonic devices. They are objects worthy of gifts and givers of merit. Just as the Buddha has not been permitted to pass quietly onto nirvana, these nuns, monks, women, and children are held in this life psychologically and even physically. They do not foreground the Buddhist values of nonattachment and impermanence, nor compassion and the belief in transmigration or rebirth. Why do practitioners not want Somdet To, Mae Nak, Baby Ae, and others to move on to the next life? Why do they employ them through rituals to remain among us?

These bodies, whether simulacra or actual corpses, are useful and powerful. They bring security and promote the value of abundance. They do not participate in what Marina Warner has identified as the "aesthetics of shock" or gory verisimilitude.[36] She examined the European fascination with horrific images in wax museums and exhibitions of medical curiosities that are meant to both scare and fascinate. She compared them in some ways to the Catholic display of martyrs being flayed, Mary with bleeding stigmata, or Christ hanging on a crucifix. Although there are Thai museums of torture and medical oddities, Thai Buddhist monastic shrines do not generally attempt to present gore. Even the mummies (of children, nuns, or monks) or statues of ghosts are not meant to frighten. They are covered in gold and wear dresses, monastic robes, or pajamas. They are surrounded by toys, cash, incense, and candles. They are not display items. They are objects of worship and sites of memory. They invoke the values of love, dedication, and loyalty. They mark historical events of triumph over death. For example, Mae Nak, despite dying in childbirth, being attacked by villagers and monks, and finally being pacified through the power of the *Jinapañjara* by Somdet To, her *winyan* (Pali *viññāna*, English "consciousness") remained active at the monastery. Phra Khru Withankitchathon believes that Mae Nak's *winyan* is caught at Wat Mahabut because people keep her there by giving her gifts and asking her for help. Her *winyan*, he explained, contra descriptions in Abhidhammic texts, is a sticky, glowing ball of energy to which your karmic actions adhere. Mae Nak had accumulated a lot of demerit in her life and is now living out her karma. However, even if she was ready to move on to the next life, her followers would not let her go. I asked if he saw this as uncompassionate. Shouldn't Mae Nak's followers want her to be peaceful and move on to her next life? To this question he had no answer. However, he saw Mae Nak as being compassionate to others. Mae Nak helped people "win," not only the lottery but in more serious ways as well. Since Mae Nak hated the military (her husband had been drafted and injured in war), many people who visit Mae Nak's shrine ask her to protect them (or more often women ask her to protect their husbands, sons, and brothers) from being drafted into military combat service, especially in southern Thailand or along the Burmese border. They want a winning number, a conscription number that will not be picked to serve on active duty. Since these numbers are handed out in April, each year the shrine is busiest then. Besides "winning" the draft lottery, people also ask Mae Nak for winning cash lottery numbers.

There are two types of lottery in Thailand, the government lottery and the one everyone actually plays. Most people play local, underground lotteries (which are not really that secret). For those who play both lotteries, Mae Nak helps. Many people, again mostly women, who visit Mae Nak ask her to inspire them to pick winning numbers (*kho huai*). Besides asking for inspiration, many purchase a special oil and candle to use in rubbing the bark of the tree under which Mae Nak's corpse is believed to be—oiling and heating the bark before rubbing it causes certain grooves of the bark to be exposed. The lines in the bark, many believe, can be counted to give a person winning *huai* numbers. On one of my visits to the shrine, I was recruited by several women led by Supa, an out-of-work mother who lived nearby, to rub their oil on the tree and tell them what numbers I saw. Supa believed that I might have better luck than her, as she had seen me prostrate to Mae Nak and therefore knew I was sanctioned to ask the tree. As a Caucasian, I was a bit of a novelty as well. As I rubbed the oil into the grooves of the bark, a crowd formed behind me trying to get a peek at the numbers that seemed to form. I saw a "9," but Supa insisted that I was seeing a "422." I told her that it was up to interpretation and that perhaps she should play both numbers. She stuck with her own. Apparently I wasn't very good at seeing the numbers in the bark. After rubbing the oil we went to purchase lottery tickets from a stand about a hundred feet away. I checked my numbers that night online (www.glo.or.th). I had lost.

For most, though, Mae Nak does not just help with numbers. She helps people win a child. Either pregnant women or women hoping to get pregnant (or simply meet a husband in order to have the chance to get pregnant in the future) visit Mae Nak and plead with her for help. Two visitors whom I interviewed one evening are good examples of the diverse reasons Mae Nak stays relevant. Kai and her husband, Montri Khachit, went to visit Mae Nak on a quiet Sunday evening on February 24, 2008. As I was chatting with an astrologer named Tittiporn, Montri, wearing a black jacket emblazoned with the English word "army" and a camouflage hat, approached me and asked me straightaway, "Are you American?" I said, "Chai krup" (Sure), and then he said, "What do you think of Thaksin?" (the former prime minister who was removed in a coup d'état in September 2006). It was late, I needed to get home, but I knew I was in for a long conversation. This type of blatant political question has been more and more common since the political upheavals of 2006. However, once we agreed to disagree and laughed about Montri's theory about how George Bush's problems have all been caused by his choice of a black dog as a pet, I decided it was my turn. He had done his ethnography for the day, now I would do mine. I asked him why he was visiting Mae Nak. This time, his wife, Kai, finally spoke up. She told me that they were thanking Mae Nak for protecting her husband, who had served in the south over the past few years as an army ranger. She had asked Mae Nak to protect him from the violence. She had. Montri would retire in April; he was stationed close to Bangkok now. It was about time to thank his protector. I noticed Kai was wearing a crucifix around her neck. She said that she was Catholic. Montri was Buddhist. Visiting Mae Nak had nothing to do with being Christian or Buddhist, they said. In fact, as I later learned from the abbot and the keepers of the shrine, many of the visitors to Mae Nak are Muslim. They all needed protection or a child or a lottery number.

Kai and Montri are not unique in their reasons for visiting Mae Nak. Maeo runs a gift and refreshment stand at the shrine to Mae Nak. She, at twenty-one years old, began helping her mother, Khun Patim, run the small stand when she was eight years old. She is in charge now and spends her days selling soda, sweets, soap, children's toys, T-shirts, photographs of the king and queen, and ritual items such as statues of Nang Kwaek and *kuman thong*. She has watched the comings and goings at the shrine for many years. While she believes the shrine has gotten much more popular since Nonzee's 1999 film *Nang Nak*, it was there before she was born and her mother's shop had been consistently success-ful for close to two decades. Maeo was struck by one question of mine about the religiosity of the shrine to Mae Nak. This question had been prompted by my conversations with the Catholic Kai on a previous visit. She admitted that she had never concerned herself with the question of whether the belief and rituals surrounding Mae Nak were "Buddhist" (*sasanaphut*) or even "religious" (*thang sasana*); however, if I really needed an answer, she supposed she could call all that is associated with Mae Nak a "belief" (*khwam cheua*). It was not Buddhist per se, but it certainly was genuine belief worthy and part of Thai culture (*wat-tanatham thai*). I could tell throughout that she was much more animated when talking about how to perform the ritual and rather bored with my questions about belief. She brought me to see Phra Sirisak, a thirty-seven-year-old monk who had resided at Wat Mahabut; she thought he might be better equipped to answer my questions. He was as perplexed by the question as Maeo. He suggested that all three of us change subjects. He and Maeo wanted to talk about how to solve problems that confronted people in general. The definition of Buddhism, religion, or magic was of no interest to them.

Phra Sirisak, who stated that he was trained by an unnamed monk and magi-cian in Kanchanaburi Province, ran a type of shop of his own. His *kuṭi* (monas-tic cell) was located in the southeastern area of Wat Mahabut near the Mae Nak shrine. Like many of the monks at Wat Mahabut, he was involved in the shrine. They helped perform the monthly funeral and blessed visitors with holy water and protective string (*sai siñcana*). Most days seemed pretty quiet for Phra Sirisak, though. He read daily newspapers and occasionally rented amulets, statues, protective potions and oils, candles, and the like. Like Maeo, he rented statues like those depicting Nang Kwaek and *kuman thong*. These small resin and plastic statues are designed to be placed in home spirit houses (*san phra phum*) and on altars. They ensure good health or a profitable business. Phra Sirisak considered himself particularly skilled at blessing and renting statues and potions that protected pregnant women and soldiers. In this way, his small business complemented Maeo's and the shrine to Mae Nak.

It also complemented the dozens of astrologers and spirit mediums who worked around the monastery. While most of these astrologer's tables and small shrines advertise the skills of a particular astrologer, like the middle-aged woman Mali or the young man named Liang Chaloensuk, and are covered with statues of Laksmi, Ganesha, a *ṛṣi* (Hindu seer), and the Chinese depiction of the *bodhisatta* Kuan Im, one boasted a sign that read, "Mo du yipsy" (Gypsy astrologer) and had a blown-up color rendition of a French-style tarot card. Another, catch-all clinic of sorts advertises expertise in not only Gypsy palm reading (*lai meu yipsy*) but also Thai astrology (*horasat thai*), Burmese astrology (*horasat phama*), and numerology (*lekasat*), all in an air-conditioned room! Mae Nak had become a magnet for a whole group of astrologers hoping both to be inspired and protected by Mae Nak, and also to cash in on some of the residual foot traffic generated by the popularity of her shrine. However, relegating these astrologers to being profiteers sadly commercializing Buddhism is seriously overlooking the entire context of Wat Mahabut.

The shrine to Baby Ae and the shrine to Mae Nak are two of eight shrines at the relatively small monastery of Wat Mahabut. Each one is different, but they all are worshipped, often by the same people. If you add the number of astrologers and fortune-tellers' tables on the monastery grounds, the number rises to three dozen places where a devotee can visit for merit, consultation, protection, or the secret to picking winning lottery numbers. If one visits the monasteries connected to Somdet To, like Wat Rakhang, Wat Indrawihan, Wat Chaiyo, there are hundreds of small shrines, each dedicated to a variety of different deities, monks, kings, and Buddhas. Each of these shrines has murals, images, objects, or historical events that make them famous. If one cannot visit these shrines, then she or he can wear amulets around their neck to protect them.

"Proper" images of the Buddha and monks, of which there are many at Wat Mahabut, share the monastic space and are visited by the same people who entreat Mae Nak. Theories about sacred and profane spaces do not work well at Wat Mahabut or at any Thai Buddhist monastery. There is the *ubosot* (Pali *uposatha*) hall, which is surrounded by *sima* stones marking the place within a monastery where new monks and novices can be ordained, but besides this, the space is relatively open, and images of the Buddha sit comfortably among images of other powerful beings.[37] In fact, one path at Wat Mahabut is a veritable gallery of images. On this path there is a small building with metal gates that houses several Buddha images as well as an image of Kuan Im, the Indian *arahant* Kaccāyana (Thai Phra Sankacchai), who is popular in Burma, Laos, and Thailand as a bringer of good luck and wealth.[38] The room also contains two images of monks, one of which is from Laos and has the *Jinapañjara gāthā* inscribed on its base, and the other is from central Thailand, with no name inscribed. There are also dozens of smaller images of the Buddha and a couple of Ganesha. Among these images are two lottery machines. The first is a Buddha image of about eighteen inches high sitting on top of an electric machine that spins and lights up when a person puts a five-baht coin in the slot near the feet of the Buddha and follows the instructions on the sign to "athithan" (contemplate, focus your good intentions, make a wish). The other is a similar machine, but instead of a Buddha image, there is an Umadevi (Hindu goddess) image. After the coin is inserted, the lights spin and a number appears as on an electronic roulette machine that tells the viewer their lucky number. This number can be applied when choosing lottery tickets.[39]

Next to this small shrine is the abbot's *kuṭi*, in front of which there are several large fish tanks. The *kuṭi* itself is a mess of magazines, images, unopened mail, books, gifts, ritual implements, and toiletries. In the center of his room is a large statue of Somdet To. The abbot, who ignored most of my questions, spends most of his days outside the monastery leading other monks in chanting protective incantations at local homes and businesses, or on the phone helping families arrange funerals. He is clearly a busy man. He certainly did receive prostrating patrons but seemed to prefer to let the other shrines in his monastery greet guests. Next to this *kuṭi* is another small, air-conditioned room that houses a large image of a former abbot of Wat Mahabut, Phra Khru Phithak Thawonkhun. The placement of this shrine suggests that there exists a lineage connection between this highly revered abbot of the monastery and all subsequent abbots. Indeed, the statue of the former abbot received more guests than the living one. Next to this shrine is the shrine of Baby Ae. Next to that shrine is a statue of Nang Torani. This is a goddess from on an Indian story of the earth goddess who protects Prince Siddhattha Gotama while he is meditating and trying to achieve Buddhahood. As the story is commonly recounted in Thailand, the goddess had absorbed an ocean full of water into her hair. To protect the Buddha, she wrings out her hair in order to create a flood to wash away an army of demons who are trying to distract the meditating prince. This story is depicted in images and murals throughout Southeast Asia. Finally, at the end of the path is a shrine to Kuan Im that is surrounded by trees and flowers with a man-made pond and fountain. In front of her shrine is a large wooden sign on which are painted the verses to chant while prostrating to her. Most Thai shrines offer helpful liturgical guides to visitors who have not memorized each and every chant. I have interviewed a number of people in front of these various shrines, and most say that they silently entreat the image after annunciating the prescribed formula. Some, though, do not bother reading the chant and prefer to simply prostrate, offer gifts, and move on to the next shrine.

Although there are also several smaller shrines as well as open-air classrooms, monastic cells, a functional and unornamented sermon hall (supposedly sponsored by King Rama IV because Somdet To favored this monastery), I will mention only one other shrine, for the land spirits (*phra phum*). This is a slightly rundown version of the *san phra phum*, or spirit houses, that are ubiquitous in Thailand, placed in front of nearly every high-rise, hotel, shopping mall, suburban and village home. The shrine at Wat Mahabut is at the base of a large *takian* tree, like those trees surrounding Mae Nak's shrine, and is populated by a wide array of images, including four of Nang Kwaek, a *ṛṣi*, a plastic Chinese Buddha image, two faux-jade lions, plastic *kae bon* dancers, red incense, flower garlands, and a bottle of Strawberry Fanta soda. The array of images and offerings was often slightly different on each of my visits and will surely be different next time I go. The images rarely move (although occasionally more are added), but the offerings are refreshed. Like the shrines to Mae Nak, her child, her husband (Mak), several Buddhas, Kuan Im, Nang Torani, and Baby Ae, the shrines are not permanent monuments but stages vibrating with a subtly shifting yet ever-growing number of characters and props.[40] If each shrine or statue were to be studied in isolation, then they could be described as cheap trinkets or poorly executed pieces of vernacular art. However, when studied in relation to one another, their associative value is clear. Each image's value is raised because each is in good company. This is not a particularly Thai Buddhist trait. There are dozens of canonical stories in which the Buddha is lauded because he is surrounded by crowds of thousands of followers as well as deities who come to listen to his sermons or bask in the glow of his golden skin. Although the image of the lone monk or Buddha meditating in a mountain cave or thick forest may be the one most recognized by a Western student of Buddhism, the Buddha and monks are most often depicted among crowds. Rarely, very rarely, is an image of a Buddha or a monk sitting alone on an altar.

At Wat Mahabut the *vihāra* containing the "main" Buddha image in the geographical center of the monastic compound was almost always locked. The surrounding shrines to Mae Nak, Baby Ae, and various other bodhisattvas, famous monks, and local deities were very well attended. I always found this strange. The center was vacant but the periphery full. However, not many of the people at Wat Mahabut I spoke with mentioned this as strange. Hardly any saw the monastery as fragmented and multifocal, as I initially did. Perhaps they saw it as ordered and unitary. It took me a while. Now I see that what I assume is orderly and rational in the Catholic church in which I grew up might seem quite macabre, chaotic, and polytheistic to non-Catholics. Who is the object of worship? The Virgin, Christ, Saint Catherine, Saint Blaise, the Eternal Flame of the Holy Ghost, the priest, the suffering Christ on the crucifix, Christ the King?

Wat Mahabut, like other Thai monasteries, is in a constant state of flux. Old photographs of the Mae Nak shrine from the 1980s (the shrine supposedly started initially when people started seeing strange footprints around the burial site of Mae Nak) show that the shrine has grown significantly. Moreover, the statue of Mae Nak (there are now two others nearby), which was once bald, now has a black wig, and her lipstick and mascara are freshened often. On her lap are two baby dolls whose clothes are constantly changed. Changes like these are normal, and this is why researchers must make it a point of visiting the same site over and over again for years.

These changes should not indicate that Thai practitioners embrace change as a fact of existence. In fact, sometimes the opposite is true. We saw that the lifelike resin image of Somdet To at Wat Indrawihan in effect hypostatizes his ritual body. At Wat Rakhang, the large market that had fish, turtles, candles, incense, and other religious offerings for rent, was completely demolished in June 2008 because the local authorities wanted the monastery to look nicer for a visit from the king. This change, I found out through later interviews, was not approved or enjoyed by the merchants or visitors. They liked the bustling market the way it was. Wat Rakhang has changed much over the past two hundred twenty plus years. First it was known as the home to King Rama I, then the home of the largest *ho trai* (monastic library) in the emerging capital, then home of Somdet To, then market for Somdet To's amulets. In the past fifty years it has been the temporary headquarters for the Buddhist Association of Thailand, at which Naep Mahaniranon (one of the most famous female sermon givers in modern Thai history) spoke weekly in the 1940s and 1950s, the home of the Burmese monk and recognized father of the Burmese Abhidhamma school in Thailand, Saddhama Jotika Dhammacariya, from 1954 to 1968, as well as the residence of some of the well-respected *maechi* (nun) scholars in Thailand.[41] But change just doesn't happen over time; each monastery can have different purposes at the same time. Wat Rakhang is presently the headquarters of one of the most important Abhidhamma schools in the country, boasts one of the most important cremation halls in Bangkok, some of the best examples of Ramakian murals, being a place where children can go release turtles and feed fish for merit, a home to a well-respected girls' high school (*rong rian satri*), a monastery that is particularly welcoming to ethnic Mon monks, and so on. Only by spending long periods of time at any one monastery can the plethora of resources be appreciated and the cacophony of voices be heard.

Another example can be seen at Wat Kaeo Fa in Nonthaburi Province, where there is an Ayutthaya-era *ubosot* that stands in a state of decay. However, it is still the ritual center of the monastery because its age and the Buddha images on its altar have a sense of gravitas (*krang*). In fact, the sense of sacred power that comes from its age and beauty has prevented the local monks and laypeople from repairing it. Moreover, the Buddha images inside it create new images. In 2007, strings were tied to the main image and then connected to several thousand small Ganesha images. These new images were infused with *khwam saksit* (spiritual power) through the chanting and connection to the older Buddha images. These Ganesha images have become very popular to amulet and image collectors. In fact, the image has also created a number of smaller amulets that have been much sought after. The old *ubosot* and Buddha images have also gathered a number of smaller shrines around them, like an elaborate shrine to a female spirit who is believed to reside in the *phikun* tree next to the *ubosot*. This shrine features Barbie dolls, plastic dancing figures, a full-size mannequin of a woman dressed in traditional clothing. There is also a shrine to Kuan Im near the *ubosot* as well as a stupa in the shape of a rice barge covered in small images, including Somdet To, Nang Kwaek, the Buddha, *kuman thong*, and even a toy "transformer" robot. Here age, heritage, and permanence are valued because they spawn or at least sanction the building of new shrines.[42]

The dizzying number of images and shrines at Wat Mahabut and at Wat Kaeo Fa may be a unique combination, but they certainly cannot compete with the number of shrines at much larger monasteries in the country, like Wat Chetuphon (Pho) and Wat Suthat in Bangkok, Wat Phra That Lampang Luang and Wat Doi Suthep in Lampang and Chiang Mai, respectively, Wat Ban Rai in Nakhon Ratchasima, Wat Wang Wiwek in Kanchanaburi, or Wat Mahathat in Nakhon Sri Thammarat. In Bangkok, perhaps the greatest number of statues to a myriad of Indic and local deities is Wat Srapathum. Wat Srapathum (or more properly, Wat Pathum Wanaram Ratchawihan) is striking. It sits in the center of the busiest high-end commercial district in Bangkok, Siam Square. This is the equivalent of Rodeo Drive in Beverly Hills, of the Champs-Élysées in Paris, or Orchard Road in Singapore. There are no less than nine luxury department stores within two blocks of the monastery. The national police headquarters is directly across the street. The high-rises surrounding it cast shadows over the entire grounds. The main juncture for the sky train is fifteen hundred feet from its front entrance. The palace of Princess Sirindhorn is behind the monastery. Despite being in this busy location, the monastery is actually a "forest" monastery of the Thammayut lineage. The monastery was originally built in a swampy area outside the main city along the Saen Saep Canal in the 1840s. It was also an area that Lao refugees were forcibly settled in after the wars with Laos between 1778 and 1827. It is ironic that this undesirable and overgrown, malarial district in the suburbs of Bangkok would become over the next one hundred fifty years the financial center of the country. As I mentioned in chapter 1, this monastery was deeply connected to Somdet To and to the Lao. Indeed, the three main Buddha images (Luang Pho Soem, Luang Pho Saen, and Luang Pho Sai), along with dozens of smaller ones, at the monastery are proudly noted as Lao war booty stolen in 1827 and placed at the monastery in 1865.[43] However, like the main image at Wat Mahabut, these main Lao images are not the only images, and not even the most popular images, visited by patrons today.

The layout of Wat Srapathum is interesting not only because it sits between high-rises, hotels, and shopping malls but also because it contains its own forest. Thammayut monasteries are associated with the forest, although many of them, like Wat Boworniwet and Wat Ratchapradit, are in the middle of Bangkok without any discernible forested ground. Wat Srapathum, however, has maintained this forest ideal, and approximately half the monastery's twenty-four acres are maintained as a *pa* (forest). The trees form a thick canopy over hundreds of images. Images of guardian *yaksa* giants, famous monks, Hindu deities, kings, and Buddhas rest between trees on small altars. This forest is not the typical one presented in studies of Thammayut-lineage forest monasteries, a lineage that supposedly disavows the power of images and the entreating of spiritual beings and past heroes. Monks do not only meditate here in isolation (there are regular meditation sessions, usually at 6:30 every evening, and several small *kuti* for monks to sit in for meditation) but also participate in the care of images and listen to the assistant abbot, Phra Thawon, speak over the loudspeaker about amulets, meditation, social ethics, and psychology. It is a relatively loud place made louder by the almost constant sound of the sky train, construction equipment, children playing, and traffic.

These images are configured to form new lineages by usurping the prestige of established ones. For example, as one enters the "forest," there are three large bulletin boards onto which are posted the photographs and short biographies of famous monks in Thai history. The majority of the biographies posted are those of Thammayut monks from all over the country; however, important monks like Somdet To and Luang Phu Tuat, among others, who were not Thammayut monks, are also displayed. Many of these monks did not know one another and did not teach one another systematically. However, by placing them in chronological order by birth, there is a suggestion that they form an actual lineage and that that lineage is connected to the present assistant abbot at Wat Srapathum, Phra Thawon. Phra Thawon, who kindly allowed me to film an interview with him, has become the de facto head of the forest section of the monastery. His photographs are posted on trees, on bulletin boards, and in large posters. He is depicted not only as part of a lineage of famous monks who had nothing to do with his direct teaching or ordination lineage but also with the present king and crown princess of Thailand. As one walks deeper into the forest, one comes across a much larger (fifteen feet high) statue of Jatukham Ramathep, next to an equally large Buddha image. In front of these images is a row of life-size images of famous monks, including Luang Phu Sao Kanthasilo, Luang Phu Man, Luang Phu Hom Sophano, Luang Phu Tuat, Luang Phu Chantsri, and Somdet To. While the first two were in the same lineage, the others were not in this lineage, and there is not much evidence that any of them knew one another. What links them is not a lineage—as suggested by their arrangement in front of the Buddha and Jatukham Ramathep—but the fact that they are all popular among a wide range of Thai Buddhists. They are all worthy of respect. Somdet To is the only image larger than the other monks, and he sits first in line next to another statue, of Brahma. For a person untrained in Thai history, this shrine creates a new history and a new lineage.

Phra Thawon can be seen as gaining prestige from this lineage. In his *kuṭi*, he greets visitors surrounded by hundreds of images. Behind his seat are statues of Ganesha, Brahma, several former monarchs, and most notably a very large statue of Somdet To. In fact, there are at least seven statues of Somdet To in the Wat Srapathum forest, two of the larger ones on the veranda of Phra Thawon's *kuṭi*. They are outnumbered only by images of the present king of Thailand, Rama IX, of the Buddha, Luang Pho Yi (a former abbot of the monastery), and Phra Thawon himself. In fact, the largest image on his veranda is a life-size photograph of himself backlit by several fluorescent bulbs. He is certainly intent on cultivating a powerful, if not contrived, lineage. Somdet To was an essential part of that lineage. I asked him about his seeming affection for Somdet To. He admitted that of course he had never met Somdet To and was not instructed by any of Somdet To's teachers. Somdet To had eaten his midday meal at Wat Srapathum several times one hundred fifty years previously, but that was the closest connection that historically could be made. However, he emphasized vigorously that Somdet To, even though he was not a Thammayut monk, was legitimately his teacher and an inspiration to the Thammayut. The separation foreign scholars make between the Thammayut and the Mahanikai lineages is overemphasized. There are a few publicized high-level disagreements over which ecclesiastical offices should be held by which lineage; however, on a day-to-day basis, there is not a deep sectarian divide. By sitting next to an image of

Somdet To and other personae, he was subtly suggesting, even if it was not consciously planned, that he was part of their lineage. He was their living representative. Understanding the associative value of being close to images and the power images absorb from one another is necessary in making sense of why certain images become popular to collect, donate, and place in prominent places. As with celebrity endorsements, placing the image of your favorite amulet, monk, king, deity, or even yourself next to the image of another, more famous figure can increase the prestige of your image or yourself.[44]

This associative value can be seen well in the consecration of a new Buddha image I participated in at Wat Srapathum in November 2006. As I kneeled with a crowd in front of the newly cast image, a monk placed the bone relics of a former monk inside the head of the image (most images are made with a hole in the top of the head for this purpose; sometimes manuscripts are rolled up and placed in a hole at the base of the image's spine as well). His handling of these bones and being in charge of the final consecration of this Buddha image gave him much merit and associative prestige. The Buddha image in turn increased in value being associated with the fame of Phra Thawon and the fact that it contained the relics of a human being. The seemingly normative hierarchies in Theravada Buddhism are constantly being shifted and reshuffled.

Perhaps the most striking thing I noticed about Wat Mahabut and Wat Srapathum is that the main Buddha images in their respective *ubosot* and *wihan* are the least visited, despite the fact that they are the oldest and most revered by art historians. Indeed, most of the time, even during daylight hours, the *ubosot* are locked, and one must request a key to enter and pay respects. The keys seem to be rarely requested. At these monasteries, and at many others, the peripheral images, either of the Buddha, or more often of famous monks, ghosts, deities, and royalty, receive more elaborate gifts and greater attention than the central images of the Buddha. Sometimes the Buddha image entreated is not the oldest or most stylistically perfect but the one that has a miracle or historically curious stories connected with it. Other times, the shrines that are the most visited are the ones that are accessible and conveniently placed near parking lots, stages, or bathrooms. There are practical reasons for this. Some of the oldest images of the Buddha are kept locked away because they sit in rooms that need to be protected because they have old murals, valuable royal gifts, or are too precious themselves to be exposed to excessive sunlight or human contact. This can be seen at monasteries in Bangkok with historically important murals, such as, for example, Wat Suwannaram, Wat Sisuddharam, and Wat Ratchaorot. If a visitor has to find a caretaker, nun, novice, or monk with a key to open up a room (often very difficult in my experience), then they will most likely offer gifts to a more convenient, outside shrine like the giant statue of Somdet To at Wat

Sisuddharam or the shrine of Kuan Im at Wat Mahabut. This can also be seen at monasteries with very entertaining or unique images, like Baby Ae at Wat Mahabut, Luang Pho Din at Wat Salakhao in Chainat, and the image of Somdet To at Wihan Somdet To in Nakhon Ratchasima, which is very convenient because it rests on the side of the major northeast highway. This roadside attraction is an entire structure (over fifteen stories high) built solely to hold the image of a monk, not the Buddha. It is not a monastery but a shrine in honor of this one image and one monk. In fact, we might be witnessing a phenomenon in modern Thailand in which the Buddha is being usurped subtly by images of local monks, royalty, or deities. I imagine these types of shrines will only increase in popularity over the next few decades.

The field of art history has largely ignored studying the images of monks and local deities in Thailand in favor of studies of Buddha images and occasionally those of Hindu deities. Furthermore, studies of Buddha images have neglected some of the most popular and colossal images in the country, like the giant standing Buddha (Luang Pho To) at Wat Indrawihan, the long, reclining Buddha at Wat Sateu, and the fifty-four-foot-tall sitting Buddha at Wat Kutithong.[45] These images, while neither the most refined nor made of precious materials, are popular with children and families, who picnic near them, and devotees of monks like Somdet To.[46] The sitting Buddha at Wat Kutithong in Ayutthaya, for example, was sponsored by Somdet To in the 1850s (because Wat Kutithong was a temporary residence of Somdet To, and his mother had supposedly lived nearby for a few years), and it is a major attraction for devotees from central Thailand. Not only do people want to visit a former residence of Somdet To's but they also want to bring their children to "play" with the Buddha. This colossal image, named Phra Phuttha Mahamuni Srimaharat, has a large machine in front of it that operates two water cannons. These cannons are operated by inserting a ten-baht coin into a slot. The water shoots about forty feet in the air, hitting the Buddha image's chest and thus washing and cooling him (indeed, the image sits in the sun in a very hot valley of Ayutthaya). Children crowd around the machine to take turns washing the Buddha.[47] They are also instructed to chant the *Jinapañjara*, which is inscribed on a large plaque in front of the water cannons. In the courtyard in front of the image, local comedy troops perform on the weekends, and there are several vendors selling refreshments. There is dancing and ample parking. In a rural area, this image is a major destination for families who may not be able to afford the large amusement parks on the edges of Bangkok. There is simple enjoyment that accompanies visits to these sites. It is hard to fit fun and laughter into theories of iconology, globalization, or habitus. The context of an image is not simply the historical context of its original construction.

By concentrating on images as reflections of particular styles or as simply sacred historical objects controlled by kings, we miss what David Morgan has called the "protocols" that develop between devotee and object.[48] These protocols are not orthodox prescriptions but certain expectations that the devotee understands regarding the proper body posture, the appropriate range of gifts, and the murmured and deferential voicing of both formal incantations and informal intentions. If a particular image develops a protocol (which I see as a component of an individual's personal religious repertoire) with an image, then the abbot of the monastery or the caretaker of a shrine can insert other images near that one. These ancillary images receive similar forms of devotion and share in similar protocols. In this way, images spawn their own material lineages. Phra Thawon's placement of images of his teacher, of Jatukham Ramathep, Luang Pho Tuat, famous Thammayut monks, and his own photograph next to the images of Somdet To absorbs Somdet To's established lineage. Somdet To himself sponsored the construction of dozens of Buddha images, which worked to connect him directly and concretely to the person of the Buddha. The corpse of Baby Ae is near the statues of Mae Nak, Luang Pho Yim, Kuan Im, and several other images. Mae Nak's statue can be seen as the mother of the other images. They certainly would not be as popular and have developed their own following if the image of Mae Nak had not drawn crowds to this very hard-to-find little monastery. In general, a single altar or a single monastery can become a repository of images of Hindu deities, Thai monarchs, local spirits, monks, and Buddha images. By sharing the same altars (or neighboring altars), they take part in the same protocol and over time can share in the same prestige.[49] One popular image may draw devotees to the monastery or shrine, but while they are there, they can develop relationships and protocols with other images.[50]

For an individual monastery to grow, it often needs to be a "full service" religious center, which means that it has to offer a plethora of different ritual centers to speak to a wide variety of visitors. Visitors to Wat Srapathum, Wat Mahabut, and other places have the opportunity to trade and rent amulets, purchase CDs or posters, prostrate to a variety of images, meditate, consult with astrologers, release fish, eels, and birds, eat ice cream, listen to chanting, obtain corpse oil or holy water, have their wrists bound with sacred string, admire murals, listen to sermons, sit in an (often air-conditioned) library, and even play soccer and innocently flirt with men and women their own age.[51] Monasteries are often lively and stimulating, and this atmosphere is created by placing a number of different images in relationship with one another so that instead of having a single altar with a central focus, there are multiple poles forming a network of visual cues. Studies of the history, iconology, and iconography of individual images will more often than not miss these protocols, lineages, networks, and relationships and therefore miss an entire part, if not the biggest part, of the way a person's religious repertoire is formed and evolves.

## BEYOND COMMERCIALISM: THINKING ABOUT AMULETS HISTORICALLY AND MATERIALLY

In June 2001 police sergeant Suthep Chantnoi of Pattaya (central Thailand) was arrested and charged with attempted murder and grand theft. He was caught after he held up at gunpoint the sixty-one-year-old Liang Sae Jia, a wealthy man who was wearing a Phra Somdet amulet around his neck. Apparently, Suthep was friends with Liang and had asked to hold the rare amulet, an early-generation (*rung*) Phra Somdet amulet made at Wat Rakhang by one of Somdet To's students in the late nineteenth century. When Liang placed the amulet in Suthep's hand, Suthep drew a concealed pistol and pulled the trigger twice. The gun jammed and Liang took off on foot without his amulet. Suthep was later identified and arrested.[52] The small clay amulet, worth approximately 8 million baht ($240,000), was recovered.

This story is one of many that have made headlines in the past few years regarding amulet theft, assault, and even murder. There are other stories of amulets causing poor farmers to go into debt collecting Phra Somdets, or old women being trampled to death by crowds rushing to collect amulets distributed at funerals. People in Pattaya were interviewed on television nightly news at the time of the incident (I was particularly interested in following this case, as I was living down the street from Wat Rakhang at the time), and two young women were quoted as saying that the amulet was still protecting Liang even after it had left his hands. That's why the pistol had failed to fire. In fact, there are hundreds of miracle stories such as this in amulet collector's magazines and related between friends in the amulet markets or while relaxing at monasteries.[53] Occasionally a monk is heard telling these stories over loudspeakers during monastery festivals. Some stories tell of people who were protected from house fires because of amulets. Others tell of those who have successfully passed entrance examinations or were cured of cancer.

Amulets are big business.[54] In Thai they are called alternatively *phra khreuang* or *phra phim*. Even though they are made mostly of clay and flowers and often measure approximately 1 x 1.5 x 0.2 inches (one can hold five or six in the palm of one's hand), some can cost upwards of 2 million dollars. Phra Somdet amulets at Wat Rakhang and Wat Indrawihan by Somdet To have consistently been some of the most valuable in the country. His amulets have also attained the most privileged place among the five highest-ranking amulets of the nation, the

Benchaphakhi (League of Five).[55] Other valuable amulets include Phra Kring amulets connected to the present king and Luang Pho Doem's ivory-handled knives. There has also been a recent rise in the value of the Jatukham Ramathep and Ganesha amulets. There are thousands of articles in popular amulet collector's magazines (there are over thirty different weekly amulet magazines published in the country, with subscriptions in the thousands). These magazines contain stories about the value and beauty of these small objects. There is a regular section in the popular Thai-language newspaper *Thai rath* called "Sanam phra" that features new amulets on the market, stories of their production, and occasionally a miracle story about how an amulet saved a person from drowning or helped her business. These amulets are usually connected to the monk that first made them. Somdet To's are the gold standard. There are more catalogs specifically referencing To's amulets than those of any other monk. Genuine ones can be "rented" for as much as 1.75 million dollars. However, there are many Somdet To amulet copies that cost as little as 10 cents. They are sold in big, open bins in the various amulet markets. Although I paid 200 dollars for a rare one once, I have also bought five for a dollar and have been given dozens as gifts. Somdet To was and is extremely well-known and has now become a commodity of the commoner as well as the nobility.

This commodification of Somdet To and other monks, nuns, deities, monarchs, and historical figures has generally been approached by scholars as a reflection of a growing crisis in Thai Buddhism and of the rise of religious commercialism.[56] This commercialization, or what Alexander Horstmann has called one aspect of the culture of "spectacular consumption," is seen as connected to the growing globalization of Thai culture. Kasian Tejapira "has argued that the current age of accelerated globalization has generated a series of conflicts within state-sponsored nationalist Thai identity . . . in the face of a perceived influx of *un-Thai* culture." Therefore, he asserts, the government has sponsored projects promoting local Thai culture. Amulet fairs and national amulet consecration rituals can be seen as part of that effort.[57] Nidhi Aeusrivongse, J. L. Taylor, Phra Phaisan, Alexander Horstmann, Pracha Hatanuwat, as well as many amateur commentators in Internet blogs, Listservs, and chat groups have lamented this commodification.[58] The covers of *Thailand: The Worldly Kingdom* and *Thaïlande contemporaine* both feature photographs of monks speaking on cell phones.[59] These are well-researched studies, but the publishers' choice of covers participates in this juxtaposition that pits materialism and modernization against Thai Buddhist tradition. Stanley Tambiah's study of the "cult of amulets" rests on the dichotomy of good forest monks who meditate and those who deal in materialism. For example, he defends Achan Man as a proper forest monk by stating that he was no "crude dispenser of charms or amulets."[60] Phra

Phaisan Visalo, a popular monk and social critic, has stated that "Thai Buddhism in the new millennium has been losing the moral and ethical grip necessary to lead its people out of the destructive globalizing forces of consumerism and materialism."[61] Sanitsuda Ekachai of the *Bangkok Post* regularly mourns the commercialization of the Thai religion. Somchai Nil-athi believes that monastic grounds are being taken over for commercial purposes.[62] Mettanando Bhikkhu, who has recently given up his robes after serving as a monk for many years, has written that "it is not surprising that instead of being a religion of peace and wisdom . . . many high-ranking monks in Bangkok are astrologers, masters of the occult arts or entrepreneurs in the amulet industry . . . The amulet market, also controlled by the Ecclesiastical Council in Thailand, is as lucrative as that of the underground lottery: billions of baht circulate in this business daily, and it is all tax-free. Buddhism in Thailand is in need of radical change."[63] Phra Dhammapitaka, one of the most highly respected scholar monks in Thailand, believes that there is a "crisis [*wikrit*] in modern Thai Buddhism . . . [because] both monks and followers practice magic not Dhamma."[64] Saichon Sattayanurak has shown that the practice of magic was popular in the Ayutthaya and Thonburi periods.[65] But instead of seeing this history as instructive for understanding Thai Buddhism today, she coins the terms *phuttha satsana thi nen bunyarit witthayakhom* (supernaturally or magically oriented Buddhism) to describe the moral crisis.[66] Both Payutto and Saichon see amulets as the prime example of this modern crisis.[67]

Most of these critics have very little appreciation for the history of Buddhist material culture and so are surprised by its apparent growth now. Most studies in English or by elite liberal reformers are characterized by shock. The critics are shocked by the prices of amulets, the excessive trading, the prominent display, and the crime caused by the trade. They seem surprised by materialism in Buddhism, as if it were a new phenomenon. This shock, as in the cases of Sulak Sivaraksa or Phra Phaisan, is one of anger at Thai society in general for being duped by this duplicitous religious commercialism. The most recent chorus over the ways in which commercialization is destroying Buddhism rose most acutely in connection with the massive popularity of a new amulet called Jatukham Ramathep. Starting in early 2006 and reaching its pinnacle in the summer of 2007, newspapers, television programs, film stars, and politicians in Thailand had regular commentaries on the popularity and economic impact of this new class of amulets from Nakhon Sri Thammarat in southern Thailand. The flurry (what Thais came to call *khai*, or "fever") of people who traveled to the south to purchase these amulets reached into the tens of thousands. When one group of these amulets went on sale two people were trampled to death as crowds rushed to the monastery cash in hand. There have been reports of people committing murder to get their hands on rare Jatukham Ramathep amulets. The amulet markets are full of inexpensive imitations and rare original runs of these amulets. There are T-shirts with images of the amulet in every major mall and market in Thailand.

The fever over Jatukham Ramathep and other amulets has largely not been investigated historically; it is reduced to the product of modern socioeconomic forces and their moral ramifications.[68] Terms like *phuttha phanit* (Buddhist business), *sasana dalat* (the religion of the market), *sasana phlom* (fake religion) are employed to separate true Buddhism from that which has been sullied by money and things. Some studies express shock in explaining it away. They reduce amulets to being empty signifiers onto which those uneducated in Buddhist doctrine place their lower-class frustrations, modern anxieties, insecurities over the Islamic insurgency or the global economic downturn. They relegate amulets to social scientific illustrations of globalization, commercialization, or doomsday prophecies about the imminent end of true Buddhist values or the deleterious effects of Westernization. They are either tools of oppressors or fake science, or sad symbols of the poor trying to compete in a dangerous world. These are condescending studies on the one hand and studies of longing on the other—longing for a Buddhism that fits more in line with a certain Protestant rationality, which eschews materiality in favor of an undefined spirituality. Scholars have not been studying amulets; they have been looking at these objects and seeing them as referents (or symptoms) to something else. Herein rests a tension. A minority of elite and vocal critics, often publishing in English and Thai, criticize the use of objects in Buddhist life for anything other than symbolic purposes. This approach effectively marginalizes any serious historical or sociological study of amulets. The history and creativity of Thai Buddhist material culture have largely been ignored by these critics.

What can we learn from amulets? The most cursory reading of Buddhist canonical texts or study of South and Southeast Asian archaeology reveals that objects have been integral in the spread of Buddhism since its inception twenty-five hundred years ago, beginning with the relics of the Buddha himself. One could argue that buildings, images, stupas, and amulets, like the Phra Pathom Chedi, Emerald Buddha, Wat Sri Chum, the Sandalwood Buddha, the Mahamuni image, the Phra Bang, the image of Queen Suriyothai in Ayutthaya, the image of King Chulalongkorn in front of the parliament building, and so on have inspired Buddhist practice and belief in Southeast Asia more than doctrine. Pilgrimages to images, the cherishing (not just the collecting) of amulets, the prostration to images, the circumambulation of stupas certainly occupy the days of more Buddhists than the close study of Pali texts. Pattana Kitiarsa has pointed out that this critique of commercialization is usually "based mainly on doctrinally defined moral Buddhist standpoints. They rely on the authority of written texts, especially the Tripitaka and authoritative conventions."[69] Instead of seeing this commercialization as a modern phenomenon or a sign of the decline of Buddhism, scholars need to both take a historical view and attend to "multiple ethnographies of multiple Buddhisms." The perception of a crisis and commercialization is shortsighted and connected to Weberian approaches to religion. Pattana provides a new direction and asserts that "to explain the emergent prosperity religions and their occult economy is to gauge the realities of their 'commodifying tactics,' read them against their own historical and sociocultural backdrops, and take them from the actors' points of view. The 'new' religious hybridities and their significations are not totally new."[70]

Pattana is right.[71] We must start to study amulets as part of the study of Southeast Asian history. Gregory Schopen, David Drewes, Akira Hirakawa, and Robert DeCaroli have shown that the earliest Buddhist communities in India, including those of nuns and monks, were involved quite extensively in the use of objects to propitiate ghosts, land spirits, deities, and demons. Indeed, John Strong and Pattaratorn Chirapravati have demonstrated that this intense concern with relics, corpses, and stupas began at the cremation of the Buddha himself. Canonical texts and early Pali commentaries frequently mention the use of holy water, the molding and entreating of images, the collection of relics, and the building of stupas. The historical and material turn is simply asking us to take amulets seriously as art historical objects. Stanley Tambiah's famous book, the first study of amulets in English of any weight, devotes almost a hundred pages to the study of famous Buddha images and amulets.[72] Herein, we see the beginnings of the historical and material turn that few scholars outside Thailand have continued. First he describes briefly a number of important images and then moves on to describing some famous amulets, including a page dedicated to some of the amulets of Somdet To. He even mentions, in a section titled "Street Machismo and the Amulet Craze," amulet markets in the 1970s and the intense trading that took place (and still does).[73] When I write about amulets, I am truly standing on the shoulders of a giant. However, Tambiah's historical turn is on a particular and peculiar type when it comes to Thai Buddhist material culture. He sums his historical approach in a 1987 response to the reviewers and critics of his studies on Buddhism in Thailand: "For better or for worse, I consider my writings on Buddhism, society, and polity as situated at the confluence of anthropology, Indology, and history . . . The challenge . . . has been to find my way towards a historical anthropology informed by indological learning."[74] One problem here is that Tambiah sees Indic history and Buddhist/Hindu history as essential to the study of Thai images and amulets.[75] For example, a little further in the essay he writes, "Let us all applaud the efforts of those linguists, philologists and grammarians who have dedicated their careers to composing meticulous translations of texts and painstaking glossaries and dictionaries . . . for the benefit and enlightenment of scholars in other disciplines."[76] From there he goes on to praise the *Sacred Books of the East* series of translations and the Pali Text Society. This obsession with Indian historical sources leads him away from his strengths, one of which is being a brilliant anthropologist. His turn toward Indic texts and Indologists takes him away from local texts and local scholars.[77] In his section on amulets, he provides little information on the Thai history of these amulets and images, cites only one Thai-language source, of which he provides no analysis.[78] He cites extensively Pali canonical texts and the great Indologists, André Bareau, Ananda Coomaraswamy, Louis de La Vallée-Poussin, among others. He looks past Thai history to Indian history, past Thai-language sources to Pali and Sanskrit sources. Moreover, by not looking at Thai sources or interviewing many Thai experts in amulet history and production, he assumes that there are "literally dozens of similar works" in Thai, when in fact within these sources and in amulet magazines one finds much debate and disagreement among Thai scholars and enthusiasts regarding the authenticity, lineage, composition, ritual production, and social history of individual amulets.

However, toward the end of his study of amulets, Tambiah uses his skills as an ethnographer to open up the possibility of a local approach, which I hope I have taken in this book, when he briefly relates "the" biography of Luang Phu Waen, a forest monk from northeastern Thailand (1888[?]–1985), and how his amulets were eventually believed to protect soldiers.[79] This turn toward local history in his study of amulets provides insight into the value of amulets.[80] Amulet enthusiasts and even serious local scholars of Thai amulets rarely, if ever, cite Indic texts or engage in a study of Indian history. They do write extensively on local monks, rituals, and texts, as we have seen in the previous chapters. We need to study the history of the monks who made these amulets, the rituals, materials, and texts involved in their production, and the local stories told of their powers. We need to take seriously what Tambiah has so effectively taught to anthropologists: pay attention to history. I ask additionally that we pay attention to history near as well as history far.

The local historical and material turn in the study of amulets has its voices; however, these are voices that are not being heard by scholars of religious studies or anthropology in Southeast Asia.[81] Pattaratorn Chirapravati has traced the history of amulets in Thailand to the use of votive tablets made of clay and metal going back to the sixth century. Evidence suggests that they were more popular among religious communities on the Malay Peninsula and in southern Thailand, as well as among the Khmer.[82] Chalong Soontravanich has noted that archaeological evidence has uncovered the use of "locally available 'natural' objects, such as cowries, a certain kind of jack fruit seed, 'mai ruak' [a local species of small bamboo] and 'wan.'"[83] There are also dozens of different types of phallic amulets often worn on a man's belt that can be acquired in virtually every amulet market. Chalong believes that Brahmanism and Buddhism brought the added ingredient of powerful words inscribed on these objects in Sanskrit and Pali in a variety of scripts. This led to the use of *takrut* (small metal scrolls, mentioned in chapter 2 and discussed in the following), *yantra* cloth, *mit mo* (small knives), as well as of *luk prakham* (string of beads), *si phung* (consecrated beeswax), and *sua* (ivory-carved tiger statuette). Of course, tattoos can also be seen developing from this tradition of wearable and mobile objects of protection. Of course amulets are part of Southeast Asian religions in general. In the Philippines and parts of Indonesia, objects known as *ating ating* are held in the hand and are supposed to protect the possessor.

In Thailand, the ranking of these amulets into categories by the royal family began in the late nineteenth century. One of the earliest ranked amulets was the Phra Kamphaeng Thungsetthi, which became one among the prestigious League of Five after it was found (or perhaps made) by Somdet To during his 1850s pilgrimage to Kamphaengphet (to visit his mother's birthplace). King Chulalongkorn also went on amulet-hunting pilgrimages and was given Phra Nang Phraya, another member of that prestigious league, in Phitsanulok Province. When an old stupa collapsed in Suphanburi it exposed a large number of Phra Phong Suphan votive tablets, also of the league, some of which were confiscated by the local authorities and presented to Rama VI. The amulets in the League of Five are prized royal gifts, thus showing that amulet trading and collection is not a pastime only of the masses. For example, the famed forehead bone, now missing, of Mae Nak is believed to be in the possession of the royal family. Chalong and another historian, Sorapol, have noted that Prince Abhakorn, a son of King Chulalongkorn's and graduate of the British naval academy, was a follower of "one of the most celebrated 'local' Buddhist saints during the early 20th century," Luang Phu Suk of Wat Pakkhlong Makham Thao in Chainat.

Chalong has also noted that this early amulet trade grew after World War II. He traces the rapid rise in the collection and trade of amulets in the 1950s and 1960s. At that time, magazines relating stories of brave police officers being protected by amulets while battling bandits in urban and rural Thailand became popular reading material in Thailand. These stories were popular because of the rise in the use of small arms and in crime in Thai society. These cheap and accessible texts coupled with the growth in the publication of detailed studies of the materials and rituals used in the production of amulets led to a greater desire among people to seek their own amulets. As more people became involved in the trade, the more the study of the history of particular amulets, especially those of Somdet To, grew. Unlike in most studies of amulets, Chalong does not reduce the rise of amulets simply to sociohistorical forces but instead emphasizes that the histories of individual amulets, individual sacred monks, and individual thieves and crime fighters need to be undertaken to explain why certain amulets are treasured and others fall into disuse.

Taking Pattana, Pattaratorn, and Chalong's historical and material-cultural approaches even further, I investigate the actual historical sources that amulet traders, purveyors, and collectors are using, as well as studying the objects themselves. Material objects are seen by some scholars and social critics as getting in the way of the simplicity, nonattachment, and quiet embracing of impermanence needed to achieve world peace and future enlightenment. I see them as something cherished by Buddhists that ought not to be ignored, reduced, or lamented. I also see them as expanding the study of Thai religion beyond Theravada Buddhism. First, there are many amulets of Chinese deities and *bodhisattas*. Moreover, there are hundreds of different types of amulets in Thailand that do not depict Buddha images or Buddhist monks. They depict Hindu deities, royal family members, local goddesses and gods.[84] Therefore, any conversation about amulets needs to include these other important historical sources. I also see amulets as instructive invokers of the values of heritage, graciousness, security, and abundance. As I have done before, I first turn to examples of amulets drawn from the tradition of Somdet To.

The only known text that can be definitively said to have been written by Somdet To himself is a handwritten collection of his *yantras*, incantations, and amulet-making recipes. The short introduction states that it is a text that displays Somdet To's talent in Buddhist hermeneutics (*phutthakhom*) and magic (using the word *saiyasat*). Moreover, the incantations and recipes are said to be useful as a manual for soldiers in war (*songkhram*). It calls the *Jinapañjara* the greatest example of a protective incantation.[85] Each incantation (*kāthā*) and *yantra* is labeled by Somdet To as to its purpose, such as "protecting against ghosts," "for closing the nine human orifices to attack," "for protection when writing your own name," "for holding on to your *viññana*" ("consciousness," but more accurately in this context "spirit," or *khwan* in Thai), "for invoking dead monks for protection," "to stop outsiders," "to stop gossip," "to protect against enemies" (*satru*), "to counteract the magic of others," and the like.[86] This is followed by a very specific set of instructions on how to make amulets, including the types of flowers, clays, soils, incantations to mix, and the words to be chanted and the implements to be used when making these protective pieces. For example, there are instructions for chanting an eight-line mixed Sanskrit-Pali incantation beginning with "Paṇidhānato paṭṭhāya . . ." (Starting with this aspiration . . . )

and ending with "Sabbaśatrū vināssanti . . ." (All of my enemies are destroyed . . . ).[87] This incantation is used to stop the slanderous words of others. It
is followed by a series of instructions, such as drawing a *yantra* in the shape of a
man with a fish's tail, writing the letter *p* on the leaf of a *Calotropis* flower and
putting the leaf under one's pillow, as well as offering 108 candles, nine limes,
and so on. This incantation is followed by instructions on drawing the well-
known "Nā-mo-bu-ddhā-ya" *yantra*. Stating that when chanting the mantra
"Ma a u," the practitioner is to "cut into" the letters *ma* and then the *a* and then
the *u*. The shapes that emerge from the transformations of these letters are the
half-moon, sun (or *bindhu-dot*) and the *unaloma* (a symbol representing the tuft
of hair between the eyes that is one of the marks of a holy person). Slowly the
*yantra* is built through a process of expanding the letters of "ma, a, u" (each
letter can invoke multiple meanings) to the five syllables of "Nā-mo-bu-ddhā-
ya." These syllables in other texts can be transformed into representations of the
five Buddhas (Kakusandha, Konagamana, Kassapa, Gautama, and Metteyya),
five parts of the body, five eons, five colors, and so on. The entire manual offers
extremely specific instructions for *yantra* drawing, amulet-recipe mixing, and
chanting. It is meant for experts who have spent time training under a master
like Somdet To. Clearly, Somdet To, one of the great Thai Pali scholars of the
nineteenth century and a royally ranked monk, devoted a considerable amount
of time to thinking about amulets. Moreover, it is stated in many biographies
that people, including nobles, came from far and wide to see Somdet To in Bangkok or on his pilgrimages to obtain one of his amulets.

   The study of the amulets of Somdet To and other famous monks like Luang
Pho Suk, Luang Pho Doem, Luang Pho Khian, and others is a major intellectual endeavor in Thailand.[88] Not only do local scholars closely investigate the
history, material features, and authenticity of amulets before national auctions,
museum exhibitions, and contests but they also publish detailed studies of them.
Soraphon Sophitkun, Akadet Khrisanathilok, Ram Watcharapradit, Thawon
Kiattaptue, Phonchai Likhitthamwirot, Thepchu Thapthong, among others,
have written extensive studies of amulets in Thai that not only provide information on the ritual production and material composition but also discuss competing historical claims regarding the authenticity and origin of particular amulets.[89] For example, Somsak Sakuldanak has given basic biographical details of
many monks (because an amulet is only as powerful as the person who originally forged and consecrated it) followed by a detailed catalog of the major amulets of individual monks. He also does explicitly what Achan Thawon at Wat
Srapathum did subtly by placing statues of different monks in rows at the monastery. Just as the statues, when grouped together, create new lineages, Somsak
creates new lineages (or perhaps "halls of fame") by writing a book in which

monks who had no connection in life are associated with one another in print. In his two-volume catalog of monks and their amulets, he includes lesser-known monks like Luang Pho Khan of Wat Nok Krachap in Ayutthaya (1872–1944) and his Phra Pit Ta (a corpulent monk, often identified as Mahākaccāyana, covering his eyes with his hands as a sign of being uninfluenced by sensual desires) amulets with nationally famous monks like Luang Pho Khun of Wat Ban Rai in Nakhon Ratchasima (b. 1923). He also makes a concerted effort to describe the biographies and amulets of monks from southern Thailand, like the lesser-known Luang Pho Klai of Wat Suan Khan in Nakhon Sri Thammarat (1876–1970) and Luang Pho Kham of Wat Prasatnikon in Chumphon (1852–1948). He even includes a monk from northern Malaysia, Luang Pho Khron of Wat Udommaram (no dates provided), whose amulets are hard to find in Thailand. He elevates the prestige of Luang Pho Khron by telling the Thai reading audience that this monk is well respected in Malaysia and his amulets, especially his own version of the Phra Pit Ta, with large ears, are treasured there.

New lineages are also created by the way amulets are physically presented at monasteries and in markets. For example, at Wat Rakhang, one of the amulets available at the monastery's market is an amulet I rented in 2005 that features the faces of four monks floating in a copper circle. Somdet To is there, as well as three other abbots of Wat Rakhang. These other abbots are not well-known; in fact, the person who rented me the amulet did not know all their names. However, she stated that they were great teachers because they were in Somdet To's lineage. However, only two of the four actually had lives that overlapped, and there is little evidence that their teachings had serious influences on one another. The prestige of these other abbots is raised by their spatial affiliation with Somdet To. This use of Somdet To to elevate the prestige of other monks and their amulets is also seen in a set of amulets I rented in March 2008 at the Wihan Somdet To in Nakhon Ratchasima. Here glass cases displaying nineteen different amulets were for rent. In the center was a large circular amulet depicting Somdet To seated in meditation. The other, smaller amulets orbiting him like lesser moons featured Luang Pho Sot, Luang Pho Mi, Luang Pho Ruang, Luang Pho Ruai, among others. These monks lived at different times, were from different regions, and even had different sectarian affiliations. However, in this case, they all occupy the same prestigious universe, all share the merit (and marketing power) of Somdet To, and become honorary members of his lineage. At Wat Tha Kradan in Kanchanaburi Province there was a consecration ceremony for a set of five amulets in 2007. These amulets, all depicting the Buddha in various poses and made of red *phong* (a powder mixed with clay and flowers), and all different shapes, brought together the collective merit of five different local monks, who alone would not have had the local or regional cachet to attract collectors. At Wat Tham Seua, in rural Kanchanaburi Province, I found a rare three-faced amulet. Usually amulets have two sides, one for the Buddha, deity, or monk image, and one for a *yantra* or date stamp. This amulet is a three-sided conelike amulet made of brass with a core made of a rolled *yantra*. It was cast in 1994 in honor of the sixtieth anniversary of the abbot's ordination. On the three sides there is a different figure: (1) a replica of the giant Buddha image at Wat Tham Seua; (2) a sculpture of Phra Khru Sitthiwimon, the famous abbot of the monastery who taught meditation in the caves and was responsible for attracting sponsors to build the four tall stupas, cable car, and giant Buddha image; (3) Luang Pho Singh, the present abbot of the monastery. Here the abbot, who had the amulet cast, connects himself not only to the Buddha but also to his own, more famous teacher. Moreover, it is not simply a representation of the Buddha but a very specific Buddha image, that of his own monastery. The amulet itself was made available for rent in front of a shrine holding statues of Luang Pho Singh and Luang Pho Cheun, as well as, for extra prestige, of Somdet To. This monastery did not even exist during the time of Somdet To and so he never could have visited it. Luang Pho Cheun and Luang Pho Singh have no firm connection to Somdet To. Their placement together on the amulet links them together for all future visitors.

Not only do amulets and statues when grouped together physically create new lineages but photographs do so as well. The Bank of Thailand sponsored a set of postage stamps in honor of the king's birthday on December 5, 2005. For approximately two dollars one could order the Tra Prasanitakon Thiraleuk Phra Puchaniyachan (Highly Revered Monks Commemorative Stamps) featuring Somdet To (central), Luang Phu Tuat (southern), Than Achan Man (northeastern), and Khrupa Sriwichai (northern). This set reveals an explicit nationalist motivation—the most famous monks from each region of Thailand are depicted under the seal of the king. This is part of a broad sentiment in Thai society that values the rather historically contrived notion of unity in diversity. The royal family and successive secular governments have engineered this sentiment for over two hundred years, and now people from different classes and regions generally take part in this participatory nationalism without explicit directives or manipulation. For example, Prasani Yuphapandit has been a shopkeeper near Wat Rakhang since 2006. Originally from Phisanulok, she moved to Bangkok to help her brother run his shop. Although she had no deep interest in the life of Somdet To or Buddhism in general, at the shop she sells photographs and posters of famous monks and other celebrities. She purchased negatives from the Siam Gallery (a major purveyor of Buddhist visual material) and then went to the local film-processing shop and printed dozens of copies to sell. The particular set of photographs she sells is quite telling: Luang Phi Yi, Prince

Damrong, Somdet To, Luang Pho Cheam, Phra Mongkon Thepmuni, Phra Phuttha Chinarat, Shiva, Luang Phu Khai, Luang Phu Iam, Than Achan Man, Luang Pho Chong, Luang Pho Cha, Luang Pho Te, the Emerald Buddha, Princess Kalyani, Luang Phu Thim, Queen Sananthewi, King Rama IX (three different poses, as a soldier, as a monk, in royal regalia), King Naresuan (a photograph of an actor dressed as King Naresuan, since he ruled two hundred years before the emergence of photographic technology), Phra Prathan (the main Buddha image of Wat Rakhang, also known as Luang Pho Yim) Luang Pho Doem, the Taoist Jade Emperor, King Taksin, a photograph of a Phra Somdet amulet, a photograph of a Jatukham Ramathep statue, King Chulalongkorn, Ganesha, and Than Achan Khao. Here we see a mixing of Taoist, Brahmanic, Buddhist, and royal personages and statues from different times and places all sold in the same bin. This is not unusual. Religious stores throughout the country, as well as a store at one of the largest shopping malls in the country, bring these monarchs, deities, and monks together on their shelves. In fact, Prasani also sold posters that feature paintings of groups of monks seated together. These monks include Somdet To, Khrupa Sriwichai, Phra Mongkon Tepmuni, Luang Phu Waen, among others. Again, most of these monks never knew one another, came from different sects and from different regions, but they are grouped together in one poster like members of an all-star monastic football team. Perhaps the greatest example of this grouping is at the National Museum of Human Imagery, where the resin, wax, and fiberglass statues of monks, kings, and gods are brought together with the images of famous musicians, artists, and historical figures in Thailand. They share in one another's prestige and partially create it, each for the others. They are their own celebrity endorsements. They have become an ensemble cast.

Akadet Khrisanathilok's three-volume study of Phra Somdet amulets is a good example of how local independent historians study amulets. They start with the object itself—the material and the methods of its production and design. Akadet makes a great effort to teach the reader how to spot fakes and warns against schemes. His concern is how the material qualities of Phra Somdet amulets reflect both local choices and the relation between material and worship. He refers to Phra Somdet as *buchaniyawatthu* (raw material for the purpose of worship). Somdet To's goal, Akadet claims, was to cause *aphinihan saksit* (sacred miracles) after his death (the amulets would act in his place) and offer the Thai people *ekalak thang tham* (something that possessed the essence or "identity" of dharma). People today in Thailand, he emphasizes, do not have the skills or proper substances, especially the *phong*, or powder of high enough sacred quality, to make these items anymore. This powder is the most important material needed to make an amulet. Somdet To used *phong khao suk* (fresh white powder) to make amulets and then distributed it to novices and monks to make their own amulets. At Wat Rakhang, one of the high-ranking monks, Phra Khru Platwichit Khantiko, guards a large stone that was used by Somdet To to grind powder (*bao khlot phong*) for making his amulets. Therefore, Somdet To saw himself not simply as the sole producer of amulets but as a person who helped others develop their own amulet lineages. As we saw with the production of images, one image is used to make others, like mothers bearing children. The powder Somdet To used could be seen as the raw material others could use to create their own material offspring. This is why Phra Somdet amulets can have multiple *rung* (generations). Phra Somdet of the first generation are considered the most valuable; however, those made by Somdet To's own students with raw material and techniques directly connected to Somdet To are also extremely valuable, like colts sired by famous thoroughbreds.

Somdet To did not only use *phong khao suk* but also *phong keson* (pollen filled powder), *phong wan* (sweet powder), *phong takrai bai sema* (lemongrass powder taken from the boundary stones of monasteries). The first was made from lotus, jasmine, plumeria, and other flower pollen (and pistils and stamens). The flowers were said to have been given to Somdet To during his alms rounds and therefore were already the products of merit. The second was made out of roots of sweet-smelling plants. These plant materials were used not only for their olfactory and visual aesthetics but also because they were medicine for curing headaches, fevers, and the like. The third is taken from lemongrass pollen, which often floats through the air. Somdet To was said to scrape this pollen off the boundary stones of monasteries, where it often collected. Therefore, these amulets possess direct medicinal value. Besides these three basic types of powder, there are also different mixtures, with names like *itthiche, patthamang, maharat*, among others, with different amounts of each petal, stamen, root, and the like. They could not only be used to hold and keep close to one's heart around a necklace but also soaked in holy water. The medicine in the powder would be absorbed by what was around it (i.e., skin and water). Akadet emphasizes that Somdet To was a practical healer. While other scholars criticize the irrational collection of seemingly worthless trinkets (based on the fact that amulets do not usually contain rare and precious material like gems or gold), Akadet links the material the amulets are made of directly to their value. Akadet offers methods and photographs to train readers in the identification of the material in amulets. For example, *phong* is identifiable by color and can be seen with a small magnifying glass (jeweler's loop). Besides the color of *phong*, there are also other substances in amulets that are easy to spot if one is trained in what to look for: oyster- and clam-shell flakes, banana flower, ground jackfruit seeds, small scraps of monks' robes, and pieces of palm-leaf manuscripts.[90]

Some of these ingredients are roasted before being added to the mixture, and each ingredient is chanted over with various incantations, including the *Nāmo buddhāya, Itipiso, Jinapañjara, Bahuṃ*, and various *parittas*. Since most amulets are barely one inch tall, correctly identifying these substances takes time, but this time is relaxing and social, as it is often interspersed with short conversations and snacks.

Akadet offers detailed drawings of different types of Phra Somdet, especially those made at Wat Rakhang, to help train traders and collectors in identifying quality and exposing fakes. One should look not only for the color and clumps and fragments of different substances but also for cracks, inscriptions, and flaws in the stamps. For example, Phra Somdet Wat Rakhang amulets generally have a stamp of a Buddha seated on a three-tiered throne (*asana* or *than*) with his hands folded in his lap and with a pronounced, sharp *ushnisha* (topknot). The arched frame around the seated Buddha is carved with two pronounced lines. All these details need to be checked. The number of tiers (usually three, but five, seven, or nine are also possible), the shape of the tiers (either straight or with upward rounded edges), the length of the ears (or the lack of ears), the width of the chest, and the length of the neck. These marks can tell you where and by whom the amulet was made. The age of the amulet can be identified by the width of the cracks, the degree to which the carving and stamp have worn away, and the smoothness of the edges. Akadet explains all these features in detail. However, this type of information has been ignored by art historians, who have concentrated on the physicality of seemingly more important images. It has also been overlooked by social critics, anthropologists, and religious studies specialists, who, if they mention amulets in their writings on Thai Buddhism at all, ignore material qualities and specific local histories of amulets. This ignores what many Thai collectors and scholars value and research.

Consecration volumes are another type of Thai publication that serve as a rich source for the study of amulets. These texts, which often have color photographs, describe in detail the rituals, liturgies, dates, materials, and personnel involved in the production of a batch of amulets. For example, in 2006, a batch of amulets of the Phra Kring style (small Buddha image with a hollow core into which is placed a small metal bead) was produced and consecrated in honor of the king's birthday (although he was not in attendance and had nothing to do with the sponsorship or arrangement of the actual production). The ritual begins, as do all amulet-making rituals, with the choosing of the time and date to gather the material, mix the ingredients, make the molds, and the like. These times are determined by Brahman astrologers. The purpose of the amulet production was not only to celebrate the king's birthday but also to "give encouragement to the members of the military and police who have volunteered to work in the three border provinces of southern Thailand."[91] The text then states that this amulet will help the soldiers think about the virtues of Buddhism. After these celebratory remarks, details of the ritual and liturgy are provided. The liturgy was taken from the formulas of Somdet Phra Phonarat (of Wat Pa Kaeo in Ayutthaya), who had instructed Somdet Phra Naresuan, the first producer of Phra Kring amulets. Using this liturgy, *yantra* drawings were inscribed, and the materials were prepared for casting. The material composition included nine different metals, including gold, the relic bones of Somdet Phra Phae, a former *sangharat*, *phong*, and a mold kept at the national sangha headquarters in Nakhon Pathom. The actual mixing of the metals and other ingredients took place in Lampang Province because there is a claim that the wax core (which melts during the casting process and thus leaves a hollow center in the image) was made from a traditional recipe from Wat Phra That Lampang Luang in northern Thailand. So that the whole country could participate in the event, the names of the seventy-six provinces were each inscribed on metal *yantra* sheets to be added to the alloy. Then in the casting process, Brahman masters were brought in to join with at least one monk from each of the seventy-six provinces. It is stated that these abundant (*udom*) and auspicious (*mongkhon*) materials were made using various superior methods (*khaledasat wicha chan sung*) by true experts (*buraphachan*). Then the newly cast amulets were moved to Wat Suthat in Bangkok, where they were consecrated with chanting drawn from the manual of Somdet Phra Naresuan and Somdet Phra Phonarat. After the seventy-six monks chanted over the 960 amulets produced (celebrating the ninth king of the Cakri dynasty and his sixtieth year on the throne), members of the Mahatherasamak-hom higher ecclesiastical council inspected the quality of the amulets. In the conclusion of the text there is a mixture of Brahmanic, royal, nationalist, and Buddhist sentiments: "The Phra Kring Luang made on this auspicious date is the highest quality and most auspicious Phra Kring amulet in existence . . . It was made for the king and for the good of the country . . . It is made [by monks] of important monasteries in accordance with the recipes of Phra Kring in order for it to be an auspicious object for the Thai people . . . This will ensure that the spirits [*thewada*] protect them . . . It has been sanctioned by the Buddha from an ancient ritual in accordance with the recipe books in the manual of Wat Suthat."[92]

The example of this ritual, of which I could describe only a brief section, shows that some amulets are made on a national scale for important occasions. This could be interpreted simplistically as an example of elite manipulation—the blatant effort to invoke loyalty to Buddhism, the royal family, and the nation all while exploiting people economically through the sale of religious trinkets made through a contrived ritual performance. It could be read as an obvious example of national theater in the guise of religion. It could be seen as a sad example of a once devoutly Buddhist populace reduced to trading in worthless trinkets and bowing down at the altar of Western commercialism. However, interpreting this ritual and the book written to commemorate it in a crudely nationalist manner would prevent us from learning why a relatively highly educated population living in a modern country values amulets.

What can we learn from amulets if we study them historically and as pieces of religious art? First, the cost of this ritual and the production of this book far outweighs the direct profits made from the actual amulets (since most of the amulets and the books were given as gifts to the royal family and high-ranking monks, Brahmans, and lay sponsors). The income from amulet sales is widely distributed. The amulets produced at these ceremonies are rented or given as gifts, and the direct profits from their rentals are usually quite insignificant. These gifts are considered some of the most gracious ways of thanking another person for their friendship, because you are giving them the gift of merit making. They might not have been able to go to the monastery or ritual you attended, so by giving them a material object from the monastery, they share in the merit. For example, an amulet with the image Phra Phuttha Chinarat was made for the anniversary of a locally well-known monk in Phisanulok and sponsored by Naresuan University in 2008. This amulet was freely distributed at the consecration and then rented later for less than three dollars a piece. Considering the amulet was gold plated and presented in an inscribed plastic case, the profits were not significant. Even a solid silver amulet stamped with Luang Pho Saeng's image (one of the teachers of Somdet To) was produced at Wat Manichonlakhan in Lopburi in 2000. The sales, I was told, did little to increase the coffers that year at this small monastery, even though each amulet cost fourteen dollars. Many people who sponsor the production of amulets and the monks who host the consecration and later distribution or sale would not go through the trouble if they were interested simply in profits. However, the production and renting of some batches of amulets can be considerably profitable. The point is that the history and production of each amulet need to be investigated before reducing the motivation to pure commercialism.

Second, if we do view the phenomenon of amulets in Thailand through the lens of economics, there needs to be a study of indirect profits as well. The consecrations of batches of amulets are rarely national events as in the previous example but are very popular local events often connected to annual monastic fairs or anniversaries. These events attract locals in various provinces, students, monks, as well as pilgrims and invited honorary guests. These people need places to eat, sleep, and shop. Therefore, there are hundreds if not thousands of people who profit from these events—food vendors, carnival-ride operators, astrologers, the renters of sound equipment, local shopkeepers, souvenir makers, candle and incense companies and vendors, florists, motel owners, charter-bus companies, dance troupes, and the like. Of course, the publishers of amulet magazines, commemorative volumes, cases, necklaces also indirectly or directly profit from this industry. Even when amulets are distributed freely, most people who visit monasteries make small or large donations. There is a considerable amount of local revenue that is produced. For example, I have been to many amulet-consecration rituals and have gone on "pilgrimages" to see certain monasteries and certain monks. I nearly always rent a few amulets for myself and as gifts for friends and often purchase local products in whatever province I happen to be, such as silk, fruit, nuts, or handicrafts. I am one of millions in Thailand who participate in this practice regularly. Wat Phra That Lampang Luang, the site of the mixing of the ingredients in the Phra Kring amulet, is a fifteenth-century monastery situated in the middle of rice paddies and fruit orchards in rural northern Thailand. It is out of the way and not on most Western-tourist itineraries. However, it is very important historically and ritually in the north. It attracts mostly Thai pilgrims seeking to view its architecture, circumambulate its reliquary, and participate in ritual consecrations and other ceremonies. It is the single-most important moneymaker in the villages that surround it. There are hundreds of shopkeepers, students, carpenters, and truck drivers who depend on it. It is responsible for the most consistent local income stream, especially when the agricultural commodities markets change so frequently and the region fluctuates between flood seasons and droughts. The same can be said of Wat Ban Rai in northeastern Thailand, Wat Wangwiwek in Kanchanaburi, Wat Chang Hai in Pattani, among many others. The economy of amulets is a desperately needed boost to the local economy. Moreover, it is not only the abbot of the monastery, local government officials, and members of local mafia families who are hording this revenue. People from all classes are profiting. Monks are not simply manipulating people into buying trinkets, they are participating in a microeconomic environment that is encouraged by many who have nothing to do with the monastery and who may or may not be interested in collecting or believe in the power of amulets, and who may not even self-identify as Buddhist. There certainly are problems with the amulet trade, as with any other: theft, fraud, obsession, and the like. These have been well discussed by others. However, in scholarly studies the negative effects of the trade too often overshadow the benefits.

Third, the amulets, old or new, that make it to the amulet markets outside monasteries are a profitable business but not a centrally controlled one like a brewery, oil company, toy factory, or automobile producer. There is no centralized group of monks who produce amulets and who are hording the raw materials or secrets of production. Amulets are produced by many monks of different ranks in many different monasteries. Amulet sales do not require elaborate store-fronts, access to foreign technology, heavy machinery, tech-repair specialists, lawyers, insurance, or a highly trained staff with salaries and benefits. It is an industry that the uneducated and nonelite can break into and become experts. Most amulet dealers I know are not wealthy. For example, Sutachai, who runs a store in the Tha Phrachan amulet market, the most well-known one in the country, crowded with renters, traders, and the curious every day, states that she usually takes in 500 to 1,000 baht a day (14 to 28 dollars). Some days she hardly sees a customer. Other days she manages to rent a large image or a rare amulet. Since she employs two assistants and must stock her shelves, she does not see her shop as being very successful. However, she loves the friends she has in the market, she makes merit, and she learns much about different teachers and an-cient things (*wattu boran*). Sutachai's shop is one of the larger ones in the market: she earns a living. The amulet dealers who set up shop by spreading a blanket on a folding table on the sidewalk are lucky, they tell me, if they rent one or two items a day for between 25 and 300 baht each. In general, the shops and the temporary sidewalk dealers do not pay high rents. Owners of the shops in the market, some of whom have been in business over forty years, can either occupy the space themselves or rent the space out to rotating temporary shops. These owners pay only 20 baht (80 cents) a day for upkeep of the market. However, a renter will need to pay the shop owner about 125 baht a day in rent (3 dol-lars). The shop spaces are tight and usually passed down from parent to child. If they are sold, which is rare, they can fetch up to 10,000 dollars. However, this is a relatively low buy-in to own your own business. Since they are rarely sold, large conglomerates or chain stores have not infiltrated the market. Taxes are extremely low since no one reports their full income and there are few receipts. Sidewalk vendors pay no taxes but pay the shopkeepers in the neighborhood inexpensive under-the-table fees.[93] There are certainly a few wealthy individuals who own a number of stalls in the larger amulet markets in the country, but for a large part this is one of the few industries in Thailand, like the street-restaurant business, that help the lower and middle classes, as well as the rich.

Fourth, there are indeed many monasteries that get rich from amulet sales, but it is where the profits go that is worth noting. Let me provide a couple ex-amples. At Wat Srapathum, Phra Thawon organized a casting of Jatukham Ramathep amulets of various colors and sizes in 2006. This ceremony and its products raised 65 million baht (almost 2 million dollars). This money has been used to build a Buddhist school for poor children in rural Bangladesh and help fund the building of a monastery in Australia. It also helped with the repairs and restoration of the nineteenth-century *ubosot* and *wihan* of Wat Srapathum itself. While Phra Thawon is certainly a self-promoter and effective marketer of amulets, in an interview with me in February 2008 he said that people who came to make merit and rent the Jatukham Ramathep amulets were well aware where this funding was going. Indeed, there are photographs of the construction of the school and monastery on large bulletin boards at the entrance of Wat Srapathum. The massive income brought in at Wat Indrawihan is generated from Phra Somdet, Jatukham Ramathep, and Phra Chiwok Koman amulet and image rentals, among other products like books, CDs, and holy-water containers. Much of these funds go to the Somdet To Foundation (Munitthi Somdet Phutthachan To Prahmarangsi), which to date has funded the building of thirty elementary schools in rural Thailand. It is not just cash that is generated, though; the people employed at monasteries (alongside the free labor of novices, *mae-chi*, and monks) are often the handicapped, destitute, or orphans. For example, a woman named Benchawan at Wat Rakhang lives at Wat Rakhang without paying rent. She told me that her husband abused her and she ran away. She lives at the monastery and spends her days sitting at a booth renting Phra Somdet amulets. She eats, largely for free, and participates in regular monastic events. She now has a large group of supportive friends. The new computers and reference desk in the library of Wat Rakhang, a place that provides free after-school tutoring programs and study space for children in this very dense and loud neighborhood of Bangkok, have been funded by the renting of Phra Somdet amulets. A young mentally disabled boy at Wat Sateu in Ayutthaya, a site of one of Somdet To's residences, helps hand out candles, flowers, and incense sticks at the Somdet To shrine. I was told by a monk there that he was abandoned by his parents when he was a baby and is now being cared for by the monks at the monastery. He also attends the monastery's elementary school, eats in the cafeteria, and is given clothes and toys, all without charge. The funding for this child comes from the ability of Wat Sateu's monks and wider rural community to "commercialize" the amulets and legacy of Somdet To.[94] This is not just a new phenomenon. The funding of one of Thailand's premier Pali grammar schools came in 1939 through the sale of amulets.[95]

The sales of Ganesha amulets and images (made by Buddhist monks) have grown in such popularity that the International Thai Studies Conference at Thammasat in 2008, an academic meeting of over four hundred foreign and Thai scholars and presided over by Princess Sirindhorn, was funded largely by the sale of Ganesha images. The original idea of this fund-raising was initiated by Dr. Anucha Thirakanont, director of the Thai Khadi Research Institute and professor at Thammasat University. He commissioned Phra Raja Khru Wamathepmuni, the head of the Brahman sect of Thailand, for the ritual consecration of the images. The design was by a sculptor from the Pao Chang Institute of Art. The wax casting and bronze came from a company called Fine Art Thailand. Three statues were produced (18,900 baht for the eleven-inch one, 7,800 baht for the seven-inch one, and 2,800 baht for the four-inch one). All were limited in quantity: 200 of the large ones, 1,000 of the middle, and 2,000 of the small. The consecration ceremony was performed at the Brahman temple by the head of the Brahman sect himself. The Brahman ceremony was also "enhanced," as Anucha stated, by a Buddhist ceremony at Wat Suthat. This is indeed the first time a secular academic conference was funded by the sale of statues of an elephant-headed deity![96] Social critics and scholars who lament the crass commercialism of the "amulet craze" often fail to mention the collateral social services enabled through the funds generated by the craze. Certainly golden stupas, elaborate murals, air conditioners, and other luxuries are also funded by amulet profits; however, materialism comes in many forms, including food for orphans and cell phones for monks. Critiques of the latter type of materialism as being Western and commercial often fail to praise the former. In this way, amulets can be seen as a great benefit to Buddhist communities rather than a local cultural corruption of traditional Buddhist values. The values of abundance, graciousness, security, and heritage are promoted to different degrees by amulets.

Besides these four economic considerations, amulets have more abstract and unforeseen dimensions that scholars would benefit from studying. Amulets create communities and texts. The wonderings, reflections, and visualizations that take place while looking at an image or walking around a monastery generate questions that can be posed to texts or help individuals develop new beliefs. The conversations that take place over the trading of amulets can be seen as emerging doctrine. Buddhist texts in Thailand are seen as having value, but amulets as being corrupting objects. This is because texts are not seen as objects but as voices. The material features of texts are often overlooked. Amulets are generated by texts. Many, if not most, amulets have inscribed in metal or clay *yantras* in Khom, Thai, or Lan Na script. Many also have information about the monastery, date, and name of the monk they were made by (or in honor of) inscribed on them. This information would go a long way in tracing local lineages and art history, but it has not been the subject of any serious non-Thai study. Other amulets were actually texts originally. These are called *takrut*. They are amulets made of rolled metal (copper, gold, silver, or lead) or palm-leaf scrolls with an inscription. The rolled inscriptions are placed inside glass or metal tubes and sealed. Phra Oot Thamakamo of Wat Sai Mai in Nonthaburi Province has recently produced a set of two *takrut* that have metal scrolls inserted inside bullets that help protect soldiers (among others).[97] These inscriptions can be *yantras,* but more often they are short *paritta* texts. My abbot presented me with one with an abbreviated *Ratanasutta* inscribed on it. There are *takrut* with a full or abbreviated *Jinapañjara* inscription. These *takrut* are rolled and either placed inside small glass or clear-resin tubes and worn around the neck or rolled, bound with sacred string, and sealed with wax, molten metal, or tree sap. This sealing process makes the texts unreadable. One of the most famous *takrut* in Thailand was produced by Phra Khru Thammanukhun Cantakesaro of Wat Indrawihan. He was born in Tak Province in 2373 (1830) and was a *phra thudong* (*dhutaṅga*, "wandering forest monk"); later he moved to the forested area near Wat In-drawihan (along the riverbank where the National Bank of Thailand's offices are now located). This used to be a forested area used by Lao refugees and *thudong* monks traveling in from upcountry, often to visit Somdet To. This ban Lao area became renowned for magically powerful Lao monks. Phra Khru Tham-manukhun resided here, may have been of Lao ethnicity, and later became the abbot at Wat Indrawihan, in 2435 (1892) at the age of sixty-two. He died at age 103 (in 2476 [1933]). He created, it is believed under the tutelage of Phra Arannik and Somdet To, a *takrut* that was eight inches long. It was a short text, covered with a clay mixture used to make Phra Somdets (*phong*). The text inscribed on the metal sheet before being coiled and wrapped in string and covered with powder and resin was the *Awut* (Pali *Āvudha*) *phra phuttha chao* (*The Weapon of the Buddha*). It warded off *phi sat* (devils). His students continued this tradi-tion and produced a number of shorter and different-color *takrut* with the same incantation. All the *takrut* are sealed and unreadable.[98]

Some clay amulets are actually made from texts. One of the more popular ingredients for amulets is the ground-up clay roof tiles from famous monaster-ies. The red, blue, orange, and other roof tiles of Thai monasteries are iconic. These clay tiles often need to be replaced. Men on scaffolding slowly replacing one tile after another is a common sight at Thai monasteries. The old tiles are taken down and smashed. The dust from the tiles is considered valuable be-cause it has absorbed the chanting of the texts inside the monastery for years. It is believed that as the monks sit under the ceilings and chant, the sound drifts upward and is absorbed. The dust from the old clay tiles is mixed with other in-gredients and shaped into amulets. When individuals donate (usually ten baht [twenty-five cents] each) new tiles to the monastery, they often write their names on the tiles using black, felt-tip pens. Therefore, eventually their names will be ground up and placed in amulets as well. In other cases, old palm-leaf manuscripts that have become tattered and unreadable are ground up into dust, and mixed with water to form a paste. This paste is one of the ingredients that can go into an amulet. Obviously, the semantic meaning of the texts in question is not important. They are illegible. However, amulets are, in this way, textual practices, and oral liturgies and physical texts are needed to make them.

Another way amulets are part of Buddhist textuality is through conversation. The stories and conversations generated from the trade, collection, and production of amulets can be seen as valuable as other Buddhist texts.[99] When people chat in Internet blogs about amulets, meet in markets in and outside of monasteries, attend consecration rituals, amulet contests, monastic fairs, and auctions, they often talk about different Buddhist teachers, monasteries they have visited, and the material qualities and power of their own amulets. Most of these conversations are ethereal and brief. However, they can be seen as Buddhist texts. The most popular Buddhist texts in Thailand are *jātaka* tales (both canonical and noncanonical), and stories drawn directly or inspired by the *Dhammapada-at-thakathā*. Local histories, such as relic chronicles, dynastic histories, and biographies of famous monks, are also popularly known (*tamnan, phongsawadan,* and the like). These are all found in manuscripts from various regions in Thailand, some dating back to the fifteenth century. They form the content of many sermons. These are all stories that relate miracles, the heroic acts of famous images, monks, and princes, and trace the mytho-historical legacy of Buddhism both locally and translocally. Conversations about amulets, especially their material composition, history, and powers, are part of this longer textual heritage of Thailand. The rituals, catalogs, detailed material analyses, stamps, photographs, museum displays, and amulet sets not only help collectors but they also attract amateurs to the field and inspire pilgrims, start conversations, and create new communities. Parents often want their teenage children to go on pilgrimages and attend monastic festivals so as to keep them away from narcotics and other less-savory pastimes. Oftentimes, my friends in Thailand are inspired to go on these pilgrimages from amulet-market hearsay, testimonies of friends, and amulet catalogs and magazines. Many who go on these pilgrimages do not rent amulets, but they go to learn about the lives, miraculous feats, and teachings of these monks. They also attend local music concerts and festivals. Conversations about amulets are a way of breaking the ice. They are also a way to commiserate and express fears. When my wife was pregnant with our second child, I had conversations with several pregnant couples at the Mae Nak shrine at Wat Mahabut regarding fears of miscarriage as we rented protective oil. I have overheard women *huang* (worry) about their husbands and sons serving in the military at the shrine while they purchase dresses and cosmetics to present to the image of Mae Nak. Students who have never met often strike up conversations about impending examinations while standing near the image of Somdet To at Wat Rakhang as they stand waiting to pick up flowers or incense or rent an amulet.

These conversations are taking place between people in Australia, Japan, Singapore, the United States, Thailand, Malaysia, and other places in online amulet trading and collecting blogs. Tour groups of amulet traders from Taiwan and Singapore are beginning to go to Wat Rakhang and Wat Indrawihan. One visitor to Wat Rakhang was so inspired by the story of Somdet To and the possible power of his amulets that he donated a painting he had done of Somdet To. This painting, executed in abstract calligraphic style with Somdet To's name in Chinese, now hangs prominently above the main door of the newly designed library.[100] These new communities sometimes formalize themselves into amulet-collecting clubs or charitable foundations. This social component and the conversations lead to the writing of new texts, the tracing of new histories, the recounting and reinterpreting (and exaggerating) of local biographies, and the increase of local pride. One can see it as energizing local textual practices and shifting understanding of heritage and expressions of graciousness.

Individuals not only feel protected wearing amulets around their necks but also can participate in an abundant material culture even if they are not wealthy themselves. For example, an ice cream vendor, Batwat, whom I met at Wat Rakhang, proudly showed me the amulets hanging on his necklace. He had a Phra Somdet, a Jatukham Ramathep, a Luang Pho Tuat, and three *takrut*, one of which he stated helped him meet his future wife! Sopon Suptongthong, a taxi driver from Bangkok, is a devotee of Somdet To. He showed me the *yantra* made at the Hindu temple Wat Khaek in Bangkok, that he had placed above his head on the taxi's roof. It was placed next to two other *yantras*, one drawn in white powder and another one made of red cloth and sealed in a plastic sheath. These, he stated, protected him against accidents, and they were also drawn by a Phra Prahm (a Hindu priest). On the dashboard he had glued a Phra Sangacchai because it brought happiness and money. He said this encouraged his passengers to give him money and *udom sombun* (abundance) for his family. Aesthetically, he also liked this image because it "yim talot" (smiled all the time). In the center of the dash he had a Phra Somdet To amulet. Somdet To, he asserted, was important because he had *metta* for the people, just like the king. He elaborated that Somdet To was much like the monk-king to all the people of Thailand! Next to the Phra Somdet, he had a Kuan Im that, he said, reminded him not to get drunk and drive! He was unsure himself why Kuan Im was believed to protect against drunk driving. He had Chiwok Koman (Jivaka) hanging from the rearview mirror because that protected him from catching colds from his passengers and getting sick. He had many Jatukham Ramatheps stuck to the windshield. He wasn't sure why he had those, he said. He just liked them. Sathapon Sawamiwat from Chachoengsao Province was the driver of another taxi I took in Bangkok. He had only one image in his taxi, a Somdet To statue on his dashboard. He liked Somdet To because he practiced both *paṭipatti* and *pariyatti*—he was a meditator and a scholar. He was *yot* (high ranking), like the king, but he loved the *chao ban* (villagers), like the king. Somdet To visited all the villages; he didn't just stay in the city. Somdet To, he also stated, was an expert in Pali-Sanskrit but used simple words in his sermons. Sathapon admitted that he didn't know much about history (he did get a few simple facts about Somdet To's life wrong) and could chant only a little, but he still loved Somdet To. One of the most interesting conversations I have ever had about Thai Buddhism was with Pithipon, a coffee shop owner in Chiang Rai (northern Thailand). As I was ordering a cup, I noticed that she was reading an English-language translation of the *Tibetan Book of the Dead*. She had received a master's degree in Bangkok and learned to read (although not speak) English. This led to a discussion about different religious traditions in Thailand. She showed me her extensive collection. She had a Chinese Jade Emperor image, a Kuan Im, statues and photographs and amulets with images of Somdet To, Luang Pho Khan, Khrupa Siwichai, Khrupa Nunchum (a Shan monk), King Chulalongkorn, and photographs from the shrine to Ṛsi Bharata, a locally famous Brahman sage in Nakhon Ratchasima Province. She did not believe that people needed to choose which religion to believe in; she valued sacred people and were drawn to their teachings and *barami* (a type of sacred power generated through specific virtuous practices). Amulets and images were not mere bricolage she had assembled from random trips. They defined her intellectual approach to religion in general.

Willa Cather famously quipped that "religion and art spring from the same root and are close kin. Economics and art are strangers."[101] I hope that I have shown that, despite Cather's quip, amulets are objects in which art, religion, and economics have come together in creative ways. Opening a discussion about amulets that takes history and materiality seriously exposes motivations and values for the production, display, and trade of amulets that cannot be reduced to mere modern commercialism, globalization, or Westernization. I see these famous monks and their amulets as simply creating new types of communities, communities of pilgrims, amulet traders, spiritual tourists, and online communities. Scholars so often separate culture and religion—culture is something that "happens" to religion, and this happening is almost always negative. I am arguing that we cannot hope to learn from Thai Buddhism if we do not take seriously its material culture and the way individual agents incorporate objects into their personal religious repertoires. The way individuals construct their repertoires consciously and subconsciously over time is part of the shifting way ethics are expressed.

# ULTRAMAN AND THE SIAM COMMERCIAL BANK:
# MURALS AND AGENCY IN MODERN THAILAND

In the northernmost province of Thailand, Chiang Rai, there are two monasteries whose murals tell very different stories. Among other phantasmagoric images at Wat Rong Khun, there is a depiction of the American actor Keanu Reeves dressed as his famous film character Neo from the *Matrix* trilogy, wearing a black trench coat and dark sunglasses. He is standing in a macho, kung fu–like pose next to a pod racer from episode 1 of *Star Wars*. Near him is a painting of Ultraman, a well-known Japanese animated hero (and, by far, my young son's favorite mural character in Thailand!). Besides these fictional, and randomly assembled, heroes there are also images of a demon holding a cell phone and the World Trade Center in New York City being hit by a commercial jet. Depictions of the terrorist attacks of September 11, 2001, and of international pop culture heroes are interspersed with paintings of AK-47 machine guns, gas pumps, flaming skulls, and satellites. These murals, which were still being completed when I visited them in March 2008, are the creation of Chalermchai Kositpipat. In fact, Wat Rong Khun itself was designed by Chalermchai. Although the *wihan* of the *wat* is similar in size and architecture to central Thai monasteries, it is completely white, with carved leaping flames, statuary of Brahmanic gods, and skulls—lots of skulls. The entrance to the monastery has a bridge over a wide pit. Hundreds of sculpted hands reach up from the pit, which is supposed to depict hell. The hands are asking for alms, for mercy. Chalermchai is a social critic whose uses painting and sculpture to point out the dangers of global culture, materialism, and greed. His work is very popular in Thailand, but he has not been well received by critics or other artists. He is a businessman who runs shops and a large gallery at the monastery selling his art. Life-size posters of him are hung in several places on the grounds. This is neither a gimmick nor simply one man's obsession; Wat Rong Khun is a functioning monastery in the process of building dorm rooms for novices and monks. On a day I was there, over two hundred monks from Phichit Province in central Thailand were visiting and chanting there. People prostrate, offer alms, and the like as they would at any other monastery.[102]

The second monastery is Wat Phra Kaeo. Unlike Wat Rong Khun, it is very old. It was built sometime between 1391 and 1432. It may be the first monastery in Thailand to have held the famous Emerald Buddha, the palladium of the modern Thai state that now sits in Wat Phra Kaeo in Bangkok. Wat Phra Kaeo in Chiang Rai is a royal monastery and is considered the most sacred place in the province. However, like Wat Rong Khun, it has new murals. The murals are housed in a new building that honors the legacy of the Emerald Buddha. Surrounding a copy of the Emerald Buddha, the walls are covered in rather cartoonish murals that depict the history of the image from the fourteenth century to the present. As the murals change from one historical period to the next, the style of painting also changes. The last mural depicts world leaders, Chinese businesspeople, camera-toting tourists, all seated or standing near the present king of Thailand, Rama IX, who is dressed in a Western suit and necktie.

These creative murals are not unique to Chiang Rai Province; in fact, they are not limited to new mural projects. Past and present, perhaps the best way to see the diversity of Thai Buddhist art is to spend time looking at murals. Central Thai murals from the eighteenth and nineteenth centuries do anything but reinforce tradition or Buddhist teachings. In fact, many murals do not depict Buddhist teachings or texts at all. These are creative sites, not repositories of supposedly orthodox ideals.[103] However, as I have argued throughout this book, "orthodoxy" is largely an ideal that is not found in any single monastery, museum, or monastic library. It is difficult to find any one monastery that does not have some evidence of supposedly non-Buddhist texts or art, whether statues of Ganesha, scenes of Chinese romances, or Persian dignitaries.

In this way, it is difficult to draw a line between what is considered "Buddhist" by viewers and producers of Thai monastic art even at some of the most famous royal monasteries, not tucked away on the walls of insignificant, rogue monasteries.[104] For example, Wat Phra Kaeo, the most important royal monastery in the country (among dozens of other monasteries) has murals depicting different scenes from the Thai version of the Sanskrit epic *Rāmāyaṇa*. The murals of Wat Kho Kaeo Suttharam in Petchaburi Province depict the cosmology of heavens and hells from the *Traiphumikathā*. In Bangkok, Wat Ratchaorot, an Ayutthaya-era monastery restored by Kings Rama II and III, has an *ubosot* in which there are intricate murals depicting Chinese deities along with Chinese still-life scenes—flower arrangements, a Chinese desk set, a quill and ink bottle, and a silk scroll with Chinese characters. These all surround a very large early Bangkok-style Buddha image and a painting of King Rama III. The murals in the *wihan* contain scenes from the Chinese epic romance *Sam kok*.[105] This is also a royal monastery. Wat Suwandararam in Ayutthaya has murals depicting the life of King Naresuan, with Brahman priests, ṛṣi casting spells over fires, bloody battles, and prison torture. Some of the murals at Wat Suthat depict scenes of Westerners arriving on ships to Bangkok.[106] Gerhard Jaiser has recently observed murals at Wat Tha Sung in Uthai Thani Province, which were painted in 1928 and cast the life story of the Buddha in the modern period. Although the murals depict the Buddha in the Indian city of Benares in the background, there are paintings of a modern car, Thai opium pipes, and cigarettes. The artist, Phra In, also included his own portrait and signature.[107] Explicit anachronism is common in Thai murals and paintings. Forrest McGill has studied the classical landscape of seventeenth-century French and Italian painting that is often in the background of Thai murals in Bangkok. A cloth-screen painting of Mara's attack on the Buddha depicts a soldier with bloodshot eyes holding a rifle in a scene that took place two thousand years before the rifle was invented. He is wearing a shirt covered in Thai protective *yantras* (in Khom script), and in his belt is a knife with a penis-shaped handle, a tool of some magicians in Thailand and Laos.[108] Another soldier is wearing a headdress made of snakes similar to headdresses worn by Brahmans in the murals of Wat Khong-karam. In the depictions of the Himavanta Forest from the *Vessantara jātaka* at Wat Khian in Angthong Province, there are depictions of Chinese physicians drinking rice whiskey and of Persian warriors. In the murals depicting the Lao epic poem *Xiang miang*, at Wat Pathumwanaram in Bangkok, Thai soldiers are wearing American colonial military uniforms, and on the pillars there are paintings of two *bhikkhunī* (fully ordained nuns), Brachabodhi and Bathachara, even though there is no evidence that there were ordained *bhikkhunī* in nineteenth-century Thailand or in sixteenth-century Laos (approximately the era the *Xiang miang* was compiled).[109] The inscriptions of the names of these two nuns are written in Khom script. Therefore, in one set of Thai murals in a Bangkok monastery we have a Lao epic that depicts men in American dress and Khom (Cambodian) script labeling Indian nuns. Time and space are collapsed according to the whims of the artist and the patron.

The murals in the many buildings of the great royal monastery Wat Chetupon (better known as Wat Pho), next to the Grand Palace, show a great diversity of noncanonical, canonical, Brahmanic, and Thai local folk stories, including paintings of various ascetic practices, scenes from Thai children's stories, the lives of thirteen nuns (*bhikkhunī*), the locations of footprints of the Buddha throughout southern Asia, scenes from the Sri Lankan chronicle *Mahāvaṃsa*, and several scenes from Sanskrit epics. Alongside these murals spread throughout the monastery are inscriptions with instructions on how to heal, predict the future through astrology, and even manuals on the craft of war. In the *ubosot* of another major royal monastery, Wat Suthat in Bangkok, there are paintings of disconnected scenes from different narratives. One scene is drawn from the Thai version of the Panji theme from Java, the *Inao*. It is of Princess Bussaba asking a Buddha statue to hear her plea and return her true love to her. Even though this scene is not in any known Javanese or Malay version of the story, here we see a creative muralist choosing a Thai Buddhist scene from a non-Buddhist, foreign drama—a scene disconnected from many others in the room.[110] Santi Phakdikham has shown that the walls of one monastic building can have paintings of a canonical *jātaka*, while the paintings on the doors of the room can have paintings from noncanonical *jātakas* and other local romance stories that have little to do with Buddhist teachings or religion in general, like the romance story of Sangthong.[111] In fact, one could argue that religious themes are often absent in murals painted on the inside of Buddhist monastic buildings! This would be like seeing murals of individual and disconnected episodes of Shakespeare's *King Lear* mixed with disconnected scenes from *Beowulf* or the *Iliad* inside a Catholic cathedral.

At Wat Indrawihan, the last monastery of which Somdet To was an abbot, there is a new set of murals. These murals were finished in 1980, and much to the dismay of art historians in Thailand, they were painted directly over the previous murals completed sometime in the 1890s. The new murals are supposedly creative interpretations of older ones (of which we have no surviving photographic record) that depicted scenes from the life of Somdet To.[112] However, these new murals, despite the abbot's claim to the contrary, do not perfectly replicate older styles; instead, many of the scenes are based on photographs of Somdet To, King Mongkut, and others. Alongside depictions of Somdet To's life, these murals include scenes of Chinese, Portuguese, and Turkish merchants sitting crowded on boats, children playing, partially hidden lovers kissing behind walls, monks casually seated on porches reading manuscripts, and people seated in circles eating snacks. There are even specific historical paintings of the building of the ninety-foot-tall standing Buddha image, Luang Pho To, and of amulets being made by Somdet To. There are scenes of Somdet To's pilgrimages to Ayutthaya and Kampaengphet, as well as of his private meetings with King Mongkut. Because Wat Indrawihan is in a neighborhood of Lao refugees, many of the women in the murals are dressed in Lao-style skirts.

One of the most telling sections is on the back wall. Here there is a section of mural paintings of foreigners. They are presented as rather hairy and corpulent, dressed in elaborate Victorian suits, and standing near a bank. This is the oldest major bank in Thailand, the Siam Commercial Bank. The muralist painted the iconic bank headquarters, designed by Italian architect Annibale Rigotti in 1906, including its English sign. This is one of the only places where a Thai mural includes English words. King Mongkut is seen seated speaking with foreigners next to the bank. The problem here is that this bank was not built until 1906, when the bank opened. King Mongkut had long been dead (as had Somdet To). Moreover, the National Bank of Thailand is located near Wat Indrawihan, not the Siam Commercial Bank. Therefore, this muralist could not have been modeling his new murals on the old ones. Nineteenth-century muralists could not have painted these scenes. They had not happened yet. In fact, there were several muralists, led by a Sino-Thai artist named Kheng Sae Ang in consultation with Phra Sophanathamawong and Somdet Phra Phutthachan Kiao Uboseno. They clearly modeled this mural set on photographs of King Mongkut, Somdet To, and foreign merchants. In this way, the modern technology of photography inspired the traditional art of mural painting. Moreover, by assembling undated photographs together, the muralists combined various historical scenes that, while individually historically accurate, never existed at the same time. A historical period is not being represented; historical photographs are being grouped together and painted nonsequentially and creatively.

While there are certainly hundreds of examples of murals drawn from *jātakas* (either canonical or apocryphal Southeast Asian *jātakas*) and scenes from the life of the Buddha, often murals in Thailand do not attempt to represent Buddhist narratives or illustrate texts at all.[113] This is often how art historians working in Southeast Asia often talk about murals, though—either as visual representations of texts or pedagogical tools for the illiterate masses. Either way they are secondary to texts. They represent a lesser form of traditional learning. Michael Baxandall and Henry Maguire have tried to show the problems with assuming that text and image are simply two different ways for depicting the same narrative. The former observed that "we [art historians] do not explain pictures, we explain remarks about pictures—or rather, we explain pictures only in so far as we have considered them under some verbal description or specification."[114] Eugene Wang has lamented the way murals have been unimaginatively studied in China. He notes that modern scholarship on the subject is based on the premise that murals are "pictorial illustrations or derivatives of sutras. Therefore, to make sense of these tableaux is to match them with sutra texts. They are accordingly filed away in our mental cabinet according to the bibliographic taxonomy of sutra sources."[115] The same can be said for scholarship on Thai murals.[116] Besides the historical studies of No Na Paknam, almost every introduction to a study of murals at a Thai monastery, especially in English, begins with the association of the mural with a particular text.[117] There are studies of Thai murals that completely ignore the particular histories, local contexts, artists' biographies of any one set of murals, choosing instead to offer a study that takes examples of murals from many monasteries that depict one text. These often neglect to mention that the particular sets of murals they are drawing evidence from contain scenes from several narratives, some of which are unknown, and may be the product of an artist's own imagination. For example, the doyen of Thai mural painting, Jean Boisselier, bases his analysis of some of Thailand's best-known mural paintings almost solely on the way in which they depict Buddhist texts and sees murals as primarily pedagogical in function.[118] Uthong Prasatwinicchai's two-volume study of the murals of the last ten *jātakas* offers a long introduction to the texts but very little on the artists who painted the murals.

Furthermore, he draws examples of murals of the ten *jātakas* from monasteries like Wat Ban Takhu, Wat Khao Yisan, Wat Mahathat (Petchaburi), among many others, whose histories and styles are not related. The only thing that links them is the choice *jātaka* to represent. The grouping of these murals is the choice of Uthong, not of the artists who painted these murals originally and who may not have seen themselves as part of a movement to teach or represent this particular collection.[119] Even the one study of the murals at Wat Indrawihan states that they were drawn from a biography of Somdet To written by Chantichai, even though many of the scenes depicted are not contained in that biography and are instead based on a random collection of stories and photographs of Somdet To.[120]

Murals are often not seen as the creators of their own narratives, as texts in themselves. However, some mural sets creatively combine elements from a number of oral and textual sources by means of the artist's imagination.[121] The murals in the *ubosot* of Wat Kongkaram (Ratchaburi Province) are a good example. The monastery, originally used by the Mon ethnic community in the area, was built in the eighteenth century. The murals on the interior walls are drawn from several sections of several different stories. There are scenes from the story of Prince Siddhattha's "great departure" into the ascetic life, from the *Traibhūmikathā* cosmology, and scenes from various *jātakas*, some included from the last ten, like the *Temiya*, *Suvannasama*, and the *Nimi*. Among these more common *jātakas* is a rendering of erotic and violent parts of the *Cullapaduma* (the 193rd story in the canonical collection). This is a racy story of husbands hacking up their wives, roasting them, and feasting on their flesh; a *bodhisatta* feeding his wife from the blood dripping from a self-inflicted wound on his knee; and even an erotic scene of a woman having sex with an armless, legless, earless, noseless man. These are combined with scenes of Persian soldiers, the Buddha subduing the evil Mara, and naked, perhaps lesbian and gay, women and men embracing and fondling. These murals form a type of creative anthology. Not only are these stories only loosely related, if at all, but also the choice of scenes seems to be based more on the unknown artist's penchant for depicting erotic sexuality than on iconic narrative triggers from each story. Moreover, each scene does not attempt to faithfully depict the Indian stories but sets these Indian characters in scenes with Persian, French, and Mon peoples, as well as with cosmopolitan Ayutthayan architecture. The fact that Mon peoples often forbid women to enter their *ubosot* suggests that this room may have been one for pornographic entertainment. It is not an isolated example, though. The artist drew many of the building and dress styles, as well as some of the story choices, not from texts but from murals at other monasteries like Wat Thong Noppakun (Thonburi), Wat Pakklongbangkaeo (Nakhon Chasi), among others.

Therefore, the "texts" the artist was drawing from were not texts in the traditional sense. He was drawing from other murals at other places in Thailand.[122] These murals reference each other; they do not attempt to accurately depict Indic Buddhist stories.

Although without evidence of artists' intentions, which we largely do not have in the historical record, we cannot determine if any one artist saw his primary duty as visually depicting a narrative. Many apparently did want to accurately tell stories through iconic scenes. However, many muralists in Thailand, past and present, may not have been concerned with teaching or representing a particular text but with executing a vision, creating an atmosphere, and invoking a mood.[123] In reality, although they certainly could have been in the past, they are rarely used today as visual pedagogical tools during sermons. The murals, high on the walls, are often hard to see and were much harder to see before the age of electric lights. Indeed, I have interviewed many monks and nuns who were unaware what texts or histories the murals at their own monasteries represented. They did not study these murals, nor were they inspired to go and read the texts these murals supposedly represented or reproduced. Moreover, murals almost never present an entire history or set of teachings in total or in sequence. In fact, the physical space of the walls, the artist's own tastes and talents, and the possible lack of textual knowledge on the part of the artist may account for the fact that rarely can a story be reconstructed by studying a mural set. There are also murals seemingly based on texts that add elements not contained in those texts. Therefore, murals could be either evidence of textual variants or sites of creative expansion of texts. It is likely that in many cases the artist was not concerned with reproducing a text in a different medium. In this way, many murals have limited value if a monk wants to use them as systematic and sequential visual aids during textual lessons. Murals are evidence of the individual repertoires of particular artists and patrons; they reveal the influences, texts, daily experiences, values, sociohistorical contexts, and teaching lineages unique to them rather than depictions of a known canon of Buddhist texts or royal histories.

## CONCLUSION

The ritual, liturgical, material, and historical evidence in chapters 3 and 4 demonstrate the importance of security and protection (*khwam plotphai, kan pongkan*), abundance (*udom sombun*), graciousness (*khwam sawatdiphap* or *kreng chai*), and heritage (*moradok*) for many Thai Buddhists. Amulets, images, incantations, *yantras*, ghosts, and sacred personages are valued often because they are believed to protect those who honor and entreat them. The *Jinapañjara*, Mae Nak, and a Phra Somdet amulet are protective. Monastic campuses, roadside shrines, liturgical handbooks are often abundant with large and ever-growing collections of new images, new patrons, and new texts. Thai Buddhist ceremonies are generally lavish, and monastic cells are often crowded with gifts, books, and incense ash. Presentation is important. The beauty of objects is emphasized. Visitors add to the beauty by offering gifts. Images are laden with gold, flowers surround altars, decorative lights and candles illuminate ritual spaces. Monks are told to keep their robes neat and the monastery grounds swept. During the day when not cleaning, eating, reading, or meditating, although it is not required, many monks sit and receive gifts from visitors and offer short sermons, lottery numbers, or rent amulets. They must look proper and be welcoming. Often abundance and graciousness struggle with each other in monasteries. As more vendors, more stray dogs, and more gifts surrounding popular images accumulate, beauty can occasionally shift to clutter. However, most monasteries settle into a comfortable balance between the need to display abundance and the need to clean so as to be welcoming and make way for new gifts.[124] Of course, as we have seen, the importance of individual images, incantations, amulets, and other ritual devices and material objects are often connected to a local heritage. Many of the images mentioned have their own local legends and are important, like Somdet To, for their connections to royal family members, famous monks of the past, particular local miracle stories, and historical events. This local heritage is often emphasized in inscriptions, plaques, posters, and in sermons.

However, these are not simply present-day cultural axioms for Thai Buddhists. Indeed, as I have discussed in previous work, Thai and local Pali chronicles from as early as the sixteenth century, like the *Jinakālamālīpakaraṇam*, *Tamnān thāt phanom*, and others often speak of the great crowds that surrounded local monasteries and followed famous monks. They recount the beauty of Buddha images, the protective power of relics, and lavish gifts presented to visiting mendicants.[125] There are many stories lauding the lives of *seṭṭhi* (wealthy people) in premodern manuscripts. These local histories are often better known by students of Buddhism in Thailand than Pali chronicles from Burma and Sri Lanka, or even stories of the Buddha and his early followers in the canon. However, even Pali canonical and commentarial stories found in local manuscript libraries also emphasize beauty, abundance, and protective power. This is not simply an aspect of Thai Buddhism past and present. From very early textual, art historical, and archaeological evidence from South Asia we can see that the celebration of abundance, the importance of beauty and graciousness, and the importance of protection were notable values of Buddhist communities.[126] In chapter 3, I provided examples of canonical and extracanonical *jātakas*, stories from the *Dhammapada-aṭṭhakathā*, and protective *parittas* popular for use in Thai liturgies and sermons. Recently, I translated an early nineteenth century bilingual Pali and northern Thai palm-leaf manuscript titled *Nisai madhurasachomphu*.[127] This popular text, based loosely on a Pali narrative collection from Sri Lanka, has long sections stressing the golden color, the sweet scent of sandalwood, the quality of the fabric, and the like of gifts offered to a Buddha, as well as long descriptions of temple festivals (especially the festival connected to the *Aryavaṃsa* sermon), mercantile activity, and the consumption of alcohol. Oskar von Hinüber has found a fragment of the another Pali text that emphasizes celebration, beauty, and abundance, the *Dasadānavatthuppakaraṇa*. This text, from the early sixteenth century, could have originated in Southeast Asia and later brought to Sri Lanka.[128] It enumerates the ten types of gifts offered to monasteries. This text is a type of *anisaṃsa*. *Anisaṃsa* (Thai *anisong*) texts are extremely common in manuscript collections and in printed editions today. This genre of texts specifically discusses the types of material objects presented to images and to monks. Of course, the famous fourteenth-century Thai cosmology *Traibhūmīkathā* has long passages on the beauty and graciousness of various kings, palaces, and deities. Premodern Thai poems like "Lilit phra lo" and "Sangthong" are exercises in abundance containing long passages describing the beauty of princesses, rivers, heroes, and elephants. In the past and sometimes still today the dramatic performances of these poems take place on monastic grounds. Of course, intricate and colorful murals in many monastic buildings both old and new show scenes of hundreds of people offering gifts, kings wearing golden crowns, rays of light emanating from the heads of Buddhas, and there is even one showing enlightened monks wearing monastic robes covered in stars.

## Conclusion

The following lofty reflection appears in the introduction to the jubilee catalog celebrating the "Primi Decem Anni" of the Museum of Jurassic Technology, a rather peculiar little museum in Los Angeles:

> In its original sense, the term "museum" meant a spot dedicated to the muses—"a place where man's mind could attain a mood of aloofness above everyday affairs" . . . However . . . in the city of Philadelphia in America, Charles Wilson Peale was forming a museum that was to become a model for the institution for years to come. Mr. Peale's museum was open to all people (including children and the fair sex) . . . He believed that . . . the learner must be led always from familiar objects toward the unfamiliar; guided along, as it were, a chain of flowers.[1]

Taking Peale's vision and expanding it in bizarre ways, this museum does not attempt to display valuable art or even the up-and-coming work of the avant-garde. Instead, it displays a combination of fraudulent historical objects and the evidence of failed theories and experiments. It is a museum of the history of bad science, of scientists, ethnographers, philosophers, and artists who have been discarded and dismissed as crackpots and charlatans. There are galleries dedicated to Geoffrey Sonnabend's baseless "theory of forgetting," the theory of "hypersymbolic cognition," and fraudulent zoological holdings such as the "stink ant." There are even rooms dedicated to the oft-dismissed seventeenth-century Jesuit polymath Athanasius Kircher and to the history of California mobile homes. This museum defies modern Foucauldian criticism of museums, which states that they have been tools of autocratic states, colonialists, and hegemonic ideologies. The Museum of Jurassic Technology does not try to create ideals and centralize. It questions what we value as knowledge, history, and art. It is not a tool of the state or a forum for a great tradition.

In attempting to describe modern Thai Buddhism, I have not tried to create an ideal or even a comprehensive gallery of features and standards. It is not that I did not try. It is just that various methods, models, tools, and approaches that I have considered over the years applying to this subject, if it is even a subject, have proved inadequate. There are too many exceptions, too many idiosyncrasies, too many monasteries, too many agents, too many points of sight. I never have enough tools of analysis in my bag.

Therefore, I have moved inductively from close investigations of individual historical moments, texts, biographies, and images to somewhat nervous forays into the realm of general statements. This has created a tension throughout this book. Could the evidence drawn from individual shrines, texts, biographies, or objects justify generalizations about Thai Buddhism more broadly? Does the accumulation of evidence constitute an argument? Or did I merely arrange a chain of rather strange flowers? I am not alone in feeling this tension. Many scholars have struggled with ways of incorporating scattered and idiosyncratic evidence drawn from archival research and fieldwork on Southeast Asian religions. Some seek to make broad statements about the ethical choices, cultural systems, political policies, ethnic relations, and cosmological metastructures of Southeast Asian peoples. Others tend to look closely at moments, objects, and texts to ensure that their studies are highly contextual, meticulously researched, and rarely speculative.

Of course most scholars offer passing comments about their inability to capture the cacophony, the multiple voices, in any religion. We warn our graduate students to design feasible dissertation projects. We apologize for what content needed to be left on the editor's floor. However, this rhetoric is often half-hearted. We participate in what Marc Augé has called "oblivion," a simultaneous "forgetting" of certain facts or alternative explanations and a conscious construction of "fictions."[2] For the ethnographer or historian, these can be conscious forgettings or fictions about the subject of study at hand. Therefore, despite the fact that we know we are telling only part of a story and documenting snippets of possible evidence, we still feel confident enough to propose overarching theories and ask our readers to trust our speculative conclusions about historical periods, cultural systems, and metaethics. If we do not do this, editors, critics, and colleagues will query, So what did you conclude? How can you sum up your book? What is the point of your study? Why should I read this? These are important questions, because without them books would devolve into simply typed-up field notes or archive catalogs. Where is the middle ground? How do we acknowledge the inconsistency of the religious choices of individual agents and offer the reader some general statements about the religious tradition or culture about which we purport to write?

I have not been able to answer these questions. However, it is the attempt to answer them that has led me to take seriously religious diversity and individual agency in Thailand. I hope I have given the reader "a sense of the highly personal, emotive, and situation-specific combinations that are made in practice."[3] To do this, I have written a book about Thai Buddhism where the Buddha is not the protagonist; a book in which all those strange "local" cults, saints, relics, rituals, ghosts, magical practices, and miracle stories in Thailand are not seen as supporting actors or extras. Indeed, if a person with no previous knowledge of Buddhism visited a place like Wat Mahabut or Wat Rakhang, they might assume that Somdet To or Mae Nak were the central objects of worship in Thai Buddhism and the Buddha a minor deity of some sort sitting alone in a locked room while Somdet To and Mae Nak greet the throngs of visitors. Of course, the person of the Buddha is extremely important in Thailand. Buddha images are the highest on most altars. His biography is retold in different ways as the ideal example of human perfection. These biographies are not just in texts but also in postcards, posters, murals, and even comic books. However, other biographies, other images, other personages, other teachings loom large. It is often assumed by scholars that local, animistic and other religions use Buddhist symbols, teachings, and monks to legitimize their practice. However, in many of the cases in this book, the Buddha is continually made relevant by the popularity and presence of other, supposedly minor, objects of worship like Mae Nak, Ganesha, Baby Ae, and Chiwok Goman. Who is legitimizing whom? Who is making whom relevant?

Thailand, according to most statistics, is around 96 percent Buddhist. This does not mean that everyone is following the same basic tradition with a few minor idiosyncrasies. Of course, the sangha as a body of monks is often presented and presents itself as possessing an ideology of sameness and employs the technologies of sameness (to the casual observer its corps has relatively standard sets of robes, bowls, shaved heads, rules, and the like). However, it is a misconception to assume more broadly that local diversity is being homogenized in the modern period with the rise of mass media, language standardization, and organizational efficiency. In fact, the great rise in the followings of Mae Nak, Ganesha, Somdet To, King Chulalongkorn, Maechi Sansanee, Jatukham Ramathep, Kuan Im, Luang Phu Man, Khruba Siwichai, Luang Pho Doem, Buddhadasa Bhikkhu, and many other saints and deities over the past century shows that modern communication and transportation technology and the mechanical reproduction of visual images has led to more diversity in Thai religiosity. From manuscript, archaeological, and epigraphic evidence, it is clear that there has always been diversity. Models of religious decline and the corruption of orthodoxy do not match the facts. However, whereas in the nineteenth century, the rituals and images connected to a local saint like Luang Pho Si or Shiva in a single village or valley would have remained local, now millions throughout the country can hear the miracle stories of a particular saint as well see the photographs of her or his amulets and relics. They can order these objects through eBay or over the phone with numbers provided in mass-produced amulet magazines. They can board a relatively inexpensive bus to another village, provincial capital, or to Bangkok to visit a saint's home monastery or a ghost's main shrine. Certainly some local traditions remain local, but many rise to national fame quickly. Some fade away just as quickly. I have showed why Mae Nak and Somdet To's fame has risen, and hopefully future scholars will trace the careers of others.

## ON REPERTOIRES AND SYNCRETISM

A repertoire is a constantly shifting collection of gestures, objects, texts, plots, tropes, ethical maxims, precepts, ritual movements, and expectations that any individual agent employs and draws upon when acting and explaining action. No one person's repertoire is identical to another's, but people do develop their repertoires within intimate familial, social, and professional networks.[4] Many people draw also from overlapping objects, tropes, and the like. Since I have drawn examples and interviewed people in monastic or other religious ritual spaces, I call these religious repertoires. This does not mean religion is completely separate from other parts of private and public life. Gestures, beliefs, texts that a person uses in a monastery can be very similar to ones used in shopping malls or living rooms. As Steven Collins often reminds me, religion is part of a person's life; it is not the only part.

What I want to emphasize in the conclusion is that a person's repertoire, religious or otherwise, can be internally inconsistent and contradictory. They are mental as much as they are physical. They include the *qualia* of a person's experience, the memories and stories one inhabits as well the realities one touches. This is why a person who actively cultivates a religious repertoire can see myths as facts and interpret facts and actual objects as miraculous and mystical. For collectors of amulets, believers in ghosts, and chanters of incantations, the world becomes a series of possibilities rather than a series of obstacles. A person who believes in the possibility of curing cancer with an amulet can also sit for hours in a hospital waiting room. A Western-educated politician can offer gifts to Ganesha, and a scholar can request ritual protection. A muralist can draw inspiration from Sanskrit love stories, royal battles, as well as from Buddhist cosmologies. A liberal and cosmopolitan Buddhist can see no problem in praying to Brahma or entreating local land spirits. This seemingly overt inconsistency, the ability to retain and maintain several seemingly mutually exclusive belief systems, is common in Thailand.[5] If we study an individual's evolving religious repertoire, then we do not need to fit their actions and beliefs into a cultural system, rationale, or single religious tradition.[6] I trust that the plethora of examples in this book have slowly revealed that heritage, security, graciousness, and abundance are valued as much as nonattachment, impermanence, compassion, indifference, and even enlightenment. However, I do not want to suggest that Thais have simply developed a new set of values to replace supposedly traditional, early Buddhist values, nor are these understood as mutually exclusive sets of values.

In Thailand, the evolution of a personal repertoire usually takes the form of accretion. Thai *religieux* seem to add to their individual repertoires but rarely subtract. Individual memories are expressed in their accumulations. A monastery is valued for its history and the display of that history through its collection of things and recorded events. A monastery accumulates images from many different traditions and many different patrons. Abundance is valued. The accumulated material can seem like mere bricolage, and sometimes it is, but often it is valuable for its connection to a powerful person, event, or patron. Choices are being made. Indeed, an altar is a living witness to a number of patrons' choices about what to give and which powerful personage to honor. Power here means the power to protect.[7] Objects with little value absorb value through association on these crowded altars, on the grounds of crowded monasteries, and in the dense pages of religious magazines. If a Somdet To amulet has been known to protect a person or entire nation, then it would be logical that another amulet made by someone trained by Somdet To or inspired by Somdet To would offer a person security as well. Rituals are performed by people with different training and beliefs, drawing on liturgies, gestures, and objects from multiple lineages regardless of whether they are rooted in Mahayana, Sri Lankan, Brahmanic, Khmer, tantric, or even Western religious traditions. The monk Sirisak who helps take care of the Mae Nak shrine at Wat Mahabut can chant canonical Pali well. He meditates in front of Buddha images, but he also makes corpse oil and arranges recurring funerals for a ghost. My friend Arthid Sheravanichkul is a scholar of Buddhism, reads canonical and extracanonical Buddhist texts, and has been ordained as a Theravada monk. However, he studies Catholicism, carries amulets from Tibet, listens to New Age sermons and music produced by Maechi Sansanee, and is a devotee of Kuan Im. He evens reads Plato and Deepak Chopra. He is comfortable with studying and even practicing multiple traditions. My abbot, Luang Pho Sombun, a poor child from a rural village and now a senior Thammayut monk and advanced meditator, once pulled me aside in the monastery when I was a young monk. He asked if I had a crucifix. He figured that since I was Caucasian, I was probably Christian. He wanted the crucifix to wear around his neck along with his other Buddhist amulets. I asked why, and he said, "So I can have a greater religious arsenal [*khlang saphawut*]; your god must be pretty powerful if he has so many followers." If we are going to map the diversity of religious practices in Thailand, we need to study more than new sects like the Santi Asok or Thammakai, new sangha reforms, or new prosperity cults; we need also to get to the level of the individual and respect the openness, conflicting rationales, and seeming inconsistency of individual Thai students and practitioners of religion.[8] We also need to be aware that individual practitioners can claim orthodoxy (in terms of "Thai heritage" or "true Buddhism") while directly contradicting orthodoxy by their actions and statements.

Why can't we expect that a person will hold and act upon simultaneous, multiple ideals. Why don't we see this as an advantage? Why is consistency or orthodoxy seen as the ideal? Certainly there is an effort to make sense of the world and of one's beliefs, but this process of making sense, of seeing the big picture, of seeing the forest, can happen over and over again with different results by the same person on the same day. A person can have no problem collecting amulets, celebrating wealth, and believing in the value of nonattachment. A person can be afraid of ghosts and believe logically that ghosts don't exist. A person can believe in enlightenment and the Buddhist soteriological ideal of total extinguishment but still believe that an enlightened being like Somdet To can hear their chanting or protect their home. A solider can have a protective tattoo and still make sure he wears his flak jacket and loads his gun. As we have seen, the level of education and the socioeconomic background have little to do with this apparent inconsistency. We cannot reduce the belief in the efficacy of magic to class, premodernity or modernity, economic conditions, cultural anxiety, political chaos. Somdet To and Mae Nak embody this inconsistency. After all, she is the bloodthirsty ghost who protects children, and he is the simple, peaceloving village monk who advised kings, protected the country, and distrusted foreigners. Perhaps it would be more accurate to abandon the dichotomy of orthodoxy and heterodoxy, to abandon the very notion that these values are inconsistent in favor of a close study of individual events, agents, and objects.

Most scholars base their careers on identifying contradictions and exposing inconsistencies. They create categories. However, these categories are usually in the form of systems. B. J. Terwiel summed up the state of the field well in 1976:

> Many authors state unequivocally that Theravada Buddhists adhere to more than one religious tradition. Apart from "otherworldly" Buddhism, these Southeast Asian peoples adhere to other strands of religion, generally classed under rubrics such as "non-Buddhist beliefs," "folk religion," "animism," or "supernaturalism." Yet, though virtually all authors recognize this situation, there is no consensus in their views on how the different subsystems are interrelated.[9]

The lack of consensus of where Buddhism begins and ends remains today. One of the problems, though, is that we are often still looking at systems or religions and not at individuals and the highly contextualized spaces in which they practice. Just as it is overly simplistic to split Thais into Buddhists, animists, and Brahmanists, it is overly simplistic to split Buddhists into liberal or conservative, urban or rural, folk or scholarly, as well as into ethnic, sectarian, or geographical and regional camps. However, designing models of syncretism does this. In the introduction I offered four criticisms of syncretism that were supported by the evidence presented in the following four chapters. Here let me sum up this criticism. Looking closely at the people, texts, actions, and things that participate in the construction of modern Thai Buddhism—whether it be amulets, images, monastic architecture, the accoutrement of shrines, personal biographies, or the implements of ritual—helps us not only to map the constantly morphing repertoires of Thai Buddhists but also to question the very notion of syncretism. Instead of seeing a Thai shrine or Thai monastery or even Thai image blending essentialized local and translocal, Indic and Southeast Asian, Brahmanic and Buddhist elements, I see these complex lives, rituals, and objects as questioning the very usefulness of metacategories like Buddhism, Brahmanism, animism, local, translocal, Indic, Chinese, Thai, and the like. In my experience and interviews, monks or laypeople prostrating in front of a shrine with statues of General Taksin, Kuan Im, Shakyamuni Buddha, Somdet To, Phra Sangkhacchai do not see the shrine as a syncretistic stage or themselves as multireligious. They do not process the images separately, with some being local, some translocal, some Buddhist, and some non-Buddhist. If they did, there would be a more tactical attempt to arrange the objects or justify practices. The builders of the shrine, for example (from actual builders of the monastery to the thousands of patrons who donate images, money, flowers, and food), are participating not in a cross-cultural or syncretistic exercise but a celebration of abundance, a promotion of heritage, a desire for security, and a rhetoric of graciousness. Making the shrine beautiful and impressive is important. They each have individual motivations and idiosyncrasies of aesthetic and practical preference, but they reinforce these broad cultural processes and performances. Whether an image is particularly Chinese or a mural shows certain Indic influence is of no concern to most practitioners besides scholars. Objects are not judged solely on their closeness to India, their age, or even the value of their material. They are important because of what they directly reference or invoke. Certain tiny amulets made of clay and flowers do not cost 2 million dollars because of their age but because of their direct, not symbolic, relation to important people like Somdet To or stories connected to their ability to protect a person from harm. Images are not judged solely on the accuracy of their depiction of the Buddha but on the relics inside, the king who consecrated them, and the monks who formerly possessed them.

Even religion does not always matter. In some cases, statues of Brahma or Ganesha or Kuan Im are as valuable, if not more valuable, than statues of the Buddha or a Buddhist monk like Somdet To because of miracles associated with them or because certain famous patrons love them. Just as each practitioner exists in a network of relationships and memories, each object exists in a network of relationships, each has its own history and its own liturgy, and each sits on a shrine surrounded by dozens of other images or on a necklace with several other amulets. Each monastic building or mural wall is part of a much larger network. Their value and importance cannot be separated from these relationships.[10] Early on in my research I ignored these relationships and stuck to the metacategories of religion. However, I soon realized that it was not only scholars who had difficulty in determining what was Hindu, Mahayana, Theravada, superstitious, orthodox, esoteric, folk, and the like. The practitioners and scholars in Thailand had trouble separating practices and objects into these categories. I noticed that when I asked a small group of people how to define certain practices, they would hesitate, debate with one another, and eventually offer me vague answers like, "Ben khwam cheua" (It is just a belief), or "Ben thamniam prabeni" (It is a custom), "Atibai yak" (It is difficult to explain), "Mai nae chai" (I'm not sure). Therefore, I started asking different questions and stopped trying to fit Thai practices into my preconceived categories. That is when the people I interviewed reveled in describing detail, history, and technique. Perhaps what scholars have been trying to define as syncretism is actually uncertainty. Sometimes hesitation is a mode of expression.

Magical, commercial, curative, protective, prognosticative, aesthetic, and preservative practices of current Thai Buddhists cannot be explained away. These practices are neither the products of an anarchic society nor the expressions of the futile aspirations of those ignorant of more refined canonical values. I have tried to give them some shape all the while acknowledging that they are not part of an integrated and prescribed system. The notion of a repertoire has helped. This approach is useful because it focuses on individual agents and the relationships that are formed between them by looking closely at their religious products (texts, rituals, liturgies, art) in highly specific contexts. However, a repertoire is not a collection of static pieces of evidence or historical curiosities frozen in time. The repertoire approach attempts to understand how texts, objects, stories, and people are cherished or ignored by different people at different times. It allows agents, places, texts, or objects to remain ambiguous, inconsistent, evolving, and unfinished. It acknowledges an agent's capacity to remain unsure about why and how she or he express her or his fears and beliefs. A Thai Buddhist shrine is a work in progress; a monastery's grounds are constantly changing. A practitioner is constantly participating in new rituals, visiting new shrines, renting new amulets, telling new stories, changing old stories, and certainly developing new opinions and ideas. Over time, new saints will emerge, new deities will be honored and feared, new amulets will be made, and new teachings will be promoted. Or perhaps new values will emerge through the morphology of accretion and choice. Both the elite and the nonelite, the worldly and the local take part in this ongoing and nonteleological process of creating Buddhism person by person, ghost by ghost.

T. S. Eliot, in a 1923 review essay of *Ulysses*, stated that Joyce's method was "a way of controlling, of ordering, of giving a shape and a significance to the immense panorama of futility and anarchy which is contemporary society."[11] Many who have read *Ulysses* might wholeheartedly disagree, seeing it, as I did when my dear mother encouraged me to read it many years ago, as a magisterial disaster. The reader of this book may also wonder if the previous pages had shape and significance, were amusingly anarchic, or a disaster. Certainly, looking at the relationships between people and objects in ritual and social spaces throughout this book has produced for me, as the opening quotation of this study stated, "unintended consequences." There are many things about Thai Buddhism still unknown to me. I followed the stories of Somdet To and Mae Nak and did not end up where I thought I would. Thai Buddhism, when not studied solely through institutions, doctrines, codes, and the canon, as it has developed since the time of Somdet To and Mae Nak may indeed seem messy. However, any close study of what people actually do will always be messier than a study of what they are supposed to do. Joyce's Dublin is messy and therefore his is an honest depiction. My mother, of course, was right.

# NOTES

## INTRODUCTION

The epigraph is drawn from "Beyond Constructivism" (2000:2).

1. I thank Arthid Sheravanichakul for sending me news of the musical's premier. See also http://entertainment.th.msn.com/news/entertainment/article.aspx?cp-documentid=2607571.

2. Some people scrape bark off this tree and grind it into paste, mix it with oil, and use the mixture for making a type of love potion. Most apply camphor oil to the tree in order to more clearly read the lottery numbers (see first section of chapter 4).

3. In other versions it is a young novice trained by Somdet To who stops her.

4. Magical practices are often attributed to the rising middle class and Thailand's economic boom period of the 1980s and 1990s. For background, see especially the complex article by Hewison, "Of Regimes" (1993). Except for works by Bizot (discussed in chapter 2), there is little equivalent to the lengthy, highly detailed studies of esoteric religion like those of Strickmann's *Chinese Magical Medicine* (2002) and Davidson's *Indian Esoteric Buddhism* (2003). There are dozens of studies of Tibetan, Japanese, and Chinese protective Buddhist magic, for which there are no equivalents in Southeast Asia.

5. For example, Jackson distinguishes the Thai Buddhist modern and postmodern periods. The former is characterized by developments in "doctrinal rationalization" and bureaucratic "centralization," while the latter is associated with "resurgence of supernaturalism and an efflorescence of religious expression at the margins of state control, involving a decentralization and localization of religious authority." See his "Enchanting Spirit" (1999). In another study, while avoiding a condemnation of these practices, he describes modern Thai Buddhism as experiencing a "disintegration of an organized, overarching religious system" and suggests there has been an "exodus from institutional Buddhism" and a "decentralization of religiosity" ("Withering Centre" [1997:76, 79]). O'Connor asserts that these royal centralizing reforms in the twentieth century "took the wat [monastery] away from locals and, by driving folk practices out of the temple, fostered today's religious 'free market.'" The temple became an agent of the nation-state—less local and more national: "Bangkok overwhelmed localism." "Interpreting Thai Religious Change" (1993:330, 336).

6. Willford ("Modernist Vision" [2005:48]) notes that many studies of local religion simply investigate the "structural modes of domination" and ignore individual religious agents' ability to act irrationally or compulsively. Erick White ("Fraudulent and Dangerous" [2005:69–92]) offers a sophisticated way of understanding the elitist attack on spirit worship and other types of supposedly low or folk religion in modern Thailand.

7. It is not only foreign critics of Thai Buddhism who present Thai Buddhists as victims but also modern Thai liberal social, internationally connected commentators (often writing in English books and newspapers). Describing Thai Buddhism and culture as being in crisis is also an effective political tool promoted by the Royal Privy Council and politicians from multiple Thai parties on the right and left. Blaming global forces, the World Bank, scantily clad tourists, and Muslims for the demise of Thai Buddhism has been de rigueur in Thai public discourse for decades.

8. Studies that posit such a state Buddhism also reify what Daud Ali (*Courtly Culture* [2004]) calls "an overly substantialist notion of the state as an abstract thing" (6). Like Ali, throughout this study, when I deal with matters of the state, I refer to "specific activities and ideas of individual men who composed it rather than any self-evident functional structure" (7).

9. *Gathering Leaves* (2008, chap. 3). Kamala Tiyavanich's exemplary studies are clear exceptions to this.

10. This book does not aim to define modernity. For extensive discussions on this, see especially Hansen, *How to Behave* (2006); Jackson, *Buddhadasa* (2003); and McMahan, *Making of Buddhist Modernism* (2008).

11. In this way I want to put the field of Southeast Asian Buddhist studies into conversation with important studies on "living religions," especially in the fields of global Christianity and Japanese religions. Here I have been particularly inspired

by the work of Cannell, *Power and Intimacy* (1999); Orsi, *Gods of the City* (1999); Tweed, *Our Lady of the Exile* (2002); Rambelli, *Buddhist Materiality* (2008); Covell, *Japanese Temple Buddhism* (2006); Wiegele, *Investing in Miracles* (2004); and Hardacre, *Kurozumikyo* (1988). See also Cuevas, *Travels in the Netherworld* (2008) for a comparative example looking at the very category of "popular" religion.

12. As cited in LaFleur, "Symbol and Yūgen" (1992:24).

13. The origins of the categories of esoteric and exoteric in the study if Buddhism in the West is beyond the scope of this book. However, App, *Birth of Orientalism* (2010: 2–3, 138–41) provides a provocative introduction to the origins of the ways in which Europeans divided Asian religions, especially Buddhism, into esoteric and exoteric forms beginning with their encounter with Japanese religions in the sixteenth century and specifically the writings of Alessandro Valignano. This divide was, in many ways, projected onto other Buddhist schools throughout Asia, even when there was no such strict division locally. A comparative approach is offered by Kuroda Toshio. His theory of *kenmitsu* (exoteric-esoteric Buddhism) is particularly useful (although not a parallel situation) when studying the Thai context. I thank Nobumi Iyanaga for his advice on Kuroda. See also Dobbins, "Legacy of Kuroda Toshio" (1996).

14. Ricoeur, *Symbolism of Evil* (1967:349).

15. In 1957, the historian Walter Vella wrote a description of Thai religion: "It is a demonstration of their marvelous religious eclecticism that the Siamese believed not only in *phi* [ghosts], in devas, and in religious magic but also in Buddhism." This unguarded description by a specialist in Thai history, but not in Buddhist Studies, reveals how a highly qualified observer of Thai society understood the religious landscape of Thailand without assuming that Buddhism was the most important tradition in the country. Vella, *Siam under Rama III* (1957:31). I was recently encouraged by comments made by Christoph Emmrich at the Theravada Buddhist Encounters with Modernity workshop (Arizona State University, February 2009). He stated, "Rather than asking what Theravāda is . . . it appears to me to be more fruitful to ask *what it does*." Emphasis mine.

16. See particularly Garfinkel, *Ethnomethodology's Program* (2002) and Latour, *Science in Action* (1988).

17. Silber, "Pragmatic Sociology" (2003:429).

18. I am particularly influenced by the work of Luise White (*Speaking with Vampires* [2000]) and that of Julia Clancy-Smith (*Rebel and Saint* [1997]). Both have studied the power and epistemology of rumor. I thank Lisa Onaga for helpful conversations on this issue.

19. Luisa White, *Speaking with Vampires* (2000:431).

20. In many ways Bourdieu's approach to culture also does not work here, as it often assumes relatively rigid and deterministic class distinctions, as well as granting too much power to social institutions. Practices related to Somdet To, Mae Nak,

and other ghosts, texts, and saints discussed here often dismantle the social barriers between classes and are productive of internal cognitive dissonance that belies Bourdieu's tendency to see social actions leading to or a preestablished harmony and reinforcing social norms.

21. Nora, "Between Memory and History" (1989:8).

22. Carsten, *Ghosts of Memory* (2007:3).

23. Silber, "Pragmatic Sociology" (2003:429).

24. Swidler, "Culture in Action" (1986).

25. Carrithers, "Anthropology as a Moral Science" (2005:434). I also thank him for a personal conversation on this issue.

26. Carrithers, "Anthropology as a Moral Science" (2005:440–41).

27. Cassaniti, in her recent dissertation ("Control in a World of Change" [2009]), attempts to define how people in two villages in northern Thailand act upon their belief in impermanence (*anicca*). Her research reveals how difficult a project like this is and how contradictory self-generated explanations for the belief in impermanence can be among Buddhists.

28. Of course, much of the questioning of the importance of belief in the study of religion can be traced back to Rodney Needham's well-known *Belief, Language, and Experience* (1972).

29. From his *History of Rasselas*, as cited in Teresa Morgan (2007:122).

30. Wittgenstein, *Philosophical Investigations* (1963:133).

31. Clark, "Theory and Its Objects" (2002:10).

32. *Kreng chai* is a very difficult to translate but extremely common Thai phrase. When a person feels *kreng chai*, that person feels bad for putting another person out or bothering another person. A gracious person does not like to put any unnecessary burden on another person.

33. See especially Hallisey and Hansen, "Narrative, Sub-Ethics" (1996:305–25). Much of this work has been inspired by the work of Hauerwas and Nussbaum. See in particular Hauerwas's (with Gregory Jones) "Introduction" to *Why Narrative?* and, with David Burrell in the same work, "From System to Story: An Alternative Pattern for Rationality in Ethics" (1997:158–90). See Nussbaum's *Upheavals of Thought* (2003:472–77) and *Love's Knowledge* (1988).

34. Here I depart from studies like Teresa Morgan's impressive *Popular Morality in the Early Roman Empire* (2007), in which she thoroughly combs early collections of proverbs, fables, gnomai, and exempla that help define the "degree of common moral ground," where we can "often talk meaningfully of the ethics of the empire as a whole" (2). First, I examine material culture and ritual technologies instead of primarily popular texts and excerpts. Furthermore, the line Morgan draws between the elite and the commoner would be much less clear in the Thai case. Still, hers is a model study the likes of which has not been attempted in Buddhist studies.

35. Nussbaum "Narrative Emotions" (1988:226).

36. Ibid., 230.

37. More recently theories of hybridity have become *en vogue* in the study of religion. There are two major theories of hybridity, both rooted in the study of literature rather than in religion. The first, attributed to Bakhtin, sees a hybrid as a single utterance that is produced from the mixing of two or more disparate utterances. The hybrid text speaks in one voice without obviously revealing its hybrid nature. The second theory of hybridity is attributed to Homi Bhabha, who, in his groundbreaking *The Location of Culture*, sees hybridity as a conscious tactic used by colonial subjects when they write from an "interstitial space." They create a single text that combines local knowledge and a mixture of terms, structures, and tropes of the colonizer. Both Bakhtin and Bhabha see hybridity as a positive quality versus a negative product emerging from purer originals. Both approaches to hybridity are lacking, because they both reduce the agent, the agent's expressions, the piece of art or literature to a unified product of diverse influences or existing in a victim-victimizer relationship. See the comprehensive overview of the history of the term "syncretism" in Leopold and Jensen, *Syncretism in Religion* (2005). J. L. Taylor ["(Post-) Modernity" (1999:163–87)] offers a sophisticated description of hybridity in Thai Buddhism.

38. See especially Samuel, *Origins of Yoga and Tantra* (2008, chap. 6); DeCaroli, *Haunting the Buddha* (2004); Cousins, "Aspects of Esoteric Southern Buddhism" (1997:185–207); Richard Cohen, "Nāga, Yakṣiṇī, Buddha" (1998:360–400); and Davidson, *Indian Esoteric Buddhism* (2003).

39. Connolly, *Pluralism* (2005:5).

40. Marcus, *Ethnography through Thick and Thin* (1998); Latour, *Science in Action* (1988); see also MacDonald and Basu, *Exhibition Experiments* (2007:7).

41. See Le Goff, *History and Memory* (1992), and Novetzke's summary of theories regarding the separation of history and memory in *Religion and Public Memory* (2008, "Introduction").

42. This is inspired by the work of Haraway, "Situated Knowledges" (1988:575–99).

43. Pitelka describing the work of Cynthea Bogel in *What's the Use of Art?* (2008:7).

44. Pitelka, *What's the Use of Art?* (2008:8), where the work of Richard Davis is described.

## 1. MONKS AND KINGS

1. I thank Nathan McGovern for calling my attention to this book.

2. The dating of Somdet To's birth is largely agreed upon by most biographies. Many provide the astrological stamp (*duang chata*) for the day of his birth. An example can be seen in (Maha Ammattri Phraya) Thipkosa, *Prawat Somdet Phra Phutthachan*

*To Phrohmarangsi* (2528 [1985], front matter). This stamp was drawn by the famous Thai astrological scholar Thep Sarikabut, who has written three volumes of detailed explanations of Thai horoscope systems alongside his relative, An Sarikabut, the author of a major study of Thai astrological calculation methods, *Khamphi horasat Thai matrathan* (2508 [1965]). See also (Phra Khru) Kalyananukun (Heng Itthacharo), *Prawat Somdet Phra Phutthachan To Phrohmarangsi* (2529 [1986]:1–2; the original, 1952, edition of this biography has an introduction by Prince Anuman Rajadhon). A more extensive explanation of the stamp can be found in Pricha Iamtham, *Prawat Somdet Phra Phutthachan To* (2542 [1999]:81–83). A good introduction to the astrological traditions of central Thailand is the three-volume master's thesis by Korkok Wongbom, "Itiphon khwam cheua thang horasat" (2549 [2006]).

3. This version was told to me by Sasithorn Phrichetthiyaporn, an official in a government ministry in Bangkok and a frequent visitor to Wat Indrawihan.

4. Many stories I heard in formal and informal interviews in Thailand between 2001 and 2008. There are dozens of collections of these stories. Amulet-trade magazines include occasional short stories about Somdet To alongside stories of other famous monks. Some include (Phra) Thammasaro Bhikkhu, *Nuang duai Phrabat Somdet Phra Chom Klao* (2511 [1967]); Anand Amantai, *Poet tamnan Than Chao Pradun Somdet Phutthachan To Phrohmarangsri* (2543 [2000]); *Chiwit kanngan laktham To* (2538 [1995]); and (especially vol. 4) Wichai Thonasaeng, *Bencha aphinya* (2538 [1995]). Small monastery histories published in-house also occasionally include stories about famous monks connected to their institutions. In Somdet To's case, there are numerous histories of Wat Rakhang and Wat Indrawihan. A difficult one to find is the short history of Wat Boromathat in Kampaengphet, where Somdet To supposedly visited (Phra) Sriwachiraphon, *Prawat Phra Boromathatnakonchum Wat Boromathat* (2548 [2005]). I thank Thanissaro Bhikkhu for providing me with some of these stories. I also want to thank Achan Suchao Ploychum of Kasetsart University and Phra Maha Silapa Dhammasippo, professor of Pali at Mahamakut Monastic University, for help finding sources of stories about Somdet To.

5. Damrong, *Ruang tang phra rachakhana phuyai nai Ratanakosin* (2466 [1923]: 111–16).

6. I thank Sompong Duangsawai and Nai Samneuk for their explanation of the history of Wat Sangwetwisayaram. The former has published two comprehensive histories of the Lamphu district of Bangkok, where Wat Sangwet is located: *Phetbanglamphu* (2545 [2002]) He gives a short history of Somdet To's novice ordination at Wat Sangwet, where Phra Bowonwiriya was his preceptor. See also *Lamphu* (2546 [2003]); Isarangkhru na Ayutthya, *Ngan phraratchathan phloeng sop phonruangtri* (2534 [1991]) has information about several places Somdet To visited as a young monk.

7. For a study of monastic educational reform, see my *Gathering Leaves* (2008, chap. 3).

8. This book has seen many editions in the form of cremation volumes or funeral books. For a biography of Thipkosa, see Anake Nawigamune, *Bangkok kap hua muang* (2547 [2004]:113–17). Other editions are too numerous to list. I generally relied on a 1974 edition.

9. In the 1952 biography mentioned in note 4, Somdet To is said to have been born in Ayutthaya and his given name was Dhidanaichai. His mother moved him to Chaiyo District in Angthong Province, and then he moved to Wat Bangkhunphrom in Bangkok in 1799 and was ordained at Wat Sangwetwisayaram. From there he moved to become fully ordained at Wat Rakhang in 1807 and continued his studies at Wat Mahathat with Phra Achan Wichian and Phra Horathibodi.

10. He actually studied, this biography states, at Wat Bangkhunphrom Nok and not at the neighboring Wat Bangkhunphrom Nai; he was ordained as a novice at Wat Rakhang when he was twelve years old. Pricha Iamtham, *Prawat Somdet Phra Phutthachan To* (2542 [1999]:71–95).

11. Only the royal academy scholar Dr. M. R. Suphavat Kasemsri (interview July 2006, Naradip Library, Bangkok) and scholar-monk Phra Maha Narongsak Sophanasithi (interview November 2006, Wat Indrawihan, Bangkok) adamantly denied that King Rama I was the father. Thongchai Likhitphonsawan provided me with a handwritten and unpublished diary by Chao Nu Theuan, a "village child" fathered by King Rama I. Chao Nu claims that his mother, from Salaloi Distict in Saraburi Province, was impregnated by King Rama I. This diary gives unique insight into the life of an unacknowledged child of a Thai monarch.

12. (Maha Ammattri Phraya) Thipkosa, *Prawat Somdet Phra Phutthachan To* (2528 [1985]:8–11).

13. (Phra Khru) Kalyananukun (Heng Itthacharo), *Prawat Somdet Phra Phutthachan To Phrohmarangsi* (2529 [1986]:2).

14. *Somdet Phra Phutthachan To Phrahmarangsi* (n.d.).

15. (Phra) Ratcharatanaphon, Suthip Chirathiwat, Chotichai Sirikannukun, *Luang Phu To* (2545 [2002]:7).

16. This claim, that an image made of a magical substance is too heavy to move, is found for other Buddha images and relics. Probably the most famous example is the perhaps mythical image of the Buddha made by King Udāyana in Kosambi. The Chinese pilgrim Xuanzang wanted to transport it to Mount Wutai, but it was impossible to lift.

17. The 1992 issue of the popular Buddhist magazine *Saksit* contains a short story about the images and the miracles (*itthipatihan*) that happened to those who offered gifts to them. Somdet To was said to forge the images and insert amulets and powerful inscriptions inside. Suwit Koetphongbunchot, "Anuphap Krua To" (2535 [1992]:2).

18. There are statues of fifty-three *bhikkhuni* (nuns) at Wat Thepdhitaram and statues of *maechi* (nuns) at Samnak Santisuk in central Thailand.

19. This biographical trope is also seen in descriptions of Phra Phayom, Ajahn Man, and Luang Ta Mahabua, among others.

20. On the forcible settling of Lao and Khmer populations, see Chawalee Na Thalang, *Prathet racha khong Siam* (2541 [1998]), and Bang-on Piyaphan, *Lao nai krung Ratanakosin* (2541 [1998]).

21. These stories appear often in the *Thai rath, Daily News, Bangkok Post* newspapers with titles like "Nails and Hooks Found Inside Man's Body" and "Witchcraft on the Rise," as well as in popular amulet-trade magazines, and recently on Web sites promoting Thai and Khmer tattoos. The popular 2007 action film *Maha-ut* also highlights the use of tattoos and swallowing nails for protection. For some background, see Becchetti, *Le mystère dans les lettres* (1991); Lucien Hanks, "Merit and Power" (1962).

22. I thank Charles Keyes for a draft of his paper "The Destruction of a Shrine to Brahma in Bangkok and the Fall of Thaksin Shinawatra: The Occult and the Thai Coup in Thailand of September 2006."

23. Khom script was used for writing Pali inscriptions in Sukhothai and later central Thailand from at least the thirteenth century. Khmer and Khom follow the same graphic principles but are not identical. Khom is also written in many different paleographic styles. The use of Khom script does not connote any knowledge of the Khmer language by a writer in Thailand. Over time, *phra yan*, tattoos, warrior shirts, *takrut*, and other protective texts were most often composed in Khom script in central Thailand. Many manuscripts of the eighteenth and nineteenth centuries have both Thai and Khom scripts on the same leaf. I thank Peter Skilling for assistance with this nomenclature. See also Vickery, "Khmer Inscriptions of Tenasserim" (1973); and for a comprehensive study of the Thai language, including its Khmer influences, see Phaya Upakit Silapasan, *Lak Phasa Thai* (2544 [2002]).

24. Chatthip Nartsupa, "Ideology of Holy Men" (1983); Cohen, "Buddhism Unshackled" (2001). Some of these stereotypes about the cunning of the Lao were promoted early on by Prince Detadison and Prince Damrong. See Schweisguth, *Étude sur la littérature siamoise* (1951:258–73), and Damrong Rachanuphap, *Chotmaihet Ruang Prap Khabot Wiangchan* (2469 [1926]).

25. Baird has written an extensive historical study of Ya Chao Tham. These two fetuses are still held by descendants of Ya Chao Tham. Ya Chao Tham also had small black round amulets known as *luk om* that he sucked on to become invisible. "From Champasak to Cambodia" (2009:41–42).

26. I have written about the linguistic, ethnic, and political "borders" of Laos in *Gathering Leaves* (2008, chap. 3).

27. Vella, *Siam under Rama III* (1957:78–79).

28. Terwiel, *Thailand's Political History* (2006:81).

29. Hayashi, *Practical Buddhism* (2003:285–87).

30. Ibid., 286.

31. Ibid., 285.

32. Ibid., 286.

33. Ibid., 292.

34. Seeger shows that there were also female forest saints living in north and northeast Thailand who reportedly had similar magical and meditational powers. Maechi Kaeu Sianglam, for example, has had a *chedi* built in her honor, and her crystallized bones are the focus of intense devotion. "Changing Roles" (2009).

35. For the history of Wat Indrawihan, see Phra Sobhanathamwong, *Khon Khwa Ha Ma Dai Ekasan* (2544 [2002]); (Phra) Sobhanathamwong, *Wat Indrawihan kap chiwaprawat Somdet Phra Phutthachan To Phrohmarangsi nai ngan chitakam faphanang ubasot* (2537 [1994]); and *Chao awat lae wat* (2549 [2006]:80–81).

36. Interview, February 6, 2008, Wat Pathum Wanaram. See also Chirawan Saengphet, *Phutthasilapakam* (2550 [2007]:27–32, 45–46). The secretariat at the monastery has produced its own history of the Lao images: *Wat Pathumwanaram Ratchaworawihan* (2548 [2005]). See also (Phra Maha) Thawon Chittathaoro, *Srapathum* (99–104). These three Lao images are the largest among dozens of other Lao images there. They are believed to have been cast in 2109 (1566) by the same artist, according to one account, Phra Thida, who was the son of the Lao king Setthathirat. However, another account states that they were made for the three daughters of the king, which seems more accurate considering *thida* means "daughter." One story about them states that during the lighting of the furnace and melting of the gold to make the images, a mysterious Brahman ascetic dressed in white appeared and added something (supposedly magically powerful) to the gold mixture. Another story states that these three images were the "children" (modeled after and made while tied with a sacred string to the "father" image) of another image, Luang Pho Suk, thus adding to their prestige and mystery. They were brought to Wat Srapathum after being in the possession of a Thai general, Phraya Pinkhlao, who stole them from Wat Phonxai in Vientiane in 1778. They were given to Wat Srapathum by King Mongkut, who was said to particularly treasure them, so much so that he made them the main images at his new Thammayut monastery. I thank Phra Mahathawon, Phra Sarot, and Phra Khamhaeng for all their assistance in tracing the history of these images. A worthy side note is the fact that at Wat Mahabut, on the grounds of which stands Mae Nak's main shrine, there is a small pavilion with a Lao image placed next to a statue of Somdet To and a plaque inscribed with the *Jinapañjara*. Moreover, the murals at Wat Srapathum depict the story of *Sri Thanonchai*, which is a story about a jester-hero who criticizes a king. This story is famous in Laos, where it is known as *Xiang miang*. The story would certainly appeal to a Lao audience, especially refugees living under a foreign monarch.

37. Other Lao Buddha images in Thailand are regularly lauded for their beauty and ritual power. For example, the history of the twenty-eight Buddha images at

Wat Apsonsawanworawihan emphasizes their Lao origin as a mark of sacrality and beauty. See *Prawat Phraprathan 28 Phra Ong*. I thank Peter Skilling for giving me a copy of this text.

38. A very large collection of small Lao images brought by Lao war captives can be seen at Wat Srapathum. There is even a manmade cave on the grounds of the monastery in which a Lao image is supposedly kept. However, access to the cave is restricted to the abbot and to the king (who visits once a year).

39. Suchao Ploichum, *Phra Kiatkhun* (2541 [1998]).

40. For examples of Lao *paritta* manuscripts, see my "Invoking the Source" (2003, chap. 2).

41. Anand Amantai, *Poet tamnan Than* (2543 [2000]:25–34).

42. *Sarakhadi prawat Somdet Phra Phutthachan To Phrohmarangsi Wat Rakhang-ghositaramworamahawihan* (2003). The actor who plays the adult Somdet To was hired for this film after he had starred in Nonzee Nimibutr's *Nang Nak*. This film's VCD pressing was initially presented as a gift to attendees at the Buddha image consecration ceremony at Wat Sri Mongthop, Angthong Province, on December 12, 2544 [2002].

43. This is a relatively well-known Thai meditative practice called *asubha kammaṭṭhāna* or *maraṇabhāvanā*. There are several monasteries, like Wat Khao Yai in Pichit and Wat Hualampong in Bangkok, that have corpses, donated by their parents, of those who have died prematurely in accidents; the corpses are hung naked on meat hooks or on racks with their torsos sliced open and their entrails hanging out. Monks are told to meditate while seated in front of the hanging corpses. For monks and laity who cannot travel to one of these monasteries, photographs of the corpses in different stages of decay are available for sale at other monasteries or in the amulet markets or Buddhist bookstores.

44. Justin McDaniel, "Paritta" (2004).

45. There are more resources in English for biographies of forest monks than for almost any other subject in Thai Buddhism. These English-language studies may have had the effect of leading many non-Thai readers to incorrectly assume that forest monks are the most common, "ideal" type of monk in Thailand.

46. The stupa built by Khru Ta Saeng in Lopburi is still a pilgrimage destination for followers of Somdet To.

47. In addition to the 227 monastic precepts, *dhutaṅga* (Thai *thudong*) monks take on 13 (sometimes 18) additional precepts.

48. There has been much scholarly study of King Rama IV (Mongkut). See, for example, Charnwit Kasetsiri et al., *Prachum prakat Ratchakan thi 4* (2547 [2004]); Kham Bunnag, *Phra ratchaphongsawadan krung Ratanakosin* (2550 [2007]); (Somdet Phra Sangharat) Ñāṇasaṃvara, *Khrop 200 pi Phra Bat Somdet Phra Poromenathon Mahamakut Phra Chom Klao Chao Yu Hua* (2547 [2004]); as well as older studies by

Moffat, *Mongkut* (1961), Prince Chula Chakrabongse, *Lords of Life* (1960); and Reynolds, "Buddhist Monkhood" (1973), among many others.

49. Somdet To criticizes wealthy Buddhists who pay for sermons but do not want to learn anything from them. See also Chantisai, *Somdet Phra Phutthachan To* (2496 [1954]).

50. See particularly Arthid Sheravanichkul's (2009) dissertation on self-sacrifice in Thai literature, "Dana and Danaparami." Comparatively, see Benn, *Burning for the Buddha* (2007); Moerman, "Passage to Fudaraku" (2007).

51. I thank John Hartmann for conversations about Phra Phayom. See John Hartmann, "Phra Phayom," http://www.seasite.niu.edu/hartmann/. Phra Wachiramethi is very popular with well-educated, upper-middle-class women in Bangkok. He has numerous short self-help books, including four books published in 2007. See also the book he wrote with the popular lay physician and Thai self-help guru Dr. Pornthip Rochanasunan, *Thuk krathop* (2550 [2007]). There are dozens of books (hagiographies, sermon collections, and so on) about or by Luang Pho Tuat and Luang Pho Khun. Probably the most famous female saint is Mae Bunruan Tongbuntoem (1894–1964). Her statue and amulets are renowned as having healing properties. See Seeger, "Changing Roles" (2009).

52. He was often hired by the wealthy and famous in the city. See Anake Nawigamune, *Prawat kanthairup* (2548 [2005]), and Saran Thongpan, "Siam nai Khwam Song Cham" (2545 [2002]). Sunthon Sathitlak or Francis Chit may have taken these photographs.

53. In early 2008 I noticed a new photograph of Somdet To emerging in the amulet markets. It depicts a very old monk barely able to sit up being helped by another monk.

54. See Tambiah, *Buddhist Saints of the Forest* (1984, sect. 2).

55. The origins of Thai cremation volumes remains a desiderata in the field. See a short overview by Olson, "Thai Cremation Volumes" (1992). Michael Montesano recently told me of a cremation volume he was given at a funeral that was a set of CD-ROMs rather than a book.

56. See particularly (Phra Khru) Kalyananukun (Heng Itthacharo), *Prawat Somdet Phra Phutthachan To Phrohmarangsi* (2529 [1986]:5–13).

57. He also sponsored the building of an *ubosot* (ordination hall) on the grounds of Wat Kao Phra Srisanphetyaram in the province of Suphanburi and a three-story school in honor of To at Wat Chaiphruksamala in the Taling Chan district of Thonburi (a neighborhood with several monasteries with active Somdet To shrines).

58. There were efforts to print laws in Thai under the reign of King Rama III in 1839 and to produce a Thai journal, the *Bangkok Recorder*, in the 1840s. For a history of Thai printing presses, see So Phlainoi, *Samnakphim samai raek* (2548 [2005]),

and the comprehensive tome complied by a committee of historians entitled *Prawatsat kanphim nai prathet Thai* (2549 [2006]).

59. I especially thank Somneuk Hongprayoon, Peter Skilling, Phra Achan Siti-kalo, Maechi Bunchuai, Suphavat Kasemsri, and the late David Wyatt for stimulating conversations on this issue.

60. *Chiwit kanngan laktham To* (2538 [1995]:187).

61. Anand Amantai, *Poet tamnan Than Chao Pradun Somdet Phutthachan To* (2543 [2000]).

62. Bastian, *Journey in Siam* (2005:63–68).

63. *Somdet Phra Phutthachan To Phrahmarangsi* (n.d.).

64. In Nonzee Nimibutr's film *Nang Nak* about Maenak and Somdet To there is a scene in which Somdet To is sitting in front of hundreds of amulets that he has just made. He tells his assistants that he has to go help the villagers being tormented by Maenak and he will return to finish blessing the amulets.

65. Chalong Soontravanich, "Regionalization of Local Buddhist Saints" (2005). I thank him for providing me with a draft of this article and for his many conversations on this issue.

66. Ruth, "Committed to the Fire" (2007:262–63). I thank Richard Ruth for sending me his chapter on the subject.

67. Jovan Maud's dissertation is especially interesting not only for what it reveals about how Luang Pho Thuat's legacy has been cultivated but also because of its connections to Chinese religions in southern Thailand. Indeed, Suchat was ethnic Chinese and saw Kuan Im as a national protector of Thailand as well. Certainly, if any monk rivals Somdet To's popularity in Thailand, it would be Luang Pho Thuat. If Somdet To is the patron saint of central Thailand, then Luang Pho Thuat has become the patron saint of southern Thailand. "Sacred Borderlands" (2007).

68. The definitive study on Suchat's Pusawan movement is Jackson, "Huppha-sawan Movement" (1988).

69. There were several articles in the *Bangkok Post* and *Nation* (the two largest English-language newspapers in Thailand) in which the authors lamented the growth of the Jatukham Ramathep phenomenon.

70. More properly, these should be called ordination lineages.

71. *Somdet Phra Phutthachan To Phrohmarangsi* (n.d.).

72. Johnson questions the ways in which King Mongkut has been depicted as a rational, "Western," modernizing king in both Thai and Western literature in "'Rationality' in the Biography of a Buddhist King" (1997). Marston's study, ("Wat Preah Thammalanka" [2008]) of the famous Cambodian monk Lok Ta Nen also reveals that the rural/urban or folk/elite division is often crossed in Southeast Asian Buddhist saint followings.

73. Thanissaro Bhikkhu, Suchitra Chongstitvatthana, and Rangsit Chongchan-sitto, personal communication.

74. Olivier de Bernon makes a parallel point about the "knowledge" of Pali in Cambodia. He writes, "It seems that before the twentieth century there has never been in Cambodia any renowned Pāli scholar-monk. When, again, the Chronicles speak of an eminent monk reported to have had an exceptionally deep knowledge of the Pāli Tipiṭaka, his knowledge is immediately associated with the practice of supernatural powers, but never to prestigious teachings, let alone to the composition of any Pāli work" ("Status of Pāli in Cambodia" [2006]:56). I thank Christi Gambil and Kelly Meister for conversations on this passage.

75. *Baytong* (2003).

76. The popular 2004 Thai film *Tawipop* best characterizes this obsession.

77. See, for example, the story with the catchy title "Taek teun du ton tan—Muan rup Luang Pho To," *Khao sot*, March 12, 2552 [2009]. I thank Supeena Alder for informing me of this story.

78. There are a number of Thai sources that discuss Phra Somdet Sangharat (Suk); for example, Suchao Ploichum, *Phra Kiatkhun Somdet Phra Ariyawongyan* (2541 [1998]). For more information on the *yantra* and protective chant he used, see (Phra Khru) Baithikawira Thanawiro, *Phra prawat Somdet Phra Sangharatyanasangwon* (2536 [1993]). Peter Skilling also obtained for me copies of "Prawat somdetphrasankharat suk kaituan" (2550 [2007]) and "Khumeu samatha-vipassanakammatthan-machchima" (2550 [2007]). The former is a lengthy biography and the latter a guide to Luang Pho Suk Kai Tuan's rather unique meditation system. Both were produced at Wat Rachasittharam. Somdet Suk's meditation teachings are described by (Phra Khru Sangharak) Wira Thanawiro (Phet Chirasan), *Jetovimutti* (2540 [1997]). These are methods of Somdet Suk's that the author states were originally written down in 2364 [1821].

## 2. TEXTS AND MAGIC

1. From the Sanskrit *ārogyāsthāna*, meaning "a place free of disease."

2. Mus, *India Seen from the East* (1975:7).

3. There are short, introductory liturgical preludes like the *Tri saraṇa*, *Namo tassa*, and *Itipiso* that are commonly memorized in Thailand. These are not lengthy chants, though. Of the major chants in Thailand, there is none better known than the *Jinapañjara*. I translate the text as "Verses on the Victor's Armor" in some instances and "cage" in others depending on the point in the poem. There is no reason one Pali word has to have only one English lexical equivalent. Originally the term *pañjara* was used by the Jains in India often for military-style "armor." The chant uses the participle "they are marked" (*saṇṭitā*) and the noun "auspicious signs" (*tilakā*), and these are terms related to marking something on the skin like a tattoo. Tattoos in Thailand, Cambodia, and Laos are often used an "armor" to protect a warrior in

battle. For a comparative introduction to the use of a written talisman or "therapeutic ensigillation," see Strickmann, *Chinese Magical Medicine* (2002, chap. 4). A comparative study of Chinese and Thai ensigillation remains a desideratum.

4. The seven are Sunday: *Namasakan phra ratanatrai*; Monday: *Trai sarana*; Tuesday: *Thawai phon phra (Itipiso)*; Wednesday: *Bahum*; Thursday: *Phra Jinapañjara gāthā*; Friday: *Khatha pongkan phai thang sip thit*; Saturday: *Khatha luang pho obhasi.*

5. Strong, *Experience of Buddhism* (1994:234) (citing Sulak Sivaraksa), and Swearer, *Becoming the Buddha* (2004:90–92). My translation differs in many verses. See also Narada Maha Thera and Kassapa Thera, *Mirror of the Dhamma* (2518 [1975]:52–58), Sri Dhammananda, *Daily Buddhist Devotions* (1993), Piyasilo, *Puja Book* (1990:132–38).

6. Some Thai-script editions have the compound *jiyāsarākatā* instead of *jayāsanākatā*, which could be translated as "having taken up (or making) their bows and arrows." I thank Luke Schmidt for pointing out this other possible reading. This reading makes sense in connection to the gerund *jetvā* (some texts read *jetavā*, which would be an irregular participle form of the root *ji*). Most likely some Thai versions have *jetavā* because the Thai language has very few consonant clusters, and central Thai pronunciation of *jetvā* sounds like "jetawā."

7. The elephant is the usual vehicle for Māra in Buddhist literature.

8. In most Thai-script editions of this text, *piviṃsu* appears instead of *piyataṃ*.

9. Some editions have the word *narāsubhā*, which could be translated as "good men and bad men" or "good men and not bad men." Most Thai translations of this verse assume a *ca* (and) here. Therefore, the Thai translation of *narāsubhā* in English is "The Buddhas and the Bulls of Men."

10. The Sri Lankan verse replaces *buddhā* with *vīrā*.

11. More commonly known as Dīpaṅkara.

12. The list of twenty-eight Buddhas is not the earliest. For more on these lists, see Skilling, "Sambuddhe Verses" (1996).

13. Many Thai-script editions separate the Pali words differently according to how they are chanted versus how they make sense grammatically.

14. The Sri Lankan verse reads "Sīre patiṭṭhito buddho dhammo ca mama locane saṅgho patiṭṭhito mayhaṃ ure sabbaguṇākaro ca dakkhiṇe."

15. *Āhuṃ* in Sri Lankan versions.

16. This particular list is not found in any other text of which I am aware.

17. *Nāma* in Sri Lankan versions.

18. *Lalāṭe* in Sri Lankan versions.

19. In some Thai versions, this word is elided.

20. *Orasa* is a *vriddhi* derivative from *uras* and means "belonging to one's own breast," that is, "one's own son or child." However, Thai translations of the text seem

to read the word differently. It seems as if some Thai translators read the word as a nominative masculine plural, "the conqueror's own sons." They seem to see the compound *jina* + *urasā* as a relatively rare neuter, s-declension, instrumental. Combined with the verb *jitavanto* (subdued or conquered), this translates literally as "subdued by the breast of the Jina" or "begotten of the victorious one." I am translating it as "pacified by the breast of the Jina" or "nursed by the breast of the Jina." This suggests that the disciples are children of the Buddha and he nourished them or pacified them with his breast. This is understood more generally in Thai as "begotten." Some Thai translations read *jinorasā* as a nominative plural compound "those nourished by the Jina." *Jitavanto jinorasā* is not found in the Sri Lankan versions. This seems to be one of Somdet To's more significant additions and may have come out of the Lan Na textual tradition.

21. The seven texts mentioned in the *Jinapañjara* are identical to the earliest lists of *paritta* texts in the *Milindapañha* but different in some ways from the Thai, Lao, Burmese, Cambodian, as well as later Sri Lankan lists (probably influenced by Siamese lists in the late eighteenth century). This indicates that the *Jinapañjara* was probably composed in Sri Lanka and brought to Thailand later. Even though the Thai generally refer to the list of *parittas* as "Seven Texts" (*Sattaparitta* or *Chet tamnan*), there are actually nine texts in the oldest-known Thai lists of *parittas*, those being the seven texts listed in the *Jinapañjara* as well as the *Maṅgala sutta* and the *Bojjhaṅga paritta*. The Thai also refer to the *Metta sutta* as the *Karaṇiyametta sutta*.

22. Sometimes written as *sosā* in Thai-script editions.

23. Literally, "are well-established encircling walls" [around me]." If we can imagine the four texts in the previous verse being watchtowers of a fortress, the "remaining [*parittas*]" (probably connoting the nine, twelve, or twenty-four protective texts common in Southeast Asian Buddhism, considering the seven *parittas* were listed by name) would be the walls between the watchtowers.

24. This could alternatively be translated as "the manifold Jinas, infused with power, made the seven encircling walls . . ." In some Thai versions, this compound reads *sattapākāralaṃkate*, which explicitly connects this text list to the seven (*satta*) *parittas*.

25. The most common translation of *vāta* and *pittā* is "wind" and "bile." However, if we look at the Indic background of these terms, we see that they were associated with a whole range of external and internal dangers. In the Buddhist context they are discussed in the *Vibhaṅga-atthakathā* (VbhA 70) and several places in the *Samādhiniddesa* of the *Visuddhimagga*. Looking at the detailed lists of these words warrants the translation "weather" and "disease," since they are generally what torments human beings every day. *Roga* (disease) is also often associated with *pittā*.

26. I translate *tejas* as "heat" rather than as "glory" or "light," as is more common, because here it is specifically connected with the heat produced through

meditation and that arises out of the "bile" stirring in the body. In the *Atharvaveda* and parts of the *Mahābharata*, *tejas* is related to the heat generated (related to *tapas*, a term that was used more widely in Indic religions for asceticism and the process and the product of ascetic activity) through asceticism, which is necessary for performing ritual or for protecting the body.

27. Verses 12 and 13 are more clearly understood in English if translated together.

28. *Jinapañjaramajjhattham* in Sri Lankan versions.

29. Sri Lankan versions do not include *anto* (at the end).

30. This is the end of the Thai version of the Somdet To tradition. The twenty-two-verse Sri Lankan versions are not common and largely unknown in Thailand.

31. This, of course, is not the only Pali chant popular in Thailand that has martial content. The *Buddhajayamaṅgalagāthā*, or as the Thais say, *Bāhuṃ*, contains verse after verse in which the Buddha is being attacked by various mythological creatures and unsavory characters like Ālavaka the giant, Nāḷāgiri the elephant, the harlot Ciñcā, the scandalous Saccaka, among others. The Buddha conquers them with peaceful words, holy water, and mental powers (*iddhi*).

32. Ñāṇasaṃvara, *Prawat Gāthā Chinapanchon* (2529 [1986]:1–31).

33. This fact has been somewhat confirmed by me in examinations of Sri Lankan manuscript catalogs and in consultation with several Sri Lankan studies specialists like Carol Anderson, Steven Berkwitz, Mahinda Deegalle, Anne Blackburn, John Holt, W. S. Karunatillake, and others. Carol Anderson sent me a copy of Lily de Silva's study of Sri Lankan protective texts ("Paritta" [1981]:5–6). De Silva does not list the *Jinapañjara* as one of the major texts used in Sri Lanka. Berkwitz sent me a Sri Lankan anthology of protective chants, and the *Jinapañjara* is in the "second tier" of *paritta* (Sinhala *pirit*) texts. Moreover, in Sri Lanka there are two *Jinapañjara parittas*, the *cula* (small) and the *mahā* (large). They are similar, except in the short version, where ten Buddhas are invoked for protection. In the *mahā* version there are the twenty-eight Buddhas invoked. The *Jinapañjara* in Thailand looks like a creative combination of these two Sri Lankan versions, which would suggest that the most popular Thai version is later; however, this cannot be confirmed. See also Schalk, *Der Paritta-Dienst* (1973) and Perera, *Buddhist Paritta Chanting Ritual* (2000). In a recent article in the Thai journal *Silapawatthanatham* a Pali scholar from Sri Lanka, with a single name that seems like a pseudonym, Langkakuman, argues that the text was composed in Sri Lanka. He explicitly states in the introduction that he does not want to offend anyone in Thailand. The evidence is rather scattered and the argument circular. He makes rather tangential connections between general *paritta* chanting in Sri Lanka, the *Catubhāṇavāra* anthology, and the *Jinapañjara*. There is a general assumption that if the *Jinapañjara* is included in modern collections of *parittas* there, it must have always been included. There is simply no evidence to prove this, and the author admits as much. However, he does

note, quite correctly, the problems with the fact that there are two different renditions of the *Jinapañjara* (his reasons for picking one as more "perfect" [*sombun*] seem unfounded [Langkakuman, "Lao ruang" (2552 [2009]:79)]). An image of Somdet To is on the cover of the journal, and the headline reads: "Krai taeng Kāthā Chinabanchon?" [Who Composed the *Jinapañjara*?]. The cover, the provocative headline, and the fact that this article is the featured piece in Thailand's most prestigious arts and culture journal show the persistent importance of the *Jinapañjara* as well as the openness with which scholars in Thailand debate the origin of the text.

34. See my "Two Bullets" (2008).

35. There were also hundreds of texts taken from northern Thailand and Ayutthaya to Burma at different periods between 1551 and 1767. Bryce Beemer is presently finishing a dissertation at the University of Hawai'i on this subject. I thank Padmanabh Jaini and Jacques Leider for help in understanding this process.

36. For more on Phra Dhammananda, see my "Some Notes on the Study of Pāli Grammar" (2011).

37. The other major study of the text is largely derivative of the *sangharat* team's edition; see Suchao Ploichum, *Prawat Gāthā Chinabanchon* (2543 [2000]). Another study that draws directly on the *sangharat's* study is Pho Sawan, *Prawat lae withi chai Phra Gāthā Chinabanchon* (2543 [2000]).

38. There is supposedly an unpublished edition completed in Moulmein based on a Burmese version of the text translated by James Gray in 1879. I have been unable to locate it.

39. I spoke at the first conference sponsored by the association in 2008. This conference was attended by over three thousand nuns, monks, and laypeople from all over Asia, as well as from Australia, Europe, and the Americas. Several times during the speeches (in Thai and translated into several languages), Thailand was pronounced as the new center of the Theravada world. The conference concluded with a huge Thai cultural dance show featuring regional Thai dances and music, as well as a dance celebrating the Thai military and the art of *muai thai* (kickboxing). It was an incredible display of wealth and organizational skill by members of the Thai sangha.

40. For example, Khana Sit Watcharin, *Kittikhun lae phra barami* (2529 [1986]:14).

41. One common story is that Somdet To discovered the *Jinapañjara* at Wat Boromathat Kampaengphet, and next to this manuscript he found two *yantra* plaques, one silver and one gold (*lan ngoen lan thong*).

42. Suwit Koetphongbunchot, "Anuphap Krua To" (2535 [1992]:1, 2, 34–38).

43. Holy water (*nam mon*) is generated in large quantities also at Wat Sateu in rural Ayutthaya. Achan Nu Kanphai, a very popular magician (*mo wiset*) and tattoo artist in Pathum Thani Province (central Thailand), uses holy water as an ingredient in his tattoos. The water is made magically powerful by the chanting of a series of short texts he refers to as the "Mon Khatha Sek Sak" (Mantra Verses for the Empowering of Tattoos),

or the "Mahawet" (Great Veda). These chants are a mixture of Sanskritized Thai and Pali interspersed with rhythmic, abbreviated syllables. At these ceremonies, which are held once or twice a year, monks also chant *parittas* in Pali while stirring pots of holy water. At the end of the ceremony, all the laypeople in attendance have their heads tied together with sacred string, which is also tied around large Brahma images, Buddha images, and monks in the room. Achan Nu Kanphai is assisted in his tattoo ceremonies (which also include spirit possession) by two senior monks from Ayutthaya. During these ceremonies many laypeople in the audience start dancing uncontrollably, supposedly possessed by spirits. He and the monks are all referred to as Kechi Achan, which is a specialized title for teachers, either lay or ordained, who have special knowledge of protective incantations. Somdet To is occasionally described as a Kechi Achan. A good study of *yantras* and incantations is by Phra Khru Baithikathep Singrak, *Tamra phetrat mahayan* (2551 [2008]). The author was trained at Wat Rakhang and taught in a method found in the notebooks of one of Somdet To's students. The cremation/funeral book of Suphan Hemachayat has a passage that describes how this laywoman chanted the *Jinapañjara* every day and how this ensured that she led an auspicious life. *Ruam lang ruang khadi lok khadi tham* (2528 [1985]:38).

44. There are thousands of copies of various *yantras* Somdet To drew found in the amulet markets. Moreover, several biographies of Somdet To and editions of the *Jinapañjara* contain printed copies of various *yantras* drawn by Somdet To. They are all in Khom script, usually square shaped (two are in the shape of a seated Buddha and one is in *prasat*, palace shape, and one is in the shape of a diamond). Some of these *yantras* are also printed on warrior shirts alongside photographs of Somdet To and drawings of tigers. Others are inscribed on thin sheets of lead or tin and rolled in *takrut*. These *takrut* are rolled tightly, sealed with wax or gold-leaf paint, attached to a chain or rope, and worn around the neck like a protective talisman. For an introduction to various *yantras* in Thailand, see Natathan Manirat, *Lek yan* (2553 [2010]).

45. There are two stores on the monastic grounds that sell amulets, ceramic and metal statues, posters, CDs, audio cassettes of Somdet To and his teachings. There are even ceramic statues of Somdet To sitting in front of a small pool. Inserted in the backs of the statues are audio cassette players that play the *Jinapañjara* on a continuous loop. The images vibrate and the speakers play the chant. The water placed in the bowl attached to the statue vibrates as well, and the impression is one of Somdet To blessing the water with the power of his words. This and other holy-water machines allow a person to make protective substances at home. Therefore, in your home or office you can replicate the ritual moment of the cave at Wat Indrawihan whenever you wish.

46. In North Hollywood, California, the largest Thai Buddhist temple in the Western Hemisphere has a shrine dedicated to Somdet To next to the main monastic hall. Inside this shrine there is water blessed by the *Jinapañjara* just as in Bangkok. About seventy miles away in the mountains of California, another large golden

image of Somdet To sits on the grounds of the ultraconservative and isolated Wat Metta, run by the American-born monk Thanissaro Bhikkhu.

47. See Tambiah, *Buddhist Saints of the Forest* (1984), and Chalong Soontravanich, "Regionalization of Local Buddhist Saints."

48. A good example of how the *Jinapañjara* is chanted by people of all classes and backgrounds is Pornthip Kanjananiyot, the executive director of Fulbright Thailand. Pornthip is fluent in English, has studied abroad, is cosmopolitan and politically active. She told me she chants the *Jinapañjara* every morning. A working-class family from Udon Thani in northeastern Thailand recently posted a video of their seven-year-old son, Andaman, chanting the *Jinapañjara* from memory. A local monk claims that the boy has been chanting it since the age of three. The video demonstrates the particular importance of this chant to Thai Buddhists: http://amulet forums.com/3-years-old-genius-t4285.html.

49. Claudio Cicuzza recently sent me photographs of a new giant statue of Luang Pho Tuat in Prachuab Khiri Khan Province. Although not as large as Sorapong's Somdet To image, it reveals, like recent giant statues of Kuan Im, that large statues are no longer limited to images of the Buddha or Buddhas. In fact, it seems as if images of saints, kings, heroes, and *bodhisattas* are taking prominent places alongside or even exceeding in size Buddha images.

50. I thank Alan Klima and Arnika Fuhrman for sending me copies of their forthcoming work on the subject.

51. *Nak* opens with a narrator stating that in the past in Thailand, people were kind and offered gifts to monks and to ghosts. The ghosts and monks were happy, and society ran well. However, in the modern world, people have forgotten the ghosts, and so they have caused havoc in society. Some ghosts, though, like Mae Nak, still want to protect humans, and so the good and the bad ghosts battle, and their battlefield is the world of the living. Nak becomes the hero that saves modern Thai society from the ghosts. Nak has become, in the animated version, a very buxom and sexy red-headed teenage girl who can fly, stretch her arms out fifty or sixty feet to save children from falling. She is a superhero. She is backed by a team of other ghosts that are popular in Thai folklore—a legless (and also sexy) floating maiden, a giant blue *preta*, a flying nymphlike ghost, among others. The nationalist theme in the film is coupled with scenes of the Thai flag behind the good ghosts as they battle foreign ghosts, and the not-so-subtle suggestions throughout the film that foreigners have led Thais astray. I thank Adam Knee for a number of fruitful conversations about various versions of the film.

52. Recently the city district borders were redrawn. The area Mak and Nak were from used to be in the Phrakanong district but now is officially in a neighboring district.

53. While there were small skirmishes between the Siamese and the Burmese in 1868 in northwestern Thailand, the main battles between the Burmese and Siamese had long ended.

54. Alternatively, she is called I Nak ("I" is a familiar term used to address a young woman), Nang (young woman) Nak, Mae (mother or middle-aged woman) Nak, and Ya (grandmother) Nak.

55. See Prince Anuman Rajadhon, *Popular Buddhism* (1986:99–124). According to Anuman, women who die in childbirth are known as *phi phrai*. This is an extremely feared type of ghost in Thailand as it is known to feed on the entrails of the living. However, she is also feared, like Mae Nak Phrakhanong, because she can appear as a beautiful woman and seduce young men. She (and her unborn ghost child) is neutralized by sealing the corpse with wax and string and submerging it in a river. Sometimes, this type of burial is reserved for the unborn ghost baby. This type of ghost is also alternatively called *phi tai thang klom* (literally, "ghosts of women who have died during childbirth). This type of ghost also appears in the Ayutthayan-era epic romance *Khun Chang Khun Paen.*

56. Bizot, *Le bouddhisme des Thaïs* (1993:59).

57. Anake Nawigamune has published several articles on the topic, including "Khun Chan khadi" (2547 [2004]); "Poet long Mae" (2546 [2003]); "Mae Nak Phrakhanong" (2547 [2004]); and a full-length book on the subject, *Poet tamnan Mae Nak* (2543 [2000]). These articles not only investigate the details about the story but also demonstrate in great detail how these stories changed over time. For example, he shows that Mak's name was Chum in a story written by a Bangkok scholar known only by the name K. S. R. Kulap (in "Amdaeng Nak" in the journal *Siam braphet* on March 10, 1899). Chum was the name of an actual historical figure who served in the military under the brigade of Prince Phitak. Earlier records state that Chum and Nak were living in Phrakhanong and had a living son named Baen. This son was ordained at Wat Chetuphon after his mother died. In another instance, in 1904, in a short story called "Nak Phrakhanong thi Song" in a book titled *Thawibanya* Nak's husband's name is given as Choti. Mak became the common name for Nak's husband when Prince Narathippa Braphanphong used the name Mak when he directed a musical about Mae Nak at the Bridalai Theater in 1912. The prince advertised this musical as a "true story" (*ruang ching*). In 1936 Anusak Hadinthon made the first film version of the story and filmed it on-site at Wat Mahabut and used the name Mak. A play staged in 1938 called "I Nak Phrakhanong" used the name Mak, and three graphic novels published by Saengdaet Press were produced based on the "facts" presented in this play. In other versions, an eighteen-year-old novice named Phuak, who was a student of Somdet To's, subdues Nak because he knew Vedic (*phrawet*) mantras.

58. Similarly, the opening line of Mark Duffield's 2005 version, *Ghost of Mae Nak*, states in Thai "This is a love story." See also *Ya Nak* (2003). Mae Nak is played by Me Phatarawarin Thimakun. Pimpaka Towira, one of Thailand's most prominent independent filmmakers, directed another version in 1997, *Mae Nak*. This unorthodox, art-house film, with very little dialogue or character development, tells

the story from a wholly different and innovative feminist perspective. She includes one character, whom she refers to as a *mo phi* (ghost doctor), who is dressed as a Thai *phra prahm* (Brahman priest) but wears Tibetan Buddhist beads, performs a protection ritual on a Chinese-style floor shrine (Thai *san chao chin* or *keng* or *piao* in the Teochiu Chinese dialect and *aam* in Hokkien), and chants a mixture of Japanese and Sanskrit chants. The actor, Pimpaka informed me, did not know Pali chanting but had learned some Japanese, so he chanted in Japanese. Neither the director nor the actor knew the exact meaning of the chants. In the film, these chants protect a house and family from Mae Nak's ghost. The historical accuracy promoted by Nonzee is abandoned by Pimpaka. She also makes other radical choices. Mae Nak is not depicted as menacing but as passive, even content. The humans in the film seem to haunt her rather than her haunting them. I thank Pimpaka Towira for helpful comments on her film and for granting me a very fruitful short interview (November 1, 2008, Riverside, California).

59. Other films that depict the use of magic have been quite popular. See my study of these films "Emotional Lives of Buddhist Monks" (2010), released mostly between 2001 and 2009, including *Arahant Summer, Nak Prok, Maha-ut, Ong bak, Ahimsa,* and *Chom khamang wet*. The *Luang Phi Teng* films (three to date) are slapstick comedies about monks fighting with both real and imagined ghosts.

60. See http://news.bbc.co.uk/2/hi/entertainment/8699394.stm. I thank Michael Keogh for sending me this story and for fruitful conversations on this issue.

61. See especially Becchetti, *Le mystère dans les lettres* (1991); de Bernon, "Le manuel des maîtres de kammaṭṭhān" (2000); and the many works of François Bizot in the bibliography.

62. Bizot has not focused his research on central Thailand, except in his introductory survey *Le bouddhisme des Thaïs* (1993) and in a short passage in his "Notes sur les *yantra* bouddhiques d'Indochine," (1981:57, 61). Terwiel's *Monks and Magic* (1975) and Tambiah's *Buddhist Saints of the Forest* (1984) generally discuss the practices of forest or village-based monks. Tambiah briefly mentions these esoteric practices in Bangkok in relation to the amulet market. Neither focuses on protective texts.

63. See particularly Jackson, "Withering Centre (1997); Jackson, "Enchanting Spirit of Thai Capitalism" (1999); Mackenzie, *New Buddhist Movements in Thailand* (2007); Sanitsuda Ekachai, *Keeping the Faith* (2001); Saichon Sattayanurak, *Phuttha Satsana* (2546 [2003]).

64. Despite some flaccid attempts to control millenarian rebels in the early twentieth century, the central royal and postroyal governments of Thailand have not tried to "ban" magical protective practices in any serious way. This is quite different from some modern African governments and Turkish policies in which "magic" and "witch doctors" have been made officially illegal at different times. See, for ex-

ample, Fisiy and Geschiere, *Sorcellerie et politique en Afrique* (1995), as well as Moore and Sanders, *Magical Interpretations* (2001).

65. See, for example, Robinson, Johnson, and Thanissaro Bhikkhu, *Buddhist Religions* (2005); Kamala, *Forest Recollections* (1997); Kitagawa, *Religious Traditions of Asia* (2002); Southwold, "True Buddhism and Village Buddhism" (1982); Bechert, "Aspects of Theravāda Buddhism" (1989); Ishii, *Sangha* (1986).

66. For example, it is commonly known that *saiyasat* has influenced Thai politics for centuries. There are even passages in three chronicles that mention the use of magic by kings to influence the outcomes of battles. Present-day uses of magic by politicians like Thaksin Shinawatra and Sondhi Limthongkul has been described by Wassana Nanuam. These rituals are highly visible, filmed by television crews, and discussed in newspapers. Shrines have been set up by protestors on both sides of the recent political turmoil in the occupied compounds of Government House and even at Suvarnabhumi Airport. Even Wat U Mong, a "liberal" meditation monastery occupied by many monks in the Buddhadasa Bhikkhu tradition in Chiang Mai has been the site of these rituals. See *Lap luang prang pak pisadan* (2552 [2009]). She has already written a sequel, because the first book sold extremely well. See also Keyes, "Magic, Mobs and Millennialism" (2009).

67. Eade, *Thai Historical Record* (1996) provides a nice glossary for some common terms used in northern Thai astrology. The classic work is *Kamphi horasat Thai matrathan chapab sombun*, by An Sarikabut (Luang Wisat) (2508 [1965]). See pages 748–75 for the Chettha Triyang Kesat and pages 1–144 for the Suriya/Manat systems of calculating good and bad times to accomplish tasks like marriages, cremations, and the like. Warriors and soldiers use the latter system (see especially pages 118–44) for predicting when it is safe to initiate a battle. These two systems may be connected to the Tamil system based on the *Varāhamihira-bṛhat-saṃhitā*. Astrological manuscripts and practitioners in Thailand often refer to their texts as coming out of the Phra Wet (Vedas). Of course, an entire section of the Vedas has to do with prognostication and ritual weapons (*Artharvaveda*). One of the most common associations is the Jina ("conqueror," name for the Buddha) with the sun. This is referring to the fact that Suriya, the Cakkavattin king, and the Jina (the Buddha, the Victor) are all associated with the sun at its highest point (noon). Noon was considered an auspicious time to start a battle. The *Jinapañjara* discusses the sun at its zenith with the Jina. Noon was considered a particularly auspicious time to initiate a battle in premodern Siam.

68. Tambiah, *World Conqueror and World Renouncer* (1976).

69. Crosby, "Tantric Theravada" (2000:141–42). See also Cousins, "Aspects of Esoteric Southern Buddhism" (1997). I thank Kate Crosby for sending me her very informative article.

70. Crosby, "Tantric Theravada" (2000:142).

71. Depictions of the five Buddhas are common in Thailand. There are posters in the modern era. I recently saw a Tipiṭaka cabinet from the nineteenth century

with the five Buddhas with their animal symbols depicted in close detail. Other scenes painted on the cabinet were drawn directly from the canonical *suttas*, and so here we see no barrier between the canonical and noncanonical. Since this cabinet would have been commissioned by a wealthy donor and displayed in a prominent, elite monastery, it shows that these images are not particularly "esoteric" or a product of folk Buddhism. I thank Forrest McGill for pointing out this cabinet to me.

72. See my "Philosophical Embryology" (2009). These candles are used in the forecasting of winning lottery numbers at Wat Kaeo Fa by Phra Achan Kesom Achinnasilo. He instructed me and about forty others who had crowded around him to add the years they were alive to the years they (or their son or husband) had been ordained to the number twenty-one (the number of years the abbot had been ordained) and to add that number to the length of the candles he was distributing at the sermon. I thank Peter Skilling for taking me to this monastery.

73. Sahlins, *Islands of History* (1985:xiv).

74. Samuel, *Origins of Yoga* (2008:9).

75. Davidson, *Indian Esoteric Buddhism* (2003:236, 247–48). He notes that esoteric texts are characterized by the use of martial language and imagery.

76. Skilling, "Ubiquitous and Elusive" (2004:16). See also Padoux, "What Do We Mean by Tantrism?" (2002:23). Kuroda Toshio argued for a similar rethinking of Japanese Buddhist history ("Shintō in the History of Japanese Religion" [1999]).

77. There has been a great growth in studies linking tantric, especially Pāśupata Śaivite, practices connected to royal power and militarism in eighth-to-eleventh-century Kashmir, Orissa, Java, and Angkor, among other places. See Davidson, *Indian Esoteric Buddhism* (2003) and Sanderson, "Śaiva Religion Among the Khmers" (2003).

78. Translated as *Manual of a Mystic* by F. L. Woodward (1916). Bizot's association of the esoteric traditions in Laos, Thailand, and Cambodia with the practices represented in the *Yogāvacara Manual* is dubious. First, the so-called *Yogāvacara Manual* is based on a single manuscript found in Sri Lanka in 1893 without a title or a definitive colophon. Moreover, the original editor of the Pali text, T. W. Rhys Davids, admits that he had serious trouble editing the manuscript because of the scribes' apparent lack of understanding of Pali/Sinhala orthography or even rudimentary Pali grammar. Moreover, Rhys Davids did not compile the edition because of the texts' popularity in Sri Lanka or his observation of the manual being used in rituals or in guided meditation but because he considered the subject matter important from "both the historical, and from the psychological point of view"(Rhys Davids, *Yogāvacara's Manual* [1896:vi]). Finally, this text does not describe protective practices related to those of the so-called esoteric traditions of mainland Southeast Asia. Instead, it is a guide to meditation and what Rhys Davids calls "ethical self-training"(vii). The practitioner, through different postures, imaginings, mentally constructed visions, and a small candle-lighting ceremony, seeks to view 112 different states of mind.

79. Bizot, Cousins, Swearer, and others have associated it with the ritual use of the Abhidhamma at funerals. For the use of the term *araham* and the *Itipiso* and *Nāmo buddhāya* incantations in Bizot's work, see his book with Oskar von Hinüber, *La guirlande de joyaux* (1994:54–67). They demonstrate clearly how the *Itipiso* incantation was transformed into *yantra* drawings based on the auspiciousness of its 108 syllables. These syllables were connected to the different parts of the body of the Buddha. See also my *Gathering Leaves* (2008, chap. 8).

80. See especially Bizot and Lagirarde, *La pureté par les mots* (1996:52–53). In the *Saddavimala*, Lagirarde and Bizot mention that there is a reference to the eighty worms that exist in the human body. These worms are associated with the eighty disciples of the Buddha and the *Vimuttimagga* text in Sri Lanka. The *Jinapañjara*'s mentioning of the eighty disciples might be an allusion to these eighty parts of the human body.

81. A recent collection on esoteric religion in Burma adds further complexity to the ways in which we define these traditions in the region. See Kawanami and Brac de la Perrière, "Power, Authority and Contested Hegemony" (2009).

82. See Skilling, "Kings, Sangha, Brahmans" (2007:209–10).

83. Interview, September 12, 2009, Philadelphia. In another conversation, she told me that her family did not go to the monastery to make merit very often because it was inconvenient and often "too gossipy." Her mother preferred inviting the *mo phi* to their house for private rituals.

84. There are not many analytical defenses of the importance of protective magical practice in Thai sources. However, in the 1950s and 1960s Bunmi Methangkun gave several sermons at the prominent royal monastery Wat Chetuphon (next door to the Grand Palace) in which he argued for the real power of ghosts and minor deities in daily life.

85. Neusner, "Introduction," *Religion, Science, and Magic* (1989:4).

86. Mauss, *General Theory of Magic* (2002:22–25).

87. Bailey, "Meanings of Magic" (2006:8). See also Graf, *Magic in the Ancient World* (1997).

88. *Itthirit* is a creative combination of a Pali (*iddhi*) and Sanskrit (*ṛddhi*), which both have the sense of psychokinetic power, as noted, is drawn from Sanskrit *Veda mantra*. *Bao sek* is a verb that means to "infuse with protective power through the act of 'blowing.'" *Pluk sek* has a similar meaning, but the practitioner infuses an object, room, statue, or a person with protective power not by blowing but by binding the person or object with string. The verb *rot nam* has a general sense of "blessing" (literally, "make sacred," *tham hai saksit*) with water made powerful through the use of mantras (*nam mon*). *Sek mon* is the Thai verb for "incanting a mantra."

89. See Lamont and Wiseman, *Magic in Theory* (1999); Morris and Wiseman, "Recalling Pseudo-psychic Demonstrations" (1995:86). The Thai word for a professional magician who entertains with cards and sleights of hand is *mayakon*. The

word *sek* is used for the action this type of entertainer does (e.g., *Kao sek mi goet dai*—"He made it appear out of nowhere").

90. Styers, *Making Magic* (2004:220). See also Erick White, "The Cultural Politics of the Supernatural" (2003). And see Todorov's classic *The Fantastic* (1975); Daston and Park, *Wonders and the Order of Nature* (2001); McClintock, *Imperial Leather* (1995); Warner, *Phantasmagoria* (2006); and Li, *Ambiguous Bodies* (2009). I thank Felicidad Bliss Cua Lim for conversations on these developments.

91. See especially Tambiah, "Magic Power of Words" (1968).

92. Styers, *Making Magic* (2004:223).

93. Ibid., 221.

94. Ibid., 222.

95. Sarah Johnston has pointed out that magic has been used as a term of "opprobrium, to marginalize and condemn individuals or groups whose religious practices [are], by the standards of the accusers, 'abnormal.'" Johnston, "Describing the Undefinable" (2004:51). Burchett has suggested that scholars abandon the term "magic" because it "lack[s] any productive value" but then admits that the there is "productivity in such faulty terminology" for scholarly debate (Burchett, "'Magical' Language of Mantra" [2008:837]). I support the second half of this argument and also find it helpful to pay close attention to indigenous terms that are often translated as "magic" in English as much as possible when describing non-English-speaking practitioners.

96. See especially Harvey, *Introduction to Buddhist Ethics* (2000:37).

97. Samuel, *Origins of Yoga* (2008:149) relies here largely on the work of Tambiah, *Buddhist Saints of the Forest* (1984).

98. DeCaroli, *Haunting the Buddha* (2004:13–14) shows that this use of *laukika* (worldly) is quite old in Indian religions. It was a rhetorical device that Vedic teachers, Jains, Buddhists, and others used against one another. Holt noted in his 2004 keynote address at the Exploring Theravada conference at the National University of Singapore that *lokottara* is often mistranslated and should be read as "pre-eminent in this world," not as "supramundane" or "nonworldly." Holt has noted that Obeyesekere observed the problems with the *lokiya-lokottara* dichotomy in his "Great Tradition" (1963).

99. Falk, "Thammacarini Witthaya" (2000:69).

100. Spiro, *Buddhism and Society* (1975).

101. Spiro, *Buddhist Supernaturalism* (1978:263). I thank Dietrich Christian Lammerts for pointing out this quote. Personal communication, July 2008.

102. Tambiah, *World Conqueror and World Renouncer* (1976:9–10). Emphasis mine.

103. Ibid., 14–15.

104. In the 2008 animated version, *Nak*, Mae Nak helps rescue a child from this suburb who has been kidnapped. She has to travel to the center of Bangkok and is struck by the modern developments there. However, back in her suburb, Mae Nak watches drive-in/outside foreign movies like *The Ring*, uses electricity and other

modern conveniences. She does not live completely disconnected from the urban and the modern, just slightly on the edge of it.

105. Davisakd Puaksom, "Kan prubtau thang khwam ru" (1997), citing Sulak Sivaraksa, "Siam versus the West" (1970). See also Pattana Kitiarsa, "*Farang* as Siamese Occidentalism" (2005:39).

106. Erick White offers an excellent overview ("Fraudulent and Dangerous" [2005:39]) of these new criticisms of "popular religion" (especially spirit mediums) in Thailand by prominent and elite Thai intellectuals. See also his "Cultural Politics of the Supernatural" (2003).

107. I thank Steve Collins for his comments on this section. See also an article by Collins and me in which we expand on this criticism of Weber's use of the term "worldly." Collins and McDaniel, "Buddhist 'Nuns'" (2010:1373–1408). Also see Thongchai Winichakul's comments on the idea of *lokiya* in "Quest for 'Siwilai'" (2000).

108. In Weiner's essay "Colonialism and the Politics of Magic," she writes, "It is the space magic occupies in the murky territory between fraud and the fear in the imaginations of modern Europeans that I explore . . . Although it is about magic in colonial Indonesia, I will have little to say about the practices of Indonesians" (Meyer and Pels, *Magic and Modernity* [2003]:130). The actual practices are seen as fraudulent products of European fear and local trickery; she gives little voice to the practitioners. Michael Taussig has made the interesting point, though, that although many local observers of magical rituals and even the magicians themselves know that they are participating in something fraudulent, they continue to attend ceremonies and fear other magicians. Their power, in many ways, is in the skilled execution of known tricks (Meyer and Pels, *Magic and Modernity* [2003:132]). The "truth" of magic is not as important as the skill in execution. In Thailand, while many people are skeptical of the efficacy of magic and the intentions of magicians, their skills and knowledge are often lauded.

109. Ginsburg, *Thai Literary Tales* (1967). I thank Henry Ginsburg for his advice and for conversations on these stories and sundry.

110. Ibid., 24–34.

111. Ibid., 40. See examples of magical ritual, especially 54, 61, 64, 65, 69.

112. Ibid., 79–80.

### 3. RITUALS AND LITURGIES

1. Griswold, "Warning to Evildoers" (1967).

2. See especially Collins, "Introduction" (1993).

3. I describe Thai funeral liturgies extensively in *Gathering Leaves* (2008, chap. 8). For a good introduction to these Phra Malai illuminated manuscripts, see Ginsburg, *Thai Manuscript Painting* (1989) and his *Thai Art* (2000).

4. See, for example, the comic book *Phra Chikong: Thong Yomlok* (Bangkok: Phutthabucha, n.d.). The cover depicts a Chinese monk (Chikong) with a long beard walking through the flames of hell surrounded by green-faced demons and suffering naked and bleeding women. The contents are gruesome, and many of the illustrated cells depict people in hell being tortured with hot irons, being crucified, and having their tongues pulled out.

5. This sutra is popular today. It is painted on murals, depicted in dioramas, and dramatized in three-day-long festivals. Today, some Chinese women are given amulets with the text of the *Blood Bowl Sutra* to hold while menstruating. In Taiwan, mock trips to hell are acted out where red wine (mimicking blood) is consumed by sons to take on the suffering of their mothers. In the 1950s, sutra fragments copied onto narrow strips of wood were discovered in sulfur deposits along the shores of a Lake Yugama, in Kusatsu, Japan. I thank Hank Glassman for discussions of the *Blood Bowl Sutra*. For other examples, see Liz Wilson, *Charming Cadavers* (1996), and Benn, *Burning for the Buddha* (2007).

6. However, recent studies by Hansen and Blackburn have warned us not to assume institutional centralization actually leads to homogenization in Buddhism. Hansen, *How to Behave* (2006); Blackburn, *Buddhist Learning* (2001). Thak Chaloemtiarana's "Making New Space in the Thai Literary Canon" (2009) shows that while the 1914 Royal Literary Act did have some effect on the ways the parameters of the Thai literary canon was defined, it did not necessarily stop the creativity and choice of subjects of early Thai novelists.

7. From the collected correspondence of Prince Damrong's twenty-three-volume collection *San Somdet Phra Chao Boromwongtoe Krom Phraya Damrong Ratchanuphap* (last edition 2505 [1962]). As cited in Griswold, "Warning to Evildoers" (1967:21).

8. See especially Peleggi, *Lords of Things* (2002) and his excellent and often overlooked *Politics of Ruin* (2002). See also Darling, *Thailand* (1971); Thongchai Winichakul, *Siam Mapped* (1994); Wyatt, *Politics of Reform* (1969); Bechert, "Neue buddhistische Orthodoxie" (1988); Ishii, *Sangha* (1985); among many others. Horstmann has gone as far as to claim that "all monasteries across the kingdom were integrated within a single administrative organization through the Sangha Act of 1902. From this point in time, salvation was . . . possible only under state Buddhism"(*Class, Culture and Space* [2002:17]) This type of antistate and antiecclesia hyperbole is not supported by available evidence.

9. The numbers of studies on Buddhism and the state in Southeast Asia are truly staggering. For background, see Bechert's two-volume *Buddhismus, Staat und Gesellschaft* (1966–1967). These two volumes have sections on Sri Lanka, Burma, Laos, Cambodia, and Thailand. There is also a third volume that is useful as a bibliographic guide for secondary works on Theravada Buddhism in general (1973). Here is just a

small sampling of some of the more prominent and recent publications in English: Apinya Fuengfulsakul, "Empire of Crystal" (1993); Harris, *Buddhism and Politics* (2005); Ishii, *Sangha, State, and Society* (1986); Jackson, "Withering Centre" and *Buddhism, Legitimation, and Conflict* (1997, 1989); Jory, "Vessantara Jataka" (2002); Keyes, "Moral Authority" (1999), (1995: 154–182), and (1971: 551–567); Kirsch (1975: 172–196); Kitagawa, "Buddhism and Asian Politics" (1962); Mackenzie, *New Buddhist Movements* (2007); Mendelson, *Sangha and State* (1975); Schober, "Buddhist Visions" (2002:113,132); Bardwell Smith, *Religion and Legitimation* (1978:147–64); D. E. Smith, *Religion and Politics* (1965); Somboon Suksamran, *Buddhism and Politics* (1982); Stuart-Fox, *Buddhist Kingdom* (1996); Tambiah, *Buddhism Betrayed*; *Buddhist Saints of the Forest*; and *World Conqueror and World Renouncer* (1992, 1984, 1976); J. L. Taylor, *Forest Monks* (1993); as well as a number of studies by Frank Reynolds, Nidhi Aeusrivongse, John Butt, among others. It seems that scholars have said all that could be said on the topic. However, Harris's collection of essays, *Buddhism, Power and Political Order* (2007) proves there is considerably more research to be done on the topic. Most of the articles in this volume do not reify the dichotomy between the elite and the nonelite in Southeast Asia, which has often dominated approaches to the subject.

10. These studies posit a slow movement toward centralized reform. See, for example, Moffat, *Mongkut* (1961); Prince Chula Chakrabongse, *Lords of Life* (1960); Wyatt, *Short History of Thailand* (1984); and Blofeld, *King Maha Mongkut* (1987).

11. Pattana Kitiarsa, "Beyond the Weberian Trails" (2009: 200–224); Reynolds, *Seditious Histories* (2006); McHale, *Print and Power* (2004); Dror, *Cult, Culture, and Authority* (2007); Philip Taylor, *Goddess on the Rise* (2004); Chandler and Kent, *People of Virtue* (2008).

12. Some of the most garish posters were produced for film versions of the story, like *Mae Nak Khanong rak*, directed by Pricha Rungruang; *Mae Nak kheun chip*, directed by Dulyarat; and the 1962 classic *Winyan rak Mae Nak* (*Mae Nak, the Lovelorn Soul*), directed by Sen Komanchun. Comic book versions of the story are even more violent in their depictions of Mae Nak. One, written by an author using the pseudonym Lungphi, depicts Mae Nak's ghost baby as a hairless green alien, in his 1955 *Nang Nak Phrakhanong*, while P. Inthrapalit's comic *Nang Nak Phrakhanong*, written in 1959, depicts her as a carefree woman strolling through villages in some scenes and as a shrouded skeletal beast in others. See Anake Nawigamune, *Poet tamnan Mae Nak Phrakhanong* (2543 [2001]), as well as the new and expanded third edition of that book (2549 [2006]). See also his *Ruang kao phap kao* (2546 [2003]:95–106) and *Thanon sai adit* (2547 [2004]:65–72).

13. For further reading about the history of these murals, see Pricha Iamtham, *Prawat Somdet Phra Phutthachan To* (2547 [2004]:46–65); (Phra Khru) Platsomkhit Siriwatthano, *Khong di Wat Rakhang* (2541 [1998]:32–33, 53). These murals were repainted by Thong Charuwichit in 2465 [1922]) based on 1814 originals. There are

other murals in the original library of Wat Rakhang. These were painted most likely in 2312 [1769] under the reign of King Rama I, as this was his original home in Thonburi, which was later converted into a library. See *Ho Phra Traipidok Wat Rakhangkhositaram* (2515 [1972]). See also Feua Hiriphithak, *Phap khian nai ho Phra Tripidok Wat Rakhangkhositaram* (2513 [1970]).

14. On my last visit to the *wihan* of Wat Sommanat, the preservation was still under way. See No Na Paknam, *Mural Paintings of Thailand* (2538 [1995]). There has been little study on the murals of the *uposatha* hall. There is a manuscript (watercolor on mulberry paper with black lacquer covers) dated to the early nineteenth century acquired by Henry Walters labeled, mistakenly, "Abhidhammavaranapitaka" instead of "Abhidhamma-vaṇṇanā-piṭaka" that depicts very similar scenes of different stages of a decomposing body with a monk seated in meditation. The details depicting birds consuming the body, as well as a caption in Khom script on the eight folio that reads "Vikhatiyam" (a type of corpse meditation), all indicate the content and the sequence of the murals may have been inspired by these earlier illuminated manuscripts (although the painting style is very different). I thank Pattaratorn Chirapravati for pointing out this manuscript to me. I also thank Hiram Woodward for sending me detailed photographs of the manuscript (no. W716 in the Walters Collection). There are also very similar murals of this meditative practice at Wat Boworniwet, specifically in the Wihan Phra Sasada. This is another *wihan* built under the direction of King Mongkut.

15. Listopad's 1984 master's thesis has an entire chapter on these murals. He convincingly argues that they are the work of Khrua In Khong, King Mongkut's mostfavored artist. "Process of Change" (1984). I thank him for mailing me his work.

16. Listopad has speculated that the mural subjects were chosen reflecting the preferred meditation practice of Phra Ariyamuni (Buddhasiri Tap). They depict in detail the stages of *asubhakammaṭṭhāna* meditation, including the stages of *lohitaka* (meditation on a bleeding corpse), *puḷavaka* (meditation on a worminfested corpse), *vipubbaka* (meditation on a festering corpse), *vicchiddaka* (meditation on a corpse cut into two), *vikkhāyitaka* (meditation on a gnawed corpse), *hata-vikkhittaka* (meditation on a scattered corpse), among others. Ibid., 18–26.

17. Meditation on corpses has been a common part of Thai Buddhist (and other Buddhist) traditions. However, one does not need an actual corpse to practice this meditation. There is also a tradition of meditation on one's own decaying body. Some monks and nuns are instructed to imagine themselves dissecting their own bodies in meditation in order to examine the different organs, and especially on the fact that the body contains feces, bile, and urine. My own abbot suggested that we could even imagine piercing our own flesh with a knife. Meditators in this practice are supposed to focus on both the "disgust" of the body and the impermanence of the flesh, fluids, and bones.

18. Listopad is of the opinion that there are three monks depicted in these murals: Phra Maha Samanawong of Wat Maha Samanaram in Phetburi, Phra Dhammarajavat of Wat Sala Pun in Ayutthaya, and Phra Upaligunapamachan of Wat Boromniwat. It is my personal opinion that the face depicted in the *hata-vikkhittaka* meditation pose in the first panel on the northern wall is Somdet To's and not Phra Maha Samanawong's. However, the other two monks could certainly be Phra Dhammarajavat and Phra Upaligunapamachan. Phra Upaligunapamachan was most famously the abbot of Wat Kalyanamit, but he was also connected to Wat Indrawihan (Wat Bangkhunphrom), where Somdet To was the abbot in his later years and where he passed away, as seen in the cremation volume for Luang Wutinayanetisat in 1932. I do not believe that photographs of Phra Maha Samanawong bear a close resemblance to the face in this mural. However, Listopad's position is supported by the fact that Khrua In Khong was born in Phetburi and therefore may have known Maha Samanawong. Listopad does admit that these murals may have been painted by one or more of Khrua In Khong's students and not him personally.

19. Indeed, as Geoffrey Samuel has pointed out, throughout the history of Buddhism, monks have often been seen as specialists on matters of death. Samuel, *Origins of Yoga* [2008:128–31]).

20. The most well-known and consistently reliable studies of Thai ritual include O'Connor, *Muang Metaphysics* (1984); Swearer, *Becoming the Buddha* (2004); Terwiel, *Monks and Magic* (1975); Phya Anuman Rajadhon, *Life and Ritual* (1961); several short studies by William Klausner, among many others. Reginald LeMay's *Asian Arcady* (1926) is often overlooked. The latter, despite being published over eighty years ago, offers one of the most unfiltered studies of Thai religious ritual available, neither overtly creating a hierarchy between Buddhism, animism, and Brahmanism nor judging the quality of Thai Buddhist practice against a vague and ideal Indic model. Since LeMay studied the everyday practice of northern Siamese Buddhism without extensive recourse to canonical Buddhism, one review of the book stated condescendingly and quaintly, "LeMay has an obvious affection for the country and sympathy with the likeable and simple-hearted Lao who inhabit northern Siam."

21. (King) Chulalongkorn, *Ruang phraratchaphithi sipsong duan* (2463 [1920]). There is a different northern Thai version describing these calendrical rites. See Mani Phayomyong, *Prapheni sipsong duan* (2529 [1986]). This study is interesting because it mimics the format of and draws its title from King Chulalongkorn's famous study. However, it mentions several unique northern Thai rituals, like the procession to the pillar of Inthakhin and the Khantok dance (which has been transformed into a tourist event since the 1970s). (Phra) Mahawirot Thammawiro offers a history of the mural paintings depicting these twelve rituals/ceremonies sponsored by King Chulalongkorn in the 1890s at Wat Ratchapradit in his *Wat*

*Ratchapraditsathitmahasimaram* (2545 [2002]:20–21). Skilling, in a personal communication (May 24, 2008) noted that the king's projected scholarly masterpiece was never completed. In 1877 (2420), the tenth year of his reign, he began to write *Phra ratchakaranyanuson*, intending to give an exhaustive description of the history and development of the royal customs and rites of the capital. He planned to devote some of his free time to it each day, but, as the demands of rulership upon his time multiplied, he eventually had to leave the ambitious work aside. In 1888 (2431), when the king was acting director of the Wachirayan Library, he initiated a plan for the members to contribute weekly articles to the Wachirayan journal, each writing on a subject he knew well. When he asked their opinion as to what he should write about, they requested he write on the royal ritual calendar; that is, effectively, to continue with the *Phra ratchakaranyanuson*. The king worked on it for another year and finished everything except the eleventh-month description. Even with the eleventh month missing, the completed work is massive, taking up 703 pages in the 1973 edition. The Wachirayan Library published the work as a single volume in 1912 (2455); a revised, second edition was published in 1920 (2463). As for *Phra ratchakaranyanuson*, it was not published until 1920 (2463), when it was prepared for publication by Prince Sommot Amarabandhu while he was head of the National Library. See *Phra ratchakaranyanuson* (2541 [1998]). A second edition was published by Khlang Witthaya in 2507 [1964]. See also *Phra ratchapithi sipsong duan* (2516 [1973]). The information about the history of the work is from Prince Damrong's foreword to the second edition, as cited in extenso in the 1998 edition. These publication details are important for understanding that this work was not the product of a singular effort at social control or nationalism. It was an evolving piece.

22. King Chulalongkorn, *Ruang phra ratchaphithi sipsong duan* (2516 [1973]: 122–214).

23. M. L. Pattaratorn Chirapravati, a scholar of Thai art and religion and a member of the royal family herself, recently described the traditional elite tonsure ceremony. This description perfectly captures the shared Brahmanic, animistic, and Buddhist aspects of many daily rituals. See her "Living the Siamese Life" (2009:29–30).

24. Ibid., 142.

25. Phoensri Duk et al., *Watthanatham pheun ban* (2536 [1993]). There are several large encyclopedias in Thai that exhaustively describe rituals throughout the country without an effort to define certain ones as legitimate based on their being "Buddhist" or "national." See especially the sixty-three-volume *Saranukhrom watthanatham Thai (Encyclopedia of Thai Culture)* (1999–2002). There are too many surveys of Thai culture to list. However, Sathiankoset's *Prapheni kiao kap chiwit* (2505 [1962]) is considered a classic. It has seen a number of new editions, the latest being 2551 (2008).

26. See (Phra) Sugandha Dhammasakiyo, *Kan seuksa Phraphutthasasana* (2548 [2005]), and the supreme patriarch's most recent book, (Somdet Phra Sangharat) Ñāṇasaṃvara, *Khrop 200 pi* (2547 [2004]). I thank Phra Sugandha for providing me with copies of these texts.

27. An extensive description of King Mongkut's belief in the magical power of the ghosts in these important images is described in the chronicle from his reign, Kham Bunnag, *Phra ratchaphongsawadan krung Ratanakosin Ratchakan thi 4* (2550 [2007]:384–91).

28. The photographs and notes from this trip are now available; see Phawat Bunnag, *Sadet praphaston R.S. 125* (2537 [1994]:24). See also (Phra Khru) Platsomkhit Siriwatthano, *Khong di Wat Rakhang* (2541 [1998]:35).

29. Arthid Sheravanichkul has shown that King Chulalongkorn wrote a series of letters to Prince Narit in the early twentieth century in which he suggested that Siam was originally occupied by primarily Mahāyāna practitioners and that Siam had diverse Buddhist influences that should be respected. He also honored local Vietnamese and Chinese monks and dedicated temples for their practice. See Arthid Sheravanichkul, "Exploring Hīnayāna-Mahāyāna" (2010).

30. Keyes, "National Heroine or Local Spirit?" (2002); and my "Two Bullets" (2008).

31. See Rutnin, *Dance, Drama, and Theatre* (1996:222–23); Brandon, *Theatre in Southeast Asia* (1967:198–200).

32. Apinan Poshyananda has been promoting the creative work of contemporary Thai artists for several decades. See, for example, his *Contemporary Art in Asia* (1997). One of the most controversial and dynamic Thai artists working on Buddhist themes is Thinnakorn Nugul. You can see some of his recent work at http://www.thaiopenstudio.com/#468728/Tinnakorn-Nugul. I thank Anthony Irwin for introducing me to his work.

33. See Anchalee Kongrut, "Master Craftsman" (2008:14).

34. This ritual is also described in the *Tamnān brāhmaṇa muang nagara srī dharrmarāja* (*Chronicle of the Brahmans of Nakhon Sri Thammarat City*) [sic], a chronicle from southern Thailand composed most likely in 1734. It states that the celebration was sponsored by King Ramadhipati of Ayutthaya in the city of Nakhon Sri Thammarat. See Wyatt, *Crystal Sands* (1975:53).

35. Subhatra Bhumiprabhas, "Old Ceremonies" (2007).

36. The importance of *uposatha* days is found in Pali texts, including the *Mūluposatha sutta* (Aṅguttara Nikāya [AN] 3.70), the *Uposatha sutta* (Aṅguttara Nikāya [AN] 8.41).

37. See my description of some of these major Buddhist holidays at http://www.tdm.sas.upenn.edu/monastery/ritual_liturgy.html.

38. Some particularly useful works include Wells, *Thai Buddhism* (1974:214–16); Terwiel, *Monks and Magic* (1975); (Phya) Anuman Rajadhon, *Life and Ritual*

(1961); Keyes and (Phra Khru) Anusaranasasanakiarti, "Funerary Rites" (1980). Rita Langer, Patrice Ladwig, Rupert Gethin, and others at the University of Bristol have recently undertaken a major research project investigating the various beliefs and practices associated with death in South and Southeast Asia. A good introductory book in Thai is Sathiankoset, *Kan tai* (2539 [1996]). I offer a study on Thai funerals, especially the use of Abhidhammic texts, in *Gathering Leaves* (2008, chap. 8).

39. Marriage rites (*pithi taeng ngan*), like funerary rites, are not described in early Buddhist texts in South Asia but are very common offering rites in Thailand that involve the chanting of selected blessings by nine monks. Their description is beyond the scope of this book.

40. They were taking place at Wat Don Tum, Wat Don Sam Ngam, Wat Don Sena, Wat Tung Krapong Hom, Wat Pu Bradu, Wat Moso Wang Kha, Wat Kho Khu, and others, for example.

41. See my "Liturgies and Cacophonies" (2007). The only other major study of Thai liturgies in a Western language is an unpublished article by Peter Skilling, "Compassion, Power, Success." I thank him for an advance copy of this comprehensive paper.

42. I recently attended a Catholic mass in Vietnam. Even though I do not speak Vietnamese, I could easily follow the ritual instructions since they were identical in sequence to the Catholic masses in Spanish and English with which I was raised.

43. Thai private liturgies, namely those performed by monks for monks sans a lay audience, like the ordination (*upsampadā*), have specific physical and verbal sequences and instructions and are explained in the *Kammavācā* texts.

44. I discuss the lack of a standardized Buddhist canon extensively in *Gathering Leaves* (2008, chap. 6).

45. Pomarin Charuworn's talk, "Dynamism of Phra Malai Chanting," at the Thai Language and Literature Conference, Bangkok, November 11, 2006, expands on Bonnie Brereton's seminal *Thai Tellings of Phra Malai* (1995). Trisin Bunkhachon's *Klon suat phak klang* (2547 [2004]) looks closely at this performance.

46. Bode, *Pali Literature of Burma* (1966:3).

47. Malalasekara, *Pali Literature of Ceylon* (1986:12).

48. See K. R. Norman, "Pāli Literature" (1983:43), and Skilling, "Rakṣā Literature" (1992).

49. Although in the last story, the bodhisattva does discourage any offerings that would require a monk or nun to break their Vinaya rules.

50. DeCaroli, *Haunting the Buddha* (2004:12–25).

51. Manuscript archives and monastic libraries overflow with liturgical guides composed on palm-leaf and mulberry paper. See my *Invoking the Source* (2003) for an overview of these collections, especially chapter 2. These liturgical guides and

anthologies came under a variety of titles, such as *chalong, parit, suat mon, kammavācā, phithi,* among others.

52. For more on *nissaya* manuscripts, see ibid.

53. One of the most important early secondary studies is Prince Damrong's *Tamnan phra parit* (2472 [1929]). Even though Damrong was, of course, a champion of modernism and often criticized excessive ritual, he saw the *parittas* has some of the most important Buddhist texts in Thailand. In the introduction, he writes that he produced this book to distribute freely as a gift (*khong cham ruai*) to thousands of novices and monks at the opening of the royal library and city museum (Ho Phra Samut lae Phiphithaphan Sathan Samrap Phranakhon) in Bangkok in 1929. This was a two-day gala affair. He distributed this book at the event in particular because he knew how popular it was and that it would be read widely and used often.

54. For additional information, see my "Paritta and Rakṣā Texts" (2004).

55. For example, I recently found a mulberry-paper manuscript in Lampang Province at Wat Pa Daeng Luang in Mae Chaem (Amphoe Mueang) that is actually a locally made liturgical handbook for a variety of rituals, including astrological prognostication. There is no date, but it was probably composed in the 1920s. It has been used by many others and added to since it was first composed. Its title is telling: "Latthi phithikam tang tang horasat" (Various Rituals and an Astrological Guide). There are dozens of handwritten notes in the margins, presumably penned by the lineage of monks and laypeople who used the manuscript. There are also hand-drawn *yantras,* incantations with abbreviated words (*akson huachai, kham yo*). There are Pali prayers followed by vernacular cues instructing the ritualist and teacher on how to use the text in rituals and liturgies.

56. Reynolds, *Seditious Histories* (2006:58).

57. See two books produced by Prince Wachirayan (printed after his death) describing King Mongkut's Ariyaka script: *Akson Ariyaka* (2501 [1958]), and *Katha chadok lae baep Akson Ariyaka* (2514 [1971]). The Bhumipol Foundation has also produced a study of various scripts: *Akson khom lae akson boran thong thin* (2519 [1976]). (Phra) Sugandha Dhammasakiyo has edited and reprinted one of Mongkut's four texts produced in Ariyaka script, *Suat mon* (2547 [2004]). I thank him for his helpful advice and for showing me some of the first editions of books produced on King Mongkut's unique printing press.

58. Despite efforts to standardize and internationalize a Thai liturgy (or pan-Theravada liturgy), King Mongkut and other royal literati wrote their own verses for liturgies. Skilling writes that "King Rama IV composed the 'Gāthā Namo 8 Bot' for recitation when making holy water, while [Prince Wachirayan, while he was a monk] wrote 'Yo cakkhumā' to replace the Sambuddhe-gāthā. At the end of the Paritta there is the stanza 'Araham sammāsambuddho' composed by King Rama IV, and the verses 'Yaṃ yaṃ devamanussānaṃ' by Somdet Phra Buddhaghosācārya (Chim)." Skilling, "Compassion, Power, Success" (11).

59. Ibid. (1). Note that Prince Damrong, like many other members of the Thai royal family in the nineteenth and twentieth centuries, wrote regularly about his travels abroad. He also often mentions his travels in his *San somdet* (2509 [1966]). In fact, the first entry in this massive collection describes correspondence he was having with religious officials in Sri Lanka. In this correspondence he actually criticizes the authenticity of the Sri Lankan textual tradition. See also his *Nithan borankhadi* (2509 [1966]).

60. For example, Skilling points out that King Mongkut issued a decree sometime between 1862 and 1868 ordering all monks in the kingdom of royal rank to perform a "calling the rain" liturgy. This was not a pan-Theravada practice, nor did Mongkut claim it was, but a practice uniquely Siamese.

61. Other editions have been less successful. For example, the *Suat mon plae*, sponsored by Mrs. Lukin Bunyachat, translated by (Phra Khru) Panthitanuwat, published in 2480 [1937], one of the earliest sizable vernacular translations of many well-known Pali recitations in Thailand, has not been reprinted.

62. See Thep Sarikabut, *Tamnan phrawet phisadan* (2537 [1994]).

63. Both were published by Khom Ma Press in Bangkok in 2549 [2006]).

64. There are differences in these two editions. First, the ordering of the prayers is different. For example, the 1994 edition includes the invitation to chant the *paritta*. Second, although there are many additions, there are also some lengthy subtractions, totaling eleven pages of text. For example, the series of prayers in preparation for meditation have been removed in the 1994 edition. Third, many of the prayers in the 1994 edition have new names that follow the Pali title, whereas the 1976 edition uses largely vernacular titles (although this is not consistent in either edition).

65. *Suat mon mueang nuea* (2537 [1994]).

66. A good example of this was the funeral for Khun Phantharak Ratchadet at Wat Mahathat Worramahawihan in Nakhon Si Thammarat on February 23, 2007. I thank Nu Khamsiang for informing me of several new liturgical books printed for festivals in the south.

67. I have been collecting and hope to produce a study of early "ethnic" liturgical guides in Thailand. Two interesting examples were created for the Vietnamese and southern Chinese Taoist communities in Bangkok. There were at least two printings of the *Tamra phithi Phra Yuan* (*Guide to the Rituals of the Vietnamese*), by (Phra Khru Khana) Namasamanachan (Bi) and Luang Anamsanghakan (Nguyen Quang [rendered Wiyong in Thai] Thanh) in the early 1930s. This guide has descriptions and translations of Vietnamese chants from a number of rituals, especially for Gong Tek, and was useful for families of mixed marriages that needed to attend funerals in both Vietnamese and Thai. Another is Wichit Matra's *Subhasit lao cheu*, which is a guide to Laozi's *Daodejing*. It was published on the occasion of the cremations of five Sino-Thai Taoists (Choi Luangrangsi, Hun Luangrangsi, Gimbao Luangrangsi, Talum

Changsawang, Wichan Matra) in 1930. There are a number of modern, especially Chinese and Thai Christian, liturgical guides as well.

68. Produced by Munnithi Luang Pho Wiriyang Sirintharo (Bangkok, n.d.).

69. Produced by V. Musicsound LP (Bangkok, n.d.).

70. This emerging global elite Buddhist class could be seen at the worldwide Vesak Celebration in Bangkok in 2006. It was sponsored by the Tourism Authority of Thailand, the Religious Affairs Department, as well as the Mahachulalongkorn and Mahamakut Monastic universities and included speeches by royal, secular, and religious VIPs and participants from forty-five countries. The liturgy at public events such as this include chants in English, Japanese, as well as in Pali. Many rituals and chants at such celebrations are syncretic inventions that have developed over the past five years. Furthermore, PowerPoint electronic text and other electronic displays are common among the technologically savvy Bangkok Buddhist elite. Pram Sounsamut's article "Buddha Bless and Dharma Products" (2008) discusses the use of hip-hop music and creative consumer products such as wristbands, animated short films, cookies, and T-shirts to teach Pali and Thai Buddhist maxims.

71. Aesthetics also includes diverse chanting styles. For example, Pomarin Jaruworn has identified twenty-two different chanting styles for the Phra Malai liturgy alone (Pomarin Charuwon, "Suat Phra Malai" [2005]).

72. Nathan McGovern's master's thesis on this shrine is essential for understanding rituals associated with this site. See "Brahmā Worship in Thailand" (2006, chap. 6). Charles Keyes produced a paper (unpublished) on the subject in 2006, "The Destruction of a Shrine to Brahma in Bangkok and the Fall of Thaksin Shinawatra: The Occult and the Thai Coup in Thailand of September 2006."

73. In the massive Red Shirt protests in March 2010, marchers from the northeast performed a series of protective rites at historically and ritually symbolic sites along their way to and within Bangkok. One of the more shocking and innovative rituals was the mass donation of two thousand liters of human blood. This blood was splashed on the steps of Government House and of the prime minister's residence in Bangkok on March 14 and 15.

74. Kultida Samabuddhi, "Sorcerer Sondhi Wards Off Evil" (2008).

75. Chang Noi, "PAD Saves the Nation" (2008). I thank Erick White for sending me this article. Chang Noi is a pseudonym for Christopher Baker. This pseudonym was made public on November 25, 2008, at a talk at the Foreign Correspondents' Club of Thailand.

76. *Ukāsa* is a strange spelling for the Pali *ukkaṃsa*.

77. See, for example, a story about the 2007 festival on the front page of the newspaper *Thai rath*: "Hae ruam wan goet Phra Phi Kanet," September, 17, 2550 [2007].

78. Information about these rituals and liturgies can be found in pamphlets at Wat Umathewi and at the Thewasathan in Bangkok. Thotsaphon Changphanitkun

has written a short book as well, *Phra Phi Kanet* (2550 [2007]). An amulet of Ganesha comes with every purchase of the book.

79. The liturgy is distributed for free in fliers next to the shrine. There are three verses, which all start with the Sanskrit *oṃ*, and besides using the Sanskrit spelling of Ganeṣa, the chant is otherwise in simple Pali. All three are straightforward litanies of praises for Ganesha, referring to him as glorious in action and thought and a great god worthy of being praised forever—"Mahādevo ahaṃ vandāmi sabbadā"[*sic*].

80. Skilling has shown that Brahmans and Buddhist monks were tied together in ritual, inscriptions, and royal declarations from at least the Sukhothai period. See Skilling, "Kings, Sangha, Brahmans" (2007).

81. See, for example, http://www.bangkokpost.com/news/politics/38036/temple -debate-rages, and http://www.bangkokpost.com/news/investigation/37614/unholy -night-in-the-temple-compound.

82. This commentary by Thanong Khantong provides a good summary of the beliefs surrounding the Ratchaprasong intersection and the Hindu shrines there. See http://blog.nationmultimedia.com/thanong/2010/04/24/entry-1. For photographs of the fire and the shrines during the protests, see http://absolutelybangkok .com/god-vs-ghost/?utm_source=feedburner&utm_medium=feed&utm_campaig n=Feed%3A+absolutelybangkok+(absolutely+Bangkok.com).

83. Foster, "Strange Games" (2006:275).

### 4. ART AND OBJECTS

1. Silpa Bhirasri, "Art and Religion," in *Comments and Articles* (1963:20–22).

2. See Stratton, *Buddhist Sculpture* (2004); Ringis, *Thai Temples* (1990); Gosling, *Origins of Thai Art* (2004).

3. An early attempt, which was largely ignored, was Textor's 1960 dissertation on "Non-Buddhist Supernatural Objects."

4. Personal communication, October 2008.

5. See Appadurai, *Social Lives of Things* (1986), especially Patrick Geary's contribution, "Sacred Commodities," and Miller, *Materiality* (2005).

6. McGowen, "Raw Ingredients" (2008:239).

7. Levine, *Daitokuji* (2005:xlix).

8. See Holbraad, "Power of Powder" (2007). Also Gell, *Art and Agency* (1998); see especially chapters 2–5, which discuss the importance of what Gell calls the art nexus. See also Layton, "Art and Agency" (2003), and Osborne and Tanner, *Art's Agency* (2007). See also Foucault, *Order of Things* (1970), and his "Different Spaces" (1998). See as well Crimp, "On the Museum's Ruins" (1983); Hooper-Greenhill, *Museums* (1992); Cunlas, "Oriental Antiquities" (1997); Phillips, *Trading Identities* (1998:49–71). For a

provocative reflection on what a comprehensive "Bangkok Museum" would entail, see Sawan Tangtrongsithikun, *Krung Thep mai mi phiphithaphan Krung Thep* (2545 [2002]). See also Alpers, "Museum as a Way of Seeing" (1991). See also Pollock and Zemans, *Museums After Modernism* (2007), especially Phillips, "Exhibiting Africa."

9. I discuss the story of one relic that refused to be moved in "Transformative History" (2002). Often monastic buildings in Thailand are constructed specifically to house particular images.

10. Miller, "Introduction," *Materiality* (2005).

11. I have witnessed a number of these consecration rites. One of the larger ones was at Wat Rakhang in 2001 in which over twelve hundred new eight-inch-tall Buddha images were consecrated after they had been bound to the main Buddha in the *ubosot.*

12. There was a conference on religion and commercialism with two hundred participants at Mahidol University in December 2008. The advertisement for the international conference stated that "it is imperative that the consumer impulse be balanced with values other than the materialistic one." I also consciously write contra to recent work by John and Jean Comaroff, "Occult Economies" (1999), and "Privatizing the Millennium" (2004:32), and Rosalind Morris, *In the Place of Origins* (2000). Scott, *Nirvana for Sale?* (2009) offers a complex study of Buddhism and wealth more broadly, whereas Richard Payne's *How Much Is Enough?* (2010), while a collection of thoughtful studies, often uncritically associates Buddhist ethics with anticonsumerism without seeing that Buddhist ethics as practiced often promotes abundance.

13. Lopez, *Curators of the Buddha* (1995:7).

14. This research was partially enabled by a National Endowment for the Humanities Digital Humanities Start-up Grant in 2007 and 2008. I visited numerous monasteries to film rituals, photograph objects, and interview nuns, novices, monks, and visitors. There were between twenty-five and forty-five panoramas taken of each monastery, along with approximately four thousand still photographs. This project is ongoing, but the initial results can be seen at http://tdm.sas.upenn.edu.

15. This title comes from Griswold: "Not many years ago I saw an amusing example of misplaced piety. In the gallery of a monastery at Ayutthaya there was a long row of apparently identical images, one of which had been singled out for particular favors by an admirer. He had presented it with a silk scarf, and he spent a good deal of time in front of it in a reverential attitude, with palms pressed together as if in prayer. Why had he singled out this particular image, which differed in no way that I could see from the dozens of others in the same row? Upon inquiry I found that a week earlier it had inspired him to place a bet on a certain horse, which won the race handily and paid off well; so now he wanted to express his gratitude and at the same time seek further inspiration . . . It is hard to believe that the founder of the Doctrine himself would have given such encouragement to gam-

bling" (*What Is a Buddha Image?* [1962:20]). Seven years previously, he had asserted that "within the tolerant fold of the Hīnayāna, which has long been the religion of Siam, there are two very different sorts of Buddhists—rationalists and pious believers . . . To them [rationalists] Buddhism is a Doctrine designed to abolish human suffering . . . The pious, on the other hand, substitute faith for reason . . . Believing in magic and yearning for supernatural protection, they see his images as living active exponents of power" ("Medieval Siamese Images" [1955:48]).

16. Kraisri Sri-Aroon, *Phra Phuttha rup* (2539 [1996]).

17. Skilling and Peleggi have recently presented two studies on Buddha images being used ritually, politically, and aesthetically. See Skilling, "Similar Yet Different" (2009: 52–54), and Peleggi, "Icons, Antiquities, and Mnemonic Sites: The Multiple Lives of Thai Buddha Images" (talk presented at the Object Knowledge: Art, Artifact, and Authority in Southeast Asia conference, Berkeley, October 29, 2009).

18. See Jaini, *Paññāsajātaka* (1981–1983:297–308). There is an interesting passage whose rhetorical force is not captured in the English translation. King Pañcāla is a little jealous that King Mahārattha has given him a gift of a beautiful Buddha image. He wants to outdo King Mahārattha and commands his court artisans: "Ahañ ca pana dvegunaṃ mahantaṃ buddhapatimaṃ kārāpetvā tass'eva rañño pesessāmī ti" (Indeed, having commissioned a Buddha statue twice as large [or twice as awesome as the one he sent me], I will have it sent to him) (300).

19. Griswold, "Medieval Siamese Images" (1955:58). See also Arthid Sheravanichkul, "Dana and Danaparami" (2009), and Ohnuma, *Head, Eyes, Flesh, and Blood* (2007).

20. Thep Sunthasarathun, *Prawat Luang Pho Ban Laem* (15–20).

21. Photographs and recent stories of Poh Teck Tung's collection of corpses from accident scenes can be seen at these three Web sites (accessed on December 29, 2009), among many others: http://www.bangkokpost.com/091108_Spectrum/09Nov2008_spec20.php; http://pohtecktung.org/; http://www.bangkoksvildeveje.dk/pohtecktung.html.

22. Guelden, *Thailand* (1995:66–71). See also Bernard Formoso, "Interethnic Relations and Shared Cultural Idioms: A Case Study of the Xiu Gu Gu Festival in Mainland China and Overseas," Asia Research Institute Working Paper 98 (2007). Available online at http://papers.ssrn.com/sol3/papers.cfm?abstract_id=1317148.

23. This is not to be confused with the practice of "roasting" the mother after she gives birth. Jane Richardson Hanks, *Maternity and Rituals* (1963:41–57); Dundes, *Manner Born* (2003:134).

24. I thank Christopher Baker and Pasuk Phongpaichit for sending me sections of their translation of *Khun Chang Khun Paen* (2010). The making of a *kuman thong* is mentioned in chapter 35 in two different versions of the poem. They note that the use of corpse or spirit oil (*nam man phrai*) is mentioned in four different parts of the poem.

25. Kamala Tiyavanich has also mentioned stories of *kuman thong* practice done by Buddhist monks in southern Thailand: *Sons of the Buddha* (2007:195). This practice seems to be particularly popular in southern Thailand and is one in which Muslims and Buddhists participate together. These practices may be related to the Malaysian practice of using *toyol* (stillborn fetuses used to make protective oils) or *gui gia*, a southern Chinese belief in the protective powers of fetuses. For Cambodian practices, I rely on Erik Davis (personal communication, 2008). See also his Ph.D. dissertation, "Treasures of the Buddha," University of Chicago, 2009.

26. English readers see, for example, http://ki-media.blogspot.com/2010/06/thai-police-arrest-suspected-seller-of.html. This story was also cited in a number of other newspapers in Thai.

27. *Mahapho* 29.491 (2552 [2009]).

28. The use of *kuman thong* is not without controversy. In 1995 there was a high-profile case in which a Buddhist novice, Samanen Han Raksachit, was arrested after he released a video tape of himself piercing, bleeding, roasting, chanting, and collecting the drippings from a baby at Wat Nong Rakam in Saraburi Province (central Thailand). These drippings, which he called *ya sane* (lust medicine), he sold to visitors to the monastery. Although he was forced from the monastery and arrested, he did not serve jail time and was arrested again in 2005 for tricking several women into sexual acts and defrauding them of money in exchange for dubious claims that he could help them attract their true loves. He is serving time now on twenty-three counts of rape, in addition to other charges. Ehrlich, "Baby Roasting Monk"; and Farrell, "Hex, the Monk, and the Exorcist." There have been several other reported cases of people collecting corpses (usually bought from illegal abortion clinics) in recent years. One of the more shocking stories was about the discovery of fourteen fetal corpses in an abandoned house in rural Ubon Ratchathani Province. On June 22, 2010, a former nurse named Ura Sutthiwong was charged with illegally selling these corpses for over a thousand baht each for use in *luk krok* or *kuman thong* ceremonies (*luk krok* is the term used by Khmer speakers in the region). See http://www.bangkokpost.com/news/local/39138/pickled-foetuses-sold-for-good-luck. As this book was going to press a story broke on the major news wires about the discovery, on November 17, 2010, of 348 corpses of aborted fetuses (other reports claimed over 1,200 were found) wrapped in plastic bags in a Buddhist monastery. Apparently, they were bought from five different illegal abortion clinics, supposedly for sale to magicians and amulet dealers. This was not a rural monastery on the border of Cambodia or Laos but a monastery in Bangkok, Wat Phai Ngoen. An undertaker, Suthep Chabangbon, although not as yet formally charged, admitted to storing the corpses in the monastery's morgue (many funerals are performed at this monastery every month) without the abbot's knowledge. Later Thai reports spoke of the hundreds of people who were visiting the monastery after the discovery to chant for the deceased fetuses and some to inquire about the availability of

the corpses for ritual use. The Pok Tek Tung group was called by the police to assist with removing the bodies. See, among many other sources, http://www.nationmulti media.com/2010/11/17/national/348-foetuses-discovered-at-wat-30142428.html.

29. Francis Giles witnessed a corpse-oil collection ritual in the early twentieth century ("About a Love Philtre" [1938]).

30. Murals of the fruit maidens being picked by flying Brahman ascetics can be seen at Wat Suthat in Bangkok. At Wat Khian in Angthong Province the ascetics are depicted as drunken Chinese healers and in one instance as a Persian warrior. The murals at Wat Prangmuni, interestingly enough, are the work of Lao artisans living in the area.

31. I thank the keepers of the shrine (mostly local homeless men supervised by the monks in residence) for guiding me around the monastery on three occasions in 2008 and 2009.

32. I thank Peter Skilling for calling these mummies to my attention.

33. When this museum first opened, the night guards of the museum would allow poor villagers to sleep in the museum since it was air-conditioned. Many of these villagers, according to Wanlop Suanwieng, slept there only one night because they were afraid that they were offending Somdet To. Others said they felt the presence of ghosts who were visiting Somdet To.

34. Drawing on Gell's idea of "technologies of enchantment," Jessica Rawson has shown that creating identical portraits of emperors in early China allowed a follower to perpetually give gifts, as an emperor was made to be always present in the world. Rawson, "Agency of, and the Agency for the Wanli Emperor" (2007).

35. See Baker and Pasuk, *Khun Chang Khun Paen* (2010).

36. Warner, *Phantasmagoria* (2006:31–46).

37. The abbot, Phra Khru Sunthapatthanaphimon, is trying to raise money to build a new *ubosot*. Outside his *kuṭi* are nine large iron balls onto which people can stick small leaves of gold. These are called *luk nimit*, and once they have enough gold and are consecrated, they will be buried under each of the nine *sima* stones surrounding the new *ubosot*.

38. For an extensive study on Kaccāyana, see Lagirarde, "Gavampati-Kaccâyana" (2001).

39. If one does not want to use the machine, one can play the most ubiquitous fortune-telling game in all of Thailand—shake the *krabok*, which holds the *siam si* sticks. This game consists of prostrating in front of a Buddha image and then hold-ing a bamboo tube containing twenty-eight sticks. It is as common an activity at any monastery as lighting candles and incense. The number of the stick that falls to the floor first is used to find a card containing a prognostication or sage advice.

40. For a study of a number of local deities in the Chao Phraya River basin, see Saiban Puriwanchana, *Tamnan bracham thin rim Mae Nam* (2552 [2009]).

41. For background, see Meister, "Burmese Monks" (2009).

42. I thank Peter Skilling for taking me to this monastery. Wat Kaeo Fa is also a popular place to get lottery numbers from the abbot, Phra Achan Kesom Achinnasilo. Wat Nong Bua in the northern Thai province of Nan is also a place where the older Buddha image particularly inspires the creation of new images.

43. Descriptions of the movement of these Lao images is in King Mongkut's chronicle, *Phra ratchaphongsawadan krung Ratanakosin Ratchakan thi 4* (2461 [1918]:98, 152, 319, 384–91).

44. Seeger has noted that at Wat Yanasangworn, a royal temple, and at the *sangharat*'s home monastery in Chonburi Province, the *sangharat* has created a room dedicated to the saints of Thai Buddhism. He has also noted that included with these male saints are two statues of prominent Thai female saints, Maechi Kaeu Sianglam and Maechi Ki Nanayon. I thank Seeger for letting me read an early draft of his article "'Against the Stream.'"

45. On various trips between 2006 and 2008 I visited three large Buddha images Somdet To had built outside Bangkok, at Wat Sateu, Wat Kutithong (also known at Wat Phitphian) in Ayutthaya, and at Wat Chaiyo in Angthong. The images are referred to as Luang Pho To because they are large (To) and were built under the supervision of Somdet To. They have been visited by several kings and queens. There are at least five other sizable statues of Somdet To at Wat Kutithong as well. I thank Thongchai Likhitphonsawan, Anake Nawigamune, and Rangsit Chonchansitto for their conversations on these visits, as well as Luang Pho Wiset, the abbot of Wat Kutithong, for presenting me with some rare *takrut* (protective lead scrolls) and amulets.

46. There is a growing following around a new, colossal image in Thailand's rural northeastern province of Roi-Et. The statue, unfinished, will be three hundred feet tall and is dedicated to Luang Phu Sri Mahaviro. He was a forest monk connected to the lineage of Achan Man.

47. Somdet To may have sponsored the largest number of giant Buddha images in the country, but he certainly was not the only monk or layperson to pursue this type of devotion. For example, at Wat Suthachinta in Nakhon Ratchasima Province, Luang Pho Thaniyo, a Thammayut wandering forest monk who was locally famous in the 1930s, commissioned a giant sitting Buddha that now sits on the side of the mountain overlooking the cement factories in the southern part of the province.

48. David Morgan, *Sacred Gaze* (2005:25–34).

49. Cognitive dissonance is a human trait well-known among neurologists. Zeki and Bartels are skeptical about the very notion of a unified consciousness. Humans exhibit an "asynchrony of consciousness, of multistage integration, and of relative perceptual sites" (230). This is most apparent when studying vision itself. On a basic

cellular level, vision is not unitary. The "majority of cells within a given processing system continue to be concerned with a given attribute of the visual scene rather than with all attributes" (230). This means that when people look at something, like an altar or a mural of the Buddha's life, they do not cognitively process the entire scene simultaneously. Instead, cognitive processing of sensory data is spread out over several nodes. Therefore, the "scene" can be made sense of at multiple levels virtually simultaneously without immediate consciousness of broader contradictions or inconsistencies. The brain consists of many microconsciousnesses "with minimal convergence or overlap." Each node "is therefore only part of a more extensive processing system, which includes, besides subcortical stations, areas in the temporal, parietal, and frontal cortices" (234). Without a central "perceptual integrator," there is often "misbinding" of data. Zeki and Bartels have shown that "anatomical evidence shows that there is no final integrator station in the brain, one which receives input from all visual [or other sensory] areas; instead, each node has multiple outputs and no node is recipient only" (225). R. M. Gaze has also noted that there is "plasticity in the nervous system" that allows sensory data, in his case visual data, to be processed and stored in one subregion of the brain without overlapping with other data processed elsewhere. Zeki and Bartels, "Towards a Theory of Visual Consciousness," (1999), and Zeki, "Neurology of Ambiguity" (2004). I thank Robert Eamon Briscoe for several conversations on visual consciousness.

50. There is a following of the resin image of the hugely popular folk (*luk thung*) singer Phumphuang Duangchan at Wat Thapkradin in Suphanburi Province. She died young in 1992, and a sizable crowd regularly offers gifts to her image at the monastery despite the fact that she was not an openly devout Buddhist monastery patron and did not write explicitly Buddhist lyrics.

51. At Wat Prommani in Nakhon Nayok, Phra Archandang Arpakaro has developed a "born-again" Buddhist ritual in which people are made to lie down in coffins for a few seconds while a shroud is placed over them and protective chanting is projected over loudspeakers. They symbolically die and are born again as they rise out of the coffin. The huge popularity of this ritual is partially due to a popular film, *The Coffin*," in Thailand, as well as to stories of people winning the lottery after being "born again."

52. Boonlua Chatree, "District Policeman Charged."

53. One does not often hear stories of when amulets fail to protect. However, one story was widespread. On April 5, 1991, a reputed mafia boss (*chao pho*), Khlaeo Dhanikun, was killed as he was riding in an Isuzu pickup truck on a major traffic artery on the edge of Bangkok (Pinkhlao/Nakhon Chaisri Road). His truck was shot with an M79 grenade launcher! They found his body with a valuable Phra Somdet Wat Rakhang amulet around his neck. This amulet, known for its protective qualities, clearly was no match for a grenade. This story was in a number of newspapers

at the time of the incident, because Khlaeo was a prominent figure in boxing corruption. A retrospective article about the event appeared in the March 3, 2006, posting of MThai, an online magazine, http://webboard.mthai.com/7/2006–03–03/ 204887.html. I thank Panida Lorlertratna for conversations on this issue.

54. Chalong Soontravanich has noted that Phra Somdets may fetch the highest prices, but a Phra Pid Ta Luang Pho Kaew, Wat Khruawan of Chonburi, sold for 7 million baht. In June 2004, an amulet made by Luang Pu Iam of Wat Nang in Bangkhunthian was priced at 6 million baht. There are national conventions, online auctions, and contests where collectors show off and rate the "beauty and authenticity" of these amulets. There are also dozens of Web sites dedicated to the display and trade of amulets. The sale of old amulets adds about 1 billion baht a year to the Thai economy, and the production and sale of new amulets accounts for as much as 10 billion baht annually. See Chalong Soontravanich, "Regionalization of Local Buddhist Saints" (2004).

55. There is a formidable literature on value/exchange and commodification theory, which is beyond the scope of this study. I have been influenced by the work of Weiner and Myers, which offers a nuanced understanding of the social construction of networks of value found in Appadurai's *Social Lives of Things* (1986). See Weiner, *Inalienable Objects* (1992), and Myers's introduction to *Empire of Things* (2001).

56. Kasian Tejapira, "Post-modernization of Thainess" (2001).

57. See, for example, Jackson, "Withering Centre" (1997); Jackson, "Enchanting Spirit" (1999); Jackson, "Royal Spirits" (1999); (Phra) Dhammapitaka, *Sing Saksit* (2536 [1993]); Sanitsuda Ekachai, *Keeping the Faith* (2001); Sulak Sivaraksa, *Phut kap sai nai sangkhom Thai* (1995); Pracha Hutanuwatr and Ramu Manivannan, *Asian Future* (2005); Pracha Hutanuwatr and Jane Rasbash, *Globilisation* (1998); Rosalind Morris, "Crises of the Modern" (2002); J. L. Taylor, "(Post-) Modernity" (1999); Srisakra Vallibhotama, "Phra Khruang (Rang)" (1994: 77–92); Nidhi Aeusrivongse, "Phuttha wibat," (2542 [1999]: 1–28); Sulak Sivaraksa. Siam in Crisis (1980); Tambiah, *Buddhist Saints of the Forest* (1984); Horstmann, "Hybrid Processes" " (1997). I thank Michael Jerryson for providing me with a copy of this last source.

58. Dovert, *Thaïlande contemporaine* (2001); Peleggi, *Thailand* (2007).

59. Tambiah, *Buddhist Saints of the Forest* (1984:136).

60. (Phra) Phaisan Visalo, *Phuttha sasana Thai* (2003:472).

61. As cited in Tunya Supanich, "Commercialising Religious Art" (2007).

62. Mettanando Bhikkhu, "Nationalists Tap A Source" " (2007).

63. (Phra) Dhammapitaka (Payutto), *Sing saksit* (2536 [1993]:86).

64. Saichon Sattayanurak, *Phuttha sasana* (2546 [2003]:51–69).

65. As cited in Pattana Kitiarsa, "Buddha Phanit."

66. See, for example, Wassayos Ngamkham, "Fake Talismans Upset Family" (2006); Nucharee Rakrun Khultida Samabuddhi, "Talismans Draw Huge Crowd" (2007).

67. Craig Reynolds has undertaken a major research project on the history of Police Maj. Gen. Khunphantarak Rajadej (Khun Phan), who passed away in 2006 at the age of 104 and is believed to have created the first Jatukham Ramathep amulet in 1987. I thank him for sending me an advance copy of his "Rural Male Leadership, Religion and the Environment in Thailand's Mid-south, 1920s–1960s."

68. Pattana Kitiarsa, "Faiths and Films" (2006:267).

69. Although Jackson has not taken a long historical approach and has focused on "prosperity religions" as a product of the economic boom and subsequent bust of the 1990s, he has recently acknowledged that the collection of amulets and the "cult" of popular magical monks should not be seen in only derogatory terms. These new religious are on the "flourishing margins" of society and are "the productive core of a new, highly popular expression of religio-cultural symbolism and ritual ("Royal Spirits" [1999:248]).

70. As a comparative point, see Skemer, *Binding Words* (2006); Bozóky, *Charmes et prières apotropaïques* (2003); and Stephen Wilson, *Magical Universe* (2000). There has been no significant comparative research on the tactile and material qualities of various amulets from different religious traditions from either the neuropsychological perspective or the historical perspective.

71. Tambiah, *Buddhist Saints of the Forest* (1984:195–292).

72. Ibid., 228–29.

73. Tambiah, "At the Confluence of Anthropology" (1987:187–88).

74. Ibid., 189. Margaret Mead and Gregory Bateson, in their studies of ritual in New Guinea and Bali, took the opposite approach. See Ness, "Bali, the Camera, and Dance" (2008:1256–57).

75. Tambiah, "At the Confluence of Anthropology" (1987:189). One possible Indic textual and ritual tradition that has strangely not been explored but that shows a family resemblance to some Thai practices today is *Atharvaveda* (AV). The *Vidhāna* and *Pariśiṣṭa* textual traditions describe how protective mantras in the *Atharvaveda* were employed in ritual. This is the type of detailed textual work that would make Indic comparisons useful. For amulets in particular, see hymns II.4–5, II.9, VI.81, VI.85, VIII.5, X.3, X.6, XIX.34–35, among others, from the Śaunakīya school of the AV. Thai practitioners do not seem to have any direct "influence" from the AV, and although the term "Phra Wet" (Vedas) is commonly used to refer to protective mantras in Thai, there is no one-to-one correspondence to particular hymns of the AV. The *Pariśiṣṭa* tradition is another story, which is part of an ongoing study of mine.

76. Turton's "Invulnerability and Local Knowledge" (1991) takes an opposite approach. He ignores nearly all possible Indic connections to notions of sacred protection in northern Thailand.

77. Tambiah, *Buddhist Saints of the Forest* (1984:376n1).

78. Ibid., 258–73.

79. In two conversations in 1996 (Cambridge) and 2007 (Bangkok) Tambiah lamented to me that he had much information in his field notes and library about Thai religion that he never had time to analyze, write about, and publish. In retirement, he hopes to take up this project and write a fourth book on Thai Buddhism. This would be a great service to the field. I thank him for his guidance and advice.

80. Although not an extensive historical study, Coedès includes a short history of *phra phim* in *Tamnan akson Thai tamnan phra phim* (2507 [1964]:35–60).

81. Pattaratorn Chirapravati, *Votive Tablets* (1999).

82. Chalong describes *wan* as "a Thai term given to a group of plants, with or without roots, which are believed to have medicinal property as well as to give those who carry it or consume it the power of invulnerability. *Wan* remains to this day one of the major ingredients in making certain Buddhist amulets that contain the power to confer invulnerability" ("Small Arms, Romance, and Crime" [2005]:31). See also Soraphon Sophitkun, "Tamnan nangsue phrakhruang" (1994).

83. See, for example, the description of the amulets of Shiva, Vishnu, and Ganesha produced by the Thewasathan, the national Brahman training center under the supervision of Chiraphat Praphanwithya. Chiraphat's book includes the liturgies (including the Sanskrit texts) and histories of these amulets. Chiraphat Praphanwithya, *Phra Siwa Phra Wisanu Phra Phighanesuan* (2545 [2002]). Often these amulets of Hindu deities are forged in rituals performed by both Buddhist monks and Brahman priests working together. For example, the Brahman expert Montri Chanthaphan, the physician Somneuk, and the monk Pho Than Somphong Thammasaro produced a set of Jatukham Ramathep amulets together in 2551 [2008] at Wat Phrahmalok in Nakhon Sri Thammarat Province for the specific purpose of curing those who had been bitten by snakes.

84. The text is reproduced as a section of Pricha Iamtham's *Prawat Somdet Phra Phutthachan To* (2542 [1999]:256).

85. Ibid., 256–59.

86. This is a creative combination of both Pali and Sanskrit. "Śatrū" is Sanskrit for Pali *sattu* and "vināssanti" should be *vinassanti* in Pali. This might be because of a confusion with the causative form of the verb *vināseti*. The author seems to be using the verb in the causative sense here. The "Sanskrit" in the middle of the Pali text is most likely because the Thai word for enemy, *satrū*, is drawn from the Sanskrit word, not the Pali. When Thais compose Pali, they often incorporate a number of Sanskrit spellings. There certainly is a Sanskrit-Thai-Pali-Khmer hybrid language in magical texts in Thailand. This is so distinctive that one could argue that it is a new Pali dialect specific to this genre.

87. Amulets are made almost exclusively by monks. However, there is one famous nun (*maechi*) named Mae Bunruan Tongbuntoem (1894–1964) who has been worshipped as an *arahant* (literally, "worthy one," i.e., "awakened one"), and it is be-

lieved that she realized the six *abhiññās* (higher knowledge). Seeger, "Changing Roles" (2009).

88. Ram Watcharapradit, *Phap Phra Chanaloet* (2547 [2004]); Soraphon Sophitkun, *Sudyot rian phrakhruang lem thi 1* (2540 [1997]); Soraphon Sophitkun, *Sudyot rian phrakhruang lem thi 2* (2544 [2001]); Phraya Sunthornphiphit, *Itthipatihan phrakhruangrang* (2515 [1972]); Triyampawai, *Pari-atthathibai haeng phrakhruang lem thi 1* (2492 [1954]); Triyampawai, *Pari-atthathibai haeng phrakhruang lem thi 2* (2498 [1960]); Triyampawai, *Pari-atthathibai haeng phrakhruang lem thi 3* (2508 [1965]).

89. Akadet Khrisanathilok, *Phra Somdet* (2549 [2006]). See especially chapter 3 of vol. 2, and vol. 3:45–52.

90. (Phra) Wisutthathibadi, *Phra Kring Luang* (2549 [2006]:27).

91. Ibid., 59–65.

92. I thank many shop owners in the market for their help in this research, as well as Thongchai Likhitphonsawan for all his advice and training in the amulet trade.

93. Somdet To money is also printed. There are reproductions of thousand-baht notes with Somdet To's image on them instead of the king's (King Rama IX's face is on every legal baht note). Other famous monks, like Luang Pho Khun, also have their own money.

94. See Newell, "Monks, Meditation and Missing Links" (2008).

95. I thank Dr. Anucha Thirakanont for his help in learning about this fundraising effort.

96. This is not a particularly new phenomenon. There have been bullet amulets available in regional amulet markets for many years. These particular bullet *takrut* were no longer available at Wat Sai Mai in 2008, but I later rented one at the Wat Srapathum monastery for 240 baht (8 dollars).

97. The ritual that is used to concentrate this particular *takrut* is described in Somsak Sakuntanat, *Takrut* (2550 [2007]:33–36).

98. See my *Gathering Leaves* (2008, chap. 4).

99. I thank Vivian Nyitray for translating this inscription for me.

100. Cather, *On Writing* (1949).

101. See Chalermchai Kositpipat, *Wat Rongkhun*; Chalermchai Kositpipat, *Roi ruang rao khong Wat Rongkhun*.

102. For a good introduction to Thai murals, see Bunsopha Chaloenniphonwanit's "Chitakam baep prapheni khong Thai" (2525 [1982]). Prani Nimsamoe's study ("Chitakam ruam samai" [2525] (1982)) of modern Thai monastic murals is a good example of a scholar concerned with the agency of artists. Surachai Chongchitngam has studied the nineteenth-century muralist Khrua In Khong, who creatively incorporated paintings of foreigners and foreign ships into his renderings of non-canonical cosmological texts. He has argued that even though Khrua In Khong's

murals were commissioned by King Mongkut and executed at two Thammayut monasteries, they do not adhere to canonical stories, thus revealing King Mongkut's tolerance despite often being labeled a canonical purist. See Surachai Chongchitngam, "Kham huang mahasamut kap Khrua In Khong" (2008). Sandra Cate's study (*Making Merit, Making Art* [2002]) of the murals at the Thai community's monastery, Wat Buddhapadipa, in Wimbledon (UK) offers an excellent introduction to the range of mural art in Thailand in general. She also discusses (chaps. 5, 6) the work of Chalermchai, among other modern Thai artists.

103. Note that many of the gilt designs on the wooden cases used to hold "Buddhist" palm-leaf manuscripts made in the nineteenth century were of Brahmanic deities.

104. See my Web site, http://tdm.sas.upenn.edu/, for a detailed depiction of the murals of the *ubosot* of Wat Ratchaorot and a bibliography of sources related to this temple and Chinese art in Bangkok more broadly. See also the September 2522 [1979] special issue of the *Muang boran* for several articles on Chinese art in Thailand.

105. Similar scenes are depicted at Wat Suwandararam in Thonburi. I thank Donald Stadtner for pointing these out to me.

106. Jaiser, *Thai Mural Painting* (2009). See also Pichaya Svasti, "Reflections of Different Cultures" (2009) (accessed September 2009).

107. See McGill, *Emerald Cities* (2009:132).

108. See No Na Paknam, *Mural Paintings of Thailand Series: Wat Pathumwanaram* (2539 [1996]). These names are drawn from the Pali names of two famous nuns mentioned in the canonical *Therigatha*. The depiction here seems to have nothing to do with the murals on the surrounding walls.

109. Robson and Prateep, "Cave Scene" (1999:585).

110. Santi Phakdikham, "Chitakam wanakhadi Thai" (2007). Great diversity of stories is not seen not only in one set of murals but in illuminated manuscripts as well. A good example is described in Wenk, *Thailändische Miniaturmalereien* (1965), which contains images from the *Traibhūmikathā*, from the life of the Buddha, and from various *jātakas*, among other narratives.

111. See (Phra) Sobhanathamwong, *Wat Indrawihan kap chiwaprawat Somdet Phra Phutthachan To* (2537 [1994]), and (Phra) Sobhanathamwong, *Khonkhwa ha ma dai ekasan somkhan khong Wat Indrawihan* (2544 [2001]). The former has detailed descriptions of every panel of the murals. There is also the recent study by Okha Buri, *Chat bhumi (lap) Somdet To* (2551 [2008]).

112. At some new monasteries, especially among the immigrant Thai communities in the United States, there are now framed, cartoonish lithographs hanging on the walls with descriptions printed on them depicting the life of the Buddha. These are hung at U.S. temples in place of traditional murals (which are often too expen-

sive, and finding qualified artists is difficult). They are similar to Catholic paintings of the Stations of the Cross popular in the 1950s. I thank Donald Swearer, who reminded me of these new narrative paintings.

113. See Baxandall, *Patterns of Intention* (1985:1), and Maguire, "Eufrasius and Friends" (2007). See also James, "Introduction," *Art and Text* (2007).

114. See Wang, *Shaping the Lotus Sutra* (2005:xiii). See also Fraser, *Performing the Visual* (2003), and Teiser, *Reinventing the Wheel* (2007). For a particularly useful overview of theoretical concerns connected to visual culture and narrative, see Bronfen, "Visuality – Textuality" (2010).

115. A major exception to this is the last book written by the late David Wyatt and an article by Robert Brown. See Wyatt, *Reading Thai Murals* (2004). Even though he concentrates on "reading" murals for historical information, he provides a good overview of the profession of a muralist. Brown has pointed out that narrative mural art in many monasteries is actually not designed to be "read" by the visitor to the monastery but is a type of offering to the Buddha image. The murals and the image must be seen as having a particular relationship. See his "Narrative as Icon" (1997). Recently, Brown and I had the opportunity to act as advisers to Melody Rod-ari on her compelling dissertation on Wat Phra Kaeo Morakhot (including the murals). See her "Visualizing Merit" (2010:145–64).

116. See particularly Zaleski, "Art of Thailand and Laos" (1997); Ringis, *Thai Temples* (1990); Matics, *Introduction to Thai Murals* (1992); Fickle, *Life of the Buddha* (1979); Silpa Bhirasri, *Origin and Evolution of Thai Murals* (1959); Nidda Hongwiwat, *Wessandon chadok* (2549 [2006]); Chuphon Euachuwong, "Chitakam Samkok" (2007); No Na Paknam, *Siamsilapa chitakam* (2538 [1995]). This last book, by No Na Paknam, contains his collected articles on Thai art published between 1974 and 1991. He often refers to the texts that murals represent. However, in two articles, one on the murals of the partition wall of Wat Suthat ("Phap kian bon lap lae fapanang thi Wat Suthat Thepwararam") and another on the murals at Wat Bangkhae Yai ("Chitakam faphanang thi Wat Bangkhae Yai changwat Samut Songkhram"), he notes that—probably because there was not a clearly identifiable textual source—these murals are a creative interpretation of daily-life scenes depicting Mon, Chinese, Shan, and other peoples who resided near the monasteries. In 2003, the journal *Muang boran* dedicated a special issue (vol. 29, no. 4) to murals that depict historical events.

117. Jean Boisselier, *Thai Painting* (New York: Kodansha, 1976).

118. Ringis *Thai Temples* (1990:124).

119. (Phra) Sobhanathamwong, *Wat Indrawihan kap chiwaprawat Somdet Phra Phutthachan To* (2537 [1994]:45).

120. Narrative additions to well-known canonical texts were of course common in murals and in other forms of Thai painting. One notable addition is seen in a Thai cloth painting held by the Asian Art Museum of San Francisco. The painting

depicting chapter 5 of the story shows several women ridiculing the wife of the elderly Brahman Jūjaka. In the original Pali text, this scene is quite short and contains
simply twelve verses in which a group of women poke fun at Jūjaka's wife for being
so obedient to an old man. There is only a subtle mention of the lack of romance
and sex in their relationship; however, the painting is quite bawdy. The women are
depicted groping one another, dancing, and holding long wooden phalluses. Many
are half naked pretending to penetrate one another vaginally in various positions.
This kind of explicit sexual display is not mentioned in the Pali text and must have
offered some shock and delight to the late nineteenth century viewers of the painting. I appreciate Forrest McGill's taking his time to show me this painting at the
museum. See Cowell, *Jātaka* (1907:271). Naked women are not limited to cloth
paintings and are also found on prominent royal temple murals, like those at Wat
Pathumwanaram, Wat Rakhang, among others.

121. See Chutima Chunhacha, *Chut chitakam faphanang* (2537 [1994]), and
Sanitsuda Ekachai, "Thailand's Gay Past" (2008:1). See also No Na Paknam, *Mural
Paintings of Thailand* (2538 [1995]), and Nit Ratanasanya et al., "Wat Khongkaram"
(2517 [1974]). I thank Donald Swearer for giving me a copy this last source.

122. There is a set of murals based on the Chinese romance *Sam kok* at Wat
Prasoet Sutthawat. Like the murals at Wat Ratchaorot, they are arranged in square
panels. However, unlike the latter, they do seem to be attempting to tell the story of
Sam Kok in sequence. This is further complicated by the fact that the murals are
arranged counterclockwise, which goes against both Chinese and Thai reading order, as well as against the pattern of ritual circumambulation around the central
Buddha image. I thank Jessica Patterson for her talk, "Battles or Brotherhood? Romance of the Three Kingdoms in Thai Temple Murals," given at the 2010 Association of Asian Studies conference in Philadelphia.

123. For a study of modern monastic and other religious museums, especially
those like the Sanctuary of Truth, Ancient City, and Erawan Museum of Lek
Wiriyabun, and my criticism of the Foucauldian notion of the "museum effect," see
my "Reconsidering the 'Museum Effect'" (2008).

124. See my "Transformative History" (2002).

125. See Schopen, *Bones, Stones and Buddhist Monks* (1997), and his *Buddhist
Monks and Business Matters* (2004).

126. There are dozens of versions of this narrative collection found in northern
Thai monastic libraries. For example, I have examined the *Madhurasachomphu* (or
*Madhurasajambudīpa*), the *Madhurasakathā*, the *Madhurasalangkā*, the *Madhurasa-
vāhiṇī* [sic] (which, despite its title, is not identical to the Sri Lankan collection of the
same name), and the *Madhurassasut*. Most are incomplete and have different numbers of stories and were most likely used as the basis for sermons. For more background on the Sri Lankan Pali collection, see Sharada Gamdhi's introduction to her

Pali edition of Vedeha Thera, *Madhurasavāhinī* (1988), and H. C. Norman, "Buddhist Legends of Asoka" (1910).

127. See his *Handbook of Pāli Literature* (1996:189). See also Ver Eecke, *Le dasavatthuppakarana* (1976).

128. I am referring to the murals in the hall of the great reclining Buddha at Wat Chetuphon (Pho) in Bangkok. These are most likely paintings of *paccekabuddhas* (Buddhas who have realized *nibbana* on their own, i.e., without a previous Buddha's help, and do not preach to others).

## CONCLUSION

1. *Museum of Jurassic Technology* (n.d.:13–15).

2. Augé, *Oblivion* (2004:22–23).

3. Anne Blackburn, personal communication, April 2009.

4. Today many young Thais plan pilgrimages and temple visits through social-networking sites like Facebook and Twitter. Since monks increasingly participate in these sites, the social constellation frameworks cross lay and monastic lines.

5. A similar logic was observed by Evans-Pritchard in his well-known study of the Azande in the Sudan. When a granary fell and killed several men, the members of his tribe knew that it was because termites had eaten away the supports of the granary and that the men were leaning against the granary to seek shade on a hot day. However, they said that it fell at that particular time on those particular men because of magic. See his *Witchcraft, Oracles, and Magic among the Azande* (Oxford: Oxford University Press, 1976), chap. 3. I thank Steven Collins for advice on this point.

6. Steven Piker wrote in a short article published in 1972 that was largely ignored by Buddhist studies scholars and Thai specialists directly about the "inconsistency" of Thai religious beliefs. He showed that "felt" contradiction or "felt" inconsistency was extremely rare. See his "Problem of Consistency in Thai Religion" (1972).

7. On the broader subject of protection and power in Southeast Asia, see particularly Tannenbaum, *Who Can Compete Against the World?* (1996); Lucien Hanks, "Merit and Power" (1962); and the highly influential article by Benedict Anderson, "Idea of Power in Javanese Culture" (1972).

8. Todd Perreira recently presented a paper (June 2008). He offers a good summary of early scholarly descriptions of Theravada Buddhism. See also Skilling, "Place of South-East Asia" (2009:49).

9. See Terwiel, "Model for the Study of Thai Buddhism" (1976:391). He also notes in his study of Wat San Chao in Ratburi Province that "it soon appeared that informants were classifying merely to please the researcher; the categories [Buddhism, Brahmanism, Animism] under discussion had little relevance in their minds" (393).

10. Two new studies on religion in China are encouraging for problematizing the very idea of religious syncretism and hybridity: Standaert, *Interweaving of Rituals* (2008:207–18), and Mollier, *Buddhism and Taoism* (2008); see her introduction.

11. Eliot, "Ulysses, Order, and Myth" (1923).

# BIBLIOGRAPHY

Abe, Stanley. "Inside the Wonder House: Buddhist Art and the West." In Lopez, *Curators of the Buddha*, 63–106.

Adun Rattanon, ed. *Kham banyai thang wichakan lae lak patibat nai kan feuk obrom kharachakan tam khrongkanpatthana khanathamachariyatham kharachakan.* Bangkok: Rong Phim Kansasana, 2534 [1991].

Akadet Khrisanathilok. *Phra Somdet: Nangseu phra kruang thi mi neua ha sara lae wichakan.* Vols. 1–3. Bangkok: Aksaraphiphat, 2549 [2006].

Ali, Daud. *Courtly Culture and Political Life in Early Medieval India.* Cambridge: Cambridge University Press, 2004.

Alpers, Svetlana. "The Museum as a Way of Seeing." In *Exhibiting Cultures: The Poetics and Politics of Museum Display*, ed. Steven Lavine, 25–32. Washington, D.C.: Smithsonian Institution, 1991.

Anake Nawigamune. *Bangkok kap hua muang.* Bangkok: Saeng Dao, 2547 [2004].

——. "Khun Chan khadi lao ruang I Nak Phrakhanong." In *Chao leuk ruang kao*, ed. Anake Nawigamune, 71–81 Bangkok: Saithan, 2547 [2004].

——. "Mae Nak Phrakhanong roem mi phua cheu Mak tang tae mua rai." In Anake Nawigamune, *Thanon sai adit*, 65–72.

——. *Nana phiphithaphan.* Bangkok: Saeng Daet Phuan Dek, 2549 [2006].

——. "Poet long Mae Nak Phrakhanong." In Anake Nawigamune, *Ruang kao phap kao*, 95–106.

——. *Poet tamnan Mae Nak Phrakhanong*. Bangkok: Nora, 2543 [2000].

——. *Prawat kanthairup yut raek khong Thai*. Bangkok: Sarakhadi Press, 2548 [2005].

——. *Ruang kao phap kao*. Bangkok: Saithan, 2546 [2003].

——. *Sombat Muang Songkhla*. Bangkok: Filasatai, 2550 [2007].

——. *Thanon sai adit*. Vol. 1. Bangkok: Saithan, 2547 [2004].

Anand Amantai. *Poet tamnan Than Chao Pradun Somdet Phutthachan To Phrohmarangsri*. Bangkok: Saengdao Sroithong, 2543 [2000].

Anchalee Kongrut, "A Master Craftsman." *Bangkok Post*, February 15, 2008.

Anderson, Benedict R.O'G. "The Idea of Power in Javanese Culture." In *Culture and Politics in Indonesia*, ed. Clare Holt, 1–69. Ithaca: Cornell University Press, 1972.

An Sarikabut. *Khamphi horasat Thai matrathan chabap sombun*. Bangkok: Silapasan, 2508 [1965]).

(Phya) Anuman Rajadhon. *Life and Ritual in Old Siam: Three Studies of Thai Life and Customs*, trans. William Gedney. New Haven: HRAF Press, 1961.

(Prince) Anuman Rajadhon. *Popular Buddhism in Siam*. Bangkok: Sathirakoses Nagapradipa Foundation, 1986.

Apinan Poshyananda. *Contemporary Art in Asia: Traditions and Tensions*. New York: Asia Society, 1997.

Apinya Fuengfulsakul. "Empire of Crystal and Utopian Commune: Two Types of Contemporary Theravada Reform in Thailand." *Sojourn* 8, no. 1 (1993): 151–83.

App, Urs. *The Birth of Orientalism*. Philadelphia: University of Pennsylvania Press, 2010.

Appadurai, Arjun, ed. *The Social Lives of Things: Commodities in Cultural Perspective*. Cambridge: Cambridge University Press, 1986.

Arthid Sheravanichkul. "Dana and Danaparami: Significance in the Creation of Thai Buddhist Literature." Ph.D. diss., Chulalongkorn University, 2009.

Augé, Marc. *Oblivion*. Trans. Marjolijn de Jager. Minneapolis: University of Minnesota Press, 2004.

Bailey, Michael. "The Meanings of Magic." *Magic, Ritual, and Witchcraft* 1, no. 1 (2006): 1–23.

Baird, Ian. "From Champasak to Cambodia: Ya Chao Tham (Chao Thammatheva), a Wily and Influential Ethnic Lao Leader." *Aséanie* 23 (2009): 31–62.

(Phra Khru) Baithikathep Singrak. *Tamra phetrat mahayan*. Bangkok: Sripanya, 2551 [2008].

(Phra Khru) Baithikawira Thanawiro. *Phra prawat Somdet Phra Sangharatyanasangwon Mahathen (Suk Kai Theuan)*. Bangkok: Mahamakut Rachawithayalai, 2536 [1993].

Baker, Chris, and Pasuk Phongpaichit. *A History of Thailand*. Cambridge: Cambridge University Press, 2005.

——. *Khun Chang Khun Paen*. 2 vols. Chiang Mai: Silkworm Books, 2010.

Bang-on Piyaphan. *Lao nai krung Rattanakosin*. Bangkok: Samnakngan Kongthun Sanapsanun Kanwichai, 2541 [1998].

Bastian, Adolf. *A Journey in Siam (1863)*. Trans. Walter Tipps. Bangkok: White Lotus Press, 2005. Originally published as *Reisen in Siam im Jahre 1863*.

Baxandall, Michael. *Patterns of Intention: On the Historical Explanation of Pictures*. New Haven: Yale University Press, 1985.

*Baytong*. DVD. Directed by Nonzee Nimibutr. Bangkok: Sahamongkol, 2003.

Becchetti, Catherine. *Le mystère dans les lettres*. Bangkok: Éditions des cahiers de France, 1991.

Bechert, Heinz. "Aspects of Theravāda Buddhism in Sri Lanka and Southeast Asia." In *The Buddhist Heritage*, ed. Tadeusz Skorupski, 19–27. Tring, UK: Institute of Buddhist Studies, 1989.

——. *Buddhismus, Staat und Gesellschaft in den Ländern des Theravada-Buddhismus*. 2 vols. Frankfurt: Metzner, 1966–1967.

——. *Buddhismus, Staat und Gesellschaft in den Ländern des Theravada-Buddhismus*. Vol. 3. Wiesbaden: Harrassowitz, 1973.

——. "Contradictions in Sinhalese Buddhism." In Smith, *Religion and Legitimation of Power in Sri Lanka*, 188–98.

——. "Neue buddhistische Orthodoxie: Bemerkungen zur Gliederung und zur Reform des Sangha in Birma." *Numen* 35, no. 1 (1988): 24–56.

Benn, James. *Burning for the Buddha: Self-Immolation in Chinese Buddhism*. Honolulu: University of Hawai'i Press, 2007.

de Bernon, Olivier. "Le manuel des maîtres de kammaṭṭhān." Ph.D. diss., Institut nationale des langues et civilisations orientales, Paris, 2000.

——. "The Status of Pāli in Cambodia: From Canonical to Esoteric Language." In *Buddhist Legacies in Mainland Southeast Asia: Mentalities, Interpretations and Practices*, ed. François Lagirarde and Paritta Chalermpow Koanantakool, 53–66. Bangkok: Sirindhorn Anthropology Centre; Paris: École française d'Extrême-Orient, 2006.

Bizot, François. "La consécration des statues et le culte des morts." In *Recherches nouvelles sur le Cambodge*. Paris: École française d'Extrême-Orient, 1994.

——. "La grotte de la naissance: Recherches sur le bouddhisme khmer, II. " *Bulletin de l'École française d'Extrême-Orient* 67 (1980): 221–74.

——. *Le bouddhisme des Thaïs*. Bangkok: Éditions des cahiers de France, 1993.

——. *Le chemin de Lankâ*. Paris: École française d'Extrême-Orient, 1992.

——. *Le don de soi-même*. Publications de l'École française d'Extrême-Orient 130. Paris: École française d'Extrême-Orient, 1981.

——. *Le figuier à cinq branches*. Publications de l'École française d'Extrême-Orient 107. Paris: École française d'Extrême-Orient, 1976.

——. *Les traditions de la pabbajjā en Asie du Sud-est*. Paris: École française d'Extrême-Orient, 1988.

——. "Notes sur les *yantra* bouddhiques d'Indochine." In *Tantric and Taoist Studies in Honour of R.A. Stein, Volume 1*, ed. Michael Strickmann. Mélanges chinois et bouddhiques, vol. 20. Brussels: Institut belge des hautes études chinoises, 1981.

Bizot, François, and François Lagirarde. *La pureté par les mots*. Chiang Mai: École française d'Extrême-Orient, 1996.

Bizot, François, and Oskar von Hinüber. *La guirlande de joyaux*. Paris: École française d'Extrême-Orient, 1994.

Blackburn, Anne. *Buddhist Learning and Textual Practice in Eighteenth-Century Lankan Monastic Culture*. Princeton: Princeton University Press, 2001.

Blofeld, John. *King Maha Mongkut of Siam*. Bangkok: Siam Society, 1987.

Bloomfield, Maurice, trans. *Hymns of the Atharva-veda*. Vol. 42 of *The Sacred Books of the East*, ed. F. Max Müller. Oxford: Oxford University Press, 1897.

Bode, Mabel. *The Pali Literature of Burma*. London: Luzac, 1966.

Boonlua Chatree. "District Policeman Charged with Attempted Murder and Theft: Stole Gold Chain with Buddha Image Worth Millions." *Pattaya Mail*. http://www.pattayamail.com/420/news.htm#hd6.

Bozóky, Edina. *Charmes et prières apotropaïques*. Turnhout, Bel.: Brespols, 2003.

Brandon, James. *Theatre in Southeast Asia*. Cambridge, Mass.: Harvard University Press, 1967.

Brereton, Bonnie. *The Thai Tellings of Phra Malai: Texts and Rituals Concerning a Popular Buddhist Saint*. Tempe: Arizona State University, Program for Southeast Asian Studies, 1995.

Bronfen, Elisabeth. "Visuality – Textuality: An Uncanny Encounter." *Image and Narrative* 11, no. 3 (2010): 7–24.

Brown, Robert. "Narrative as Icon: The Jataka Stories in Ancient Indian and Southeast Asian Architecture." In *Sacred Biography in the Buddhist Traditions of South and Southeast Asia*, ed. Juliane Schober, 64–112. Honolulu: University of Hawai'i Press, 1997.

Bunsopha Chaloenniphonwanit. "Chitakam baep prapheni khong Thai nai yut Ratanakosin." In *Silapawatthanatham Thai lem thi 6*, ed. Decho Suananon, 1–12. Bangkok: Khrom Silapakon, 2525 [1982].

Burchett, Patton. "The 'Magical' Language of Mantra." *Journal of the American Academy of Religion* 76, no. 4 (2008): 807–43.

Cannell, Fenella. *Power and Intimacy in the Christian Philippines*. Cambridge: Cambridge University Press, 1999.

Carrithers, Michael. "Anthropology as a Moral Science of Possibilities." *Current Anthropology* 46, no. 3 (2005): 433–56.

Carsten, Janet, ed. *Ghosts of Memory: Essays of Remembrance and Relatedness.* Oxford: Blackwell, 2007.

Cassaniti, Julia. "Control in a World of Change: Emotion and Morality in a Northern Thai Town." Ph.D. diss., University of Chicago, 2009.

Cate, Sandra. *Making Merit, Making Art: A Thai Temple in Wimbledon.* Honolulu: University of Hawai'i Press, 2002.

Cather, Willa. *On Writing: Critical Studies on Writing as an Art.* Omaha: University of Nebraska Press, 1949.

Chalermchai Kositpipat. *Roi ruang rao khong Wat Rongkhun,* DVD. Chiang Rai: Wat Rongkhun, n.d.

——. *Wat Rongkhun: Srang sin pheua phaendin.* Bangkok: Amarin, n.d.

Chalong Soontravanich. "The Regionalization of Local Buddhist Saints: Amulets, Crime, and Violence in Post World War II Thai Society." In *Proceedings of the Japan Society for the Promotion of Science and National Research Council of Thailand Core University Program Workshop on Flows and Movements in East Asia,* 115–39. Kyoto: Center for Southeast Asian Studies, Kyoto University, 2004.

——. "Small Arms, Romance, and Crime and Violence in Post WW II Thai Society." *Southeast Asian Studies* 43, no. 1 (2005): 26–46.

Chandler, David, and Alexandra Kent, eds. *People of Virtue: Reconfiguring Religion, Power and Moral Order in Cambodia Today.* Honolulu: University of Hawai'i Press, 2008.

Chang Noi. "PAD Saves the Nation from Supernatural Attack." *Nation,* November 10, 2008.

Chantisai. *Somdet Phra Phutthachan To Phrohmarangsi.* Bangkok: Hong Horachan, 2496 [1954].

*Chao awat lae wat nai prathet Thai 2526–2547.* Bangkok: Prakhamati, 2549 [2006].

Charnwit Kasetsiri et al. *Prachum prakat Ratchakan thi 4.* Bangkok: Toyota Foundation Thailand, 2547 [2004].

Chatthip Nartsupa. "The Ideology of Holy Men in North East Thailand." *Ethnological Study* 13 (1983): 111–34.

Chawalee Na Thalang. *Prathet ratcha khong Siam nai ratcha samai Phrabat Somdet Phra Chulachom Klao Chao Yu Hua.* Bangkok: Samnakngan Kongthun Sanapsanun Kanwichai, 2541 [1998].

Chayan Phichiansunthon, Maenmat Chawalit, and Wichiang Chiruang. *Kamthibai tamra Phra Osot Phra Narai.* Bangkok: Amarin, 2544 [2001].

Chiraphat Praphanwithya. *Phra Siwa Phra Wisanu Phra Phighanesuan.* Bangkok: Thewasathan Botphrahm, 2545 [2002].

Chirawan Saengphet. *Phutthasilapakam na Wat Pathumwanaram Rachaworawihan.* Bangkok: Chulalongkorn University Press, 2550 [2007].

*Chitakam Faphanang Phra Ubosot Wat Indrawihan Phra Aramluang.* Bangkok: Wat Indrawihan, n.d.

*Chiwit kanngan laktham To Phrohmarangsri.* Bangkok: Thammasapha, 2538 [1995].

(Prince) Chula Chakrabongse. *Lords of Life.* London: Alvin Redman, 1960.

(King) Chulalongkorn. *Ruang phraratchaphithi sipsong duan.* Bangkok: Rongphim Thai, 2463 [1920].

(King) Chulalongkorn. *Ruang phra ratchapithi sipsong duan.* 14th ed. Bangkok: Sinlapa Bannakhan, 2516 [1973].

Chuphon Euachuwong. "Chitakam Samkok nai sala Chao Kian An Keng." *Muang boran* 33, no. 3 (2007): 50–58.

Chutima Chunhacha, ed. *Chut chitakam faphanang nai prathet Thai Wat Khongkharam.* Bangkok: Muang Boran, 2537 [1994].

Clancy-Smith, Julia. *Rebel and Saint: Muslim Notables, Populist Protest, Colonial Encounters (Algeria and Tunisia, 1800–1904).* Berkeley: University of California Press, 1997.

Clark, T. J. "Theory and Its Objects: On Thomas Crow's *The Intelligence of Art.*" *Documents* 21 (fall 2001 / winter 2002): 5–10.

Coedès, George. *Tamnan akson Thai tamnan phra phim: Kan khut khon thi phongteuk lae khwam samkhan to prawatsat samai boran haeng prathet Thai sin Thai samai Sukhothai Rachathani run raek khong Thai.* Bangkok: Khrurusapha, 2507 [1964].

Cohen, Paul. "Buddhism Unshackled: The Yuan 'Holy Man' Tradition in Northern Thailand and the Nation-State in the Tai World." *Journal of Southeast Asian Studies* 32, no. 2 (2001): 227–47.

Cohen, Richard. "Nāga, Yakṣinī, Buddha: Local Deities and Local Buddhism at Ajanta." *History of Religions* 37 (1998): 360–400.

Collins, Steven. "Introduction" to E. Denis, "Brah Māleyyadevattheravatthuṃ." *Journal of the Pali Text Society* 18 (1993): 1–17.

Collins, Steven, and Justin McDaniel. "Buddhist 'Nuns' (*Mae Chi*) and the Teaching of Pali in Contemporary Thailand." *Modern Asian Studies* 44, no. 6 (2010): 1373–1408.

Comaroff, John L., and Jean Comaroff. "Occult Economies and the Violence of Abstraction: Notes from the South African Postcolony." *American Ethnologist* 26, no. 2 (1999): 279–303.

——. "Privatizing the Millennium: New Protestant Ethics and the Spirits of Capitalism in Africa, and Elsewhere." In *Religion, Politics, and Identity in a Changing South Africa,* ed. David Chidester, Abdulkader Tayob, and Wolfram Weisse, 23–44. Munich: Waxmann, 2004.

Connolly, William. *Pluralism.* Durham: Duke University Press, 2005.

Cousins, Lance. "Aspects of Esoteric Southern Buddhism." In *Indian Insights: Buddhism, Brahmanism and Bhakti,* ed. S. Hamilton. and P. Connolly, 185–207. London: Luzac Oriental, 1997.

Covell, Steven. *Japanese Temple Buddhism: Worldliness in a Religion of Renunciation.* Honolulu: University of Hawai'i Press, 2006.

Cowell, E. W. ed. *The Jātaka; or, Stories of the Buddha's Former Births*. Vol. 6. Cambridge: Cambridge University Press, 1907.

Crick, Francis, and Christof Koch. "The Neural Correlates of Consciousness." In *The Oxford Companion to the Mind*, ed. Richard Gregory, 222–24. Oxford: Oxford University Press, 2004.

Crimp, Douglas. "On the Museum's Ruins." In *The Anti-Aesthetic*, ed. H. Foster, 43–56. Port Townsend: Bay Press, 1983.

Crosby, Kate. "Tantric Theravada: A Bibliographic Essay on the Writings of François Bizot and Others on the Yogāvacara Tradition." *Contemporary Buddhism* 1, no. 2 (2000): 141–98.

Cuevas, Bryan. *Travels in the Netherworld: Buddhist Popular Narratives of Death and the Afterlife in Tibet*. Oxford: Oxford University Press, 2008.

Cunlas, Craig. "Oriental Antiquities/Far Eastern Art." In *Formations of Colonial Modernity in East Asia*, ed. Tani Barlow, 413–46. Durham: Duke University Press, 1997.

(Phra Chao Boromwongtoe Krom Phra Samomtomonphan Krom Phra) (Prince) Damrong Ratchanuphap. *Chotmaihet ruang prap khabot Wiangchan*. Bangkok: Sobhanaphiphatthanakon, 2469 [1926].

——. *Nithan borankhadi*. Bangkok: Khurusapha, 2509 [1966].

——. *Ruang tang phra rachakhana phuyai nai Ratanakosin*. Bangkok: Rongphim Sophanaphiphatthanakon, 2466 [1923].

——. *San somdet*. Bangkok: Khurusapha, 2509 [1966].

——. *Tamnan phra parit*. Bangkok: Rongphim Sobhanaphiphatthanakon, 2472 [1929].

Darling, Frank, and Ann Darling. *Thailand: The Modern Kingdom*. Singapore: Asia Pacific Press, 1971.

Daston, Lorraine, and Katharine Park. *Wonders and the Order of Nature, 1150–1750*. Cambridge, Mass.: MIT Press, 2001.

Davidson, Ronald. *Indian Esoteric Buddhism: A Social History of the Tantric Movement*. New York: Columbia University Press, 2003.

Davis, Erik. "Treasures of the Buddha." Ph.D. diss., University of Chicago, 2009.

Davis, Richard. "From the Lives of Indian Images." In *Religion, Art, and Visual Culture*, ed. S. Brent Plate, 176–81. New York: Palgrave, 2002.

——. *Muang Metaphysics: A Study of Northern Thai Myth and Ritual*. Bangkok: Pandora, 1984.

Davisakd Puaksom. "Kan prubtau thang khwam ru khwam ching lae amnat khong chonchan nam Siam pho. so. 2325–2411" [The Readjustment of Knowledge, Truth, and Power of the Elites in Siam, 1782–1868]. Master's thesis, Chulalongkorn University, 1997.

DeCaroli, Robert. *Haunting the Buddha: Indian Popular Religions and the Formation of Buddhism*. Oxford: Oxford University Press, 2004.

de Silva, Lily. "Paritta: A Historical and Religious Study of the Buddhist Ceremony for Peace and Prosperity in Sri Lanka." In *Spolia Zeylanica, Bulletin of the National Museums of Sri Lanka*, ed. P. H. D. H. de Silva. Colombo: Department of Government Printing, 1981.

(Phra) Dhammapitaka (Payutto). *Sing saksit thewarit patihan*. Bangkok: Phutthatham Foundation, 2536 [1993].

Dobbins, James. "Exoteric-Esoteric (Kenmitsu) Buddhism in Japan." In *Encyclopedia of Buddhism*, ed. Robert Buswell, 271–75. New York: Macmillan, 2003.

——, ed. "The Legacy of Kuroda Toshio." Special issue, *Japanese Journal of Religious Studies* 23, no. 3-4 (1996).

Dovert, Stéphane, ed. *Thaïlande contemporaine*. Paris: L'Harmattan, 2001.

Dror, Olga. *Cult, Culture, and Authority: Princess Liễu Hạnh in Vietnamese History*. Honolulu: University of Hawai'i Press, 2007.

Dundes, Lauren, ed. *The Manner Born: Birth Rites in Cross-Cultural Perspective*. Lanham, Md.: AltaMira Press, 2003.

Eade, J. C. *The Thai Historical Record: A Computer Analysis*. Tokyo: Center for East Asian Cultural Studies for UNESCO, 1996.

Eck, Diana. "Excerpts from Darshan." In *Religion, Art, and Visual Culture*, ed. S. Brent Plate, 171–75. New York: Palgave, 2002.

Ehrlich, Richard. "Baby Roasting Monk Caught Tricking Women Into Sex." http://www.scoop.co.nz/stories/HL0507/S00277.htm.

Eliot, T. S. "Ulysses, Order, and Myth." *The Dial*, November 1923. Reprinted in *Selected Prose of T.S. Eliot*, ed. Frank Kermode, 175–78. New York: Harvest Books, 1975.

Falk, Monica Lindberg. "Thammacarini Witthaya: The First Buddhist School for Girls in Thailand." In *Innovative Buddhist Women: Swimming against the Stream*, ed. Karma Lekshe Tsomo, 61–71. London: Curzon, 2000.

Farrell, James Austin. "The Hex, the Monk, and the Exorcist." http://www.chiangmainews.com/ecmn/viewfa.php?id=2206.

Feua Hiriphithak. *Phap khian nai ho Phra Tripidok Wat Rakhangkhositaram*. Bangkok: Fine Arts Department, 2513 [1970].

Fickle, Dorothy. *The Life of the Buddha Murals in the Buddhaisawan Chapel*. Bangkok: Fine Arts Department, 1979.

Fisiy, Cyprian Fonyuy, and Peter Geschiere. *Sorcellerie et politique en Afrique*. Paris: Karthala, 1995.

Foster, Michael Dylan. "Strange Games and Enchanted Science: The Mystery of Kokkuri." *Journal of Asian Studies* 65, no. 2 (May 2006): 251–75.

Foucault, Michel. "Different Spaces." In *Aesthetics, Method, and Epistemology*, ed. James D. Faubion, trans. Robert Hurley et al., 175–85. London: Allen Lane, 1998.

——. *The Order of Things*. London: Routledge, 1970.

Fowler, Sherry. *Murōji: Rearranging Art and History at a Japanese Buddhist Temple*. Honolulu: University Hawai'i Press, 2005.

Fraser, Sarah. *Performing the Visual: The Practice of Buddhist Wall Painting in China and Central Asia, 618–960.* Stanford: Stanford University Press, 2003.

Frenkel, Vera. "A Place for Uncertainty: Towards a New Kind of Museum." In Pollock and Zemans, *Museums After Modernism,* 119–30.

Gabaude, Louis. "A New Phenomenon in Thai Monasteries: The Stūpa Museum." In *The Buddhist Monastery: A Cross-Cultural Survey,* ed. Pierre Pichard and François Lagirarde, 169–86. Paris: École française d'Extrême-Orient, 2003.

———. *Une herméneutique bouddhique contemporaine de Thaïlande: Buddhadasa bhikkhu.* Paris: École française d'Extrême-Orient, 1988.

———. "Where Ascetics Get Comfort and Recluses Go Public: Museums for Buddhist Saints in Thailand." In *Pilgrims, Patrons, and Place: Localizing Sanctity in Asian Religions,* ed. Phyllis Granoff and Koichi Shinohara. Vancouver: University of British Columbia Press, 2003.

Gaonkar, Dilip, ed. *Alternative Modernities.* Durham: Public Culture / Duke University Press, 2001.

Garfinkel, Harold. *Ethnomethodology's Program.* New York: Rowman and Littlefield, 2002.

Geary, Patrick. "Sacred Commodities: The Circulation of Medieval Relics." In *The Social Lives of Things: Commodities in Cultural Perspective,* ed. Arjun Appadurai, 169–94. Cambridge: Cambridge University Press, 1986.

Geertz, Clifford. *Local Knowledge: Further Essays in Interpretive Anthropology.* New York: Basic Books, 1983.

Gell, Alfred. *Art and Agency: An Anthropological Theory.* Oxford: Oxford University Press, 1998.

Giddens, Anthony. *The Consequences of Modernity.* Cambridge: Polity Press, 1995.

Giles, Francis. "About a Love Philtre Known to the Siamese as Nam Man Phrai— Spirit Oil." *Journal of the Siam Society* 30, no. 1 (1938): 24–28.

Ginsburg, Henry. *Thai Art and Culture: Historic Manuscripts from Western Collections.* Honolulu: University of Hawai'i Press, 2000.

———. "Thai Literary Tales Derived from the Sanskrit Tantropākhyāna." Master's thesis, University of Hawai'i, 1967.

———. *Thai Manuscript Painting.* London: British Library, 1989.

Gosling, Betty. *Origins of Thai Art.* Bangkok: River Books, 2004.

Goubman, Boris. "Postmodernity as the Climax of Modernity: Horizons of the Cultural Future." Paper presented at the Twentieth World Congress of Philosophy, Boston, August 10–15, 1998.

Graf, Fritz. *Magic in the Ancient World.* Trans. Franklin Philip. Cambridge, Mass.: Harvard University Press, 1997.

Griswold, A. B. "Medieval Siamese Images in the Bo Tree Monastery." *Artibus Asiae* 18, no. 1 (1955): 46–60.

——. "A Warning to Evildoers." *Artibus Asiae* 20, no. 1 (1967): 18–27.

——. *What Is a Buddha Image?* Bangkok: Khrom Silapakon, 1962.

Guelden, Marlane. *Thailand: Into the Spirit World.* Singapore: Times Editions, 1995.

——. *Thailand: Spirits Among Us.* Singapore: Marshall Cavendish International, 2007.

Habermas, Jürgen. *Der philosophische Diskurs der Moderne.* Frankfurt: Suhrkamp, 1989.

"Hae ruam wan goet Phra Phi Kanet." *Thai rath,* September, 17, 2550 [2007].

Hallisey, Charles, and Anne Hansen. "Narrative, Sub-Ethics, and the Moral Life." *Journal of Religious Ethics* 24, no. 2 (1996): 305–25.

Hanks, Jane Richardson. *Maternity and Its Rituals in Bang Chan, Thailand.* Cornell Thailand Project, Interim Reports Series 6. Ithaca: Department of Asian Studies, Cornell University, 1963.

Hanks, Lucien. "Merit and Power in the Thai Social Order." *American Anthropologist* 65 (1962): 1247–61.

Hansen, Ann. *How to Behave: Buddhism and Modernity in Colonial Cambodia, 1860–1930.* Honolulu: University of Hawai'i Press, 2006.

Haraway, Donna. "Situated Knowledges: The Science Question in Feminism as a Site of Discourse on the Privilege of Partial Perspective." *Feminist Studies* 14, no. 3 (1988): 575–99.

Hardacre, Helen. *Kurozumikyo and the New Religions of Japan.* Princeton: Princeton University Press, 1988.

Harris, Ian. *Buddhism and Politics in Twentieth-Century Asia.* London: Pinter Books, 2005.

——, ed. *Buddhism, Power and Political Order.* London: Routledge, 2007.

Harvey, Peter. *An Introduction to Buddhist Ethics.* Cambridge: Cambridge University Press, 2000.

Hauerwas, Stanley, and L. Gregory Jones, eds. *Why Narrative? Readings in Narrative Theology.* Eugene: Wipf and Stock, 1997.

Hayashi Yukio. *Practical Buddhism among the Thai-Lao.* Kyoto: University of Kyoto Press, 2003.

Hewison, Kevin. "Of Regimes, State, and Pluralities: Thai Politics Enters the 1990s." In *Southeast Asia in the 1990s: Authoritarianism, Democracy and Capitalism,* ed. Kevin Hewison, R. Robinson, and G. Rodan, 161–89. Sydney: Allen and Unwin, 1993.

Hinüber, Oskar von. *A Handbook of Pāli Literature.* New York: de Gruyter, 1996.

Holbraad, Martin. "The Power of Powder: Multiplicity and Motion in the Divinatory Cosmology of Cuban Ifá (or *Mana*, Again)." In *Thinking Through Things: Theorising Artefacts Ethnographically,* ed. Amiria Henare, Martin Holbraad, and Sari Wastell, 189–225. Oxford: Routledge, 2007.

Holt, John. *Buddha and the Crown: Avalokitesvara in the Buddhist Traditions of Sri Lanka.* Oxford: Oxford University Press, 1991.

Hooper-Greenhill, Eilean. *Museums and the Shaping of Knowledge*. London: Routledge, 1992.

*Ho Phra Traipidok Wat Rakhangkhositaram*. Produced by a committee at Wat Rakhang. Bangkok: Wat Rakhangkhositaram, 2515 [1972].

Horstmann, Alexander. *Class, Culture and Space: The Construction and Shaping of Communal Space in South Thailand*. Piscataway, N.J.: Transaction Publishers, 2002.

———. "Hybrid Processes of Modernization and Globalization: The Making of Consumers in South Thailand." Paper presented at the International Conference on Globalization, Development and the Making of Consumers: What Are Collective Identities For? The Hague, March 13–16, 1997.

———. "Magic and Modernity in Southern Thailand: Reconfigurations of a Multireligious Performance and Art Genre." Informal Northern Thai Group bulletin minutes of the 315th meeting, Tuesday, September 8, 2009.

Hutanuwatr, Pracha, and Ramu Manivannan, eds. *The Asian Future: Dialogues for Change*. London: Zed Books, 2005.

Hutanuwatr, Pracha, and Jane Rasbash, eds. *Globilisation from a Buddhist Perspective*. Colombo: Buddhist Publication Society, 1998.

Ingawanij, May. "*Nang Nak*: Thai Bourgeois Heritage Cinema." *Inter-Asia Cultural Studies* 8, no. 2 (2007): 180–93.

Isarangkhru na Ayutthya. *Ngan phrarachathan phloeng sop phonruangtri ekachai*. Bangkok: Wat Mai Amatarot, 2534 [1991].

Ishii, Yoneo. *Sangha, State, and Society*. Honolulu: University of Hawai'i Press, 1986.

Jackson, Peter. *Buddhadasa: Theravada Buddhism and Modernist Reform in Thailand*. 2nd ed. Chiang Mai: Silkworm Books, 2003.

———. *Buddhism, Legitimation, and Conflict: The Political Functions of Urban Thai Buddhism*. Singapore: Institute of Southeast Asian Studies, 1989.

———. "The Enchanting Spirit of Thai Capitalism: The Cult of Luang Phor Khoon and the Post-Modernization of Thai Buddhism." *South East Asia Research* 7, no. 1 (1999): 5–60.

———. "The Hupphasawan Movement: Millenarian Buddhism among the Thai Political Elite." *Sojourn* 3 (1988): 134–70.

———. "Royal Spirits, Chinese Gods, and Magic Monks: Thailand's Boom-Time Religions of Prosperity." *South East Asia Research* 7, no. 3 (1999): 245–320.

———. "Withering Centre, Flourishing Margins: Buddhism's Changing Political Roles." In *Political Change in Thailand: Democracy and Participation*, ed. Kevin Hewison, 75–93. London: Routledge, 1997.

Jaini, Padmanabh, ed. *Paññāsajātaka (Zimmè Jātaka)*. 2 vols. Oxford: Pali Text Society, 1981–1983.

Jaiser, Gerhard. *Thai Mural Painting, Volume 1: Iconography, Analysis, and Guide*. Bangkok: White Lotus Press, 2009.

James, Liz, ed. *Art and Text in Byzantine Culture*. Cambridge: Cambridge University Press, 2007.

Jayawickrama, N. A. *Epochs of the Conqueror*. London: Pali Text Society, 1978.

Johnson, Paul Christopher. "'Rationality' in the Biography of a Buddhist King: Mongkut, King of Siam (r. 1851–1868)." In *Sacred Biography in the Buddhist Traditions of South and Southeast Asia*, ed. Juliane Schober, 232–58. Honolulu: University of Hawai'i Press, 1997.

Johnston, Sarah. "Describing the Undefinable: New Books on Magic and Old Problems of Definition." *History of Religions* 43 (2004): 50–54.

Jory, Patrick. "The Vessantara Jataka, Barami, and the Bodhisatta-Kings: The Origin and Spread of a Thai Concept of Power." *Crossroads: An Interdisciplinary Journal of Southeast Asian Studies* 16, no. 2 (2002): 36–78.

Kaisit Phisanakha. *Chiwaprawat borom Khru Phaet: Chiwok Komanphat*. Bangkok: Saradi, 2545 [2002].

Kakar, Sudhir. *Shamans, Mystics and Doctors: A Psychological Inquiry into India and Its Healing Traditions*. Chicago: University of Chicago Press, 1991.

(Phra Khru) Kalyananukun (Heng Itthacharo). *Prawat Somdet Phra Phutthachan To*. Bangkok: Damrongtham, 2496 [1952].

——. *Prawat Somdet Phra Phutthachan To Phrohmarangsi*. Bangkok: Wat Kalyanamitworamahawihan, 2529 [1986]).

Kamala Tiyavanich. *Buddha in the Jungle*. Seattle: University of Washington Press, 2004.

——. *Forest Recollections: Wandering Monks in 20th Century Thailand*. Honolulu: University of Hawai'i Press, 1997.

——. *Sons of the Buddha: The Early Lives of Three Extraordinary Thai Masters*. Cambridge: Wisdom Books, 2007

Kammakan Nak Prawatsat [Committee of Historians]. *Prawatsat kanphim nai prathet Thai: Siam phimphakan*. Bangkok: Matichon, 2549 [2006].

Kasian Tejapira. "The Post-modernization of Thainess." In *House of Glass: Culture, Modernity, and the State in Southeast Asia*, ed. Yao Souchou, 155–61. Singapore: ISEAS, 2001.

Kawanami, Hiroko, and Bénédicte Brac de la Perrière, eds. "Power, Authority and Contested Hegemony in Burmese-Myanmar Religion." Special issue, *Asian Ethnology* 68, no. 2 2009.

Kent, Eliza. "Hinduism and Indian Ecstatic Religions." In *Encyclopedia of Shamanism*, ed. Mariko Walker and Eva Friedman. Santa Barbara: ABC-CLIO, 2004.

Keyes, Charles. "Buddhism and National Integration in Thailand." *Journal of Asian Studies* 30, no. 3 (1971): 551–67.

——. "Hegemony and Resistance in Northeastern Thailand." In *Regions and National Integration in Thailand, 1892–1992*, ed. Volker Grabowski, 154–82. Wiesbaden: Harrassowitz, 1995.

——. "Magic, Mobs and Millennialism." *Bangkok Post*, April 4, 2009.

——. "Moral Authority of the Sangha and Modernity in Thailand: Sexual Scandals, Sectarian Dissent, and Political Resistance." In *Socially Engaged Buddhism for the New Millennium: Essays in Honor of the Ven. Phra Dhammapitaka (Bhikkhu P.A. Payutto) on His 60th Birthday Anniversary*, 121–47. Bangkok: Sathirakoses-Nagapradipa Foundation and Foundation for Children, 1999.

——. "National Heroine or Local Spirit? The Struggle over Memory in the Case of Thao Suranari in Nakhon Ratchasima." In *Cultural Crisis and Social Memory*, ed. Shigeharu Tanabe and Charles Keyes, 113–36. London: Routledge, 2002.

Keyes, Charles, and (Phra Khru) Anusaranasasanakiarti. "Funerary Rites and the Buddhist Meaning of Death: An Interpretative Text from Northern Thailand." *Journal of the Siam Society* 68, no. 1 (1980): 1–28.

Kham Bunnag, comp. *Phra ratchaphongsawadan krung Ratanakosin Ratchakan thi 4*. 2461 [1918]. Reprint, Bangkok: Chase Enterprise, 2550 [2007].

Khana Sit Watcharin. *Kittikhun lae phra barami Somdet Phra Phutthachan to Wat Rakhang lae Wat Indrawihan*. Bangkok: Watcharin, 2529 [1986].

Kirsch, Thomas. "Economy, Polity and Religion in Thailand." In *Change and Persistence in Thai Society: Essays in Honor of Lauriston Sharp*, ed. G. Skinner and T. Kirsch, 172–96. Ithaca: Cornell University Press, 1975.

Kitagawa, Joseph. "Buddhism and Asian Politics." *Asian Survey* 2, no. 5 (1962): 1–11.

Kitagawa, Joseph Mitsuo. *The Religious Traditions of Asia: Religion, History, and Culture*. London: Routledge, 2002.

Klima, Alan. *Funeral Casino: Meditation, Massacre, and Exchange with the Dead in Thailand*. Princeton: Princeton University Press, 2002.

Korkok Wongbom. "Itiphon khwam cheua thang horasat to withichiwit khong khon Thai." Master's thesis, Mahidol University, 2549 [2006].

Kraisri Sri-Aroon. *Phra Phuttha rup pan tang nai Siam prathet*. Bangkok: Silapawatthanatham, 2539 [1996].

Krom Silapakon [Department of Fine Arts Editorial Team]. *Chareuk Tamra Ya: Wat Ratchaorosaram Ratchawihan*. Bangkok: Krom Silapakon, 2545 [2002].

Kultida Samabuddhi. "Sorcerer Sondhi Wards Off Evil: Followers Don White, Clean, Pray for Victory." *Bangkok Post*, November 10, 2008.

Kuroda Toshio. "Shintō in the History of Japanese Religion." In *Religions of Japan in Practice*, ed. George Tanabe Jr., 451–67. Princeton: Princeton University Press, 1999.

Lacan, Jacques. *Écrits: The First Complete Edition in English*. Trans. Robert Finks. New York: Norton, 2007.

LaFleur, William. "Symbol and Yūgen: Shunzei's Use of Tendai Buddhism." In *Flowing Traces: Buddhism in the Literary and Visual Arts of Japan*, ed. James

Sanford, William LaFleur, and Masatoshi Nagatomi, 16–46. Princeton: Princeton University Press, 1992.

Lagirarde, François. "Devotional Diversification in the Thai Monastery: The Worship of the Fat Monk." In *The Buddhist Monastery: A Cross-Cultural Survey*, ed. P. Pichard. Paris, EFEO, 2003.

——. "Gavampati et la tradition des quatre-vingts disciples du Bouddha: Textes et iconographie du Laos et de Thaïlande." *BEFEO* 87, no. 1 (2000): 57–78.

——. "Gavampati- Kaccâyana: Le culte et la légende du disciple ventripotent dans le bouddhisme des Thaïs." 2 vols. Ph.D. diss., Sorbonne, Paris, 2001.

Lamont, Peter, and Richard Wiseman. *Magic in Theory*. Hertfordshire: University of Hertfordshire Press, 1999.

Langkakuman. "Lao ruang muang (Sri) Langka Gāthā Jinapañjara." *Silapawatthanatham* (2552 [2009]): 67–81.

Latour, Bruno. *Science in Action*. Cambridge, Mass.: Harvard University Press, 1988.

Laughlin, Charles, and Eugene d'Aquili. *Biogenetic Structuralism*. New York: Columbia University Press, 1974.

Layton, Richard. "Art and Agency: A Reassessment." *Journal of the Royal Anthropological Institute* 9 (2003): 447–64.

Le Goff, Jacques. *History and Memory*. Trans. Steven Rendall and Elizabeth Claman. New York: Columbia University Press, 1992.

Lek Wiriyabun. *Guide to Muang Boran*. Bangkok: Viriya Business Company, 2004.

LeMay, Reginald. *An Asian Arcady: The Land and Peoples of Northern Siam*. Cambridge: Heffer, 1926.

Leopold, Anita Maria, and Jeppe Sinding Jensen, eds. *Syncretism in Religion: A Reader*. New York: Routledge, 2005.

Levine, Gregory. *Daitokuji: The Visual Cultures of a Zen Monastery*. Seattle: University of Washington Press, 2005.

Levy, Daniel. "Yan in Northern Thailand." Undergraduate thesis, Harvard University, 2000.

Li, Michelle Osterfeld. *Ambiguous Bodies: Reading the Grotesque in Japanese Setsuwa Tales*. Stanford: Stanford University Press, 2009.

Listopad, John. "The Process of Change in Thai Mural Paintings: Khrua In Khong and the Murals in the Ubosoth of Wat Somanasa Vihāra." Master's thesis, University of Utah, 1984.

Lopez, Donald S., Jr., *Curators of the Buddha: The Study of Buddhism under Colonialism*. Chicago: University of Chicago Press, 1995.

MacDonald, Sharon, and Paul Basu, eds. *Exhibition Experiments*. Oxford: Blackwell, 2007.

Mackenzie, Rory. *New Buddhist Movements in Thailand: Toward an Understanding of Wat Phra Dhammakaya and Santi Asoke*. London: Routledge, 2007.

Maguire, Henry. "Eufrasius and Friends: On Names and Their Absence in Byzantine Art." In James, *Art and Text in Byzantine Culture*, 139–60.

(Phra Acharn) Maha Boowa Nyanasampanno, ed. *The Venerable Phra Acharn Mun Bhuridatta Thera*. Trans. Siri Buddhasukh. 2nd ed. Sakhon Nakhon: Wat Pa Ban That, 1982.

(Phra) Mahawirot Thammawiro. *Wat Ratchapraditsathitmahasimaram Ratchaworowihan*. Bangkok: Rongphim Krom Phaenthi Tahan, 2545 [2002].

Malalasekara, G. P. *The Pali Literature of Ceylon*. London: Royal Asiatic Society, 1928.

Mani Phayomyong. *Prapheni sipsong duan Lanna Thai*. Chiang Mai: Khrongkan Sun Songsamoe Silapawatthanatham, Mahawitthayalai Chiang Mai, 2529 [1986].

Marcus, George. *Ethnography through Thick and Thin*. Princeton: Princeton University Press, 1998.

Marston, John. "Wat Preah Thammalanka and the Legend of Lok Ta Nen." In Chandler and Kent, *People of Virtue*, 85–108.

Matics, K. I. *Introduction to Thai Murals*. Bangkok: White Lotus Press, 1992.

Maud, Jovan. "Sacred Borderlands: A Buddhist Saint, the State, and Transnational Religion in Southern Thailand." Ph.D. diss., Macquarie University, 2007.

Mauss, Marcel. *A General Theory of Magic*. Trans. Robert Brain. 1972. Reprint, New York: Routledge, 2002.

May, Glenn. *Inventing a Hero: The Posthumous Re-Creation of Andres Bonifacio*. Madison: University of Wisconsin Press, 1996.

McClintock, Anne. *Imperial Leather: Race, Gender, and Sexuality in the Colonial Contest*. London: Routledge, 1995.

McDaniel, June. "Interview with a Tantric Kali Priest: Feeding Skulls in the Town of Sacrifice." In White, *Tantra in Practice*, 72–80.

——. *Making Virtuous Daughters and Wives: An Introduction to Women's Brata Rituals in Bengali Folk Religion*. Albany: SUNY Press, 2003.

McDaniel, Justin. "The Curricular Canon in Northern Thailand and Laos." Special issue, *Manusya: Journal of Humanities* 4 (2002): 20–59.

——. "The Emotional Lives of Buddhist Monks in Modern Thai Film." *Journal of Religion and Film* 14, no. 2 (2010). http://www.unomaha.edu/jrf/vol14.no2/McDanielEmtionBuddhist.html.

——. *Gathering Leaves and Lifting Words: Monastic Education in Laos and Thailand*. Seattle: University of Washington Press, 2008.

——. "Invoking the Source: Nissaya Manuscripts and Sermon-Making in Laos and Northern Thailand." Ph.D. diss., Harvard University, 2003.

——. "Liturgies and Cacophonies in Thai Buddhism." *Aséanie* 18 (2007): 119–50.

——. "Paritta and Rakṣā Texts." In *Encyclopedia of Buddhism*, ed. Robert Buswell, 634–35. New York: Macmillan, 2004.

——. "Philosophical Embryology: Buddhist Texts and the Ritual Construction of a Fetus." In *Imagining the Fetus*, ed. Vanessa R. Sasson and Jane Marie Law, 91–106. Oxford: Oxford University Press, 2009.

——. "Reconsidering the 'Museum Effect' in Modern Thai Buddhism and Art." *Rian Thai: International Journal of Thai Studies* 1, no. 1 (2008): 53–70.

——. "Some Notes on the Study of Pāli Grammar in Thailand." In *Embedded Languages: Studies in the Religion Culture, and History of Sri Lanka; Essays in Honor of W. S. Karunatillake*, ed. Carol S. Anderson, Susanne Mrozik, W. M. Wijeyaratne, and R. M. W. Rajapaksha, 69–108. Colombo: Godage Books, 2011.

——. "Transformative History: The *Nihon Ryoiki* and the *Jinakalamalipakaranam*." *Journal of the International Association of Buddhist Studies* 25, no. 1 (2002): 151–207.

——. "Two Bullets in a Ballustrade: How the Burmese Have Been Removed from Northern Thai Buddhist History." *Journal of Burma Studies* 11 (2008): 85–126.

McGill, Forrest, ed. *Emerald Cities: Arts of Siam and Burma, 1775–1950*. San Francisco: Asian Art Museum, 2009.

McGovern, Nathan. "Brahmā Worship in Thailand: The Ērāwan Shrine in Its Social and Historical Context." Master's thesis, University of California, Santa Barbara, 2006.

McGowen, Kaja. "Raw Ingredients and Deposit Boxes in Balinese Sanctuaries: A Congruence of Obsessions." In *What's the Use of Art?* ed. Jan Mrázek and Morgan Pitelka, 238–71. Honolulu: University of Hawai'i Press, 2008.

McHale, Shawn. *Print and Power*. Honolulu: University of Hawai'i Press, 2004.

McMahan, David. *The Making of Buddhist Modernism*. Oxford: Oxford University Press, 2008.

Meister, Kelly. "Burmese Monks in Bangkok: Opening an Abhidhamma School and Creating a Lineage." *Religion Compass* 4 (2009). http://www.blackwell-com pass.com.

Mendelson, E. Michael. *Sangha and State in Burma*. Ithaca: Cornell University Press, 1975.

Mettanando Bhikkhu. "Nationalists Tap a Source of Empty Pride." *Bangkok Post*, February 7, 2007.

Meyer, Birgit, and Peter Pels, eds. *Magic and Modernity: Interfaces of Revelation and Concealment*. Stanford: Stanford University Press, 2003.

Miller, Daniel, ed. *Materiality*. Durham: Duke University Press, 2005.

Mitchell, Donald. *Buddhism: Introducing the Buddhist Experience*. Oxford: Oxford University Press, 2002.

Modak, B. R. *The Ancillary Literature of the Atharva-Veda*. New Delhi: Rashtriya Veda Vidya Pratishthan, 1993.

Moerman, Max. "Passage to Fudaraku: Suicide and Salvation in Premodern Japanese Buddhism." In *The Buddhist Dead*, ed. Jacqueline Stone and Brian Cuevas, 266–96. Honolulu: University of Hawai'i Press, 2007.

Moffat, Abbot Low. *Mongkut: The King of Siam*. Ithaca: Cornell University Press, 1961.

Mollier, Christine. *Buddhism and Taoism Face to Face*. Honolulu: University of Hawai'i Press, 2008.

Moore, Henrietta L., and Todd Sanders, eds. *Magical Interpretations, Material Realities: Modernity, Witchcraft and the Occult in Postcolonial Africa*. London: Routledge, 2001.

Morgan, David. *The Sacred Gaze: Religious Visual Culture in Theory and Practice*. Berkeley: University of California Press, 2005.

Morgan, Teresa. *Popular Morality in the Early Roman Empire*. Cambridge: Cambridge University Press, 2007.

Morris, Robert, and Richard Wiseman. "Recalling Pseudo-psychic Demonstrations." *British Journal of Psychology* 86, no. 1 (1995): 113–25.

Morris, Rosalind. "Crises of the Modern in Northern Thailand." In *Cultural Crisis and Social Memory: Modernity and Identity in Thailand and Laos*, ed. Shigeharu Tanabe and Charles F. Keyes, 68–94. London: Routledge, 2002.

——. *In the Place of Origins: Modernity and Its Mediums in Northern Thailand*. Durham: Duke University Press, 2000.

Mulholland, Jean. *Herbal Medicine in Paediatrics: Translation of a Thai Book of Genesis*. Canberra: Faculty of Asian Studies, Australian National University, 1989.

——. *Medicine, Magic, and Evil Spirits: A Study of a Text on Thai Traditional Paediatrics*. Canberra: Faculty of Asian Studies, Australian National University, 1987.

——. "Thai Traditional Medicine: Ancient Thought and Practice in a Thai Context." *Journal of the Siam Society* 67, no. 2 (1979): 80–115.

Munitthi Bhumipol [Bhumipol Foundation]. *Akson khom lae akson boran thong thin*. Bangkok: Munitthi Bhumipol, 2519 [1976].

Mus, Paul. *India Seen from the East: Indian and Indigenous Cults in Champa*. Clayton, Aus.: Center for Southeast Asian Studies, Monash University, 1975.

*The Museum of Jurassic Technology: Primi Decem Anni Jubilee Catalogue*. Los Angeles: Society for the Diffusion of Useful Information, n.d.

Myers, Fred, ed. *The Empire of Things: Regimes of Value and Material Culture*. Santa Fe: School of American Research Press, 2001.

(Phra Khru Khana) Namasamanachan (Bi) and Luang Anamsanghakan [Nguyen Quang Thanh]. *Tamra phithi Phra Yuan*. Bangkok: Rongphim Sobhanaphiphatthanakon, 2474 [1931].

(Somdet Phra Sangharat) Ñāṇasaṃvara (Nanasangwon). *Khrop 200 pi Phrabat Somdet Phrapomenthon Mahamakut Phra Chom Klao Chao Yu Hua*. Bangkok: Mahamakut University Press, 2547 [2004].

——. *Prawat Gāthā Chinapanchon*. Bangkok: Mahamakut University Press, 2529 [1986].

(Somdet Phra Sangharat) Ñāṇasaṃvara, with assistance from Phra Sugandha (Dr. Anil Sakya). *Khrop 200 pi Phra Bat Somdet Phra Poromenathon Mahamakut Phra Chom Klao Chao Yu Hua*. Bangkok: Surawat, 2547 [2004].

Narada Maha Thera and Kassapa Thera, eds. *The Mirror of the Dhamma*. 2nd ed. Colombo: Gomes Trust, May 2518 [1975].

Natathan Manirat. *Lek yan: Phaen phang an saksit*. Bangkok: Sathaban Pipithanphan kan rian ru haeng Chat, 2553 [2010].

Needham, Rodney. *Belief, Language, and Experience*. Chicago: University of Chicago Press, 1972.

Ness, Sally Ann. "Bali, the Camera, and Dance: Performance Studies and the Lost Legacy of the Mead/Bateson Collaboration." *Journal of Asian Studies* 67, no. 4 (2008): 1251–76.

Neusner, Jacob, Ernest Frerichs, Paul Virgil McCracken Flesher, eds. *Religion, Science, and Magic: In Concert and in Conflict*. New York: Oxford University Press, 1989.

Newell, Catherine. "Monks, Meditation and Missing Links: Continuity, 'Orthodoxy' and the Vijjā Dhammakāya in Thai Buddhism." Ph.D. diss., School of Oriental and African Studies, 2008.

Nidda Hongwiwat. *Wessandon chadok: Thosachadok kap chitakam faphanang*. Bangkok: Saengdaet Phuandek, 2549 [2006].

Nidhi Aeusrivongse. "Phuttha wibat." In *Kan patirup Phra Phuttha Satsana nai prathet Thai*, ed. Nidhi Aeusrivongse and Pramuan Phengchan, 1–28. Bangkok: Kongthun Raktham, 2542 [1999].

Nit Ratanasanya et al. "Wat Khongkaram." *ASA: Journal of the Association of Siamese Architects* 3, no. 1 (2517 [1974]): 19–53.

No Na Paknam. *Mural Paintings of Thailand Series: Wat Khongkaram*. Bangkok: Muang Boran, 2538 [1995].

——. *Mural Paintings of Thailand Series: Wat Pathumwanaram*. Bangkok: Muang Boran, 2539 [1996].

——. *Mural Paintings of Thailand Series: Wat Sommanat Wihan*. Bangkok: Muang Boran, 2538 [1995].

——. *Siamsilapa chitakam lae sathupchedi*. Bangkok: Muang Boran, 2538 [1995].

Nora, Pierre. "Between Memory and History: Les Lieux de Mémoire." *Representations* 26 (1989): 7–25.

Norman, H. C. "Buddhist Legends of Asoka and His Times." *Journal of the Asiatic Society of Bengal* 6 (1910): 57–72.

Norman, K. R. "Pāli Literature." In *A History of Indian Literature*, vol. 7.2, ed. Jan Gonda. Wiesbaden: Harrassowitz, 1983.

Novetzke, Christian Lee. *Religion and Public Memory: A Cultural History of Saint Namdev in India*. New York: Columbia University Press, 2008.

Nucharee Rakrun Khultida Samabuddhi. "Talismans Draw Huge Crowd to Cremation." *Bangkok Post*, February 23, 2007.

Nussbaum, Martha. *Love's Knowledge: Essays on Philosophy and Literature*. Oxford: Oxford University Press, 1988.

——. "Narrative Emotions: Beckett's Genealogy of Love," *Ethics* 98, no. 2 (1988): 225–54.

——. *The Upheavals of Thought: The Intelligence of Emotions*. Cambridge: Cambridge University Press, 2003.

Obeyesekere, Gananath. "The Great Tradition and the Little in the Perspective of Sinhala Buddhism." *Journal of Asian Studies* 22 (1963): 139–53.

O'Connor, Richard. "Interpreting Thai Religious Change: Temples, Sangha Reform and Social Change." *Journal of Southeast Asian Studies* 24, no. 2 (1993): 330–39.

Ohnuma, Reiko. *Head, Eyes, Flesh, and Blood: Giving Away the Body in Indian Buddhist Literature*. New York: Columbia University Press, 2007.

Okha Buri. *Chat bhumi (lap) Somdet To prisana chak bhap chitakam*. Bangkok: Smart Books, 2551 [2008].

Olson, Grant. "Thai Cremation Volumes: A Brief History of a Unique Genre of Literature." *Asian Folklore Studies* 51 (1992): 279–94.

Orsi, Robert. *Between Heaven and Earth: The Religious Worlds People Make and the Scholars Who Study Them*. Princeton: Princeton University Press, 2006.

——. *Gods of the City: Religion and the American Urban Landscape*. Bloomington: Indiana University Press, 1999.

Osborne, Robin, and Jeremy Tanner, eds. *Art's Agency and Art History*. Oxford: Blackwell, 2007.

Padoux, André. "What Do We Mean by Tantrism?" In *The Roots of Tantra*, ed. Katherine Anne Harper and Robert L. Brown, 17–24. Albany: SUNY Press, 2002.

(Phra Khru) Panthitanuwat. *Suat mon plae*. Bangkok, 2480 [1937].

Parinya Uthichalanon. *Khu meu prakop kanchai ya*. Bangkok: Parinya Uthichalanon, n.d.

Paritta Chalermpow Koanantakool. "Contextualizing Objects in Monastery Museums in Thailand." In *Buddhist Legacies in Mainland Southeast Asia*, ed. François Lagirarde and Paritta Chalermpow Koanantakool, 149–67. Bangkok: Princess Maha Chakri Sirindhorn Anthropology Centre/École française d'Extrême-Orient, 2006.

Parnwell, Michael, and Martin Seeger. "The Relocalization of Buddhism in Thailand." *Journal of Buddhist Ethics* 15 (2008): 79–176.

Pasuk Phongphaichit and Chris Baker. *Thailand: Economy and Politics*. Kuala Lumpur: Oxford University Press, 1995.

Pattana Kitiarsa. "Beyond Syncreticism: Hybridization of Popular Religion in Contemporary Thailand." *Journal of Southeast Asian Studies* 36, no. 3 (2005): 461–87.

——. "Beyond the Weberian Trails: An Essay on the Anthropology of Southeast Asian Buddhism." *Religion Compass* 4 (2009). Available online at http://www.blackwell-compass.com/subject/religion/section_home?page=2&volume=all & section=reco-buddhism.

——. "Buddha Phanit: Revisiting Thailand's Prosperity Religion and Occult Economy." Unpublished paper, cited with the author's permission.

——. "Faiths and Films Countering the Crisis of Thai Buddhism from Below." *Asian Journal for Social Science* 34, no. 2 (2006): 264–90.

——. "*Farang* as Siamese Occidentalism." Asia Research Institute Working Paper Series 49, National University of Singapore, September 2005. Available online at http://www.ari.nus.edu.sg/publication_details.asp?pubtypeid=WP&pubid=513.

Pattaratorn Chirapravati. "Living the Siamese Life: Culture, Religion, and Art." In McGill, *Emerald Cities*, 27–46.

——. *Votive Tablets in Thailand: Origin, Styles, and Uses*. Oxford: Oxford University Press, 1999.

Payne, Richard. *How Much Is Enough? Buddhism, Consumerism, and the Human Environment*. Cambridge, Mass.: Wisdom Books, 2010.

Peleggi, Maurizio. *Lords of Things: The Fashioning of the Siamese Monarchy's Modern Image*. Honolulu: University of Hawai'i Press, 2002.

——. *The Politics of Ruin and the Business of Nostalgia*. Bangkok: White Lotus Press, 2002.

——. *Thailand: The Worldly Kingdom*. Bangkok: Reaktion Books, 2007.

Perera, Ariyapala. *Buddhist Paritta Chanting Ritual*. Colombo: Buddhist Cultural Center, 2000.

(Phra) Phaisan Visalo. *Phuttha sasana Thai nai anakot: Naeonom lae thang ook chak wikrit*. Bangkok: Sotsri-Saritwong Foundation, 2003.

Phawat Bunnag. *Sadet praphaston R.S. 125*. Bangkok: Amarin, 2537 [1994].

Phillips, Ruth. "Exhibiting Africa After Modernism." In Pollock and Zemans, *Museums After Modernism*, 80–103.

——. *Trading Identities: The Souvenir in Native North American Art from the Northeast*. Seattle: University of Washington Press, 1998.

Phoensri Duk, Phaitun Sinlarat, Piyanat Punnat, and Waraphon Chuachaisak. *Watthanatham pheun ban khati khwam cheua*. Bangkok: Chulalongkorn University Press, 2536 [1993].

Pho Sawan. *Prawat lae withi chai Phra Gāthā Chinabanchon*. Bangkok: Ban Monggon, 2543 [2000].

*Phra ratchapithi sipsong duan*. Bangkok: Fine Arts Department, 2516 [1973].

Pichaya Svasti. "Reflections of Different Cultures." *Bangkok Post,* September 13, 2009. http://www.bangkokpost.com/travel/travelscoop/23779/reflections -of -different-cultures.

Piker, Steven. "The Problem of Consistency in Thai Religion." *Journal for the Scientific Study of Religion* 11, no. 3 (1972): 211–29.

Pitelka, Morgan, and Jan Mrázek, eds. *What's the Use of Art? Asian Visual and Material Culture in Context.* Honolulu: University of Hawai'i Press, 2008.

(Somdet Phra) Pituccha Chao Sukhumalamarasri. *Katha blae ben khlong.* Bangkok: Rongphim Tha Phra Chan, 2475 [1932].

Piyasilo [Piya Tan Beng Sin], ed. *The Puja Book.* Vol. 1. Petaling Jaya: Friends of Buddhism Malaysia, 1990.

(Phra Khru) Platsomkhit Siriwatthano. *Khong di Wat Rakhang.* Bangkok: Wat Rakhang, 2541 [1998].

Pollock, Griselda, and Joyce Zemans, eds. *Museums After Modernism: Strategies of Engagement.* Oxford: Blackwell, 2007.

Pomarin Charuwon. "Suat Phra Malai: Botbat khong khatikam lang khwam tai to wannakam lae sangkhom." In *Phithikam tamnan nithan phleng: Botbat khong khatichon kap sangkhom thai,* ed. Sukanya Succhaya, 113–62. Bangkok: Chulalongkorn University Press, 2548 [2005].

Pottier, Richard. *Yû dî mî hèng: Essai sur les pratiques thérapeutiques lao.* Paris: École française d'Extrême-Orient, 2007.

Pram Sounsamut. "Buddha Bless and Dharma Products: A New Trend of Teaching Dharma in Thailand." *Rian Thai* 1, no. 1 (2008): 107–28.

Prani Nimsamoe. "Chitakam ruam samai khong Thai." In *Silapawatthanatham Thai lem thi 6,* ed. Decho Suananon, 13–38. Bangkok: Khrom Silapakon, 2525 [1982].

Prapod Assavavirulhakarn and Peter Skilling. "Tripitaka in Practice in the Fourth and Fifth Reigns." Special issue, *Manusya: Journal of Humanities* 4 (2002): 60–72.

Prathip Phayakkhaphon. *Tamra ya mo Thai.* Bangkok: Chong Heng, 2476 [1933]. Reprint, Bangkok: Bukkhonanoe Printing, 2008].

*Prawat Phraprathan 28 Phra Ong Wat Apsonsawanworawihan.* Bangkok: Wat Apsonsawanworawihan, n.d.

Pricha Iamtham, ed. *Prawat Somdet Phra Phutthachan To Phrohmarangsi.* Bangkok: Hong Samut Haeng Chat, 2542 [1999].

Pricha Iamtham. *Prawat Somdet Phra Phutthachan To Phrohmarangsri.* Bangkok: Maradok Thai, 2547 [2004].

Prothero, Stephen. *The White Buddhist: The Asian Odyssey of Henry Steel Olcott.* Bloomington: Indiana University Press, 1996.

Radin, Paul. *Crashing Thunder: The Autobiography of an American Indian.* Ann Arbor: University of Michigan Press, 1999.

Raendchen, Oliver, and Jana Raendchen, eds. *"Baan-müang*: Administration and Ritual." Special issue, *Tai Culture* 3, no. 2 (1998).

(Phra) Rajanirodharangsee [Venerable Ajahn Tate]. *The Autobiography of a Forest Monk*. Trans. Phra Ariyeseko. Nongkhai: Wat Hin Mak Peng, 1993.

Rambelli, Fabio. *Buddhist Materiality: A Cultural History of Objects in Japanese Buddhism*. Stanford: Stanford University Press, 2008.

(Phra) Ratcharatanaphon, Suthip Chirathiwat, Chotichai Sirikannukun, eds. *Luang Phu To*. Bangkok: Wat Indrawihan, 2545 [2002].

Rawson, Jessica. "The Agency of, and the Agency for the Wanli Emperor." In Osborne and Tanner, *Art's Agency*, 95–114.

Ram Watcharapradit, ed. *Phap Phra Chanaloet kan prakuat ngan nithatsakan prakuat kan anurak phrabucha phrakhruang lae rian khanachan khrang yingyai*. Phitsanulok: Department of History, Naresuan University, 2547 [2004].

Ray, Reginald. *Buddhist Saints in India*. Oxford: Oxford University Press, 1999.

Reynolds, Craig. "The Buddhist Monkhood in Nineteenth Century Thailand." Ph.D. diss., Cornell University, 1973.

——. *Seditious Histories: Contesting Thai and Southeast Asian Pasts*. Seattle: University of Washington Press, 2006.

Rhys Davids, T. W., ed. *The Yogāvacara's Manual of Indian Mysticism as Practiced by Buddhists*. London: Pali Text Society, 1896.

Ricoeur, Paul. *The Symbolism of Evil*. Trans. Emerson Buchanan. New York: Harper & Row, 1967.

Ringis, Rita. *Thai Temples and Temple Murals*. Oxford: Oxford University Press, 1990.

Robinson, Richard, Willard Johnson, Thanissaro Bhikkhu, eds. *Buddhist Religions: A Historical Introduction*. London: Wadsworth, 2005.

Robson, Stuart, and Prateep Changchit, "The Cave Scene or Bussaba Consults the Candle." *Bijdragen tot de Taal-, Land- en Volkenkunde* 155, no. 4 (1999): 579–95.

Rod-ari, Melody. "Visualizing Merit: An Art Historical Study of the Emerald Buddha and Wat Phra Kaew." Ph.D. diss., University of California, Los Angeles, 2010.

Roudinesco, Elisabeth. "The Mirror Stage: An Obliterated Archive." In *The Cambridge Companion to Lacan*, ed. Jean-Michel Rabaté. Cambridge: Cambridge University Press, 2003.

*Ruam lang ruang khadi lok khadi tham*. Bangkok: Khalet Thai, 2528 [1985].

Ruth, Richard. "Committed to the Fire: Thailand's Volunteer Soldiers in the Vietnam War, 1967–1972." Ph.D. diss., Cornell University, 2007.

Rutnin, Mattani Mojdara. *Dance, Drama, and Theatre in Thailand: The Process of Development and Modernization*. Chiang Mai: Silkworm Books, 1996.

Sahlins, Marshall. *Islands of History*. Chicago: University of Chicago Press, 1985.

Saiban Puriwanchana. *Tamnan bracham thin rim Mae Nam*. Bangkok: Chulalongkorn University Press, 2552 [2009].

Saichon Sattayanurak. *Phuttha sasana kap naeokit thang kanmuang nai racha samai Phrabat Somdet Phraphuttha Yotfa Chulalok (2325–2352)*. Bangkok: Samnakphim Matichon, 2546 [2003].

Salguero, C. Pierce. *Traditional Thai Medicine: Buddhism, Animism, Ayurveda*. Bangkok: Hohm Press, 2007.

Samuel, Geoffrey. *The Origins of Yoga and Tantra: Indic Religions to the Thirteenth Century*. Cambridge: Cambridge University Press, 2008.

Sanderson, Alexis. "The Śaiva Religion Among the Khmers." *Bulletin de l'École française d'Extrême-Orient* 90-91 (2003): 349–462.

Sanitsuda Ekachai. *Keeping the Faith: Thai Buddhism at the Crossroads*. Bangkok: Post Books, 2001.

——. "Thailand's Gay Past." *Bangkok Post*, February 23, 2008.

Santikaro Bhikkhu. "Buddhadasa Bhikkhu: Life and Society through the Natural Eyes of Voidness." In *Buddhist Liberation Movements*, ed. Sallie King and Christopher Queen, 147–89. Albany: SUNY Press, 1996.

Santi Phakdikham. "Chitakam wanakhadi Thai nai phra ubosot Wat Ratchaburana." *Muang boran* 33, no. 3 (2550 [2007]): 78–92.

*Sarakhadi prawat Somdet Phra Phutthachan To Phrohmarangsi Wat Rakhangghositaramworamahawihan*. VCD. Directed by Kaeo Laithong. Bangkok: Dream Vision, 2003.

Saran Thongpan. "Siam nai khwam song cham." *Muang boran* 28, no. 3 (2545 [2002]): 14–21.

*Saranukhrom watthanatham Thai*. Vols. 1–63. Bangkok: Thai Wanich Bank, 1999–2002.

Sathiankoset. *Kan tai*. Bangkok: Siam Press, 2539 [1996].

——. *Prapheni kiao kap chiwit*. Bangkok: Siam Printing, 2505 [1962].

Sawan Tangtrongsithikun. *Krung Thep mai mi phiphithaphan Krung Thep*. Bangkok: Silapawatthanatham, 2545 [2002].

Schalk, Peter. *Der Paritta-Dienst in Ceylon*. Lund: Bröderna Ekstrands Tryckeri, 1973.

Schober, Julianne. "Buddhist Visions of Moral Authority and Modernity in Burma." In *Burma at the Turn of the Twenty-first Century*, ed. Monica Skidmore. Honolulu: University of Hawai'i Press, 2002.

Schopen, Gregory. *Bones, Stones and Buddhist Monks: Collected Papers on the Archaeology, Epigraphy and Texts of Monastic Buddhism in India*. Honolulu: University of Hawai'i Press, 1997.

——. *Buddhist Monks and Business Matters: Still More Papers on Monastic Buddhism in India*. Honolulu: University of Hawai'i Press, 2004.

Schweisguth, Pierre. *Étude sur la littérature siamoise*. Paris: Imprimerie Nationale, 1951.

Scott, Rachelle. *Nirvana for Sale? Buddhism, Wealth, and the Dhammakāya Temple in Contemporary Thailand*. Albany: SUNY Press, 2009.

Seeger, Martin. "The Changing Roles of Thai Buddhist Women: Obscuring Identities and Increasing Charisma." *Religion Compass* 3, no. 5 (2009): 806–22.

Sharf, Robert. *Living Images: Japanese Buddhist Icons in Context*. Stanford: Stanford University Press, 2002.

Silber, Ilana Friedrich. "Pragmatic Sociology as Cultural Sociology." *European Journal of Social Theory* 6, no. 4 (2003): 427–49.

Silpa Bhirasri. *Comments and Articles on Art*. Bangkok: National Association of Plastic Arts of Thailand, 1963.

——. *The Origin and Evolution of Thai Murals*. Bangkok: Fine Arts Department, 1959.

Skemer, Don. *Binding Words: Textual Amulets in the Middle Ages*. State College: State University of Pennsylvania Press, 2006.

Skilling, Peter. "Compassion, Power, Success: Random Remarks on Siamese Buddhist Liturgy." Unpublished paper, cited with the author's permission.

——. "Kings, Sangha, Brahmans: Ideology, Ritual, and Power in Premodern Siam." In Harris, *Buddhism, Power and Political Order*, 182–215.

——. "The Place of South-East Asia in Buddhist Studies." In *Buddhism and Buddhist Literature of South-East Asia: Selected Papers*, ed. Claudio Cicuzza. Materials for the Study of the Tripitaka, vol. 5. Bangkok: Fragile Palm Leaves Foundation/Lumbini: Lumbini International Research Institute, 2009: 46–68.

——. "The Rakṣa Literature of the Śrāvakayāna." *Journal of the Pali Text Society* 16 (1992): 109–82.

——. "The Sambuddhe Verses and Later Theravādin Buddhology." *Journal of the Pali Text Society* 22 (1996): 151–83.

——. "Similar Yet Different: Buddhism in Siam and Burma in the Nineteenth Century." In McGill, *Emerald Cities*, 47–74.

——. "Ubiquitous and Elusive: In Quest of Theravāda." Talk delivered at the Exploring Theravāda Studies Conference, Asia Research Institute, National University of Singapore, 2004. Cited with the author's permission.

Smith, Bardwell, ed. *Religion and Legitimation of Power in Thailand, Laos, and Burma*. Chambersburg, Penn.: Anima Books, 1978.

Smith, D. E. *Religion and Politics in Burma*. Princeton: Princeton University Press, 1965.

(Phra) Sobhanathamwong. *Khonkhwa ha ma dai ekasan somkhan khong Wat Indrawihan*. Hua Hin: Hua Hin San, 2544 [2001].

——. *Wat Indrawihan kap chiwaprawat Somdet Phra Phutthachan To Phrohmarangsi nai ngan chitakam faphanang ubasot*. Bangkok: Amarin, 2537 [1994].

Somboon Suksamran. *Buddhism and Politics in Thailand: A Study of Socio-Political Change and Political Activism of the Thai Sangha*. Singapore: Institute of Southeast Asian Studies, 1982.

Somdet Phra Phutthachan To Phrahmarangsi. VCD. Bangkok: S.T. Video, n.d.

Sompong Duangsawai. *Lamphu*. Bangkok: Chaloenwithyakan, 2546 [2003].

——. *Phetbanglamphu*. Bangkok: Chaloenwithyakan, 2545 [2002].

Somsak Sakuntanat, ed. *Takrut khlang chom khlang wet*. Bangkok: Ban Khru, 2550 [2007].

So Phlainoi. *Samnakphim samai raek*. Bangkok: Kho Nangseu, 2548 [2005].

Soraphon Sophitkun. *Sudyot rian phrakhruang lem thi 1*. Bangkok: Matichon, 2540 [1997].

——. *Sudyot rian phrakhruang lem thi 2*. Bangkok: Matichon Press, 2544 [2001].

——. "Tamnan nangsue phrakhruang chak adit thung pacchuban." *Sinlapawatthanatham* 15, no. 3 (1994): 90–92.

Sorat Hongladarom. *Phra Phaisachayakhuru waithuraya praphatthakhatasut [Bhaiṣajyaguru vaidūryaprabharājāya sūtra]*. Bangkok: Munitthi Phandara, 2548 [2005].

Southwold, Martin. "True Buddhism and Village Buddhism in Sri Lanka." In *Religious Organization and Religious Experience*, ed. J. Davis, 137–50. London: Academic Press, 1982.

Spiro, Melford. *Buddhism and Society*. Berkeley: University of California Press, 1975.

——. *Buddhist Supernaturalism*. Philadelphia: Institute for the Study of Human Issues, 1978.

Sri Dhammananda, K. *Daily Buddhist Devotions*. 2nd ed. Kuala Lumpur: Buddhist Missionary Society, 1993. Reprint, Taipei: Corporate Body of the Buddha Educational Foundation, 1996.

Srisakra Vallibhotama. "Phra Khruang (Rang): Phutthabucha rue phutthaphanit." *Silapawatthanatham* 15, no. 3 (1994): 77–89.

(Phra) Sriwachiraphon. *Prawat Phra Boromathatnakonchum Wat Boromathat Phra Aram Luang*. Kampaengphet: Wat Boromathat, 2548 [2005].

Stadler, Felix. "Beyond Constructivism: Towards a Realistic Realism; A Review of Bruno Latour's *Pandora's Hope*." *The Information Society* 16, no. 3 (2000). Available at http://felix.openflows.com/html/pandora.html.

Standaert, Nicholas. *The Interweaving of Rituals: Funerals in the Cultural Exchange between China and Europe*. Seattle: University of Washington Press, 2008.

Stengs, Irene. *Worshipping the Great Moderniser: King Chulalongkorn, Patron Saint of the Thai Middle Class*. Singapore: National University of Singapore Press, 2009.

Stratton, Carol. *Buddhist Sculpture of Northern Thailand*. Chicago: Serindia, 2004.

Strickmann, Michel. *Chinese Magical Medicine*. Ed. Bernard Faure. Stanford: Stanford University Press, 2002.

Strong, John. *The Experience of Buddhism*. London: Wadsworth, 1994.

Stuart-Fox, Martin. *Buddhist Kingdom, Marxist State: The Making of Modern Laos*. Bangkok: White Lotus Press, 1996.

Styers, Randall. *Making Magic: Religion, Magic, and Science in the Modern World*. Oxford: Oxford University Press, 2004.

*Suat mon mueang nuea chabap sombun.* Chiang Mai: Thanathong, 2537 [1994].

Subhatra Bhumiprabhas. "Old Ceremonies to Be Revived as Giant Swing Returns History Relived." *Nation,* September 10, 2007.

Suchao Ploichum. *Phra Kiatkhun Somdet Phra Ariyawongyan Somdet Phra Sangharat (Sri) Wat Rakhang Khositaram.* Bangkok: Mahamakut Monastic University Press, 2541 [1998].

——. *Phra Kiatkhun Somdet Phra Ariyawongyan Somdet Phra Sangharat (Suk).* Bangkok: Mahamakut Rachawithayalai, 2541 [1998].

——. *Prawat Gāthā Chinabanchon.* Bangkok: Mahamakut University Press, 2543 [2000].

Suchip Bunnanuphap. *Phra Traipidok Chabap samrap Prachachon.* Bangkok, Mahamakut University Press, 1996.

(Phra) Suddhidhammaransi Gambhīramedhācariya [Lee Dhammadaro]. *The Autobiography of Phra Ajaan Lee.* Trans. Thanissaro Bhikkhu [Geoffrey DeGraff]. N.p.: Wave Audio-Visual Exchange, 1994.

(Phra) Sugandha Dhammasakiyo [Anil Sakya]. *Kan seuksa Phraphutthasasana nai Prathet Thai: Phrabat Somdet Phrachom Klao Chao Yu Hua kap Khana Thammayut.* Bangkok: Mahamakut University Press, 2548 [2005].

——. *Suat Mon.* Bangkok: Mahamakut University Press, 2547 [2004].

Sulak Sivaraksa. "The Crisis of Siamese Identity." In *National Identity and Its Defenders: Thailand, 1939–1989,* ed. Craig J. Reynolds, 41–58. Victoria, Aus.: Aristoc Press, 1991.

——. *Phut kap sai nai sangkhom Thai.* Bangkok: Commission on Religion for Development and Santi Pracha Dhamma Institute, 1995.

——. *Siam in Crisis.* Bangkok: Komol Keemthong Foundation, 1980.

——. "Siam versus the West." In Sulak Sivaraksa, *Siam in Crisis,* 196–202. Originally published in *Solidarity* (Manila) 6, no. 4 (April 1970).

(Phraya) Sunthornphiphit. *Itthipatihan phrakhruangrang khongkhlang.* Bangkok: Silapabannakhan, 2515 [1972].

Surachai Chongchitngam. "Kham huang mahasamut kap Khrua In Khong: Meua chon chan nam Syam chai withyasat ben khreuang meu nai kan yang ru khwam ben ching khong Phutthasasana." *Silapawatthanatham* 34, no. 3 (2008): 44–70.

Sutthiphong Tontyaphisalasut. *Pramuan dhamma nai Phra Traipidok.* Bangkok: Rong Phim Kan Sasana, n.d.

Suwit Koetphongbunchot. "Anuphap Krua To: Sutyot saksit haeng krung Ratanakosin." *Saksit* 9, no. 217 (January 16, 2535 [1992]): 1–39.

Swearer, Donald. *Becoming the Buddha.* Princeton: Princeton University Press, 2004.

Swidler, Ann. "Culture in Action: Symbols and Strategies." *American Sociological Review* 51 (1986): 273–86.

Tambiah, Stanley. "At the Confluence of Anthropology, History, and Indology." *Contributions to Indian Sociology* 21 (1987): 187–216.

——. *Buddhism Betrayed: Religion, Politics, and Violence in Sri Lanka*. Chicago: University of Chicago Press, 1992.

——. *Buddhism and the Spirit Cults in North-east Thailand*. Cambridge: Cambridge University Press, 1970.

——. *The Buddhist Saints of the Forest and the Cult of Amulets: A Study in Charisma, Hagiography, Sectarianism, and Millennial Buddhism*. Cambridge: Cambridge University Press, 1984.

——. "The Magic Power of Words." *Man* 3, no. 2 (1968): 175–208.

——. *World Conqueror and World Renouncer: A Study of Buddhism and Polity in Thailand against a Historical Background*. Cambridge: Cambridge University Press, 1976.

*Tamra kanphaet Thai doem phaetsongkhro*. Bangkok: Rongphim Si Thai, 2541 [1998].

Tannenbaum, Nicola. *Who Can Compete Against the World? Power-Protection and Buddhism in Shan Worldview*. Ann Arbor: Association of Asian Studies, 1996.

*Tawipop*. DVD. Directed by A. Chalermthai. Bangkok: Tai Entertainment, 2004.

Taylor, J. L. *Forest Monks and the Nation-State: An Anthropological and Historical Study in Northeastern Thailand*. Singapore: Institute of Southeast Asian Studies, 1993.

——. "(Post-) Modernity, Remaking Tradition and the Hybridisation of Thai Buddhism." *Anthropological Forum* 9, no. 2 (1999): 163–87.

Taylor, Philip. *Goddess on the Rise: Pilgrimage and Popular Religion in Vietnam*. Honolulu: University of Hawai'i Press, 2004.

Teiser, Stephen. *Reinventing the Wheel: Paintings of Rebirth in Medieval Buddhist Temples*. Seattle: University of Washington Press, 2007.

——. *The Scripture on the Ten Kings and the Making of Purgatory in Medieval Chinese Buddhism*. Honolulu: University of Hawai'i Press, 1996.

Terwiel, Bas Jarend. "A Model for the Study of Thai Buddhism." *Journal of Asian Studies* 35, no. 3 (1976): 391–403.

——. *Monks and Magic: An Analysis of Religious Ceremonies in Thailand*. London: Curzon, 1975.

——. *Thailand's Political History*. Bangkok: River Books, 2006.

Textor, Robert. "An Inventory of Non-Buddhist Supernatural Objects in a Central Thai Village." Ph.D. dissertation. Cornell University, 1960.

Tha Prian. *Mo Chiwok Komanphat: Mo luang pracham Rachasamnakratchakhru*. Bangkok: Duang Kaeo, n.d.

Thak Chaloemtiarana. "Making New Space in the Thai Literary Canon." *Journal of Southeast Asian Studies* 40 (2009): 87–110.

(Phra) Thammasaro Bhikkhu. *Nuang duai Phrabat Somdet Phra Chom Klao*. Bangkok: Wat Boworniwet, 2511 [1967].

(Phra Maha) Thawon Chittathaoro. *Srapathum*. Bangkok: Wat Srapathum, n.d.

Thep Sarikabut. *Tamnan phrawet phisadan*. Bangkok: Silapabannakhan, 2537 [1994]. Reprint, 2547 [2004].

Thep Sunthasarathun. *Prawat Luang Pho Ban Laem*. Bangkok: Prayuruang, n.d.

(Maha Ammattri Phraya) Thipkosa. *Prawat Somdet Phra Phutthachan To Phrohmarangsi*. 1930. Reprint, Bangkok: Wat Thepsirintharawat, 2528 [1985].

Thongchai Winichakul. "The Quest for 'Siwilai': A Geographical Discourse of Civilizational Thinking in Late 19th and Early 20th Century Siam." *Journal of Asian Studies* 59, no. 3 (August 2000): 528–49.

——. *Siam Mapped: A History of the Geo-Body of a Nation*. Honolulu: University of Hawai'i Press, 1994.

Thotsaphon Changphanitkun. *Katha Mahasetthi: Suat laeo ruai*. Bangkok: Khom Ma, 2549 [2006].

——. *Kruang rang Mahasetthi: Pucha laeo ruai*. Bangkok: Khom Ma, 2549 [2006].

——. *Phra Phi Kanet: Brasopkan lae pathihari*. Bangkok: Comma Books, 2550 [2007].

Tian, Xiaofei. *Tao Yuanming and Manuscript Culture: The Record of a Dusty Table*. Seattle: University of Washington Press, 2005.

Todorov, Tzvetan. *The Fantastic: A Structural Approach to a Literary Genre*. Trans. Richard Howard. Ithaca: Cornell University Press, 1975.

Trisin Bunkhachon. *Klon suat phak klang*. Bangkok: Chulalongkorn University Press, 2547 [2004].

Triyampawai [pseud.]. *Pari-atthathibai haeng phrakhruang lem thi 1: Phra somdet Phutthachan*. Bangkok: Saha Upakorn Kanphim, 2492 [1954].

——. *Pari-atthathibai haeng phrakhruang lem thi 2: Phra rot lae phrakhruang sakun lamphun*. Bangkok: Khlang Withaya, 2498 [1960].

——. *Pari-atthathibai haeng phrakhruang lem thi 3: Phra nang phraya lae phrakhruang samkhan phitsanulok*. Bangkok: Phrae Withaya, 2508 [1965].

Tunya Supanich. "Commercialising Religious Art." *Bangkok Post*, August 5, 2007.

Turton, Andrew. "Invulnerability and Local Knowledge." In *Thai Constructions of Knowledge*, ed. Manas Chitakasem and Andrew Turton, 155–82. London: School of Oriental and African Studies, 1991.

Tweed, Thomas. *Our Lady of the Exile: Diasporic Religion at a Cuban Catholic Shrine in Miami*. Oxford: Oxford University Press, 2002.

(Phaya) Upakit Silapasan. *Lak Phasa Thai*. 10th ed. Bangkok: Watthana Panich, 2544 [2001].

Urban, Hugh. "The Power of the Impure: Transgression, Violence and Secrecy in Bengali Sakta Tantra and Modern Western Magic." *Numen* 50 (2003): 269–308.

Vanchai Tan. *The Erawan Museum: Convergence of Dreams, Faith, and Gratitude*. Bangkok: Viriya Business, 2006.

Vedeha Thera. *Madhurasavāhinī: A Stream of Sweet Sentiments.* Transcribed into Roman script from the Sinhalese by Sharada Gamdhi. Delhi: Parimal, 1988.

Vella, Walter. *Siam under Rama III.* New York: J. J. Augustin and the Association of Asian Studies, 1957.

Ver Eecke, Jacqueline, ed. and trans. *Le dasavatthuppakarana.* Paris: École française d'Extrême-Orient, 1976.

Vickery, Michael. "The Khmer Inscriptions of Tenasserim: A Reinterpretation." *Journal of the Siam Society* 61, no. 1 (1973): 51–70.

(Phra) Wachiramethi. *Thamma dap ron.* Bangkok: Amarin, 2550 [2007].

——. *Thamma lap sabai.* Bangkok: Amarin, 2550 [2007].

——. *Thamma tit pik.* Bangkok: Amarin, 2550 [2007].

(Phra) W. Wachiramethi and Pornthip Rochanasunan. *Thuk krathop thamma krathian.* Bangkok: Amarin, 2550 [2007].

(Somdet Phra Mahasamanachao Krom Phraya) Wachirayanwororot. *Akson Ariyaka.* Bangkok: Mahamakut Withayalai, 2501 [1958].

——. *Katha chadok lae baep akson Ariyaka.* Bangkok: Wat Boworniwetwihan, 2514 [1971].

Wang, Eugene. *Shaping the Lotus Sutra: Buddhist Visual Culture in Medieval China.* Seattle: University of Washington Press, 2005.

Warner, Marina. *Phantasmagoria: Spirit Visions, Metaphors, and Media.* Oxford: Oxford University Press, 2006.

Wassana Nanuam. *Lap luang prang pak pisadan: Saiyasat patiwat awitchatipatai.* Bangkok: Bangkok Post Publishing, 2552 [2009].

Wassayos Ngamkham. "Fake Talismans Upset Family of Late Officer." *Bangkok Post*, February 23, 2006.

*Wat Pathumwanaram Rachaworawihan: Praditthan Phra Phuttharup saksit chak fang Lao 3 ong Phra Soem Phra Saen Phra Sai.* Bangkok: Wat Pathumwanaram Rachaworawihan, 2548 [2005].

Weiner, Annette. *Inalienable Objects: The Paradox of Keeping-While-Giving.* Berkeley: University of California Press, 1992.

Wells, Kenneth. *Thai Buddhism: Its Rites and Activities.* Bangkok: Suriyabun, 1974.

Wenk, Klaus. *Thailändische Miniaturmalereien: Nach einer Handschrift der indischen Kunstabteilung der Staatlichen Museen Berlin.* Wiesbaden: Steiner, 1965.

White, David Gordon, ed. *Tantra in Practice.* Princeton: Princeton University Press, 2000.

White, Erick. "The Cultural Politics of the Supernatural in Theravada Buddhist Thailand." *Anthropological Forum* 13, no. 2 (2003): 205–12.

——. "Fraudulent and Dangerous Popular Religiosity in the Public Sphere: Campaigns to Prohibit, Reform, and Demystify Thai Spirit Mediums." In *Spirited Politics: Religion and Public Life in Contemporary Southeast Asia,* ed. Andrew

C. Willford and Kenneth M. George, 69–92. Ithaca: Southeast Asia Program, Cornell University, 2005.

White, Luise. *Speaking with Vampires: Rumor and History in Colonial Africa.* Berkeley: University of California Press, 2000.

Whitehouse, Harvey. *Modes of Religiosity: A Cognitive Theory of Religious Transmission.* Walnut Creek, Calif.: AltaMira Press, 2004.

Wichai Thonasaeng, ed. *Bencha aphinya.* Bangkok: Sahamit, 2538 [1995].

Wichit Matra. *Subhasit lao cheu.* Bangkok: Sobhanaphiphatthanakon, 2473 [1930].

Wiegele, Katharine. *Investing in Miracles: El Shaddai and the Transformation of Popular Catholicism in the Philippines.* Honolulu: University of Hawai'i Press, 2004.

Willford, Andrew. "The Modernist Vision from Below: Malaysian Hinduism and the 'Way of Prayers.'" In *Spirited Politics: Religion and Public Life in Contemporary Southeast Asia,* ed. Andrew Willford and Kenneth George, 45–68. Ithaca: Southeast Asia Program, Cornell University, 2005.

Wilson, Liz. *Charming Cadavers: Horrific Figurations of the Feminine in Indian Buddhist Hagiographic Literature.* Chicago: University of Chicago Press, 1996.

Wilson, Stephen. *The Magical Universe: Everyday Ritual and Magic in Pre-Modern Europe.* London: Hambledon, 2000.

(Phra Khru Sangharak) Wira Thanawiro (Phet Chirasan). *Jetovimutti: Baeb lamdap samrap Wat Aranawasi.* Bangkok: Mahamakut Ratchawithayalai, 2540 [1997].

(Phra) Wisutthathibadi [Head of Committee]. *Phra Kring Luang: Nangseu ruam phap phithikan sathapana Phra Kring Luang chat phim pen anuson kanbampen kuson uthit ya pun bunchim na watniyomyatra.* Bangkok: Wat Suthasanathephawararam, 2549 [2006].

Wittgenstein, Ludwig. *Philosophical Investigations.* Oxford: Blackwell, 1963.

(Phra Chao Borom Wongtoe Krom Luang) Wongsathirachasanit lae (Phra Worawongtoe Phra Ong Chao) Saisanitwong. *Tamrasaphakhun Ya lae Tamra Ya Phra Ong Chao Saisanitwong.* Bangkok: Wacharin Kanphim, 2534 [1991].

Woodward, F. L., M. A. Cantab, and Caroline Rhys-Davids, eds. *Manual of a Mystic: Being a Translation from the Pali and Sinhalese Work Entitled "The Yogavavachara's Manual."* London: Pali Text Society, 1916.

Wyatt, David. *Crystal Sands: The Chronicles of Nagara Śrī Dharrmarāja.* Ithaca: Southeast Asia Program, Cornell University, 1975.

——. *The Politics of Reform: Education in the Reign of King Chulalongkorn.* New Haven: Yale University Press, 1969.

——. *Reading Thai Murals.* Chiang Mai: Silkworm Books, 2004.

——. *A Short History of Thailand.* New Haven: Yale University Press, 1984.

*Ya Nak.* DVD. Directed by Tophong Thapkhamhaeng. Bangkok: Sanook Studio, 2003.

Zaleski, Valérie. "The Art of Thailand and Laos." In *The Art of Southeast Asia*, ed. Bernard Wooding, 93–150. Paris: Éditions Citadelles et Mazenod, 1997.

Zeki, Semir. "The Neurology of Ambiguity." *Consciousness and Cognition* 13 (2004): 173–96.

Zeki, S., and A. Bartels. "Towards a Theory of Visual Consciousness." *Consciousness and Cognition* 8, no. 2 (1999): 225–59.

Zinoman, Peter. *Colonial Bastille.* Berkeley: University of California Press, 2001.

# INDEX

*Abhidhamma chet kamphi*, 3, 152
Abhidhamma texts, 88, 104, 254n79
abundance, value of: in art and objects,
 158, 166–167, 176, 196, 208, 211, 226,
 228–229; consumerism and, 268n12;
 cultural repertoires and, 13–15, 18, 21,
 26; *Jinapañjara* and, 76, 88; Somdet
 To amulets and, 67–68; Thai
 Buddhism and, 117, 120, 219, 220–221
Achan Cha, 37, 67, 102, 109
Achan Kham, 48, 49
Achan Lee, 109
Achan Mahabua (Luang Ta Mahabua),
 102, 151, 238n19. *See also* Than Achan
 Mahabua
Achan Man, 26, 37, 66, 102, 151, 190,
 272n46. *See also* Than Achan Man
Achan Fan Acaro, 38

Achan Man Bhuridatto, 37, 42, 50,
 238n19
Achan Sing, 38
Achan Thet, 38, 42
Akadet Khrisanathilok, 197, 200–201, 202
Ali, Daud, 232n8
alms, 80, 133, 135–136, 138, 213
amulets: and Buddhist textuality,
 208–211; and commercialism,
 189–193, 196, 204–207, 211–212,
 274n54, 275n69; consecration of,
 202–205; funerals and, 151, 189;
 of Hindu deities, 151, 190, 191–192,
 206–208, 211, 275n67, 275n83; as
 historical objects, 192–196, 208,
 275n75, 276n83; in League of Five,
 189–190, 195; lineage and, 198–199,
 201, 208; Phra Kring, 190, 202–203;